CW01017946

Resist to the End

Royal Asiatic Society Hong Kong Studies Series

Royal Asiatic Society Hong Kong Studies Series is designed to make widely available important contributions on the local history, culture and society of Hong Kong and the surrounding region. Generous support from the Sir Lindsay and Lady May Ride Memorial Fund makes it possible to publish a series of high-quality works that will be of lasting appeal and value to all, both scholars and informed general readers, who share a deeper interest in and enthusiasm for the area.

Other titles in RAS Hong Kong Studies Series:

Reluctant Heroes: Rickshaw Pullers in Hong Kong and Canton 1874–1954
Fung Chi Ming

For Gods, Ghosts and Ancestors: The Chinese Tradition of Paper Offerings
Janet Lee Scott

Hong Kong Internment 1942–1945: Life in the Japanese Civilian Camp at Stanley
Geoffrey Charles Emerson

The Six-Day War of 1899: Hong Kong in the Age of Imperialism
Patrick H. Hase

Watching Over Hong Kong: Private Policing 1841–1941
Sheilah E. Hamilton

The Dragon and the Crown
Stanley S.K. Kwan with Nicole Kwan

Public Success, Private Sorrow: The Life and Time of Charles Henry Brewitt-Taylor (1857–1938), China Customs Commissioner and Pioneer Translator
Isidore Cyril Cannon

East River Column: Hong Kong Guerrillas in the Second World War and After
Chan Sui-jeung

Resist to the End
Hong Kong, 1941–1945

Charles Barman

Edited by Ray Barman

香港大學出版社
HONG KONG UNIVERSITY PRESS

Hong Kong University Press
14/F Hing Wai Centre
7 Tin Wan Praya Road
Aberdeen
Hong Kong

© Ray Barman 2009

ISBN 978-962-209-976-0

British Library Cataloguing-in-Publication Data
A catalogue record for this book is available from the British Library.

Secure On-line Ordering
http://www.hkupress.org

Printed and bound by Condor Production Ltd., Hong Kong, China.

To my wife and children, Winifred, Pamela, Richard,
Derek, Raymond and Carol, the men of many nationalities that
fought in the battle and suffered as prisoners of war under
the Japanese and finally to The Royal Regiment of Artillery

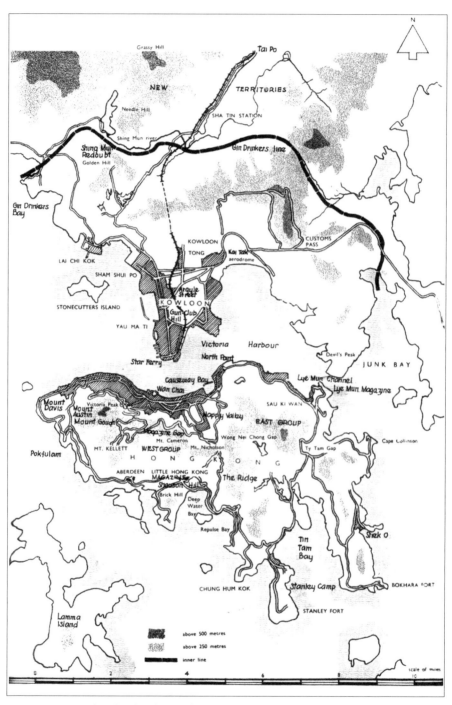

Hong Kong: The Island and part of the New Territories. Illustration by Brigade Major
J. H. Monro MC from the *Royal Artillery Commemoration Book, 1939–1945*.

Contents

Foreword for the Series

Coming soon after Chan Sui-jeung's excellently researched *East River Column: Hong Kong Guerrillas in the Second World War and After*, this latest title in our series also stems from the Second World War. Much has been written of Hong Kong's experience from the Japanese invasion in December 1941 to the liberation almost four years later. There are well-written histories, and there are the official records from that time. However, few accounts are more valuable than those of people who were there at the time, faithfully recording what happened and their impressions and feelings. *Resist to the End* is based on such a record, that of Charles Barman. Having joined the Royal Artillery in 1919, Barman was already a veteran and experienced soldier by the time he was posted to Hong Kong in 1936. His recollections of his time here, in peace, in war and in an internment camp, therefore reflect a greater appreciation and understanding of life than those of many of the tragically young men with whom he shared many of these fundamentally formative experiences.

Originally written as a private record, Barman's diaries remained exactly that for almost 40 years until a more generally readable version was lovingly coaxed out of him by his proud and supportive family, particularly his son Ray. The result is far more than a facsimile of the diaries themselves, although that would be interesting enough in itself. Ray Barman has done a lot of editing of the text and verification and expansion of some of the detail by reference to military and other sources. The result is what may be a familiar story to those who have read about the invasion and surrender of Hong Kong, but with the unique addition of the first-hand account of this observant and resourceful man. For those of us who will never have to live under such conditions, the matter-of-fact descriptions of what must have been a living hell will be particularly poignant.

The Royal Asiatic Society Hong Kong Branch and Hong Kong University Press are very proud of what they have achieved so far with the Studies Series. More and more people, both here and abroad, are finding that Hong Kong and its unique history and culture provides a rich and fascinating field of study. An increasing number of schools are including the history of our city and its surroundings in their curricula, for which we should be able to take some credit. We will continue to bring to the public original works that will enhance this area even further.

The publications in the Studies Series have been made possible initially by the very generous donation of seeding capital by the Trustees of the Clague Trust Fund, representing the estate of the late Sir Douglas Clague. This donation enabled us to establish a trust fund in the name of Sir Lindsay and Lady Ride, in memory of our first vice president and his wife. The Society itself added to this fund, as have a number of other generous donors.

The result is that we now have funding to bring to students of Hong Kong's history, culture and society a number of books that might otherwise not have seen the light of day. Furthermore, we continue to be delighted with the agreement established with Hong Kong University Press, which sets out the basis on which the Press will partner our efforts.

Robert Nield
President
Royal Asiatic Society, Hong Kong Branch
February 2009

About This Book

This book is a diary of an eyewitness account, which endeavours to describe the heroic defence of Hong Kong during the period between 8 and 25 December 1941 and as prisoners of war for the period 1941–45. This record was maintained and events entered whenever possible to the date, then returned underground.

Initially, this book was compiled by my father for the family's eyes only. In fact there were two manuscripts, firstly the one that is published here and secondly a very personal small pocket book written specifically for my mother, which was buried with her after she died in 1981. None of the family read that version.

It was after 1981 that we 'children' coaxed our father into compiling his diary into a readable account. He almost completed the work before he died in 1987, and it stayed in that unfinished form until 1996 when at various intervals I started to research, edit and compile the manuscript the best I could.

I endeavoured to check the information he wrote by various means, the Royal Artillery Museum, the RA librarian at Woolwich (Paul Evans, to whom I spoke at length on the phone), the War Memorial and National Library in Canberra, the Mitchell Library in Sydney, the families of Roy Holmes (particularly Clifford Holmes) and BSM Johns (thanks to Denzil Johns).

I would also like to thank Tony Banham of Hong Kong for his valuable assistance in this project and to my wife Sylvia for her patience and support and the many hours spent at the computer.

The original version of the diary was written in the camp itself, but after repeated burials to keep it hidden from the camp guards, the paper became very fragile and the writing almost illegible. Immediately after the Japanese surrender, therefore, my father found a stock of paper and rewrote the original in longhand. It was this version that he later typed up. There are a few differences between the longhand and typed versions. For instance, in the original diary he alludes to certain soldiers' poor performances during the battle and internment. He omitted this from the typewritten diary for obvious reasons.

To inform the lay reader I have expanded on a very few sentences on the text, but only from the point of view of clarifying information (rather than adding to the story). For instance, in the very first line of the first page of the war diary between the words 'Barracks, at' I inserted: 'the home of the 1st Regiment HK/SRA'; I believe that was necessary for the reader's understanding.

Finally, this event occurred so many years ago that a lot could be lost in the sands of time. One thing for sure, my father did not have the lives of a cat. In fact, he had the lives of two or three cats. As Maj Squires and Cmdr Millett said to him, 'Someone is certainly looking after you, Q.'

Ray Barman, son of Charles Barman
Narooma NSW
Australia

Abbreviations

Rank

AB	Able Seaman
Bdr	Bombardier
BQMS	Battery Quartermaster Sergeant
Brig	Brigadier
BSM	Battery Sergeant Major
Bug	Bugler
Capt	Captain
Cmdr	Commander
Cpl	Corporal
CRA	Commander Royal Artillery
CSM	Company Sergeant Major
(E)	Engineer (Naval)
FO	Flying Officer
Flt Lieut	Flight Lieutenant
Gnr	Gunner
GOC	General Officer Commanding
GPO	Gun Position Officer
GSO	General Staff Officer
Hav	Havildar (Indian Sergeant)
Hav Maj	Sergeant Major (Indian)
IOR	Indian Other Rank
Jem	Jemadar (Indian Second Lieutenant)
L/Bdr	Lance Bombardier
L/Cpl	Lance Corporal
Lieut	Lieutenant
2/Lieut	Second Lieutenant
Lieut Col	Lieutenant Colonel
Lieut Cmdr	Lieutenant Commander
L/Naik	Lance Bombardier or Lance Corporal (Indian)
L/Sea	Leading Seaman

L/Sgt	Lance Sergeant
MG	Master Gunner
Maj	Major
Mne	Marine
Naik	Bombardier or Corporal (Indian)
NCO	Non Commissioned Officer
OIC	Officer in Charge
OR	Other Rank
PO	Pilot Officer
Pte	Private
QMS	Quartermaster Sergeant
Regt	Regiment
RQMS	Regimental Quartermaster Sergeant
RSM	Regimental Sergeant Major
Sgt	Sergeant
Sgt Maj	Sergeant Major
Sig	Signaller
Spr	Sapper
S/Sgt	Staff Sergeant
Subadar	Lieutenant (Indian)
Subadar Maj	Captain (Indian)
Sub Lieut	Sub Lieutenant
Tel	Telegraphist
Tpr	Trumpeter
VAD	Volunteer Aid Detachment
W/Cmdr	Wing Commander
WO1	Warrant Officer (Class 1)
WO2	Warrant Officer (Class 2)

Units

AA	Anti-Aircraft
BAAG	British Army Aid Group
FA	Field Artillery
HKDDC	Hong Kong Dockyard Defence Corps
HKRNVR	Hong Kong Royal Naval Voluntary Reserve
HK/SRA	Hong Kong Singapore Royal Artillery
HKVDC	Hong Kong Volunteer Defence Corps
HQ	Headquarters
HQCC	Headquarters China Command

HQCCRA	Headquarters China Command Royal Artillery
IAMC	Indian Army Medical Corps
RA	Royal Artillery
RADC	Royal Army Dental Corps
RAEC	Royal Army Education Corps
RAF	Royal Air Force
RAMC	Royal Army Medical Corps
RAPC	Royal Army Pay Corps
RAOC	Royal Army Ordnance Corps
RASC	Royal Army Service Corps
RAVC	Royal Army Veterinary Corps
RCS	Royal Corps of Signals
RCCS	Royal Canadian Corps of Signals
RE	Royal Engineers
RIASC	Royal Indian Army Service Corps
RM	Royal Marines
RN	Royal Navy
RNVR	Royal Naval Volunteer Reserve
RROC	Royal Rifles of Canada

Miscellaneous

BRH	Bowen Road Hospital
CBS	Central British School
CWGC	Commonwealth War Graves Commission
Cwt	Hundredweight
How	Howitzer
MTB	Motor Torpedo Boat
NAAFI	Navy Army Air Force Institute
OP	Observation Post
POW	Prisoner of War
VCC	Vehicle Concentration Centre
WMH	War Memorial Hospital

About the Author

Charles Edward Barman was born at Canterbury, Kent in England on 14 May 1901, the eldest of four children. He was the son of a gardener, Richard Thomas, and Emily Barman from Tenterden, an area of Kent where many people of the Barman name still live.

Charles had two brothers, Richard and George, and a younger sister, Elsie. As a boy, he attended the local primary school at Canterbury and attended services at the Cathedral.

He had a reputation for playing practical jokes; once roping the front doors together at the Cathedral thus preventing the congregation from getting out. He left school at the age of fourteen with an average educational standard, to earn a living to sustain the family — a necessity as his mother was going blind. Charles was mad about horses and obtained additional work as a 'strapper'. His mind was set on enlisting in the Army and although he attempted to apply early, he was told to wait until he reached the required age. When he reached that age he applied for enlistment in the Royal Hussars, preferably in Churchill's old unit — the 4th — but was rejected (as he once said, 'there were no vacancies'), but possibly this rejection was also due to his lack of education as the Hussars were an elite unit. Therefore, he enlisted in the Royal Horse Artillery at Canterbury in October 1919, and transferred to Royal Field Artillery in January 1920.

He was promoted to Lance Bombardier and posted to Ireland with the 81st Field Battery RA of the 5th Field Brigade, who were redesignated the 5th RA Mounted Rifles. There, they were ordered to support British troops during the rebellion. The Regiment was housed under canvas with the horses stabled in Phoenix Park, Dublin. They were formed into troops to patrol the outlying areas of the city, locating suspected small arms and ammunition caches buried under the peat moss in the countryside and amongst the graves in the various cemeteries located around.

Whilst serving, he regularly sent money home to the family including paying fees for his brother George who gained a scholarship to Cambridge University, finally obtaining a position as Master of Mathematics and

Geography at the University and later at Worksop College Nottinghamshire. Charles himself very quickly passed the Army 3rd, 2nd and 1st Education Certificates, as these would improve his prospects of promotion.

Promoted to Bombardier, Charles was posted to India on the troop ship SS *Derbyshire* on 4 October 1921, together with thirty other ranks, to join the various artillery units stationed at places between Bombay and Peshawar, North West Frontier (such as Jhansi, Jubulipore, Lahore, Rawalpindi and the farthest outpost — Landi Kotal — that overlooked the Khyber Pass). Later, he was posted to 119th Field Battery of the 27th Field Brigade, which was stationed at Nowshera and Peshawar during the years 1921–1925.

Charles never forgot the outbreak of bubonic plague of 1922, and the removal of dead bodies by six-horsed wagons to huge fires prepared on the banks of the river Kabul. About twenty bodies were laid on each pyre where they were cremated. This thankless job went on for about four days, when the city of Nowshera was finally burnt to the ground, thereby burning the plague out.

The disastrous earthquakes of 1922 and 1924 also caused a heavy loss of life. The quakes covered an area running from Peshawar and along the rivers Kabul and Indus to Attock Bridge. That of 1922 was Charles's first such experience, and when it struck he thought the end of the world had arrived. The surrounding area showed huge movements of the ground like giant sea waves. He could not stand, and had to crawl to escape from the Barracks which were disintegrating behind him. As he gained the veranda of the building he fell into a huge crack that opened up in front of him, from which a Bombardier Shinstone very smartly pulled him out just before the earth began to close on him. The quake of 1924 struck when they were watering about 150 horses at the edge of the river Kabul. The horses instantly stampeded, causing the deaths of four British drivers and one British gunner. Well over twenty horses had to be destroyed due to their terrible injuries; others were lost in the jungle and no doubt became prey to the tigers roaming this area. Two guns used for tying and securing horses completely disappeared, and the tents of the whole camp collapsed. Some Ghurkhas in a camp a few miles away, finished up on an island caused by the diversion of the River Indus.

During his time on the North West Frontier, Charles also witnessed an officer being shredded by a tiger, with its claws exposing the bones of his back. On another occasion, a British officer had his throat slashed by a Pathan, who Charles then had to subdue in a hand-to-hand encounter. Not everyone could adapt to the situation; two soldiers at the Khyber Pass committed suicide by jumping off a cliff, and even Charles was surprised when he woke from a two-hour siesta to find a cobra curled up under the sheet at the bottom of the bed.

After serving in this region for over five years, with a loss of a good number of men caused by enemy action, earthquakes and tropical diseases, the 27th Field Brigade moved to Mhow in Central India — about half way between Mumbai (Bombay, as it was then known) and Delhi — in 1925.

Charles met his wife-to-be on a tennis court in Mhow that same year. Merlyn (Peg) Harland had been born in Mhow in 1908, her mother being Indian and her father — who was an engineer on the Indian railways — had been born in Reading, UK. Their friendship blossomed with horse-riding as well as tennis and spending time with her parents. This courtship was short and they married towards the end of 1925 at All Saints Church of England Church in Mhow, which to this day remains, as do all the records including the births of their first three children in Mhow, Winnie, Pam and Richard.

His wife being Anglo-Indian had its drawbacks, as this was frowned upon by some people, both British and Indian, at the time. This was one of the reasons Charles declined a commission three times, but the main reason being that with three and eventually five children, his hand would have been in his hip pocket all the time.

The 27th Field Brigade was then posted home to England, but Charles was retained in Mhow for a few months after the takeover of their duties by the 8th Field Brigade who had recently arrived in India. He was then posted to the 12th Field Brigade in Meerut where he joined the 25th Field Battery as acting RQMS.

He became quite fluent in Hindi and Urdu and had a smattering of some of the many other languages in his ten years in India, an asset that was later to be a distinct advantage during his years in Hong Kong.

Following promotion to BQMS, he was posted to 70th Field Battery stationed at Fenham Barracks, Newcastle upon Tyne, England, where his fourth and fifth children, Derek and Ray, were born. Here, during the depression, Charles introduced a soup kitchen outside the back gate. He formed a roster including ORs, all the cooks of the messes, with Sergeants to replace him as necessary to collect all the leftover food for issue to the civilians. Any soldiers caught disposing of food was immediately charged. The small queue which formed at first outside the gate soon grew when the word got around, to the extent that he had tickets issued to those people that missed out, to ensure they would be first in line the next day. Later, Charles became depot quartermaster at Redesdale Artillery Practice Camp in Northumberland before, in 1936, being posted to 4th Medium Battery of the 1st HK/SRA stationed at Kowloon, Hong Kong, as Battery Quartermaster Sergeant.

Introduction

By the late 1930s, the Japanese had conquered South China. Hong Kong was still at peace, and the border with China ran along the Sham Chun River. Fortunately it was impossible for the Japanese to launch a surprise attack upon the New Territories and Hong Kong, as British observation posts established on the hills overlooking the river plain were able to observe any significant concentration of enemy troops. These observation posts noted, around 5 December 1941, that a large mass of Japanese forces were building up across the river. Their report triggered off the Hong Kong garrison's emergency plans. Orders were then given for all units to deploy and occupy Battle Stations.

The Hong Kong garrison at that time consisted of six infantry battalions, being from the 1st Middlesex Regiment, 2nd Royal Scots Regiment, Winnipeg Grenadiers Regiment, Royal Rifles of Canada, 5th/7th Rajputs Regiment (Indian), and 2nd/14th Punjabis Regiment (Indian).

There was also The Hong Kong Volunteer Defence Corps, a considerable force of the Royal Artillery, a naval base with nothing more formidable than destroyers, a small RAF detachment with a handful of biplane bombers, and all the supporting units (such as ordnance men, signallers, engineers, medics, pay staff, etc.) that an isolated and self-contained garrison needed.

The army was initially deployed in two brigades: the Mainland Brigade, under Brigadier Wallis, was in Kowloon and the New Territories, while the Island Brigade, under Brigadier Lawson, was distributed across Hong Kong Island.

The mobile field artillery for Hong Kong was predominantly provided by the 1st Regiment of the Hong Kong and Singapore Royal Artillery manned by Sikh and Mohammedian gunners in the command of British Officers and Senior NCOs. This consisted of five batteries: 1st Mountain Battery, 2nd Mountain Battery, 3rd Medium Battery, 4th Medium Battery, and 25th Medium Battery.

The Regiment comprised in all 28 field guns with a mixture of 3.7-inch, 4.5-inch, and 6-inch howitzers.

In the event of an all-out attack by the Japanese, the plan was that these batteries would be deployed as follows: the 1st and 2nd Mountain Batteries were to occupy positions on the mainland to support the troops manning the forward defences. The 3rd Medium Battery was to occupy positions on the eastern part of Hong Kong Island and under control of 'Eastern Administrative Pool'. The 4th Medium Battery was to immediately occupy positions at Mount Austin and Mount Gough, on the western side of Hong Kong, with one section of guns at each site. The 25th Medium Battery was to occupy a position near the road bridge in Prince Edward Road, Kowloon, and to carry out counter bombardment duties in support of the forward line of defences in the New Territories, and if necessary to support the withdrawal of troops to the island of Hong Kong.

At the same time, the residence of Sir Robert Ho Tung would be taken over and used as 'West Administrative Pool'. This residence was situated on the west of the island of Hong Kong and not very far from the well-known Victoria Peak. Charles Barman was instructed to take over this building and the surrounding estate from the Secretary to Sir Robert Ho Tung (who resided there at all times), and the whole of the house and estate would be used for:

1. Accommodation for British Officers, Indian Officers, British and Indian other ranks and technicians
2. Storage of British and Indian rations
3. Storage of small stores, etc.
4. Storage of petrol and oils, etc.
5. Storage of reserve clothing and bedding
6. Storage of small arms, e.g. Thompson sub-machine guns, 0.38 revolvers, 0.303 rifles, including ammunition and grenades
7. The surrounds of the estate to be used for vehicles and assembly park
8. A telephone exchange to be connected to the following:
   (a) Battle headquarters
   (b) West Group headquarters
   (c) Wong Nei Chong Counter bombardment headquarters
   (d) Wanchai Gap headquarters
   (e) All gun positions deployed around the west of the island
   (f) An area to be selected to stable mules of 2nd Mountain Battery including areas for the storage of fodder, grain and harnesses
   (g) A detail of duties for British and Indian ranks within the residence including the surrounds of the estate
   (h) The siting of machine gun posts and defensive positions around the perimeter of the estate

In case of a complete withdrawal of defence forces from the mainland, the 1st Mountain Battery would occupy a position allocated to them in the eastern part of the island and the 2nd Mountain Battery and the 25th Medium Battery would occupy positions in the western half of the island. The two 4.5 Howitzer's and vintage 18 pounders being used as defence in the Kowloon area would re-establish positions at 'Sanatorium' and 'Matilda' sites in the western part of Hong Kong.

The supply of artillery and small arms ammunition was located on Hong Kong Island at the following magazine locations:
1. RAOC Depot, Queen's Road
2. RAOC Depot, Lei Yu Mun
3. RAOC Depot, Little Hong Kong
4. 4 Medium Battery HK/SRA at their depot

The magazines at Queen's Road were situated near the Hong Kong Naval Dockyards, while the magazines at Lei Yu Mun were near the 5th AA Artillery Barracks at the eastern entrance to the harbour. The magazines at Little Hong Kong were situated in the south centre of the island in an area not far from Shouson Hill and overlooked by Mount Nicholson. The magazines at Lei Yu Mun and Little Hong Kong were extremely well built and constructed underground. Large stocks of artillery ammunition of all types, including small arms ammunition and high explosives, were stored in huge underground departments leading off a series of passageways. However, the planners of these sites did not consider how vulnerable the highways would be for the convoys to and from the gun positions.

By early December 1941, all the positions to be occupied by the island and the Mainland Brigade were fully stocked with equipment, stores, clothing and non-perishable food, with a build-up of shell and cartridges amounting to 300 per gun. Reserve stocks were also stored in the east and west administrative pool. A source of further supplies could also be obtained from the RAOC and RASC depots scattered around the island and the mainland.

Exercises were carried out continuously at the various positions and all units were at 'action stations', leaving only a few men in barracks for security reasons. In the case of the mainland defences, all commanders were in direct contact by telephone to battle headquarters.

The total defence strength on 8 December 1941 was approximately 14,000 men. No modern Air Force or Navy had been allotted to the defence of the colony. They were faced with a ground force of approximately 60,000 experienced Japanese troops, most of whom were four-year battle tuned, together with a modern air force and navy.

As Winston Churchill would say, in a telegram to the commander-in-chief and governor of Hong Kong, Sir Mark Young: 'We expect you to resist to the end. The honour of the empire is in your hands.'

The Battle

8 December 1941

I returned to Gun Club Hill Barracks, [the home of the 1st Regiment HK/SRA][1] at about 1.00 a.m. this morning, after making further deliveries of ammunition and supplies to the gun positions that have been established on the Island of Hong Kong, in the event of an outbreak of hostilities in the Far East, including the estate of Sir Robert Ho Tung situated in the 'Peak District' which will be taken over and known as West Administrative Pool.[2]

I ensured that the lorries used for this purpose were returned to the garages, finally dismissing the men to their respective barrack rooms. After a few hours sleep in my quarters, I proceeded to the Sergeants' mess for breakfast at about 7.45 a.m. which was prepared for me by the Chinese Compradore employed there. The dining-room main window faced to the well-known Lei Yu Mun Pass in the far distance, being the main entrance to the harbour of Hong Kong. From this dining-room window, one could obtain a beautiful view of the harbour facing east to the island from Kowloon.

I commenced my breakfast at about 8.00 am when I heard in the far distance a drone of a great number of planes, which appeared to be coming from the east in the vicinity of Lei Yu Mun Pass. The noise from these planes increased in volume and suddenly about fifty of them hurtled out of the brilliant blue sky. As they became closer I identified them to be Japanese torpedo bombers. Suddenly, this large formation broke up, with one flight of approximately twelve planes flying westwards towards the island of Hong Kong, with about six to eight heading for Gun Club Hill Artillery Barracks flying directly over the Sergeants' Mess. The remainder of the formation headed in the direction of Kai Tak Aerodrome that was situated off to my left. Within a very short time the planes above the barracks were flying very low and started dropping bombs in all directions. In this attack, a string of bombs demolished the cookhouses of the Sikhs and Mohammedan's killing two Indian gunners and one Chinese and severely wounding three other Indian gunners.

A large number of bombs were dropped upon the infants' school, situated at the south end of the married quarters which was completely destroyed. All my children had attended this school prior to the evacuation of all families from Hong Kong to Australia via the Philippines. After the raid, I arranged to remove the dead and wounded to the medical base at Whitfield Barracks, this being about two miles from Gun Club Hill. In about an hour, another raid took place with the Japanese planes flying low over the parade ground strafing it with machine gun fire and at the same time dropping more bombs that caused huge craters in the gun park area. We could hear huge explosions vibrating and coming from Hong Kong and the areas of Shamshuipo and Kowloon City. In the distance we could hear the wailing and screaming of women and children who were massing and fleeing with men down the side streets below the barracks and past the Roman Catholic Church in Chatham Road.

The planes were easy to identify as being Japanese, being distinguished by large yellow round markings under the wings. At this stage I had rather a problem with the thirty Sikhs who were a batch of recruits that had recently arrived from India to join the Regiment. They became completely demoralised with the sudden attack, as of course did everyone. To ease the nervous tension of these disastrous scenes I moved them around on various jobs that had to be carried out immediately, such as the loading of stores that had to be removed across to West Administrative Pool on the island of Hong Kong. By mixing them amongst the Mohammedan gunners in the loading of the lorries at my disposal, it appeared to have settled their minds temporarily, although they still looked quite anxious. As these were very young Sikhs, I decided to house them at West Administrative Pool and not post them out to the various gun positions but instead, to retain them for the forthcoming convoys that will surely be necessary in the very near future and for general duties around the pool. During the lull in these air attacks, I collected whatever could be carried on the lorries and finally assembled the Indian NCOs and gunners for further instructions.

I instructed Havildar Sher Khan to take charge of five lorries and about twenty-five gunners, to proceed to West Administrative Pool on the island of Hong Kong. I told him to closely guard the stores on the lorries and instructed him to use the men if necessary to disperse the crowds of Chinese, who by now must have gathered at the wharfs of the ferries and who could become a hindrance in moving the vehicles on to the vehicular ferry. Due to the chaotic situation amongst the Chinese populace in Kowloon, it was impossible for me to forecast where I would be under the circumstances. Air raid sirens appear to have gone haywire, as one minute you can hear the 'all clear' and the next 'air raid warnings'. Heavy clouds of smoke can be seen drifting in from all directions and the fire engines can be heard in the far distance. My foremost intentions at this point, were to collect as much ammunition from the magazines at West Fort adjacent to Whitfield Barracks (that could be entered from Nathan Road, Kowloon),[3] the ammunition etc. being delivered to the 25th Medium Battery in action near the overhead bridge that spans Prince Edward Road. To accomplish this, I had to confiscate five lorries with drivers from Whitfield Barracks and together with the four lorries of mine at Gun Club Hill Barracks; I would have sufficient vehicles to transport the ammunition. I had sufficient number of gunners for loading purposes.

Just as I was about to leave Gun Club Hill Barracks, Mr and Mrs (Joe) Henson approached me and requested me to allow his wife and himself to escape to the Island of Hong Kong on one of the lorries. They were a fairly aged couple, each about 65 years of age. Joe Henson was an employee with the RASC Barrack Department at Sha Tau Kok, a suburb of Kowloon for quite a number of years. I told Joe to collect whatever personal belongings they may have and to embark upon the first lorry of the convoy, which was in charge of Havildar Sher Khan. I instructed the Havildar to transport them to Hong Kong and drop them off near the Shanghai Bank in Queen's Road or at a place of their choosing. I felt very sorry for both of them, particularly as they were getting on in years and also for having witnessed such a sudden and devastating attack by the Japanese. I think they should have accepted the advice of the Hong Kong Government in June 1940 that all civilian nationals should evacuate to a country of their choice. It was compulsory that all wives and children of those men serving in the HM Forces to be evacuated to Australia via the Philippines on the first of June 1940. Now of course, if the Japanese are successful in overrunning Hong Kong, the Hensons will have to suffer the period of confinement as internees.[4]

Increasing flights of Japanese planes continued to strafe and bomb Hong Kong and Kowloon indiscriminately causing widespread destruction of buildings and heavy loss of life amongst the Chinese population. Dense, black clouds of smoke are lying heavily over the whole area. The shells from the 9.2-inch coastal guns from Stanley and Mount Davis are at this time whistling overhead and no doubt being directed by observers on to targets on enemy formations in the New Territories. The guns of 5th AA Battery are also blazing away at the flights of Japanese planes that appear to be increasing by the hour. As I moved down Nathan Road to gain entrance to West Fort, I came in contact with a dreadful scene of mutilated bodies of the dead and the dying, lying scattered along the roads and pathways. Vehicles of all types were completely wrecked and burning fiercely. The defence units are doing their best to remove the injured to hospitals and other medical bases. The Health Department is endeavouring to remove the dead as quickly as possible to prevent disease and epidemics spreading. The fire brigade are attempting to control the huge fires that are raging in the heavily populated areas in Kowloon. The whole scene looks a complete shambles in such a short period of time. The Jubilee married quarters in Hankow Barracks received direct hits from the bombing causing quite a number of casualties amongst the remaining military personnel.

Eventually I arrived at West Fort to withdraw ammunition. This Fort stored 6-inch How and 3.7-inch How shells, also small arms ammunition and amatol for the Royal Engineers for demolition purposes. It was about 7.00 p.m. when I arrived at the magazines with my four lorries plus the loading parties of British and Indian gunners. I had about an hour's daylight to load the vehicles, so therefore I had to force the quick loading of the ammunition. At about 9.00 p.m., all lorries were loaded and ready to proceed to 25th Medium Battery in action along Prince Edward Road. As the first lorry moved forward to a position just past the main gate, all hell broke loose. A flight of Japanese planes came suddenly out of the semi-moonlight sweeping low over Whitfield Barracks and West Fort dropping loads of bombs right along the coastline of the harbour. This sudden attack must have caused hundreds of casualties amongst the Chinese population living in these areas and near to the Barracks. At the time, the only place we could take cover was in the underground rooms of the magazines that stored shell and high explosives. After the raid, we felt very lucky; as I am sure the intended target by the Japanese was West Fort. They also missed the lorries that were already loaded to full capacity with high explosives.

Outside the Barracks and in the far distance, we could hear the terrible screaming and crying of a great number of Chinese coming from the district that had been bombed and from which flames could be seen for miles around. I decided to re-route the convoy of lorries to the west of the barracks so as to avoid the huge sparks coming from the burning buildings and settling upon the lorries containing the explosives. I met a Chinese inspector who was in charge of a civil defence unit. He was giving instructions on the removal of dead bodies from the devastated area and I suggested very quickly to him, that it would be advisable to remove all wounded casualties firstly to the hospital or other medical bases and to leave the dead to the health department. He agreed with me even though I was unable to stay and watch him carry out this task. The heavy pall of smoke coming from the bombed-out areas caused a real 'pea souper' fog that blanketed the sky for miles around. As I moved the convoy along Austin Road and into Nathan Road, to proceed to Prince Edward Road, in the semi-darkness we came slap-bang into masses of Chinese fleeing towards the Yaumati Ferry, who were endeavouring to board her or any other sea-craft on hand to make their escape to Hong Kong Island. Finally, after massed obstructions, I was able to deliver the ammunition to the 25th Medium Battery position and then return to Gun Club Hill Barracks.

9 December 1941

It is now the early morning of 9 December 1941 and when we returned to Gun Club Hill Barracks via Nathan Road, we saw lorries and vehicles of all types, fully crammed with wounded British and Indian troops with bedraggled able-bodied troops following on foot. They all looked utterly exhausted in these early hours of the morning. At Gun Club Hill at about 6.30 a.m., with the convoy of lorries standing at my office door, was Lieut Vinter[5] who informed me that a further amount of 6-inch shell cartridges was required by the 25th Medium Battery as they had already blazed away near on 200 shells since I had left them in the late hours of yesterday. Therefore, I gathered the lorries and loading parties and once again proceeded to the magazines at West Fort. I entered the barracks by the north side so as to avoid the devastated areas nearby on the east and south. At this stage, the Japanese were keeping up their air raid attacks upon Hong Kong Island. Within the two hours I had, the lorries were loaded without any opposition from the air and we proceeded on to the 25th Medium Battery who we could hear blazing away as we moved along Prince Edward Road and were no doubt engaging long-distance enemy targets. Our 9.2-inch coastal guns were also blazing away on the enemy positions. As we passed the isolated areas that were previously bombed by the Japanese, we had to use rags to cover our mouths and noses to smother the dreadful smell from decomposed bodies lying across and along the sides of the roads.

There were still streams of vehicles pouring in from the forward positions carrying British and Indian troops. Quite a number were from the Royal Scots, 2/14th Punjabis and 5/7th Rajputs. As I turned into the south of Prince Edward Road from the dirt track near the C.B.S. (Central

British School)[6] and not far from Kowloon Hospital, I noticed that the Chinese masses had thinned out considerably and thereby was able to continue my journey much easier than I anticipated. When I arrived at the 25th Medium Battery position, I reported to the Gun Position Officer of my intentions and future movements depending on the situation. The six-inch How Shell and cartridges were offloaded. I then asked the GPO what stocks of ammunition he had on hand at the site and he said that he was down to about 100 shells per gun. This meant that I would have to arrange a further supply. I told him that I would endeavour to make a further supply probably late in the afternoon, or during the hours of darkness. As I left this position and about to enter Prince Edward Road near the overhead bridge, a flight of planes suddenly appeared and commenced bombing and strafing the main highway, presumably trying to locate the 25th Medium Battery position that I had just left.

As I turned into the road near the bridge, strings of bombs rained down upon the fleeing Chinese who were endeavouring to take shelter under the bridge, but unfortunately, one group received a direct hit killing all but a few. As a result, I was prevented from moving my vehicle forward because the Chinese bodies were jammed against the chassis of my car. A piece of shrapnel from a bomb killed one of my gunners outright. He received a gash in the side of his neck, which nearly severed his head. The gunner on my left in the forward seat received a splinter in the right eye. I received small pieces of shrapnel in my right arm and shoulder. A piece of metal or small stone struck me in the nose feeling as though a needle had penetrated my forehead. I suffered a terrific bout of sneezing with blood spurting everywhere. One gunner riding in the rear of my vehicle received a piece of bomb that removed a portion of his right shoulder. One large piece of bomb buried itself into the abdomen of an aged Chinese woman, which completely disembowelled her and at the same time her blood and flesh splashed right across our car and over our faces. I took my casualties to the Kowloon Hospital about a mile away where they were admitted, the dead gunner being placed in the morgue. The doctor told me that I should also be admitted for observation, but I declined, as I could call for dressings when necessary. The doctor did remove bits of shrapnel and grit from my right arm and shoulder followed by an anti-tetanus injection. He dressed up my nose, which made me look like a stuffed pig, and with two black eyes I must have looked a fine sight. During my absence at the hospital, the gunners took the opportunity and wisely so, to hose off the dried flesh and blood from my car, which no doubt would eventually attract large groups of flies. I was finally able to proceed to West Fort and withdraw further

6-inch How shell and cartridges for delivery to 25th Medium Battery late that night.

After making this delivery, I then returned to Gun Club Hill Barracks, where I allowed the gunners to collect any clothing or other articles of a personal nature. I went to my quarters at No. 10; where I recovered whatever personal belongings I could gather quickly which included the photographs of my dear wife and family. I secured these photographs in the folder of my gas mask haversack where I intended they would remain always. As time was running out, which was limited because I had received instructions to take over Sir Robert Ho Tung's Estate at the Peak on Hong Kong Island immediately and also to establish that the Yaumati vehicular ferry was still operating from Kowloon that was so necessary at this stage as it was the only means of moving transport and guns etc. across to Hong Kong Island. Also I did not know as to whether the masses of Chinese refugees had decreased by now, which could be a problem for the movement of troops and mobile equipment from the defences. Prior to this, I prepared the gunners and NCOs for the move to Hong Kong Island with all the available transport I had that was now loaded with stores. I proceeded to the ferry at the Yaumati wharf, which by now was free of congested traffic and refugees and without any problems the transports were moved onto the ferry.

Luckily at this time, the air raids had abated in this area and they now appeared to be confined to the New Territories and to the East of Hong Kong Island. The journey across the harbour was completed without incident where the lorries were driven onto the wharf at Hong Kong Island. As I moved the transports from the wharf towards Queen's Road — and towards the Peak tramway terminal to get on to the main Peak highway that leads to Magazine Gap Bridge which was my objective — suddenly, a flight of about twenty planes swooped along the foreshores of the harbour strafing and bombing right along the coastal front and in the direction of the village of Aberdeen. I hastily ordered the lorries under cover near a bank with an avenue of huge trees secreting the convoy and practically opposite the Peak tramway terminal. Following this sudden attack and the 'all clear' siren, I moved the convoy along the zigzag Peak Road towards Magazine Gap Bridge where I would turn off to the south side of the island and out of view from the mainland of Kowloon. It was imperative that I take over the residence of Sir Robert Ho Tung as soon as possible, so as to establish the 'West Administrative Pool'. I contacted the Secretary to Sir Robert Ho Tung, a Chinese by the name of Ah Cheung, for an inventory of the estate and for his presence in the taking-over and checking of the inventory.

Mr Ah Cheung and his wife was an aged couple and had been in the employ of Sir Robert for many years. They were very pleasant and assisted me tremendously in the layout of the estate, and the rooms of the residence. He requested that he and his wife be allowed to stay in their quarters whilst we were in occupation. I agreed to that as they were completely isolated from the main part of the building, but I pointed out that they would have to be prepared to accept the bombing and artillery bombardments that would arise if the Japanese were successful in gaining a foothold in Kowloon or on the island where they could unmercifully shell and bomb the whole of the foreshores of Hong Kong. They fully understood the situation and that if it was necessary, they would take shelter in the basements of this huge building.

I have just heard that our Air Force, which comprised of five obsolete planes (two Walrus amphibians and three Wildebeeste dive bombers), was destroyed at Kai Tak Aerodrome. They never got into the air.

10 December 1941

I planned the full use of this house and the huge area of the surrounds organising the following:

Accommodation for three reserve officers who were permanent residents in Hong Kong and in the Business world.
1. Accommodation for British NCOs and other ranks.
2. Accommodation for Indian Officers, NCOs and other ranks.
3. Accommodation for Chinese who were on the staff of Sir Robert Ho Tung.
4. Cooking arrangements for 1, 2, 3 above.
5. Latrines for 1, 2, 3 above.
6. The installation of emergency water pump chlorination system by Spr Nichols, RE,[7] who was held responsible for its operation and serviceability.
7. Storage facilities for food, clothing and equipment etc. plus petrol and oil filling points. Also small arms ammunition storage.
8. Suitable rooms to be selected for 1, 2, 3 and 4 above for decontamination purposes in case of gas attacks etc.

The reserve officers were as follows:
2/Lieut Parks, Royal Artillery
2/Lieut Simpson, Royal Artillery (from Hong Kong University)
2/Lieut Andrews, Royal Artillery[8]

I arranged for the following duties to be carried out during my absence which I could foresee being for long hours for me as the campaign intensified.

2/Lieut Parks would be in charge during my absence.

S/Sgt May (now Acting BQMS) is responsible for the withdrawal of perishable and non-perishable rations from the officer in charge of the RASC depot in Queen's Road Hong Kong daily or whenever possible.

Subadar Mohammad Khan to be responsible for feeding and rationing the Mohammadian gunners.

S/Sgt Fitter Gollege will be responsible for the maintenance and the servicing of the guns at Mount Austin and Mount Gough gun positions and all other associated equipment.

S/Sgt Farrier Holmes is responsible for the feeding and the welfare of the mules under his charge that are to be stabled in the grounds of the estate.

S/Sgt Wilson will take charge of all clerical administration and the telephone exchange.

Mr Ah Cheung and his wife will be responsible for the feeding of the Chinese personnel in and around the estate.[9]

Maj Proes at Wong Nei Chong Gap headquarters informed me on the phone that I was to ensure that all gun positions were fully stocked with shell and cartridges. This meant I would have to withdraw as much ammunition as possible from the magazines available on the island and at West Fort in Kowloon. He told me that the latest information to hand is that the Japanese are attacking fiercely at night, penetrating our forward defence positions in the New Territories and near Fanling. However, these attacks have been halted by very effective fire from the 9.2-inch guns of 12th Coast Regiment. In the communiqué he says that severe casualties have been inflicted upon the Japanese forces by the 9.2-inch guns and our 6-inch How's having contributed their share. One can hear the huge shells whistling overhead and the gun flashes just light up the sky resembling a firework display. From the Peak and in the darkness one can see Kowloon fully ablaze from the continuous bombing in the last two days and Hong Kong itself is burning fiercely at points in the East and West of the island.

11 December 1941

During the early hours of this morning, the guns at Mount Austin and Mount Gough have been blazing away these past three hours with the coastal guns also doing their share. As the Japanese artillery gain ground and to a position where they can readily bombard the island, we shall be under constant artillery barrages and relentless air attacks.

I received a telephone call from Maj Proes who was in charge of headquarters at Wanchai Gap. He informed me that a problem had developed at the Mount Austin gun site. Jemadar Kishen Singh had reported to him that the guns are unable to engage enemy targets upon the mainland due to the house at 'No. 11 The Peak', which is obstructing the crest clearance of the guns. I told him to contact the Royal Engineers for a demolition squad to remove part or all of the building, but he said there were no squads available at the moment and that at this present time they are all under pressure on other priority jobs. This house at present is being used by thirty other ranks of the Royal Army Pay Corps in the charge of one officer. I told Maj Proes that this problem being of extreme urgency, that I would demolish the top of the building to a height of about eight feet by shelling it with one of the 6-inch How guns lying below. He was a bit concerned about this proposal but finally agreed for me to carry out the job as per my advice. I explained that I would lay one of the guns directly on to the top of the building by open sites and shell the highest portion of the brickwork until I had completely cleared sufficient space to allow the guns to gain crest clearance. I further said that as the building would be about thirty yards in front of the guns, I would have to fire from this distance by attaching a lanyard to the firing mechanism of the gun to avoid the possibility of debris falling back onto the men and guns. Maj Proes agreed and told me to go ahead.

At the time, I was about three miles from the Mount Austin gun position and therefore I asked Maj Proes to phone the OIC of the Pay Corps at No. 11 The Peak to evacuate all of his men from the building immediately and to explain to him my intentions. On my way over Magazine Gap Bridge, I was spotted by two Japanese planes. I told the four Indian gunners riding with me to lie down on the floor of the vehicle and to get as much cover as possible. Within a few seconds, the planes commenced strafing me along the highway to the Peak where there is no cover whatsoever for about one and a half miles. All I could do was to zigzag the car along the road to avoid the bullets that were being sprayed at me from right to left of the road and in front of the vehicle. How lucky I was to be able to reach safety under a small overhead bridge where I sheltered for about fifteen minutes until the planes withdrew at which time I continued my journey to Mount Austin.

I was quite relieved to escape from these attacks and the Indian gunners gave me a pat on the shoulder saying 'Shah Bash Sahib' (meaning, 'well done', or 'very good'). As I turned the car to the left at the Peak tramway terminal and onto the narrow pathway leading up to the Mount Austin gun site, I passed the men of the Royal Army Pay Corps coming from the Peak, which indicated to me that the order from Maj Proes to No. 11 to evacuate the building had been carried out and thereby giving me the all-clear-to-proceed with the task of demolishing a portion of the house to give clearance to the guns which was essential to engage the enemy forces concentrating in great force upon Kowloon and beyond into the New Territories. Meanwhile, Battle headquarters has been trying to contact me for a convoy movement of ammunition to take place this evening. I informed Maj Squires[10] that I would be at the appointed rendezvous as ordered and that I would phone him as soon as I had completed the task at Mount Austin gun site. As soon as I arrived at the Mount Austin site, I informed Jem Kishen Singh what I was going to do. I told him to order the gunners to open up the breaches of each gun and ensure that the barrels of the 6-inch How's were clear so as to enable me to lay the guns on the portion of the building to be demolished. After I had sighted the guns, I arranged to secure the light drag ropes on charge to the equipment, which gave me at least thirty feet to be attached to the firing levers of each gun. I ordered the guns to be loaded and to prepare for firing. The lanyards were handed over to two or three gunners to take hold to pull the lanyards on the order of fire. I ordered 'FIRE', the result of the first two shells striking the building was fairly satisfactory, having removed quite a large amount of brickwork to a reasonable height and quite successful in width. I ordered the guns to be reloaded and traversed about fifteen degrees to the left. Once again, I gave the order to 'FIRE' and the result was extremely good. When the dust was cleared; we saw that a thirty-yard breach had been made to a height of about eight feet. This left a large enough gap to allow clearance for both guns, which were now able to engage the enemy on the mainland.

Within a very short time, the guns were blazing away over the crest of Victoria Peak. I informed Maj Proes that clearance had been achieved to allow the guns elevation. The Maj was delighted with the success and informed Battle headquarters accordingly. As I walked away from the gun position towards the pathway running down from No. 11 The Peak, an agitated officer of the Royal Army Pay Corps, Capt Thompson,[11] shouted to me with annoyance saying, 'Quartermaster, you never gave me time to finish having a shit.' During this abusive language, he was still attempting to tuck his shirt into his shorts. His face was livid and red with rage. I said to him, 'Did you not receive orders from Maj Proes to vacate the premises?' He said, 'Yes, but I did not think you would be so damn quick to shell the building.' Anyway, I did not have time to discuss his complaint and I told him so. I finally departed, leaving this officer in the process of adjusting his shirt and shorts. I reported the incident to Maj Proes and he and the other officers at headquarters burst out laughing. Whenever this officer was seen or spotted amongst the groups, the men would say, 'There goes that officer that was blown out of the shithouse by the quartermaster.'

The demolition squad from the Royal Engineers arrived on the site just before I left and they were quite surprised to see that the job had been done. The sapper officer told me that considering it was a very primitive attempt, I had carried out an excellent job.

It was now evening of 11 December and upon my return to West Administrative Pool, I was told that the convoy of twenty-four lorries had been cancelled for the time being, thank goodness, as at this stage I was completely exhausted, as it was impossible to have any real sleep since 8 December. The RAOC instead, had withdrawn the 6-inch How shells which had been delivered to the Mount Gough gun position. As I entered the huge estate of Sir Robert Ho Tung, I was met by S/Sgt May, who had recently been promoted to A/BQMS, he said to me, 'Charles, for goodness sake get some rest.' Apparently, he prepared for me a couple of sandwiches and a cup of tea, but when he brought them to me he noticed that I had gone into a deep sleep in an armchair still clutching my Tommy gun. 2/Lieut Simpson told May and S/Sgt Gollege and in the presence of S/Sgt Farrier Holmes to let me rest and not to wake me until it was absolutely necessary. I had about thirty minutes sleep when BQMS May woke me to tell me that Maj Temple at Wong Nei Chong Gap headquarters wanted me on the telephone, the time being about 7.00 p.m. He wanted me to collect clothing and equipment, etc., from the RAOC Depot, Queen's Road, Hong Kong.

The following items had to be collected:

1. Binoculars, compasses, revolvers, etc., required for officers of the HKVDC units who had recently joined West Group on 8 December.
2. Clothing and armbands, etc., for Chinese followers.
3. Non-perishable rations to be drawn from RASC supplies and to be delivered to all positions.

Due to air attacks, which were increasing daily, the movements of the vehicular ferry was being restricted because of the build-up of traffic towards the wharf and near the embarkation area, which was completely blocked. The situation was so serious that I contacted two officers informing them of this situation and advised them to contact Battle Headquarters by telephone of this problem — suggesting civilian and military police control the area. This advice was passed on and after a lapse of about thirty minutes, a force of civilian and military police moved in and dispersed the congested vehicles into smaller groups off the main thoroughfares leading to the entrances onto the vehicular ferry. Eventually, after a long wait, I was able to embark on the ferry with my five lorries and men and shortly we left the wharf and headed for Kowloon. When the vessel was in mid-harbour we heard the sudden blast of sirens from the mainland and the island. Suddenly, a flight of Japanese planes appeared and commenced bombing and strafing along the foreshores of Hong Kong harbour. They dropped everything they were carrying from Aberdeen to Lei Yu Mun and then followed up by machine-gunning about every form of sea-craft they could see. Seeing that the vehicular ferry would be an obvious target, the coxswain put the ferry into a zigzag course at the fastest speed possible towards Kowloon. By the time we reached Kowloon Wharf, the planes had disappeared.

Due to the strafing and bombing, the Chinese crowds had sought cover and we were able to disembark without obstruction. We then headed to Gun Club Hill Barracks without any serious incidents.

Quite a large number of battle-weary troops were making their way down the highways of Kowloon to the ferries for transportation over to Hong Kong Island and to occupy the defence positions allocated to them. There were quite a number of lorries and other vehicles carrying wounded and destined for the military hospital at Bowen Road[12] on the island. We also passed trucks of all types carrying mortified dead bodies of Chinese that caused everyone to cover up their faces and mouths to avoid the stench. When we arrived at Gun Club Hill Barracks, we noticed that further air raids had taken place during our short absence. The Gun Park and other buildings had been completely demolished which included my office and store block.

We could now hear the Japanese guns in the far distance and I fear that our troops are gradually retiring to other defence lines established nearer to Kowloon. It appeared to me that the GOC, Major General Maltby,[13] would have to withdraw the remaining survivors of the Mainland Brigade to the island in the very near future. I collected whatever stores were remaining in the buildings at Gun Club Hill and loaded the five lorries at my disposal and finally proceeded towards the vehicular ferry in Jordan Road. As we moved down the road between the officers and sergeants' messes into Chatham Road, the first shells of the Japanese Artillery started to bombard the area in the vicinity of the marina, which runs parallel with the Kowloon Railway. I turned right into Austin Road and straight across Nathan Road, then on to the vehicular ferry in Jordan Road with the five lorries fully loaded en-route to Hong Kong Island.

Shells from the Japanese long-range batteries were now dropping in and around the Star Ferry Wharf and in the areas around the Peninsula Hotel. Once again this caused further panic amongst the Chinese living there and now fleeing from these districts and they began to mass on the main roads to the harbour foreshores. To avoid these masses, I directed the convoy down the side streets towards the vehicular ferry with very little obstruction. Luck was on our side and we made the ferry without hindrance and were able to board the vessel immediately. The vessel made the crossing without being caught in an air attack, which could happen at any time. As soon as we disembarked at the wharf in Hong Kong, I made haste with the lorries towards Peak Road and then on to West Administrative Pool. It was now about 11.00 p.m., and as we reached Magazine Gap Bridge, which was off to the right from Peak Road and out of view of the mainland, suddenly a flight of Japanese planes appeared and at once commenced low-level attacks on my convoy. I zigzagged my car along the road hoping that the drivers of the lorries following me would do the same and at the same time put on speed. Luckily, we escaped the low-level attacks unscathed and made the cover of the trees and embankments. The low-level attacks ceased and the planes disappeared allowing me to make West Administrative Pool without further incident. I asked L/Naik Lall Khan if there were any casualties, he said, 'Naheeng (no) sahib.' After unloading the lorries, I dispersed the gunners who were now exhausted as much as I was.

BQMS May and S/Sgt Gollege arranged a meal for me after which I headed for a bed in one of the small rooms in this enormous-sized house. May and Gollege sat on the bed and gave me all the news to what had happened since I was there last. I asked if there were any problems and they both said, 'Nothing serious, Charles.' May said to me, 'Charles, the Mount Gough and Mount Austin gun positions are running short of shells and cartridges and will need re-supplying as soon as possible.' I told them both that I would deal with this matter after having something to eat and if possible a short rest.

香港俘虜收容所 6

1. 30 cwt lorry (Driver Mohd Khan).
1. 15 cwt truck (-"- Shahib Uddin).
1. 8 cwt truck (Myself & 2nd Driver Mohd Zaman).
2. 3 ton Lwid Lorries (2 Chinese drivers).

The guard consisted of 1 Havildar and 8 men, also a fatigue party of 10 Sikhs and 16 P.M's.
The job was completed at about 3.a.m. in the morning.
My eyes were very tired and strained, due to the darkness and driving along the perilous roads that exist from one end of the Island to "The Peak."
During the trip to Lyemun for the a/m ammunition and on the main road, nearly opposite the "Taikoo Sugar Refinery," the leading lorry was caught in a concertina wire barrier, this was due to the fact that there were no sentries anywhere about to guide the convoy through the barriers. There were still no sentries on this barrier when I returned. As the wire was so entangled around the rear axle of the lorry, this caused me a 2 hour delay. I reported this matter of the non-existence of sentries on this particular barrier to Battle Headquarters.

11th December 1941.

(a) At 8.a.m, collected additional sandbags, barbed wire and angle pickets for delivery to positions on the Island from R.A.O.C. Depot, Queens Road. I reported to Major Proes. R.A. that these stores had been drawn and delivered. At this time he also informed me that No2 gun of "Austin" position could not clear the crest owing to a house No No "The Peak", was obstructing the line of fire. He ordered me to make arrangements with Fortress. R.A. at Battle Headquarters, for demolition of this house immediately. I requested Fortress, Battle H.Q. telephone No 368 to hasten demolition of this house as immediate fire was required to be bore on targets of enemy artillery located in the Laicha Kak area on the Mainland, these targets being observed from the "Victoria Peak O.P." The demolition of this house was not forthcoming, so I reported to Major Proes and suggested that I destroy the top of the house by shellfire from the position, he replied by saying, "yes". Knowing fully well that the house in question was in occupation and in use as Headquarters of the Royal Army Pay Corps, I immediately telephoned them and said, "that they were to evacuate the house at once as I was proceeding from West front very shortly for "Austin," with instructions from Major Proes to destroy the top portion of No10 "The Peak" without delay, at the same time I would explain the reason for on my arrival. On my arrival at Austin I could see that the personnel of the Army Pay Corps were well under way of removing their Headquarters to another position in "Austin Barracks." Meanwhile I gave orders to the Jemadar and Havildar, to prepare lanyards from lines natural whipcord

Page example of the Chinese block in top right hand corner (see also p. 261)

12 December 1941

After making delivery of 4.5 and 6-inch shell and cartridges to the gun positions at Mount Austin and Mount Gough, in the early hours of the morning, I contacted Maj Temple OIC Counter Bombardment Headquarters at Wong Nei Chong Gap to make my usual daily report upon casualties, supplies and ammunition expended at the various gun

positions etc, in the western half of Hong Kong. To wind up my
conversation with Maj Temple, he said to me in a jovial manner,
'Quartermaster, have you had any car accidents recently?' I said, 'No, sir,'
his reply was, 'Well, Q, you can drive like blazes without any fear of
losing your drivers licence.' My reply was, 'One has to drive in this
business when shells and bombs are constantly falling all around you,
and by the way sir, I lost one man and two seriously wounded by the
bombing attacks near the 25th Medium Battery position in Prince Edward
Road. If you are referring to my looks sir, I caught some splinters and
two black eyes, with a pug nose and at the moment I am dressed up
around the face like a man from outer space. The Indian gunners are
really amused to see me dressed up like this, but in a couple of days the
bandages around my head and face will be removed.'

At about 2.00 p.m., I received a telephone message from Capt Fox,
the adjutant of Mainland headquarters, to withdraw 600 hand-grenades
from the RAOC Depot, Queen's Road, Hong Kong, which are required
urgently at all positions on the mainland and on the island.

They are for distribution as follows: Mainland 350; Island 250.

As Indian officers and other ranks are not familiar in the use and
operation of hand-grenades, Capt Fox requested me to give them a brief
instruction on how to handle them, particularly as this type of explosive
are not normally used by Artillery units. I advised them of how to use
and operate the grenade and that once the safety pin was removed, it
was vital that it be thrown immediately to its intended target. I also
instructed them to throw the grenade by the overhand movement. In
the late evening, Lieut Bompas, RA of 4th Medium Battery HK/SRA was
ordered to proceed for duty on the mainland.

At 11.00 p.m., I received orders to proceed from West Administrative
Pool where I had lorries as follows:

1-cwt	Driver	Mohammad Khan
1–15-cwt	Driver	Shahib Uddin
2–3 ton	Drivers	2 Chinese
1–8-cwt car	myself	and driver Mohammad Khan

The accompanying guard consisted of one Havildar and eight men,
also a loading party of ten Sikhs and ten Mohammedans. During the
journey to Lei Yu Mun Magazines via Peak Road and Causeway Bay, we
could hear the guns from Stanley Fort and Mount Davis blazing away at
the Japanese forces advancing on Kowloon from the New Territories. At
this stage, I can foresee that the Island of Hong Kong will soon be wide
open for a direct assault by the Japanese in the near future using the full

force of their artillery, infantry and air force in an attempt for a full-scale invasion across the harbour.

Upon my return from the magazines with the convoy of lorries fully loaded with 6-inch How shell and cartridges, the leading lorry became entangled with one of the concertina barbed wire barriers that were erected across the road and near Tai Koo refining establishment. Normally these barbed wire barriers were supposed to be guarded by sentries but as they were absent, the driver of the lorry unavoidably in the dark crashed straight into it. The barbed wire became completely entangled around the rear axle of the lorry and it took near on two hours to have it released. Due to this obstruction and obvious delay, I instructed the other lorries to bypass and to proceed to a rendezvous at the base of Peak Road and near the terminal of the Peak tramway and to await my arrival. With this part of the island being in direct view of Kowloon, movements along this road became easy targets for the Japanese artillery and bombing raids. Later, I reported the absence of sentries on the barbed wire barriers for my own benefit and more importantly for my men, as we are the main users of this particular highway and it is the only means for me to access the gun positions to the west of Hong Kong. It was essential that this route for any transports be manned along the way. Finally, after releasing my lorry I reached the remaining lorries near the Peak tramway terminal, and proceeded along the route to the gun positions at Mount Gough and Mount Austin where the deliveries were made. Due to the night travelling, without lights on the vehicles, and the difficulty of keeping on the road and well clear of the precipitous cliff edges that exist around the island, one's eyes tend to become very sore and bloodshot, which of course is also aggravated by the lack of sleep. The vehicular ferry service was extremely bad by this time with so many people and military services using it to full capacity, particularly from Kowloon to Hong Kong, which is now always completely full with troops and transports withdrawing from the mainland. It takes about an hour to make the journey across to Hong Kong and vice versa to Kowloon and the delays caused by air raids and shelling leaves a serious congestion of traffic along Connaught Road Hong Kong, and even more so at the ferry terminal on the Kowloon side in Jordan Road. The wharf in Jordan road is jammed with withdrawing troops and transports from the forward defences in the New Territories. I estimate that the ferry could take aboard approximately twenty to twenty-five vehicles of all sorts, some towing guns, plus about 600 passengers. Due to the area of embarkation on these ferries, particularly at the Kowloon end, the congestion of traffic became a very serious problem and a prime target for the Japanese air raids.

Due to the urgency of the stores I was carrying over to the island, an air raid suddenly took place in the Kowloon area behind us and when halfway across, the coxswain dropped the anchor. As the ferry was packed with approximately twenty-four lorries of all sorts, fully loaded with ammunition and towing guns, etc., with troops of Canadian, British, Indian soldiers and other odd bods, I thought it inadvisable to stop in the middle of the harbour where we would be an excellent target for enemy aircraft. Whilst I was on the portside of the gangway, watching the bombings of Kowloon and Hong Kong, a flight of planes came in from the south and commenced strafing and bombing the full length of the harbour. They dropped their bombs at low level but they fell well behind the ferry. An officer of the RAOC came up to me and said, 'Quartermaster, this damn ferry has stopped in mid-stream and if they make a return attack we are just a sitting duck.' The officer and I went up to the wheelhouse and confronted the coxswain where I immediately ordered him to get the ferry moving at once, but he refused to do so. With this refusal and without hesitation, I drew my revolver and in no uncertain terms threatened to shoot him if he did not obey my instructions and get his second-in-command to take over. With this warning he began moving the vessel towards Hong Kong Island.

The officer agreed with my action and I said to him that he should report this incident to Battle Headquarters as soon as possible. Another flight of planes appeared from the direction of Lei Yu Mun and commenced low-level attacks along the shores of Kowloon. They strafed all craft leaving the wharfs that were conveying our troops and equipment heading for Hong Kong Island. With this onslaught, and attack on the mass exodus from the mainland, one could see the havoc being caused amongst the retreating forces. Craft of all shapes and sizes could be seen sinking, with bodies being thrown into the harbour with not a chance of saving them. One pontoon carrying mules and Indian gunners of the 2nd Mountain Battery, including their 3.7-inch guns, completely capsized in the middle of the harbour.

One of these planes made a low-level attack upon our ferry and machine-gunned it from fore to aft. A burst of fire from this plane struck the starboard side of the ship and caused a great number of casualties amongst the Chinese civilians trying to escape and take shelter on the lower deck carrying the motor transports including the 6-inch How guns of the 25th Medium Battery that was being drawn by 8-ton Scammel lorries fully loaded with ammunition. If one of the armour piercing shells from this plane had struck the ammunition we certainly would have been blown sky high. Shells penetrated the hull of the vessel, which caused a terrific loss of life, mostly Chinese, but there were also casualties amongst the British and Indian forces. Finally the vessel reached the wharf in Hong Kong where I arrested the coxswain. The RAOC Officer reported the incident and the action we had taken against the coxswain to a staff officer of battle headquarters. The staff officer ordered a Hong Kong police officer to arrest the coxswain and charge him with being a fifth column agent who had apparently been working for the Japanese before the outbreak of hostilities. The ferry was then taken over by the police and manned by a crew from the Royal Navy. Maj Temple was informed and he furnished a report to Maj Proes at West Group headquarters. I called in to West Group headquarters and made my report to Maj Proes. From there, I proceeded with a convoy to the RAOC Depot.

By this time long-range guns were heavily shelling the Island of Hong Kong along the foreshores of the harbour, and were now being subjected to continuous bombardment. As I left West Group headquarters and moved down the main road from Magazine Gap, which overlooks the harbour in the distance, I could see shells bursting along the coastline and upon the craft carrying the retreating forces from the mainland. As I arrived in Queen's Road and near the RAOC Depot, shells began to fall upon the Royal Engineers Barracks and the Royal Naval Dockyards opposite. I was able to get my five lorries and men under cover in the depot under a high gravel bank to wait for a lull in the shelling. When the shelling abated, I got my men to hastily load whatever equipment that was available and finally left the depot in Queen's Road to make my way if possible to the Peak tramway terminal at the base of the main road leading to the Peak via Magazine Gap.

As we turned away from the shoreline, I noticed troops, guns and wounded, etc., being unloaded from small craft at various points. I recognised a Sergeant Major of the Royal Scots and asked him, 'What is the position like in the forward defences?' He said, 'Charles, we cannot hold the little yellow bastards because they were advancing along the whole front with Chinese peasants being forced at gunpoint in front of them.' On the mainland one could hear vast explosions and continual sound of rifle, machine gun and mortars in the distance.

I have seen and have been told that the Royal Navy are now crewing and operating the vehicular ferries. The ferries are now receiving loads of wounded arriving back from the battle zones and also other troops that have been withdrawn from our forward defence lines, which presumably have been overrun by the Japanese. The remnants of Royal Scots, Punjabis, Rajputs and artillery units with guns can be seen moving to various points along the shores of Hong Kong. The harbour now appears to be free of small craft that did exist a few days ago when the Chinese were fleeing the mainland to the Island. The Chinese population is now non-existent in Kowloon and it looks as if the whole of the masses have moved over to Hong Kong Island. Goodness knows what will happen to them if the Island comes under heavy aerial and artillery bombardment.

The whole area to the west of Hong Kong is one of burning buildings. The Japanese are advancing fairly rapidly on all fronts in the New Territories and our troops continually withdraw across the harbour to the island. My intention was to return by ferry to the mainland with my convoy of lorries to obtain further supplies of 6-inch shells from West Fort, but seeing the last remaining guns of the 25th Medium Battery moving down Nathan Road to the Yaumati Ferry and the huge congestion in the streets, I realised that a full-scale withdrawal from the mainland was imminent and therefore I cancelled the move to West Fort. Our Lewis gun posts established around the estate of Sir Robert Ho Tung engaged the Japanese aircraft but were not successful in bringing any down. I told 2/Lieut Parks that I thought these flights were reconnaissance missions and possibly a prelude to an all-out attack on West Group. I told him that all outside activities during the day must be kept down to a minimum so as to avoid as much detection as possible from the air. After hearing of the low-level aerial activity over this area, I am sure that the Japanese have earmarked us for future bombing attacks. 2/Lieut Parks advised me that quite a number of personnel had been withdrawn from here for other duties in the defence system. Therefore, it was necessary for me to reorganise and change the duties of the remaining British and Indian troops here. I hastily re-arranged the duties as follows, because my future movements were uncertain:

1. Sgt Waterhouse[14] 3rd Medium Battery HK/SRA — in charge of petrol and oil supplies, dumps and filling points

2. S/Sgt Gollege 4th Medium Battery HK/SRA — in charge of urgent repairs and maintenance of all transport and to stand by for urgent repairs to guns in action at the various positions when necessary

3. BQMS May 4th Medium Battery HK/SRA — in charge and supervising cooking arrangements for British and Indian gunners plus Chinese volunteers

4. S/Sgt Blofield RAOC — in charge of maintenance and repairs to guns and equipment at all positions assisted by S/Sergt Gollege as necessary

5.	Spr Nichols Engineers	in charge of emergency supply of water and the chlorination as necessary assisted by a Chinese sapper of the Royal Engineers
6.	No. 3665 L/Naik Ghulam Mohi-Ud-Din 4th Medium Battery at HK/SRA	in charge and responsible for food supply to all the Sikh and Mohammedan personnel in conjunction with L/Naik Dalip Singh 3754 and all those serving the gun positions. An 8-cwt car is to be maintained and fully serviced and on hand at the West Administrative Pool.[15]
7.	S/Sgt Wilson 4th Medium Battery HK/SRA	in charge of all Administrative duties and telephone switchboard. The telephone would be manned at all times with a roster drawn up and that messages were to be despatched immediately.
8.	Standing Orders for West Admin. Pool	It is the responsibility of 2/Lieut Parks that orders are given to all British and Indian ranks prohibiting unnecessary movements in the grounds of the estate during daylight hours so as to avoid drawing attention to enemy aircraft as a military objective. I informed 2/Lieuts Parks, Simpson and Andrews of these instructions and requested that these orders must be enforced during my absence.

I received a telephone message from 2/Lieut Platts, the adjutant of West Group headquarters at Magazine Gap to withdraw additional Thompson sub machine guns and 0.45-inch ammunition urgently from the RAOC depot, Queen's Road, Hong Kong. These were to be distributed to all gun positions and other defence areas immediately and also to all gunners travelling in convoys instead of the usual 0.303-inch rifles. I rounded up three five-ton lorries and a loading party of about ten men and with me leading in a 15-cwt lorry accompanied by a Naik and two other Indian gunners proceeded to the depot on Peak Road, via Magazine Gap. As I turned into the highway with the convoy leading down towards Hong Kong proper, the shelling had eased somewhat and therefore I was able to travel fairly safely without having to take cover en-route. All we could hear was the far distant rifle and mortar fire, with the occasional artillery fire. I arrived at the depot with an uneasy feeling that all hell was going to break loose, and no sooner had I entered the depot that this occurred.

The Japanese opened up with an artillery barrage that covered the areas from the Naval dockyard to the Royal Engineers Barracks. As per the usual drill, the lorries scattered to cover under the buildings that had been damaged during previous bombardments. After about half an hour, the shelling eased and became spasmodic. I immediately took advantage of this break and loaded the vehicles with the Thompson submachine guns from the ruins where they were stored. To ensure I was well stocked with cartridges for the submachine guns I confiscated a further 4,000 rounds in case of emergency. In addition, I claimed another 0.38-inch revolver and ammunition that I laid upon the space in my vehicle between the seats for immediate use. All the surplus small arms ammunition I stored in a metal container plus 25 grenades carried in the rear of my vehicle.

Further shelling commenced and as I had obtained all I could, I thought it was wise to get away from the depot before the Japanese really opened up with another heavy barrage, which we had previously experienced. We passed the areas of large buildings which had been devastated and abandoned cars, lorries and dead bodies were strewn everywhere. It was not the Hong Kong showing bright lights as we used to see in the past, but a city completely destroyed by a murderous onslaught of continuous bombing and shelling. The fire brigades, health and civil defence units were just non-existent with the result that all one could see was blazing and smouldering blocks of buildings. The non-removal of dead who were lying everywhere completely mortified and when passing, we had to cover our mouths and noses to prevent the awful stench getting down our throats. The convoy was able to make the way to Magazine Gap despite the shelling; making only two stops to take cover for safety. I eventually issued the small arms and ammunition to the defence positions as instructed. Up to this stage, perishable foods for British and Indian troops had been drawn from RASC depots established around the island and delivered to all positions.

When I arrived back at West Administrative Pool, 2/Lieut Parks informed me that 2/Lieut Simpson had been wounded at the Matilda observation post and had lost four fingers to the left hand. The OP was demolished by low flying bombing attacks from about six planes that killed all the signallers on duty there. 2/Lieut Simpson has been admitted to the Bowen Road Military Hospital. After about two hours' break at West Administrative Pool, I received orders to proceed to the magazines at Lei Yu Mun and to withdraw 300/6-inch How shell and cartridges that is required for the gun positions at Mount Gough and Mount Austin. I gathered a convoy of 10/3-ton lorries for this consignment and took the route to Lei Yu Mun via Wong Nei Chong Gap thereby avoiding the main Peak Road. This highway took me out to near North Point and along Causeway Bay and at this point, came into clear view of the enemy observation points on Kowloon across the harbour and of course wide open to be shelled. The convoy entered the fishing village of Shaukeiwan which is at the far side of the island and at the base of Lei Yu Mun. In order to gain the entrance to the magazines at Lei Yu Mun one has to use the steep incline from Shaukeiwan which is a good quarter mile in length and in view by the enemy on the mainland across Lei Yu Mun pass, being the main channel entrance to the harbour. I assembled the convoy under cover in a large culvert behind the village where I gave all the drivers, guards and loading parties the situation and briefed them regarding moving up the steep incline and entry to the magazines. I instructed that each lorry would move independently from our place of cover, and each one would return to this place fully loaded and await further orders. I made the entrance with the first lorry at the magazines and directed it to the store where the type of shell required was stored.

I then went to the small office that was situated inside the main gate at the entrance to telephone Maj Squires at Battle headquarters to advise him that I had arrived at the magazines and that I would report to him when the convoy was fully loaded and ready to move. We had just completed the loading of the seventh lorry when the Japanese commenced shelling Lei Yu Mun from the Devil's Peak area upon the mainland. I quickly instructed the driver of the seventh lorry to make a quick exit to the culvert where all the remaining lorries were and to inform the driver of the eighth lorry not to move until there was a lull in the shelling. After a lapse of about an hour, the bombardment stopped and within about 15 minutes the eighth lorry arrived at the magazines.

During this pause we were able to load the last and tenth lorry and commenced our homeward journey to the gun positions at Mount Gough and Mount Austin. I contacted Maj Squires and advised him that all deliveries were completed. I returned to West Administrative Pool where I was able to snatch a couple of hours sleep and told BQMS 'Clancy' May to withhold all non-urgent messages so as to allow me to have a rest. After about two hours' rest, Clancy awakened me with a nice meal and a cup of tea. At about 9 p.m. I was visited by Capt Thursby[16] of the Kings Own Shropshire Light Infantry who was on the staff at Battle headquarters. He was making enquiries regarding the issue of anti-gas clothing and equipment and if an issue had been made to all defence positions. I confirmed that this had been done a few weeks before the outbreak of hostilities. When Capt Thursby left, I made an issue of clothing and other necessary items to all British officers, NCOs and Indian other ranks.

I checked by phone to all gun positions the total rounds of shell and cartridges held and the amounts that had been expended. These returns of expenditure and stocks held were required daily at West Group headquarters, which was essential so as to replenish with further supplies in order to avoid the gun positions being without ammunition. I was under the direct control of Battle headquarters who were responsible for the withdrawal of ammunition and the arrangement of the necessary convoys of lorries held at the RASC vehicle pool at various points around the island when orders would be given to me to organise the rendezvous for the collection of these lorries, armed guards and loading parties as necessary. These convoys would be made up to strength of about twenty to twenty-five lorries with armed guards totalling four to a vehicle, plus a senior NCO in charge. The loading party would consist of about twenty men, mostly Indian Gunners. The only two main magazines remaining on the island were at Little Hong Kong, near Aberdeen, which is on the south-western side of the island and one at Lei Yu Mun on the east of the island. If Lei Yu Mun were lost to the enemy, the magazine at Little Hong Kong would be our only remaining source of supply.

13 December 1941

During the early hours of this morning at about 2.00 a.m., I received an urgent message to supply 6-inch How shell and cartridges to the sites at Mount Gough and Mount Austin. At about 2.30 a.m., I assembled a small convoy of small lorries fully manned with guards and loading parties. I then proceeded to Lei Yu Mun via Peak Road and Causeway Bay highways. On the way you could hear in the far distance of Kowloon, an amount of spasmodic rifle and mortar fire and also intermittent shelling of the island from the mainland.

The flashes from the Japanese guns could be seen from various points along the coastline and exploding along the foreshores of the harbour causing further fires to buildings, which were now illuminating the east, and west of Hong Kong Island facing Kowloon. Our guns could be heard responding from around the island. I arrived at the magazines at Lei Yu Mun and was able to get the lorries loaded with shell and cartridges with very little interference. I finally left the area as quickly as possible briefing the drivers before moving off to ensure at least fifty yards between vehicles. When I reached the base of the road that led back up to the magazines, the barracks which normally housed the 5th AA Regiment, Royal Artillery and the convoy was about to pass through the fishing village of Shaukeiwan, the Japanese opened up with a barrage on to the magazines and barracks from the Devil's Peak district which was across the Lei Yu Mun Channel. Luckily, the shells went over our heads into the embankment. Nevertheless, I moved the convoy at increasing speed along the road to North Point. Within a very short space of time, the Japanese switched their bombardment towards that area causing me to order the lorries off the road to cover behind a small culvert with the hope of avoiding a direct hit on one of the lorries fully loaded with explosives. Should a direct hit occur on one or more of the lorries amongst the surrounding semi-high buildings, there would be complete devastation to this area and no doubt a great loss of life to those residing there.

There was a lull in the shelling of the North Point area, during which I quickly moved the lorries away and headed to Peak Road, which I had to make before daylight. If caught on this road during daylight we would be at the mercy of the Japanese artillery directed from observation posts in Kowloon. I decided to continue up Peak Road safely reaching the top, which more or less terminated at Wanchai Gap.

We had a clear run along the south-west of the island out of view of the enemy artillery and all we had to face was air attack along this part of the road, but fortunately this did not occur and therefore we delivered the ammunition to the gun sites without incident.

I also spoke to Lieut Simpson who was at RA Central and an officer in the last World War, as a matter of fact; he commanded a battery on the Macedonian front. He is an extremely nice fellow and I have enjoyed his company on many a pleasant evening during peacetime.

Later, I took the opportunity to try and rest for a few hours and believe me I do need it as I am just about fagged out.

14 December 1941

Shortly after midnight of 14 December, I received orders from battle headquarters, to rendezvous at North Point with a convoy of lorries, to transport Indian officers and other ranks of the 2nd/14th Punjabis who had recently arrived across from Kowloon. I arrived at the place of rendezvous at the designated time and met Maj Gray,[17] who commanded the company. There appeared to be about 80–90 other ranks, completely worn out, but still quite at ease even after fighting a rear guard action for the last four days. I took them all to West Administrative Pool, for rest and food which I arranged with Havildar Muzaffar Khan as these men were Mohammedans. During my discussion with Maj Gray, he told me that they had fought all the way from Tai Po in the New Territories, where they first came in contact with the Japanese on 9 December. He further told me that he deployed his company in the market village at Tai Po, as he believed the Japanese would advance this way to the south. Normally a busy place, Tai Po was totally deserted. Using his arms by way of explanation, he said north of the village was a hill over which the Japanese were most likely to appear via the track. Every machine gun and rifle of his men pointed at this hill and track. His forecast proved correct, for the Japanese appeared marching in column of route without any attempt to check their surroundings. He said there must have been a full battalion of around 1,000 men behind which followed a battery of artillery carried by pack mules. When the Japanese were at a distance of about 300 yards, he roared the order to 'FIRE' which the men did as fast as they could reload their weapons. This murderous fire continued unabated for a full two to three minutes, with only a few Japanese escaping unscathed by retreating back over the hill. The mules also bolted into the distance carrying all their supplies. It was first blood to my company Maj Gray explained, and not a man lost to boot. However, Gray did say that after this convincing victory, things started to go wrong from this point on.

He appreciated what had been done for his men and were ordered to take up defence positions in and around Wong Nei Chong area. I never saw him again.

I met up with Lieut Bompas RA at West Administrative Pool who has just returned from the mainland and he told me that he had to swim Lei Yu Mun Channel. He said that a lighter conveying mules and guns capsized in the channel whilst evacuating the mainland from the Devil's Peak area during the hours of darkness. He could not say how many casualties there were amongst the mules and the men as he only just managed to save his own life by the skin of his teeth. His temporary rig-out amused me, as he arrived in a pair of khaki shorts and a white tennis pullover, which he obtained from someplace on the island, leaving his wet clothes as exchange. Anyway, after re-clothing him again and issuing him new equipment, etc., we both sat down and enjoyed a couple of bottles of beer in the early hours of about 4.00 a.m. During this interlude, Capt Avery RA arrived and told us that he has been ordered over to RA Central for further instructions and I fancy he is being transferred to 'East Group'. Capt Avery and Lieut Bompas are excellent officers and are both doing good work in this campaign.

I had orders to collect the following items from the RAOC depots at Brick Hill and the Ridge for distribution to defence positions: 400 blankets, 250 anti-gas capes, 40 sets of anti-gas clothing, cooking utensils, personal clothing and necessities, etc.

In addition, I will have to arrange to withdraw rations for British and Indian officers and gunners. Also an issue of 6-inch How and 3.7-inch How shell and cartridges for delivery to the following gun positions that will be occupied by 2nd Mountain and 25th Medium Batteries who will take over the gun position sites following their withdrawal from the mainland: Tiger Balm, Caroline Hill, Stanley Gap and Victoria Peak.

At this moment, concentrated fire is now being directed from all guns onto the Shing Mun Redoubt, which has fallen into the hands of the advancing Japanese forces who are moving down the highways of the New Territories towards Kowloon. I wonder what has happened to Lieut Willcocks[18] and staff who were in the Redoubt and were directing artillery fire upon the enemy. I think there were fifty or more officers and other ranks that were housed within this strongpoint, being the last line of defence in this area.

Early in the afternoon I was returning to West Administrative Pool, when we came under heavy shellfire and as a result a great number of casualties were inflicted upon the Canadians at Wanchai Gap and also devastating the roads leading into that area. As I approached Wanchai Gap, a small car overtook me on my right and which was being driven by an officer of the Royal Scots Regiment, received a direct hit from a shell, which completely wrecked the car and killed the officer instantly.[19] The wrecked car lay about sixty yards in front of me, which caused a blockage and the movement of the convoy of about thirty lorries fully loaded with high explosives. I signalled to the men to remove the wrecked car with the remains of the body being covered by a groundsheet. I reported the casualty to headquarters who arranged to remove the body from the area. On passing St Albert's Convent that had been established as a hospital, a shell struck the building, killing one VAD nurse and wounding several others.[20] This incident was taken care of by the hospital authorities.

15 December 1941

The total evacuation of the remaining Mainland Brigade including troops and artillery were completed in the early hours of this morning with few casualties, the retreating forces were quickly dispersed on Hong Kong

Island to their allotted positions of defence on the east and the west of the island. It was reported that 2nd Mountain Battery had lost some of their guns and mules and also some troops when crossing the harbour somewhere in the region of the Lei Yu Mun Channel. This report has yet to be confirmed.

The Shing Mun Redoubt was well constructed and completed with concrete underground passages and rooms to house and store ammunition and equipment, etc. It was built upon similar lines in a smaller way to the well-known 'Maginot Line' in France. The Redoubt accommodated approximately 50–60 officers and other ranks, whose purpose was for observation and report the progress and Japanese movements during the battle. Even though it was formidable, the Japanese appeared to have overrun it very easily. I well remember when I lost my bearings upon Golden Hill which is situated near this post during an exercise in the New Territories in late 1939. At that time, the whole of this area was covered in dense fog and similar weather would no doubt have assisted the Japanese.

Battle headquarters have issued orders to all batteries to put down a heavy barrage of fire upon the area of Shing Mun Redoubt and along the whole of the 'Gin Drinkers Line' which is now in the hands of the Japanese. The 'Gin Drinkers Line', was the first line of defence stretching for over ten miles in the New Territories, which lies north of Hong Kong. It runs east to West direction. It was so named after Gin Drinkers Bay to the West, where in peacetime particularly on Sundays, picnics were held during which copious amounts of gin were consumed.

The vibration that is being felt all around the island resembles a violent earthquake. The 9.2-inch Coastal Batteries are discharging their heavy projectiles of approximately 300 lb, each which are presently whistling over our heads. The Japanese artillery is also replying with their long-range guns, which are causing wide-scale damage to buildings on the island; also, their Air Force are carrying out round-the-clock bombings. It appears that the Japanese batteries are stationed somewhere in the vicinity of Kai Tak Aerodrome and Kowloon City. I again proceeded to Little Hong Kong Magazine with a convoy of lorries to collect 6-inch How and 3.7-inch How Shell and cartridges for the gun positions at Tiger Balm, Caroline Hill, Stanley Gap and Victoria Peak. On the way, I called into the Brick Hill RAOC depot where I met an old friend of mine QMS Daniels[21] of the Royal Engineers who was not wearing a steel helmet, which he had lost during a skirmish with the Japanese on the mainland. I had a spare one in my car so I gave it to him for protection.

The staff at Brick Hill RAOC depot has been continuously supplying stores to all units since 8 December, and in the last few hours they have been issuing vital stores to the remnants of the withdrawing troops that recently arrived from the mainland. These units included the Royal Scots, 2/14th Punjabis, 5/7th Rajputs, etc., who were re-equipped as much as possible. The staff at the depot were as follows: QMS Daniels, L/Sgt Ewens OIC depot, L/Cpl Ealey, Pte Stopforth,[22] and eight Chinese volunteers.

The duties of rationing West Group Administration and the whole of their positions was handed over to BQMS Searle,[23] 4th Medium Battery HK/SRA. During my absence, West Administration Pool had come under heavy bombing attack from low-flying aircraft that appeared to come from the direction of the New Territories, which I assumed, was in Japanese hands. During this raid, five Indian gunners were wounded and BQMS Searle received shrapnel wounds to his left foot.

These casualties were admitted to Bowen Road Military Hospital. Two mules were badly injured; one being gutted by flying shrapnel and the other had its leg broken at the hip. I ordered S/Sgt Farrier Holmes to destroy them immediately and bury the carcases in the grounds surrounding the building. The Indian gunners manning the Lewis guns that had been established around the area made an attempt to shoot down the planes but without success. It was reported that two planes did go down in the harbour, but the gunners were not credited with these kills.

The huge clouds of smoke drifting across to the west of the island are now becoming very unpleasant, more so, because it is now raining very heavily. It is like driving through a London pea-souper fog to gain access to the defence positions. It also appears that the Japanese have destroyed the huge oil tanks, so as to enable them to invade the island at any time from now with the assistance of this smoke screen. The island is now under a continuous heavy bombardment by land, sea and air. All the commercial and residential buildings and other installations are burning fiercely around the whole of the centre and west of Hong Kong Island. The guns at Mount Austin and Mount Gough positions continue to bombard the Japanese batteries situated on the mainland somewhere in the Lai Chi Kok and Kai Tak districts.

One can hear the continuous cries and anguish of the Chinese women and children fleeing from the centre of Hong Kong towards Aberdeen where they are hoping to find some sort of temporary shelter from the continuous bombardment. The rationing had now been handed over to BQMS May who has replaced BQMS Searle, the latter now being in hospital.

I received a phone call from the Mount Austin gun position advising me that one of the 6-inch How's was out of action. I sent S/Sgt Fitter Gollege and S/Sgt Fitter Phillips to the position to carry out repairs to the dial sight bracket, which had become faulty thereby causing inaccurate fire when engaging enemy fire on the mainland.

16 December 1941

Received orders at 7.00 a.m. to collect a convoy of twenty lorries from the Vehicle Concentration Centre (VCC) at Happy Valley racecourse and to proceed to Lei Yu Mun Magazines at the eastern end of the island to withdraw ammunition and again issue to the gun sites at Tiger Balm, Caroline Hill, Stanley Gap, Mount Austin, Mount Gough and Victoria Peak. In addition, to issue the following items to the personnel at the defence sites that were taken over by our infantry after their evacuation from the mainland: blankets, anti-gas clothing, personal clothing, other necessities, etc.

During this assignment, air attacks continued every hour throughout the day. The distance between each position was approximately three-four miles; this caused me to take evasive action many times along the highways by getting the lorries under cover as much as possible, but taking advantage of any lull whilst the aircraft were also concentrating on trying to locate the batteries at the various gun positions mentioned above plus those at Mount Kellett and Sanatorium. These gun positions were cleverly concealed in valleys and behind very narrow razor-like ridges, which were not easily detectable either by air or shellfire. The guns' barrels at these sites I would say must be red hot with so much firing and it looks as if I shall have to be on my way again to withdraw further supplies of ammunition. S/Sgt Farrier Holmes is quite busy attending to the mules under his charge which are stabled well under cover below Sir Robert Ho Tung's house and near a well-covered creek lined with trees and bushes.

The Japanese reverted back to a more practical form of warfare. The shelling increased in intensity and a furious barrage of mortar fire came from the Kowloon waterfront. Clearly, this was a softening-up process as a curtain raiser to a full-scale landing on the island. This landing was not slow in coming, but the first attempt by the Japanese was a dismal failure as the concept was too bold to the point of being suicidal and was summarily and bloodily dealt with by our troops holding the defences along the foreshores. The attempted assault was carried out by fanatically brave men. Estimates of their numbers vary from one to two companies, but not a single Japanese set foot on the island. Many of the Japanese troops making the invasions swam across the channel, pushing crude rafts made of petrol tins which carried their equipment.

I saw others from my vantage point, where I was under cover with a convoy of lorries waiting to move at the first opportunity to Little Hong Kong Magazine to collect further supplies of ammunition making the journey in a weird assortment of craft such as small rubber boats, sampans and junks. As this armada arrived at the middle of the harbour the defenders poured a murderous fire into the Japanese. A junk punctured by hundreds of bullets was holed and sank, sampans were hit and overturned and machine gunners and riflemen sprayed the water, which by now was red with blood. The channel became a dark shambles of shrieking struggling and drowning Japanese, until the last yelling voice was silent and the last clawing hand still, was the order to cease fire given. This was a tremendous boost to the defenders whose nerves had been most cruelly shaken during this uneasy period of waiting. Major General Maltby's men had drawn first blood in the battle for Hong Kong Island.

Later in the day I returned to Lei Yu Mun Magazine to obtain further supplies of ammunition for the various gun positions. On the return trip we came under a disastrous air attack from a large group of planes. All lorries were fully loaded with shell and cartridges and each one endeavoured to take cover amongst the trees and buildings en-route to the gun positions. I lost three lorries and twenty men in this action, due to direct hits.

From the devastating explosions, surrounding buildings were demolished and quite a number of casualties amongst the Canadians holding[24] defence positions in the area. There have also been quite a number of casualties amongst the Chinese occupying the buildings. Battle headquarters was alerted and groups of troops were soon at the devastated area to remove the dead and wounded. Eventually the remainder of the convoy proceeded under cover of darkness to the gun sites where the ammunitions were offloaded. A burial party located an area for disposal of the dead and the wounded were transferred to Bowen Road Military Hospital. The green and red discs were removed from the dead and forwarded to headquarters.

When travelling at nights without lights, through the deserted streets and isolated villages, it was impossible to avoid running over the scattered groups of dead Chinese bodies that had been caught up in this bombing and shelling. One could feel your vehicle bumping over bodies that one could not see, some may have been dead and quite possibly, some may have been alive. Late in the evening I received a telephone call from West Group headquarters to collect a convoy of ten 5-ton lorries from the Vehicle Concentration Centre (VCC) at Happy Valley and to withdraw 6-inch How shell and cartridges from Lei Yu Mun Magazines. Capt Wiseman, in charge of the centre will arrange to hand over the lorries to me, plus one NCO and twelve ORs as guard who are to be drawn from the Royal Rifles of Canada. Incidentally, Capt Wiseman was operating on an artificial leg and he moved around without any difficulty. I decided to use Causeway Bay and North Point to reach the fishing village of Shaukeiwan. On nearing the village a sudden bombardment developed, the shelling coming from across the Lei Yu Mun Channel on to the high ground, which was where the Barracks of the 5th AA Regiment was stationed. On our way through the fishing village, I saw three distinct electric light flashes from one of the houses that we were passing at the time, this being probably a signal to the Japanese forces on the mainland, informing them of a convoy passing through. At that stage I dare not stop to investigate and hold up the movement of the lorries in case we would be pinned down as a target. I immediately hastened the lorries to the west end of the village to a well-covered area in a large valley. The lorries were stacked close up to a bank, which was very high and well covered with trees. The shells were falling well over the ridge that was protecting the men from shrapnel fallout.

As soon as the bombardment abated, I checked the lorries and personnel to see if there were any casualties but fortunately there were none. The only disturbing problem I had was the absence of three Chinese drivers who had deserted; however, having had previous experience of desertions amongst the Chinese employed as drivers, I carried reserve Indian drivers as replacements. I realised that the Chinese could not stand up to the shelling and bombing. During a lull in the present shelling and the time being about midnight, I decided to take advantage of this lull to move the lorries up to the magazines for loading one at a time and when each lorry was loaded, it would return to this rendezvous and the driver would inform the next driver to proceed to the magazines for loading. This system would go on until each vehicle was loaded. With these instructions fully understood by all the drivers, I left the place of concealment followed by the first lorry and proceeded up the steep incline to the entrance gates of the magazines. I directed the lorry to the chamber that stored the 6-inch How shell, etc. and got the men under way for loading. From there, I made my usual telephone call to Maj Squires at Battle headquarters to inform him of my arrival and the progress and reasons for my delay.

Finally, I was able to get all lorries loaded with the exception of the tenth and last one that was near completion of being loaded which was to follow me down the steep incline and then onwards to the rendezvous. At the base of the incline, I suddenly heard a terrific explosion, which came from the top and near the main gates of the magazines. This appeared to be a direct hit on the lorry from a further commencement of artillery barrage. The lorry moved out of control near the rise of the steep incline, overturned and disappeared over the cliff in a drop of about 400 ft. killing everyone on board. As no assistance could be given, my thoughts now were to get the remainder of the convoy on the move to their respective sites. I instructed all drivers to keep a good distance between all vehicles and all to rendezvous at the Peak tramway terminal. We commenced our journey as quickly as possible along the Causeway Bay and North Point route. About two hours later all lorries rendezvoused at the Tramway Terminus and from there, made our way up Peak Road eventually reaching the top without incident.

Later, all drivers reported that they had delivered the ammunition to the sites as ordered.

17 December 1941

The day started normally for the defenders with the humdrum sounds of the bombing and shelling. The steady drain of casualties with the cursing of sleep-starved men and the rumours. The rumours alternated between facile optimism and extreme pessimism as to whether or not the Chinese forces were on their way to relieve them in a matter of hours, and also whether a powerful American fleet was at this moment steaming with haste towards Hong Kong. As I was proceeding along the Causeway Bay highway with a convoy of twenty-five lorries fully laden with shell and cartridges with the lorries moving at approximately fifty yards interval between each when suddenly an uneasy quietness swept over Hong Kong. The shelling from the Japanese had ceased and all one could hear from here or there was a shell screaming overhead or a machine gun stuttering in the far distance. What a relief not to hear the noise of battle being silenced, which had been going on for days.

Looking across the Harbour from North Point, Havildar Muzaffar Khan sitting beside me said 'Sahib, dekko' (meaning 'look'), pointing his finger in the direction of Kowloon where we spotted a small launch chugging across the harbour with a large white banner on which was emblazoned 'PEACE MISSION'. This was of course the reason for the

sudden cessation of the bombardment and was the second time the
Japanese had offered the unconditional surrender of Hong Kong. This
would mean that there would be a cessation of hostilities, therefore giving
me about four hours to deliver the ammunition to defence positions
before the demands, if not accepted by Major General Maltby or the
Governor of Hong Kong Sir Mark Young, expired. I was sure that these
demands would not be accepted, so in all haste, I got the lorries moving
up Peak Road as quickly as possible. At about 6.30 p.m., the whole of
Hong Kong came under further bombardment from the land, sea and
air. Later, an official communiqué was issued to all headquarters and
defence posts that the Japanese had come from Kowloon under cover of
a white flag, bringing a letter, inquiring if His Excellency the Governor
was willing to negotiate surrender, whereupon the Governor summarily
rejected the proposal. The Governor then repeated the following, as he
had done in the previous offer of surrender.

THE COLONY IS NOT ONLY STRONG ENOUGH TO RESIST ALL
ATTEMPTS OF INVASION, BUT ALL THE RESOURCES OF THE BRITISH
EMPIRE AND OF THE UNITED STATES OF AMERICA AND THE
REPUBLIC OF CHINA ARE BEHIND US AND THOSE WHO HAVE
SOUGHT PEACE CAN REST ASSURED THAT THERE WILL NEVER BE
ANY SURRENDER TO THE JAPANESE.'

We, of course all realised that these were brave words, as there was
little enough to back them, as there were no more resources available
for the defence of Hong Kong by the British Empire. In the evening I
received orders from Maj Squires from West Administrative Pool to
commandeer an 8-ton Scammell lorry from the RAOC depot at the Ridge
along Repulse Bay Road and withdraw a 60-pounder including fifty
rounds of shell and cartridges. While I hastily proceeded to the depot in
a 15-cwt accompanied by Havildar Muzaffar Khan and four Indian
gunners, I suddenly realised that this ancient piece of ordnance was
required for a specific purpose. We located the gun but found it difficult
to locate the equipment required for the gun to operate after so many
years in storage. This ancient piece of artillery was of 1914 manufacture,
as was the ammunition. Apparently, Major General Maltby, GOC of
Troops Hong Kong, had been informed that there were three Japanese
transports lying at anchor in the harbour just off North Point presumably
thought to be carrying troops for a possible invasion at that part of the
island in the very near future.

The GOC passed this information onto Brig T. McLeod,[25] who was
in command of all artillery units in Hong Kong. He was instructed to
destroy them at all costs. Hence, the need for the 60-pounder which was

selected for this purpose and is to be positioned at a site decided by Lieut J. Vinter on the foreshores of the beach at North Point. This movement to be carried out during the hours of darkness.

The following ranks of the RAOC were at the Ridge depot:

Lieut Col McPherson (OIC)
QMS (Vic) Morris (Chief Clerk)
QMS Haynes (Master Artificer)
Lieut Markey
L/Cpl Bliss
Mr (Cyril) Walker (Foreman 'E' Group)
Mr Collinson (Foreman 'Clothing' Group)
Mr Redding (Foreman 'K' Group)
QMS Singleton (Foreman 'B' Group)[26]

There were other personnel also whose names I have now forgotten. With the exception of Lieut Col McPherson, the above personnel were very good friends of mine. The Ridge, in my opinion, was not the ideal location for an ordnance depot, as it was extremely vulnerable to air and land attack.

We towed the 60-pounder by the 8-ton Scammel lorry, the normal vehicle used for gun towing. Lieut Vinter was detailed for this operation with a detachment of one Jemadar, one Havildar, two Naiks and twelve gunners. He told them that the site was to be occupied with as least noise as possible. Lieut Vinter took command of the gun after it was towed to the site. The site selected faced the ships that were at a distance of about 500 yards.

Once the gun was fully established and prepared for action, it was lined with open sights on the first transport. With the chamber loaded with shell and cartridge the gun opened fire on the first transport, but on contacting the hull, it did not explode, so Vinter decided to shell all ships by hitting them below the water line which he did with great success. After firing a number of shells at the first ship, it suddenly burst into flames and exploded. He then traversed to the second ship, which received direct hits causing it to sink aft first, finally going down with its bow shooting out of the water. Vinter then engaged the third transport which also received about a dozen shells and it burst into flames. We noticed Japanese troops scrambling overboard in the bright lights of the burning ships. There were many troops on these ships, but exactly how many we could not ascertain. Eventually, the Japanese on the mainland realised what was happening and immediately opened up with a barrage of artillery fire on to the North Point area. Vinter, in all haste, gave

orders to hook up the gun to the Scammell and withdraw to Causeway
Bay Road and to head to West Group headquarters and report the success
of the mission. Brig McLeod congratulated Vinter for the action including
the Indian officers and gunners who acted so bravely during this
operation, particularly when they came under heavy fire during and after
the action.

It was on this day in the late afternoon when I was returning to
West Administrative Pool and on my way to Wanchai Gap and about
fifty yards from the temporary bridge built across a fairly wide creek,
which was necessary to keep the road open to the Peak, we came under
a heavy artillery barrage from the mainland.

As I was passing Wanchai Gap headquarters, an officer of the Royal
Engineers had just left his car with a view of taking cover amongst the
rocks in the vicinity. He appeared to run in a crouching position when a
large portion of shrapnel from a shell completely decapitated his head
from his shoulders. The headless body continued to move forward for
about a yard or so when it finally collapsed.

I arranged with my men to move his body further into the rock
formation just off the road as soon as the bombardment eased. I reported
the casualty to Maj Proes at the nearby headquarters and told him that I
could not identify the officer because he was not wearing the usual red
and green identity discs. Anyway, he reported the casualty to Battle
headquarters who no doubt made arrangements for the removal of the
body. I resumed my journey to West Administrative Pool when I
witnessed a convoy of lorries in charge of L/Sgt of the Royal Engineers,
being heavily bombed by a group of Japanese aircraft that caused the
destruction of about five lorries with a great number of men being killed
and wounded. I attended the scene and with the assistance of my men,
we removed the dead and wounded to the War Memorial Hospital and
reported the incident to the nearby Wanchai Gap headquarters.

Upon leaving the headquarters, I passed a detachment of the Royal
Scots Regiment with a Sgt Maj Sutherland[27] in charge, who were moving
to an allotted position on the island and in the direction of Mount
Cameron. In passing I said, 'Sandy, where are all your men?' He said,
'Quite a number were killed and wounded at the position we were holding
near the Shing Mun Redoubt which was overrun by the Japanese.' With
best wishes to each other, we proceeded on our ways.

It has been reported that small groups of Japanese troops have
infiltrated the island and the defences have been warned of possible
sabotage to supply depots and ammunition dumps, etc. We have sent
out patrols into the jungle areas to search and destroy these Japanese,

who I believe would be operating in the Pokfulam district, which would be the ideal place to land, particularly as it is near Lamma Island off the west coast of Hong Kong Island and only a short distance away. The search will be conducted by the Royal Scots or Middlesex Regiment. I rang Maj Temple at Wong Nei Chong Gap headquarters and informed him that the highways running from east to west of the island, particularly the road leading up to the Peak, were badly pitted with shell holes and jammed with abandoned lorries of all types that were obstructing the movements of transport. He arranged immediately with Battle headquarters for the Pioneer Corp units to repair and clear the roads as soon as possible.

At about 8.30 p.m. I received a telephone message from Wanchai Gap to collect a convoy of lorries from the Vehicle Concentration Centre (VCC), at Happy Valley for the purpose of conveying 3.7-inch, 4.5-inch and 6-inch How ammunition from Lei Yu Mun Magazines. At about 10.00 pm on approaching Shaukeiwan village, I noticed that a large rubber factory with its surrounding buildings were ablaze, which was caused by enemy shellfire from the mainland. Due to the continuous shellfire from the mainland, I used the Shek O Road route.

Furthermore, there was heavy machine gun fire which appeared to be coming from the Star Ferry area on the mainland and I believe the Japanese had machine guns planted in the clock tower situated nearby. On reaching the road below Lei Yu Mun, I could see by the glare of the burning rubber factory, that the gun track leading up to the barracks had been bombed heavily during the day which had severed the track in two places and making this portion of the track practically impassable for transport. As my convoy would be seen by the glare of the fire, which was in full view of the mainland, I gave orders that lorries would move at 200-yard intervals into the magazine. I also instructed each driver to proceed cautiously when approaching the bomb craters, as any error on their part would mean instant death on the rocks below. I also noticed that the guardroom, offices, stores and other buildings were practically in ruins caused by the recent heavy bombardments. On reporting to L/Cpl O'Connell[28] RAOC and in charge of the magazines, he said, 'No issues of ammunition were being made from the magazines tonight.' To confirm if this was correct, I telephoned Maj Squires at Battle headquarters but Maj Ryan RA[29] answered the phone and he confirmed that no ammunition was to be issued from Lei Yu Mun magazine until further notice.

He instructed me to collect my convoy and move off as quickly as possible, as all batteries were about to commence concentrated fire onto the Lei Yu Mun Pass areas where according to recent reports, the Japanese were attempting to make a landing. Within a few minutes of getting my lorries underway, the Japanese opened up with a barrage of shelling and heavy machine gun fire from the direction of Devil's Peak, this peak overlooking the pass. On the way out of the magazines, I met S/Sgt Peters[30] of the RAOC, who had attempted to repair one of the beach searchlights that had apparently been put out of action by machine gun fire during the day. Peters remarked to me, 'Damn that place, Charlie, it is too hot around there,' and it was and no mistake. This attempted landing was finally frustrated towards early morning.

During all these actions, the drivers of my lorries were very good and especially skilful when driving over the difficult ground of the Lei Yu Mun gun track.

As I was stalled for drawing ammunition from Lei Yu Mun, I proceeded directly to Little Hong Kong Magazine by the Shek O Road route to withdraw ammunition as ordered, eventually delivering this to Caroline Hill and Stanley Gap positions. We were continually intercepted by our sentries stationed at strategic points along the road as was the case now all over the island. When travelling at night and without lights one could only hear the noise of the lorry engines and the shelling, etc. Therefore, one had to keep his ears and eyes wide open for any challenges that were to be expected from the sentries, or else you were liable to be shot by one of your own men. An example of shooting your own men, was in the case of Band Master Gordon of the 2nd Royal Scots, who was shot dead by one of his own men for not answering the usual challenge at a place called 'Skeats ground', which is situated along Castle Peak Road. He was buried practically at the same spot he was shot.

As it was reported that a small detachment of Japanese troops had landed in the Aberdeen-Pokfulam area, I decided to use one of the jungle tracks to Little Hong Kong Magazine. The Japanese would have little or no knowledge of these routes through the jungle. When I joined the main road just a short distance from the magazines, we came under machine gun and rifle fire from my left in the direction of Brick Hill. The Indian Naik Ahmad Din who was seated beside me in the front seat was hit and collapsed onto the gearbox on my left side. My left hand was hit dislodging it from the steering wheel causing me to temporarily lose control of vehicle. To avoid crashing into the trees on the other side of the road, I braked causing the car to spin before coming to a stop. The two Indian gunners in the rear seat pulled Ahmad Din into an upright position. I got out of the vehicle and urged the lorries to keep moving. As I was about to board my vehicle, I was hit on the right foot by machine gun or rifle fire. I could hear the bullets ricocheting off the road.

I jumped into my vehicle and moved at great haste into the magazines. Ahmad Din was offloaded onto a stretcher and attended to by a medic. He had a severe wound in the back just below the left shoulder. In the meantime, the lorries were being loaded with ammunition with Havildar Muzaffar Khan who took charge of the loading. During this period I pulled off my right boot to find my sock soaking in blood, the injury appeared minor, however; I washed and bandaged the wound. I looked at my left hand, which was aching, but there was no wound, although the third finger was bruised. It was then I realised that my wedding ring was missing obviously severed by the bullet. Later I found my ring on the floor of my vehicle. I reported to Maj Marsh[31] (Middlesex Regiment) informing him I would return by the same route through the jungle track (also known as Cookhouse Lane). He said he would give covering fire and added 'best of luck "Q" '. I informed each driver to keep at least 100 yards distance from the lorry ahead. I left the magazines at around 1.00 a.m., the convoy completing delivery to the gun positions by 3.30 a.m. without further incident. At 5.30 a.m. on 18 December I submitted my ammunition return, which was the usual procedure.

During the past week I have been constantly in touch with Maj Squires and Master Gunner O'Connell who are stationed at battle headquarters and they want up to date statements of stocks of ammunition held at all gun positions in the western part of the island. Depending on this information they can arrange to build up these sites with adequate amounts of ammunition so that stocks are not completely exhausted, whereby we would be unable to engage the enemy, either on the mainland or in case of invasion of Hong Kong Island.

When receiving orders to move the convoys whether empty or fully loaded with high explosives, I have had to determine the routes to and from the magazines which are under surveillance by observation posts by the Japanese at various points on the mainland, mostly in the region of Kowloon. Most of these highways are pitted with shell holes, particularly Peak Road leading up towards Magazine Gap. From that point the road becomes hidden from view from Kowloon or any other point on the mainland. It was imperative that I endeavour to clear all highways before daylight, particularly Peak Road which is a main target for enemy artillery leaving shell holes that become a major problem to cross with heavy laden lorries. To overcome this problem, I arranged for all vehicles to be issued with planks, which can be used if necessary to cross these potholes that are enormous at some places. I hope the pioneer units are on the move to fill in these holes as soon as possible. Luckily, I have had only four direct hits on lorries moving along this route, with of course a great loss of drivers, guards and loading parties.

18 December 1941

At 8.00 a.m. I proceeded to Kennedy Road magazines with a convoy of lorries to collect 4.5-inch How ammunition which was delivered by 10.00 a.m. to Sanatorium and Mount Kellett gun positions.

During this time, heavy shelling was taking place at the following places: RAOC Ordnance Depot, Queen's Road, Stubbs Road, and Magazine Gap and Wanchai Gap Roads.

As Peak Road was in full view of the enemy, precautions were taken in camouflaging all vehicles. At 11.00 a.m. I received a telephone message to collect 6-inch How shell and cartridges from the magazines at Little Hong Kong that are required urgently at the gun positions at Mount Gough and Mount Austin. For this consignment, I used my own transport consisting of four 3-ton lorries and my own 15-cwt vehicle. Four Indian gunners accompanied me in my vehicle. I gave instructions to the drivers to step up the speed when proceeding down the highway from Magazine Gap and if they did come under shellfire, to just keep moving. Whilst avoiding the shell holes in the road, it was now becoming impassable in some places and therefore it was necessary to hastily put down the planks of timber over these holes to enable the lorries to cross. By now, the gunners and drivers were becoming very adept in the use of this planking. I give full praise to these men taking part in these operations and not one of them had stalled during the runs.

I decided to withdraw any further supplies of ammunition from Little Hong Kong by daylight and to use the Lei Yu Mun Magazines by night. The pain in my right foot is now becoming unbearable. Capt Hoyland[32] suggested I attend the medical centre nearby, this being the War Memorial Hospital. The civilian doctor there was unable to x-ray my foot, but has soaked the swollen part in a strong solution of iodine and strengthened the foot and ankle with bandages. He said it also may be fractured and should be rested, but I explained to him that it was essential that I keep the convoys on the move as ammunition is much needed at the gun sites in the western part of the island in this most critical time. I would endeavour to rest the foot whenever possible. The doctor gave me a supply of iodine and bandages, plus tablets to ease the pain. Being as the foot is so swollen, I am wearing a canvas rubber shoe on the right foot, which makes it more comfortable.

The movements of the convoys are becoming increasingly hazardous and casualties to date have totalled twenty-four killed comprising five British, seventeen Indian and two Chinese lorry drivers plus six severely wounded. In addition, a short time ago I lost a lorry fully loaded with 3.7-inch How shell and cartridges which went over a cliff from the roadway leading down from Lei Yu Mun Magazines, killing all ten men and a driver who were crushed under the weight of the shells from the vehicle; also, a lorry that received a direct hit along Causeway Bay Road exploded and completely disintegrated, killing everyone aboard. We were lucky that the blast did not cause a chain reaction to the remaining vehicles in the convoy, which were fully loaded with high explosives. Finally, we were able to proceed and deliver the ammunition to the sites it was destined for. I reported the casualties to Battle headquarters who arranged for burial parties to be sent to the various scenes.

It is most probable, that the Japanese may attempt to cross the narrow channel at Lei Yu Mun, the seaway entrance to the harbour and from there no doubt will go ashore below the high ground of Lei Yu Mun Barracks and the magazines. The fishing village of Shaukeiwan, which lies on the shores, would surely be an ideal place to land a strong force. From there they could attack the barracks and defences from the rear and spearhead along Shek O Road towards Repulse Bay and then to Stanley Peninsula via Wong Nei Chong Gap, thereby cutting the main line of defence and communications from east to west of the island. If the magazines do fall to the Japanese, I should be denied any further supplies from there, leaving me the last remaining magazine at Little Hong Kong. The magazines at Lei Yu Mun were well constructed with fairly large compartments for the storage of thousands of shells and components including small arms ammunition and other similar explosives. The storage rooms were erected from the main passages leading from the main gates extending from the north-end entrance to the south and to the wharf that was built upon the shoreline at the bottom that led to the Lei Yu Mun Channel. Ships, barges and lighters transporting explosives were offloaded at the wharf for eventual storage within the rooms of the building. Owing to the nature and various types of explosives, special chambers were built to isolate these groups. The magazines at Little Hong Kong are constructed on similar lines and built under a heavier rock formation, completely surrounded by very hilly terrain and so concealed to avoid detection by enemy aircraft.

At about 6.00 p.m. I received instructions from Maj Proes to immediately telephone Wong Nei Chong Gap for orders regarding removal of ammunition from the magazines at Lei Yu Mun and to collect twenty-five to thirty lorries to form the convoy plus a loading party of thirty Chinese coolies and a guard of one officer and thirty men fully armed with sub-machine guns. The officer in charge of the guard being Capt Potts[33] of the Hong Kong Volunteer Defence Corps (HKVDC). The ammunition for removal was to be delivered to the remaining gun positions in the western half of the island in separate convoys to be decided. Whilst the loading of the lorries was taking place, one of the Chinese drivers either switched on the lights of his lorry by accident, or it may have been intended. The driver was immediately cautioned by Capt Potts and told that if this occurred again, he would be placed in police custody. The more I pondered about the driver's actions, the more I suspected that he was an agent of the 5th Column that was widely spread throughout Kowloon and Hong Kong.

I voiced my thoughts with Capt Potts. Within a very short time, as the convoy was passing through the fishing village of Shaukeiwan, we came under a heavy barrage of Japanese artillery fire from the mainland across the Lei Yu Mun Channel. Therefore, it was quite possible that the light from the Chinese driver's vehicle was a signal to agents operating of the mainland, which was the likely cause for this sudden bombardment. Later I heard from Capt Potts that the driver in question had disappeared at the vehicle concentration centre and no doubt to avoid being handed over to the police authorities. After delivering the ammunition to the various gun positions, the lorries were returned to the Vehicle Concentration Centre (VCC).

I proceeded to make a further run with my own transport back to Lei Yu Mun Magazines with a smaller convoy than usual, consisting of four lorries and myself in the 15-cwt car. The vicinity of Shaukeiwan appeared fairly quiet. I proceeded up the steep incline to the main gates with great speed, where I told the drivers to take cover under a great number of trees. I informed the lead driver of the first lorry that I was now going to the office nearby to phone Maj Squires at Battle headquarters of my arrival.

As soon as I lifted the phone, I heard Squires say suddenly, 'Q, get out of the magazine area as soon as possible, the Japanese are attempting a landing across the Lei Yu Mun Channel and all our batteries on the island are going to lay down a heavy artillery barrage on that area immediately, so move out as quick as you can.'

I ran back to the lorries and got them moving quickly, giving instructions to Havildar Muzaffar Khan to direct them to cover down the steep incline and form up in the culvert situated behind the village which we had used before. I returned to my 15-cwt car and informed the Indian driver to keep the engine running, while I made a hasty check of the ammunition held in the foremost compartments of the magazines that were near the main entrance gates. During the spot check the Japanese landed at the bottom end of the magazine area near the wharf. These landings were supported by Japanese artillery and air from across the Lei Yu Mun Channel and at the same time our own guns laid down a heavy barrage upon the Japanese landings. I could see the Japanese troops in the distance, running forward up the slopes near the wharf, towards the underground entrances leading to the various compartments that stored all types of ammunition. Other troops advanced up the sandy beaches towards the barracks situated on the heights of Lei Yu Mun. I could hear the Japanese infiltrating into the passageways of the underground magazines, jabbering in their guttural voices in their search of a number of storerooms holding the stocks of numerous grades of shells. I realised that I would have to move quickly to avoid being captured. I made a quick exit to my car that was standing approximately twenty yards outside the main gates. I made the dash that completely surprised the Japanese when they saw me leaving the building and they were slow to react to fire upon me. Shahib Uddin, my driver, was moving the vehicle forward as I jumped onto the running board where I hung on grimly with bullets following us until we turned the corner that led us down the steep incline towards the village at the base. Within a very short time, I got the convoy moving inland towards Little Hong Kong as the alternative for withdrawing ammunition required at the sites of Mount Gough and Mount Austin. The weather was dreadful, with heavy showers of rain, making it difficult to see the road through the windscreen. To make matters worse, the Japanese had unleashed an artillery barrage on the oil tanks near North Point setting them ablaze, causing a huge pall of smoke to envelope the North part of the island assisted by the strong winds. These conditions could only assist the Japanese providing ideal cover in their efforts to establish a foothold on the island. I phoned Maj Squires from the pillbox of Maj Marsh to say that I had made a successful getaway from Lei Yu Mun. Squires then told me to visit the gun positions at Tiger Balm and Pagoda regarding the stocks of shells etc. remaining there and to replenish if necessary. I replenished all the sites and then I headed for West Administrative Pool using the Causeway Bay route. I received news, that at about 10 p.m., the Japanese had landed at several points on the island. Three separate landings took place between North Point and Lei Yu Mun. I left Pagoda 6-inch How gun position a short time earlier, which at the time was under intense machine gun and rifle fire.

Accompanying me in the 15-cwt was Havildar Muzaffar Khan with two Indian gunners. Unknowingly, I was in amongst the Japanese troops landing at North Point. I did not recognise these troops at first, but Havildar Khan who was beside me on the front seat said 'dushman, sahib' (meaning 'enemy') and as he said this, I saw through the flashes of guns and mortar fire, four to five Japanese soldiers through the windscreen, who I am sure thought that my car was one of theirs. I knew that it would only be a matter of seconds before they realised who we were. Therefore, I had to act first and quickly, so I warned the men to be ready to open fire on our left side. When the Japanese soldiers were at a distance of about thirty yards, I accelerated quickly to our right and ordered 'FIRE', which the men did without hesitation, killing or seriously wounding all the soldiers. I continued very smartly out of this area en-route to Peak Road, passing more Japanese troops. A quick glance at these little fellows who were well groomed and appeared to be tough and seasoned fighters. When I reached the base of Peak Road, I pulled over for a few moments and congratulated the men on their courage and resourcefulness and although the two gunners looked rather shaky, they were all smiling and appeared quite pleased with themselves.

Upon my return to West Administrative Pool, I noticed that the road leading into the estate had been bombed and I knew at once that Japanese aircraft had located our headquarters. The huge craters outside the building and in the roadway would have to be filled in as soon as possible. The air raid had upset the wives of Capt Fox and S/Sgt Wilson, who were in temporary residence there. I ordered them to be removed to a far safer place and therefore selected the War Memorial Hospital about a mile away, which they gladly accepted and was a relief to me as well, particularly as Mrs Wilson had a baby daughter named Wendy.[34] The Chinese caretaker and his wife who were originally employed by Sir Robert Ho Tung on the estate requested to stay, even though I told them it would be far safer at the hospital, but they both declined to move there, so I let them stay.

19 December 1941

In the early hours I received orders to collect ammunition from the magazines at Little Hong Kong. I was to collect the lorries and to rendezvous at the Queen Mary Hospital at Aberdeen where an armed guard of one NCO and two men per vehicle would be waiting. I am to provide three men from West Admin Pool for the loading of each lorry;

these men were a mixture of Sikh and Mohammedan gunners. I will also have four Indian gunners fully armed travelling in my car. I arrived at the university at Aberdeen,[35] this being the forward line of defence that faced the main road leading to the magazines at Little Hong Kong. Cmdr Millett of the Royal Navy was in command of this headquarters and was also in direct contact with Maj Marsh of the Middlesex Regiment in a concrete pillbox near the main gate of the magazines. Marsh reported the progress of the Japanese that were gradually infiltrating this area and at the moment were holding a line from 21 Shouson Hill to Brick Hill, with machine gun and mortar posts installed overlooking the two-to-three-mile strip of 'no man's land' as I used to call it between the Magazines and Aberdeen. This road being the direct route to Repulse Bay and the Stanley Peninsular where the barracks and 9.2-inch coastal guns were emplaced. With the Japanese holding this high ground they were inflicting heavy casualties amongst our troops withdrawing towards Aberdeen. Through my binoculars, I could view quite an accumulation of abandoned vehicles and dead lying around, causing quite a blockage to this part of the road. It is now quite obvious, that withdrawing ammunition from Little Hong Kong Magazine during daylight will present the most dangerous period for a convoy, and the only option being was late at night or in the early hours of the morning and under the cover of darkness.

I left the convoy at a rendezvous point near the university at Aberdeen and proceeded in my car accompanied by the four Indian gunners to reconnoitre the blocked site which one could see was a complete shambles of damaged and burnt-out vehicles. The area was littered with so many dead bodies lying in, across and around the vehicles. I returned to headquarters at Aberdeen where I rang and informed Maj Marsh of this scene, and suggested to him that if he could contact Sgt Bedward of the Middlesex Regiment who was in command of an area with a great number of machine guns overlooking those of the Japanese on Shouson Hill and Brick Hill, that if Sgt Bedward could bear continuous fire on the Japanese positions this would allow me to be able to clear a path through this area with as few casualties as possible to my vehicles and men and of course allow any of our retreating forces free passage. Maj Marsh said he would arrange this and therefore I told him that I was now proceeding. Sgt Bedward kept a continuous and heavy machine gun fire upon the Japanese positions thereby giving me the opportunity to clear some of the disbanded lorries blocking this highway allowing me to get my convoy through, under the cover of darkness to the magazine despite concerted efforts by the Japanese to prevent me to do so, but with the concentrated fire by Bedward's machine gunners ably supported by my own men, we arrived virtually unscathed and loaded the ammunition onto the lorries in quick time.

I gathered the drivers and remaining personnel and briefed them regarding where to rendezvous at the University of Aberdeen, where from there, we would move on to the gun positions for which the ammunition was destined. I reported to Maj Marsh who was in his concrete pill box, quite near the main gates of the magazine to tell him I was now leaving to return to Aberdeen, upon which he ordered a concentrated barrage of covering fire from Sgt Bedward's unit upon the Japanese positions. I decided to use the route through the jungle which was the best to take under the circumstances because we had cover of a dense jungle growth and at this stage against Japanese patrols operating in this area. The track was very muddy, caused by heavy rains which we had experienced in the last few days. With these conditions in mind, we had to avoid being bogged down through the weight of the fully loaded lorries. As I looked up towards the village of Aberdeen, I noticed two most ragged individuals coming over the hill nearby who looked completely exhausted. A few more soon followed looking about the same. In this party was an officer and in the semi-darkness, I recognised him to be from the 5th AA Regiment, Royal Artillery. He said to me, 'The Japanese are landing at Lei Yu Mun from across the mainland.' I told him, 'They have already landed about four hours ago and also along the shores of Causeway Bay and North Point.' They apparently were from a searchlight section of the 5th AA and had escaped the advancing Japanese near the village of Shaukeiwan.

After reporting to Cmdr Millett, I gathered the convoy and proceeded on our way, passing the Queen Mary Hospital on our right. For the first time, we came under sniper fire from Lamma Island on our left, but no casualties. Once again, it was essential if possible, to get the lorries off Peak Road before daylight. I eventually reached Peak Road, when the first lorry of the convoy was caught in a barbed wire barrier set across the road. This was caused by a sentry not being on duty at this post, whose presence was necessary to allow any transport through. Being a barrier of concertina wire, it just wound itself around the rear axle of the lorry. A Havildar came upon the scene from this defence position that was held by the 2/14 Punjabis and I asked him if he could provide wire cutters to release the wire so as to enable the convoy to continue onwards and get out of this area before dawn, before we became a target for the Japanese artillery. The Havildar contacted the British officer in charge of this post, who was Capt Blair[36] who regretted the absence of the sentry and would take disciplinary action against him . . . To make the problem worse, the Captain found that he had no wire cutters at the post, which there should have been. After struggling with hammer and chisel, I was able to release the wire from the axle to allow the lorry to proceed on its way with the remaining convoy following.

We arrived at the Peak without further incident, from where I dispersed the lorries to their allotted sites. After about two to three hours, each driver reported to West Administrative Pool and stated that all deliveries had been made.

I reported the incident with Capt Blair to Maj Proes at headquarters and told him that I had used some rather bad language towards this officer during the process of releasing the truck and he said he would report me. I told Capt Blair he could do what the hell he liked, but my job was to get this convoy off the road before dawn. Maj Proes said, 'Even though you did use obscene language, quartermaster, I would probably have used more than you could imagine under the circumstances. I will see Capt Blair and prevent his attempt to report this incident to Battle headquarters and I am sure he will not because I will make him realise that he was at fault.' This was to be the last time I spoke to Maj Proes.

The drivers were dismissed to get some well-earned rest; I also took the opportunity to get some rest. On my return to West Administrative Pool, I heard that the following officers had been killed or wounded: Capt Avery RA (killed); Capt Atkinson RA (wounded).

The above officers were attacked by the Japanese whilst assisting our own troops in the defence of 'Post Bridge', a house along Repulse Bay Road, the owner being Mr Tinson[37] who was also killed. It was around 10.00 a.m. when I was talking on the phone to Maj Temple at Wong Nei Chong Gap headquarters when I heard a terrific explosion that practically deafened me in the left ear that cut off my communication with him suddenly, this being my last contact with him. I spoke to one of the survivors I later met near Wanchai Gap and he told me that the headquarters had been completely destroyed and overrun by the enemy. The Japanese had used hand grenades throwing them into the air vents of the concrete blockhouses, killing all the officers and staff inside. This was a very sad end to all those in this most vital post. Amongst those killed were Maj Temple, Maj Proes and Capt Fox, who were all excellent officers. We are now completely cut off from the eastern part of Hong Kong.

I received orders to remove 4.5-inch shell and cartridges from Kennedy Road Magazines using transport of five 3-ton lorries. Three journeys were made using Peak Road, which at this time was constantly under intermittent air and artillery attacks. These trips were extremely nerve-wracking with the drivers of the lorries moving as quickly as possible so as to reach the cover of Magazine Gap to avoid the shelling from the mainland. As the Japanese advanced from the eastern part of the island we expect the bombing attacks to increase with bombardments from the sea off the south of the island. Finally the lorries in convoy reached their destinations after witnessing the devastation of houses and buildings that were burning fiercely upon the hillsides of Hong Kong. A thick pall of smoke was covering most of the western part of the island, which helped to secrete the convoy from ground and air attack. The Bowen Road Military Hospital received quite a number of direct hits during the shelling which partially demolished some of the wards and the dining room. Quite a number of patients were killed in these attacks. I noticed during these trips to and from Kennedy Road Ordnance and RASC Depots and through the areas of Wanchai and Queen's Road were practically deserted by the Chinese. The Ordnance depot was a complete shambles and in these devastated buildings, there were still some remaining RAOC representatives doing their level best to meet demands for stores required by the various units. One of these shells landed in the office portion of the magazines, which only a few minutes before was occupied by Pte Smith[38] of the RAOC. I said to him, 'You were extremely lucky there lad.' By now, stocks of stores and ammunition were getting less as the hours went by. I told all the staff to withdraw to the Peak area and grab any seats on the vehicles where possible, most of them finally accepted the offer and they were accommodated in the rooms of West Administrative Pool.

At about 8 p.m., I proceeded to Kennedy Road Magazines to collect and salvage 3.7 and 4.5-inch shell and cartridges and any other stores of ammunition remaining lying in the rubble of the demolished buildings caused by the recent concentrated shellfire. I used my own lorries on this occasion and as usual I was in the 15-cwt. Accompanied by three Indian gunners whom I must praise for their loyalty and dedication in carrying out this type of work under the most trying circumstances. Two of these gunners, Shahib Uddin and Mohammed Zaman[39] have been with me since the start of hostilities. The withdrawal of these stores coupled with the rain from the still burning oil tanks on the harbour front made the work very unpleasant, but finally, the task was completed in the early hours of the morning. The night driving is playing havoc with my eyes, which have become very sore and bloodshot. I am finding it very hard to keep awake at the wheel, so I have decided to get Shahib Uddin to take over the driving for a while.

A box of ammunition during the loading, dropped upon my haversack, smashing the frame and glass of the photograph of my dear wife and family, which I have carried all these days since 8 December. I have managed to obtain a large envelope in which I have placed the photograph and deposited the same in my gas mask haversack.

We returned before daylight to West Administrative Pool despite the journey being somewhat slow due to the heavy mist and burning oil causing a real 'pea souper'.

20 December 1941

In the early hours of the morning, I received a message to deliver ammunition to the gun positions at Mount Kellett and Sanatorium. The Japanese were now concentrating their fire on Albany, May and Garden Roads, giving me the opportunity to move the convoy along Peak Road as quickly as possible to the protection of a small culvert situated at Magazine Gap. With the Japanese artillery concentrating their fire elsewhere, I continued my journey delivering the ammunition to the gun positions. On our return trip to West Administrative Pool, and only a short distance to Magazine Gap, the convoy came under shellfire from the mainland. I had no choice but to keep going, increasing my speed and hoping the lorries behind would do the same. We finally reached the safety of the culvert at Magazine Gap where I decided to pause until there was a lull in the shelling. After about twenty minutes the shelling abated and we hastily continued our journey to the Peak and West Administrative Pool. The Indian gunners were very pleased and shouted 'Shah Bash Sahib'.

As the situation was becoming critical, the ammunition dumps spread at points in the Peak area had to be removed because of the increasing air attacks. These dumps had to be removed over the most rugged and rocky terrain that existed in this part of the island and it was very hard for the working parties carrying out this task under awful conditions due to heavy rain and mud, where one sank up to well over the ankles. In addition, the heavy density of the fog, which covered the whole district, meant that the Japanese were unable to use their artillery and air raids were disrupted for which we were very thankful.

At about 7 p.m., I received orders from Battle headquarters to proceed to Aberdeen and collect 10/5-ton lorries with loading parties and guards. I was to proceed to Pokfulam, which was a well-known dairy farm area during the years before the outbreak of hostilities. Apparently, two hundred 6-inch How shell and cartridges have been dumped there for some unknown reason. I was instructed to deliver the 6-inch How shells and cartridges to the gun positions at Mount Austin and Mount Gough.

I arrived at Aberdeen headquarters, where the lorries with loading parties and guards were waiting. Some of the men appeared unsettled and anxious. I told them we had a job to do, so the quicker we complete the task, the sooner we will be on our way. I spoke to Cmdr Millett, who informed me that the Japanese have now a solid foothold in this area and to keep a sharp lookout.

I located the shells and cartridges and we proceeded to load the lorries. The loading was going smoothly, when all of a sudden the Japanese artillery opened up with a heavy barrage from the mainland or possibly Mount Nicholson. Fortunately, their fire was not accurate, but just as the loading was completed, the Japanese began to use 4 inch mortars for the first time in the area, which appeared to come from Mount Cameron. With the loading completed, the convoy moved off as quickly as possible to the gun positions at Mount Austin and Mount Gough without loss, delivering the ammunition at around 11 p.m.

21 December 1941

Major General Maltby has received a cable from Churchill, which reads, 'RESIST TO THE END'.

The eastern part of Hong Kong was now in enemy hands. By now, the western half of Hong Kong was limited to eight field guns, these being the 6-inch How's at Mount Gough and Mount Austin, the 3.7-inch How's at Sanatorium and Mount Kellett and the two 4.5-inch How's at Sanatorium.

Later in the morning enemy aircraft approached and released three strings of bombs, most of which fell into the roadway below the house. One bomb made a direct hit on the north side of the building, causing damage to the technical stores, etc. The building fairly rocked under these bombs and two Indian gunners were slightly injured by flying glass and shrapnel and naturally were suffering from shock as we all were.

The casualties were immediately removed by ambulance to the War Memorial Hospital. The odd Chinese, who were with us, naturally became panic-stricken and disappeared completely into the scrub lying outside the estate. In this large building I had about 120 Indian gunners, which included one Jemadar, Havildars, Naiks and L/Naiks. Fifty percent of the gunners were raw recruits and only arrived in Hong Kong a month before the outbreak of hostilities and quite a number also had escaped from Wong Nei Chong when it fell to the Japanese. I also had three British officers, who were reservists and permanent residents in Hong Kong, having business connections here.

The officers were 2/Lieut Parks, 2/Lieut RKM Simpson and 2/Lieut Andrews. Joining us later was Capt Hoyland who was a regular officer of the 5th AA Regiment. In addition, I also had the following British personnel who I have mentioned before in this diary:

S/Sgt (Fitter) Gollege 4th Medium Battery HK/SRA

BQMS May 4th Medium Battery HK/SRA

S/Sgt Wilson 4th Medium Battery HK/SRA Artillery Clerk

Sgt Blofield RAOC

BQMS Searle 2nd Mountain Battery HK/SRA

S/Sgt Holmes (Farrier) 4th Medium Battery HK/SRA

Spr Nichols Royal Engineers

Sgt Waterhouse 3rd Medium Battery HK/SRA

Also stabled within the estate were twelve pack mules of the 2nd Mountain Battery HK/SRA that normally carried the 3.7-inch How guns, the mules being in charge of S/Sgt Holmes.

A short time later, a further attack took place when a flight of about twelve planes released their bombs upon the building and surrounds inflicting casualties amongst the men and mules. One string of bombs, made a direct hit upon a lorry carrying twelve or more Indian gunners whom had just arrived and taken cover under the archway to the main entrance of the house. All the gunners and NCOs were killed instantly and burnt beyond recognition, the lorry becoming an inferno, as did the bodies that were just cremated. This vehicle was just like a burning oven stuck within the archway. Those personnel in the house quickly took cover in the enormous underground passages, which gave a certain amount of protection for the time being. Within a very short time again, further bombs were dropped, one group of which hit the main entrance doorway that led into the huge hall and where a large number of Indian gunners and NCOs were attempting to take cover, but the blast killed twelve to fourteen instantly, including Havildar Muzaffar Khan whose falling body hit me towards the wide stairway that led up to a number of small rooms on the first floor, which were used as the concubine quarters when Sir Robert Ho Tung was in residence.[40] Havildar Muzaffar Khan's body no doubt saved my life in that it shielded me from the full blast that came through the main door with such force. Where the bombs

struck, they set the wide and huge stairway alight which I had to ascend
to see if any of the personnel who may have been in the rooms, which
had been allotted to them, but I found them to be empty and assumed
they had taken cover elsewhere.

When descending the fiercely burning stairs it started to collapse, I
quickly clambered back up to the first floor. Despite the noise from the
burning and collapsing stair, I heard distinct cries for help. I gained the
outside grounds via a drainpipe and went in search of where I could
hear the cries for help.

I located the body of S/Sgt Farrier Holmes lying with the blood
flowing from a deep wound from the side of his throat, which showed a
large piece of bomb splinter protruding from his neck. He said, 'Help
me, Charlie,' but as I moved him under the protection of the verandah,
he died in my arms.

I was very saddened by this awful event, having lost a good friend. I
then searched around for any further casualties and found seven Indian
gunners near the mule lines severely wounded. In addition, five mules
were killed outright and eight were lying or standing with broken legs
and with their bodies badly mutilated by bomb splinters.

I returned to the building where I met Capt Hoyland, whom I
understood had arrived about three hours before the air attack and was
apparently a survivor from Wong Nei Chong Gap headquarters that had
fallen to the Japanese. I said, 'Well, sir, this is disastrous and I shall now
have to immediately go and locate another building up Peak Road for
West Administrative Pool and most likely have to find one to house the
Indian gunners and also one for the British ORs.' However, the first
thing that must be done is to put the mules out of their misery. Capt
Hoyland said, 'This is terrible, quartermaster,' and I said, 'This is bloody
war, sir.'

As soon as possible, we shot the mules that were badly injured.

Meanwhile, BQMS May and other British ranks returned to the
recently bombed-out estate. BQMS May said to me, 'There is a message
for you from Battle headquarters that you are to proceed to the Vehicle
Concentration Centre (VCC) near Hong Kong University and to collect
twenty lorries with guards using your own loading parties and then to
proceed to Little Hong Kong Magazine to withdraw shells for the
6-inch, 3.7-inch and 4.5-inch How's and to be at the VCC by 6.00 p.m.'

In the presence of S/Sgt Gollege and BQMS May, I said to Capt
Hoyland, 'I must now leave you, sir, to arrange the burial of bodies
during the hours of darkness in a suitable area in the grounds of the
estate near the vacant land near the creek and the mules further on.' My

first task was to remove the red and green identity disks from the bodies and forward them to Battle headquarters as soon as possible. No sooner had I made arrangements for the disposal of the bodies when another flight of planes came over and strafed us with machine gun fire, followed by bombs. During this raid, BQMS Searle and five Indian gunners were wounded near the body of S/Sgt Holmes, the blast of which lifted me into a deep creek nearby. The attack was over in about fifteen minutes. I told S/Sgt Gollege to make arrangements to move BQMS Searle and the five Indian gunners to the War Memorial Hospital which was about 300 yards away. I returned to the house for a review of the damage and for any survivors there may be from the recent raid. As I entered the main hall, I noticed that the enormous figure of the statue of Buddha was tilted to one side against the wall. This Buddha must have weighed ten tons or more and stood to a height of about thirty feet, and having a circumference at the base of about eighteen feet. On looking at the tilted side of the statue, I recognised the Chinese Secretary, Mr Ah Cheung had been completely crushed against the wall and his wife silently crying beside him. I put my hand on her shoulder in a gesture of comfort. She elected to stay with her husband until his removal and burial.

I got some of the Chinese to ease the statue and free the body for burial in the area. I told Capt Hoyland and S/Sgt Gollege that I must now be on my way to the VCC to collect the lorries for convoy as directed and if all goes well I will return in the morning. Before leaving West Administrative Pool, I reported to Maj Duncan[41] that Sir Robert Ho Tung's house had been badly damaged and was now unsuitable as headquarters or accommodation and that I had moved the Indian gunners over to the Masonic building ensuring that cooking facilities were suitable and accommodation satisfactory. The British officers and ORs were now accommodated in a house known as 'The Mount', which was quite suitable as a headquarters and near the building I had selected for the Indian gunners. I also told him that the wounded had been transferred to the War Memorial Hospital and that Capt Hoyland was now arranging for burying the dead including the mules.

I have just received orders that the collection of the convoy from the VCC has now been cancelled and has now been reported that the gun position at Mount Austin is without ammunition as the last remaining 100 cartridges had been destroyed by aerial bombing and shellfire from the mainland. Therefore, I was to replace this gun position with ammunition. I informed Maj Duncan of my intentions to proceed to the magazines at Little Hong Kong as soon as possible and that I would take the 15-cwt together with four Indian gunners including my 2nd driver Shahib Uddin.

Before leaving for Little Hong Kong, I arranged with Havildar Maj Unwar Khan to return to Sir Robert Ho Tung's house to ensure that the fifty Indian ORs were present to bury the Indian dead at dusk and to assist in the disposal of the mule carcasses, also to collect whatever rations remaining in the ruins plus any stores and equipment that could be salvaged and to remove them to the newly established West Administrative Pool headquarters.

Due to the extreme urgency for the replacement of the cartridges at Mount Austin gun position, I informed Lieut Dawson[42] that I would replace the ammunition from my stocks held at West Administrative Pool and then replenish my stock from Little Hong Kong Magazine. On my way to Mount Austin with this consignment, and proceeding up the steep and narrow incline when about a third of the way up heavy bombardment commenced. To avoid this, I had to accelerate the vehicle to the top of the rise, which was only a short distance from the hidden gun position where there was reasonable cover. For some time, the Japanese artillery had been endeavouring to silence the guns at Mount Austin and at Mount Gough without any success.

These guns have been causing heavy destruction amongst their troop formations advancing towards Kowloon to their positions in that area. Being that these two positions were in action in ideal locations, the Japanese artillery was unable to locate them from the air. When there was a lull from the shelling, I, with the Indian gunners riding in the rear of the 15-cwt moved very quickly with the cartridges which we offloaded and transferred behind the guns. No sooner had I left, the guns were blazing away at the Japanese positions on Kowloon. Jemadar Kishen Singh in charge of the site told me that the scrub surrounding the cartridges that were destroyed was done by the scrub catching fire during bombing attacks near the position.

Before leaving the site, I contacted Lieut Dawson on the field telephone and informed him as I had the 15-cwt at hand, that I would proceed to Little Hong Kong Magazine to withdraw the 100 cartridges to replace those from my stocks at West Administrative Pool. I mentioned to him that as the 15-cwt was a small vehicle, I would have a better chance to succeed by slipping through and penetrating the thick jungle to the magazines thereby avoiding the Japanese machine guns holding the line at Shouson Hill and Brick Hill which had full command of the road leading to Repulse Bay and eventually Stanley. This road was partly blocked with the wrecks of lorries and cars where the Japanese were inflicting heavy casualties upon the retreating British, Indian and

Canadian troops. When I did arrive at Aberdeen, I made my usual report to Cmdr Millett, explaining my intentions and whether he had the latest report on the advancing Japanese. He said that the enemy were advancing from the Wong Nei Chong area and were encircling Mount Nicholson and the main magazines at Little Hong Kong; he feels that they will be heading to this point very soon. I explained to Cmdr Millett the urgency of my mission to collect 6-inch How cartridges from the magazines and said that I would attempt to gain entrance through the jungle via a narrow muddy track that was completely overgrown. He wished me the best of luck and thought I was wise to avoid the blockage along the main road. As I was leaving the University of Aberdeen, I met a Sergeant of the Middlesex Regiment, who was in charge of a platoon and was hastily moving his men into the building. The sergeant said to me, 'Quartermaster, you have not an earthly chance of making the Little Hong Kong Magazine because the Japanese are advancing along the roadway towards Aberdeen.' I said, 'Thanks, sergeant, but I will have to take that chance and if I cannot make the bend in the road, I will certainly return back here smartly and defend the post.' He said, 'Good luck and I hope you can make it.' I left the grounds of the university and proceeded on a straight portion of the main highway heading in the direction of Repulse Bay and reached a point in the road where I turn off on to the jungle track to the magazines. As I arrived at this point, I spotted a group of Japanese at a distance of about two miles, overlooking a Bren Gun Carrier, which no doubt they had only just captured a short while ago.

At the same time, I recognised a blockage by a number of vehicles at about a mile and a half distance, which appeared to have become enormous since I was last here, and no doubt caused by attacks on forces withdrawing from the Wong Nei Chong district.

As I turned off the road to take cover provided by the jungle track, I was met with bursts of machine gun fire on either side coming from Shouson Hill and Brick Hill, which ripped through the thick jungle bushes, the bullets striking the undergrowth from all directions. The jungle was very muddy and it took me all my time to prevent the car from skidding all over the place and also trying to prevent being bogged down in the density of the undergrowth that was hard to penetrate along the edges. We could hear the bullets striking the thick scrub behind us. Eventually, I came out of the jungle quite near the main gates of the magazines and not far from the blockhouse of Maj Marsh's headquarters. However, I was now exposed and was forced to take cover behind a large rock formation as the Japanese fire intensified. I ordered the men to return fire and could also hear fire being returned by our men in and around the magazines. After a period of sustained fire for about twenty minutes, the situation became quieter, although one could hear gunfire in the distance. I decided to take the risk of making the short distance to the gates and to the magazine holding the cartridges, which I did at great haste. Without further delay, we loaded the vehicle with over 200 cartridges as quickly as possible.

I told Maj Marsh that I would have to leave shortly come what may for the return journey to Aberdeen and eventually West Administrative Pool. He said he would give me covering fire and wished me good luck. I left the magazine and headed to the jungle track which was about 150 yards away, suddenly as we moved deeper into the scrub, we were attacked by about six to eight Japanese that came into view from out of the thick jungle and as they grouped in the centre of the track, all I could do was to drive straight at them, which took them by surprise. Two of the Indian gunners riding in the rear opened up with their Tommy guns causing casualties that I could not determine due to the movement of the car, which at this stage was hard to control on a very rough track. One Japanese armed with a sword that presumably was an officer or a senior NCO, rushed at the vehicle and jumped onto the running board grabbing hold of the frame of the vehicle and with his right hand flashed his sword to an upright position with an attempt to slash my head. With the presence of mind, I grasped the .38 revolver laying on the seat beside me that I always carried as a spare and deliberately threw it strongly with my left hand into his face with the result that it deterred him from using the blade upon me and at the same time dislodging him from the car where he fell heavily on the track. He was then killed by one of the Indian gunners riding in the rear who blasted him with his Tommy gun. The Indian gunners continued to fire despite two of them being wounded in the first attack, the remainder of the Japanese disappeared into the jungle. I continued to move very quickly on to Aberdeen headquarters, and despite several bursts of enemy fire coming from my left, I arrived safely where I made my usual report to Cmdr Millett giving him details of this episode. 'Well,' he said, 'they are getting closer, Q.' I said, 'Yes, and if it had been a very large patrol I may not be here now.'

Cmdr Millett made arrangements for the two Indian gunners to be moved to the medical centre at Queen Mary Hospital, from there I proceeded on my way to West Administrative Pool arriving at around midnight to offload and store the 6-inch How cartridges.

22 December 1941

Early this morning, I heard that a personal friend of mine, Master Gunner Cooper of 'Belcher Battery' has been killed. Apparently the gun [that] Cooper was standing by at the time received a direct hit from a Japanese shell, killing him and most of the detachment of twelve men.[43]

At about 5.00 a.m., I received orders to proceed to Kennedy Road ammunition dump and clear any 4.5-inch How shells and cartridges that could be found amongst the damaged underground storage emplacements and to deliver them to Sanatorium gun position as soon as possible.

I have just heard that a personal friend of mine, S/Sgt Nicholson of the Royal Engineers has been killed outright.

I used my vehicles, comprising of four 3-ton lorries and my 15-cwt, we reached Kennedy Road without incident and searched the remains of the buildings locating 4.5-inch shells in one of the storage rooms. Hastily the shells of which there was about 250–300 were loaded. During the return journey along Peak Road, two lorries broke down due to mechanical problems at various points along this road. With this delay, it would mean that the remaining lorries would be in full view of the enemy batteries on Kowloon. To avoid this, I informed the drivers of the other trucks to continue to their destinations to offload the shells, etc., that they were carrying and to return immediately to the broken-down lorries on Peak Road where the ammunition they were carrying would be offloaded and transferred to their vehicles and to continue the journey to the required destinations. Just as dawn broke, we were able to clear the last broken-down lorry and were able to gain the top of Peak Road just a few minutes before the Japanese opened up with an artillery bombardment.

We just managed to make Magazine Gap bridge and obtain cover from the surrounding hills and out of view of the enemy. On our return to West Administrative Pool, 2/Lieut Parks said to myself, drivers and loading parties to take a complete rest, and I needed it too as I was absolutely exhausted. The last fifteen days have begun to take its toll upon me.

The ration situation was beginning to become very serious now and I gave orders to Sgt Holberry and BQMS Yearling,[44] who have just recently joined us from the Wong Nei Chong district that rations must be obtained immediately from Hong Kong University. Holbery and Yearling returned about four hours later, with British and Indian rations that were issued to all defence positions immediately. These issues were necessary to build up the reserve stocks at all sites. It was also essential that all those personnel in the West Group areas should maintain at least two days' rations in their haversacks. I finally cleared Kennedy Road depot of all equipment and ammunition using the 15-cwt car and the 8-cwt car for this purpose, as these vehicles were ideal because they were quicker and easier to manoeuvre than the larger lorries, particularly on Peak Road that was badly pitted with shell holes. This road was now becoming the major target of the Japanese artillery and was now under constant bombardment. When travelling on this road, I expect to be blown up at any time and find myself coming to grief on the rocks below. If the police caught me at the speeds I do now in peacetime, my driver's licence would have been suspended for life.

At about 6.00 p.m., I received orders and instructions to report to Capt Otway, Royal Engineers, at the headquarters of Lieut Col Field[45] at Magazine Gap to collect a convoy of lorries required for removing ammunition from Little Hong Kong Magazine. I received six lorries, driven by gunners from the 5th AA Regiment RA plus lorries from my own group, which included my 15-cwt car and to proceed to Aberdeen headquarters where I met Capt Otway, and we reported to Cmdr Millett RN. Capt Otway wanted to know the present situation regarding the Japanese holding the high ground of Shouson Hill and Brick Hill. Cmdr Millett said he was fairly certain that Japanese patrols were operating in the jungle district, because BQMS Barman came in contact with them yesterday. I then told Capt Otway, I was sure there was Japanese on and around Mount Nicholson and Mount Cameron and have forces within the thick scrub nearby. Cmdr Millett advised Capt Otway to use the jungle route, which would take you directly to the main gates to the magazines and near the headquarters of Maj Marsh. Having knowledge of this track, I pointed out on a map the areas where we would most likely encounter Japanese patrols, which by now must be increasing in numbers since the fall of Wong Nei Chong Gap. Everyone was issued with rubber shoes, these being ideal for jungle warfare which of course all the Japanese troops wore similar footwear, which was made to stand up to the rugged terrain and assisted the movements of troops, which was not like ours where one could hear for quite a distance the heavy British boots.

As the jungle was so thickly overgrown, which skirted the track; it would be very hard for the Japanese to penetrate in large numbers even though they appeared to be very close at this stage. As we proceeded, on the road from Aberdeen, we could hear the din of mortars and rifle fire in the distance, which appeared to be coming from Mount Nicholson and Mount Cameron areas. As we reached the entry to the jungle track, the convoy came under heavy fire from Brick Hill which was quickly returned by our guards and loading parties.

I urged the drivers to keep moving, thus gaining cover in the jungle track. Surprisingly, we reached the exit of the track without further incident, but as soon as we gained the main road leading to the Magazine, which was only a short distance away, the convoy again came under fire. This fire was returned by our guards and loading parties, assisted by Sgt Bedward's machine gunners in and around the Magazine.

After quickly loading, I arranged with Capt Otway that I take the lorries loaded with 3.7-inch and 4.5-inch shell to Mount Kellett and Sanatorium gun positions and that he move the last three lorries loaded with 6-inch How ammunition to a rendezvous point, near the vicinity of the Government Dairy Farm situated at Pokfulam, where I was to return and collect the lorries to deliver the ammunition to the gun positions at Mount Austin and Mount Gough. After advising Maj Marsh of our intentions, he told me that the direct route to Sanatorium was now not an option as the Japanese are controlling this area and advancing towards Little Hong Kong and Aberdeen. Therefore, I decided to head for West Administrative Pool and leave the lorries there for delivering the ammunition to Mount Kellett and Sanatorium the next day. We all shook hands wishing each other good luck. I was the first to leave with my convoy under covering fire from Sgt Bedward's men. I headed for Aberdeen using the jungle track again arriving without incident, where I reported to Cmdr Millett advising him what took place. I then proceeded to West Administrative Pool returning to Pokfulam area in my vehicle accompanied by the Indian drivers only to pick up the convoy.

The three lorries of this convoy gave me quite a considerable amount of mechanical trouble enroute and all broke down. I sent my driver Shahib Uddin with my car on to West Administrative Pool, to inform Capt Hoyland of these breakdowns and to send three other lorries for the transfer of the ammunition. Finally they arrived where the shells were offloaded onto the lorries and we were able to continue on to the destinations ordered. Meanwhile, and unbeknown to me, Cmdr Millett had received a message from Battle headquarters for me to take over a barge and lighter fully loaded with 9.2-inch shell and small arms ammunition that was required at the beleaguered fort at Stanley which is situated along the coast of the island and to the south from Aberdeen, a distance of approximately seven miles. Being as I was late in receiving this message and in arriving at the Aberdeen headquarters when Cmdr

Millett and myself heard a terrific explosion that came from the wharf of the harbour at Aberdeen, where the barge and lighter was anchored with near 40 tons of explosives on board. Cmdr Millett then said, 'Well, Q, with that explosion we have just heard, it means you will not be required to go to Stanley and the delay has saved your life and those of the Indian gunners who were going with you.' Later on, Maj Bill Squires told me, 'You were very lucky, Q, someone must have been watching over you.'

After this incident, Cmdr Millett briefed me regarding the situation along the area between headquarters at Aberdeen and Shouson Hill, etc. Reports received recently confirms that the Japanese units were advancing from Wong Nei Chong Gap towards Repulse Bay road where they were well emplaced in that district and it looks as if their objective is Aberdeen and the lowlands to the west of the island below Victoria Peak. If this is successful, they will completely encircle the positions held by our troops. At this point of time the Japanese were using their mortars very effectively on our defences and upon the routes along Peak Road, Pokfulam and leading to the Little Hong Kong Magazine.

23 December 1941

At about 8.45 a.m. I proceeded to the dairy farm at Pokfulam with transport and a loading party to collect what available ammunition that had been dumped there. The transport comprised of the following: two 30-cwt lorries, one 15-cwt truck, and one 8-cwt truck.

When I arrived at the dairy farm, all I could locate were about 280 rounds of 4.5-inch How shell. As for the 6-inch How shell, there were none, after an extensive search I eventually gave up.

Due to the heavy bombing of the Victoria Gap area, I was unable to move the shells from the dairy farm until about 12.00 noon. As soon as this heavy bombardment had abated, I moved the ammunition to Mount Kellett and Sanatorium gun positions completing the deliveries by 2.30 p.m.

At approximately 5.00 p.m., I was ordered to collect 10/5 ton lorries with guard of 1 NCO and 12 men from the 12th Coast Regiment RA from Hong Kong University at 7.00 p.m. From there, I was to proceed to Little Hong Kong Magazine, and to remove whatever 3.7-inch, 4.5-inch and 6-inch How shells that was available.

I briefed the drivers and the guards, and informed the drivers to keep a distance of at least fifty yards between vehicles and that if any of the lorries broke down with mechanical failure, the faulty lorry or lorries would be left temporarily, and whatever happened all vehicles would rendezvous at Hong Kong University.

It appears that the Japanese are now in control of the island of Lamma, from where we are coming under quite a considerable amount of sniper fire and mortar shelling on the convoys passing through. Upon my arrival at Aberdeen, I made my usual report to Cmdr Millett and where I hope to get further information regarding the situation of Japanese held positions at Shouson Hill and Brick Hill. As far as he knew, the latest report was that remnants of retreating forces were still coming in. The blockage by wrecked lorries and other vehicles could be seen through my binoculars which were now built up to a size of about ten times since I last viewed the area. The derelict vehicles could be seen spread across the road, with bodies strewn here and there, which by now must be black due to burning and decomposing rapidly and I can imagine the awful stench that must be coming from that area now. I could foresee that the jungle track was now not a viable option as the entrance to the magazines, because by now, the Japanese would now be in control of this part of Little Hong Kong and therefore it would be very unwise of me to use this route, as I am sure we could not make it and without doubt, the convoys would be completely overrun by the Japanese. With this in mind, it meant I would have to penetrate the blockage and somehow clear a passage through for the transport to pass. This would mean I would have to carry out reconnaissance of the blocked area, before moving any convoys through to gain the turnoff point in the road to the magazines. At this point of time, I decided to go forward and examine the position in my 15-cwt accompanied by six Indian gunners to assist in the movement of any obstacles that would prevent the passage of transport moving through. So I told Cmdr Millett of my intentions, and he agreed with me that this was the only way to enable me to get through to the magazines without the possibility of being caught in a trap in the jungle which no doubt now existed at this time.

I briefed the drivers and guards, etc., what I was preparing to do to ensure where possible a safe passage through for the convoy. I told the NCO in charge of the guard that he was to give me at least thirty minutes to proceed and reconnoitre the position and if I did not return, within a reasonable time, to take the convoy to the Vehicle Concentration Centre at Hong Kong University and to explain these orders to Capt Wiseman who was in charge. After ensuring the men in my truck were fully armed with 0.45 Tommy guns, I proceeded enroute to the obstruction site with Sgt Tavendale, whom I had previously decided to remain with the lorries, but changed my mind to leave L/Bdr Thompson[46] instead. I then moved off to reconnoitre the site of the obstructions.

Tavendale was seated upon my left with six Indian gunners riding in the rear. I cautiously approached the area without incident in a dark and overcast night. Up to this point, everything was fairly quiet and all one could hear was the occasional sporadic rifle, mortar and machine gun fire plus a certain amount of shelling which appeared to be coming from the Wong Nei Chong valley and the far distant hills of Mount Nicholson and Mount Cameron, both of which overlooked the huge buildings of the magazines. When I arrived at the obstruction site, it was just a complete shambles of wrecked vehicles that were lying at all angles across the roadway. Some of the lorries and smaller vehicles had their engines still running, which gave me reason to believe that they had only recently been ambushed during daylight hours. One could smell the stench of decomposed bodies spread here and there and lying across the vehicles and in the cabins. Some of the bodies had been burnt beyond recognition. We found two lorries obstructing the passage of transport that had to be removed as soon as possible. There were smaller trucks blocking the way that we had to remove, and during this thankless task, we had to cover our mouths and noses. Some of the bodies that had been there for a number of days just collapsed into pieces on the movement of the vehicles. Those that had been killed a few hours before were moved reverently to one side of the road to allow the transports to pass through.

We eventually cleared a suitable passage for the convoy. What amazed me was that during the whole of this operation, we had not come under fire from Japanese-held positions about a mile away, probably because it was dark and being about 1.00 a.m., they were unable to sight their machine guns on us, so they would probably wait until the early hours of daylight, when no doubt they would attack with vengeance. After the blockage had been cleared enough for the lorries to pass, we heard a distinct cry of a child that appeared to be coming from a small creek running along the edge of the road that was overgrown. After a careful search in the dark, we located a small child lying across the body of its Chinese mother, who was laying face down in the creek.

I picked up the child, who was a boy, after releasing it from the tight hold of its mother, who of course had been dead for quite a few hours. I told one of the Indian gunners to empty a large metal container to store the child in for safety. Naturally, seeing us caused him to be frightened, otherwise he appeared unharmed. Once he saw the biscuits we had there was no doubt that he was ravenously hungry, so goodness knows when the last time he had been fed. We eventually got a smile from him and appeared to show us that he knew he was in good hands. I thought the boy was about four years of age.

I returned to Aberdeen, and instructed the NCO L/Bdr Thompson to send one lorry at a time with intervals between each to be at least 20 minutes and that he was to follow in the last lorry of the convoy. Before leaving again in the 15-cwt, I asked one of the staff at the headquarters to mind the child until my return as I believe that I had someone to care for him, that being Mrs Ah Cheung at West Administrative Pool. Cmdr Millett said, 'Best of luck, Q, have a drink before you go,' but I declined. Cmdr Millett had just received a report that the Japanese were advancing on a front from Wong Nei Chong Valley towards Aberdeen via Repulse Bay Road. He also said that he had spoken to Maj Marsh at headquarters near the main gates to the magazines and he said if necessary, he had arranged for covering fire from our outlying defences on your way to the magazines and on your return here with the ammunition.

Before leaving, I told Sgt Tavendale to travel in the first truck with me leading in the 15-cwt and to take command should anything happen to me. The situation appeared quiet and I had no difficulty threading my way through the road blockage although my vehicle was much smaller than the rest in the convoy. Shahib Uddin, my reserve driver, who was beside me, said, 'Dushman sahib' (enemy) pointing to the edge of the jungle to our left, where a Japanese patrol suddenly appeared. Fortunately, there was a disbanded 5-ton lorry at the edge of the road, behind which I took cover immediately, as it was evident that they had spotted my vehicle.

I left the engine running and ordered the Indian gunners to take cover behind the lorry. I immediately ordered them to open fire on the Japanese who were in an exposed position and their only cover was to re-enter the jungle, which they did after I saw four or five Japanese fall. I told the men to continue firing into the jungle, which they did relentlessly. Only Minutes had passed, which to me seemed like hours when I ordered 'cease fire' and awaited the first lorry, which I am sure must have heard the firing. When it arrived I told Sgt Tavendale of the incident and then proceeded on to the magazines, coming under fire from south of the main road in the Brick Hill area. The four Indian gunners accompanying me were magnificent, not flinching and keeping up a relentless barrage of fire. On nearing the magazine, I received support fire from our men in and around the magazine, entering the gates at a fair speed. I said 'well done' to the Indian gunners who appeared quite pleased and patted me on the shoulder. I awaited the remainder of the convoy but only eight of the lorries arrived. After supervising the loading of the lorries with ammunition, I told Sgt Tavendale that before we move off, I would back track along the road to search for the missing lorries.

There appeared to be a lull in the Japanese onslaught, so I left the magazine in the 15-cwt accompanied by the four Indian gunners and although there was sporadic firing by the Japanese, I eventually found one lorry stuck in a creek by the side of the road and another in a similar position further on. Both had been abandoned. After searching for the men I eventually gave up. I instructed Shahib Uddin my reserve driver to drive the vehicle back to the magazine. On the journey, I glanced over to him and his eyes were peering intently into the darkness with his face almost on the steering wheel causing a wry smile to come to my face. We returned as quickly as possible to the magazine only to find the missing men there.

L/Bdr Thompson hastily gave me an account as to what had happened and he said that both lorries had been ambushed by a patrol of Japanese who suddenly appeared from the thick jungle taking them completely by surprise. Thompson and the gunners used their sub-machine guns very effectively, inflicting casualties upon the enemy, the survivors of which disappeared into the jungle. Our casualties were four wounded, including Thompson who had a possible fracture to the right ankle. The men's wounds were dressed and they were housed in an adjacent blockhouse to await their removal to St Mary's Hospital near Aberdeen.

The men looked completely exhausted when we left the magazine on the return journey, including the wounded men. At the junction of the main road and only a short distance from the magazine, I turned right to proceed to Aberdeen, when a patrol of Japanese suddenly appeared on the road not more than forty yards ahead.

Instinctively, I drove straight at them knocking one soldier flying and scattering others. My men were quick to react, opening fire on the Japanese with their Tommy guns and causing a number of casualties. I dare not stop continuing on towards Aberdeen. I asked Shahib Uddin, my reserve driver, to see if the convoy was intact, with a quick check he said, 'Ach chaa Sahib', meaning OK. We arrived without further incidents, although one could hear a constant barrage of fire. We arrived at headquarters of Aberdeen where I was relieved to see the convoy was intact; however, three men were wounded during the skirmish. I congratulated each man on their efforts. Incidentally, L/Bdr Thompson's father was BSM Thompson who previously was a sergeant in the 1st Regiment HK/SRA. The Thompson family before the war was well known to my family and used to live on the 2nd floor, which was one below us in the married quarters at Gun Club Hill Barracks.

After making my report to Cmdr Millett, informing him of the attacks to and from the Magazines, including the loss of the last two lorries on the way to the Magazine, he asked me if I had met Sgt Walker[47] of the Hong Kong Volunteer Defence Corps (HKVDC), who was in charge of an armoured car and who was apparently sent forward to meet me and to assist in the withdrawal of the convoy if necessary, which was assumed would be under heavy fire from the Japanese positions at Shouson Hill and Brick Hill. As Sgt Walker was under the impression I would be using the jungle track and not the road, he naturally took this for granted not knowing that I had already made a clearance through the blockage of derelict and wrecked cars. I told Cmdr Millett that I had not seen Sgt Walker or the armoured car. I decided to make a search of the road and fortunately I located Walker in his armoured car stuck in a ditch; we were able to pull the car out of the ditch by drag ropes that I always carried in a case of emergency. I thanked him for his attempt to give me assistance, but he said, 'The assistance was the other way around, and it's my thanks to you.'

I met up again with the little Chinese boy and found that he appeared to be quite all right, the staff at the headquarters having fed him well during my absence. The boy was again housed in the metal container and wedged safely behind the seats of my vehicle and the convoy departed to the gun positions at Mount Gough and Mount Austin arriving before daylight where the ammunition was offloaded. Upon my arrival at the recently established West Administrative Pool I handed the little Chinese boy over to the old Chinese lady, Mrs Ah Cheung, the wife of the fellow that had been crushed by the statue of Buddha in the recent bombing of Sir Robert Ho Tung's house. She said she would care for the boy and it was not long before the boy adapted himself with those in the building, but naturally was still very frightened of the noise of the shelling which was increasing every hour. We christened him 'Johnny'.

The aerial bombing was also taking its toll upon the western half of the island where the Japanese were endeavouring to silence the last four gun positions, which are still causing havoc amongst the Japanese defences upon Kowloon and other areas on the mainland. I have just heard that Lieut Bompas has been killed in the area of Stanley. I was very sorry to hear this, another good man gone.

24 December 1941

I was in a deep sleep when I was awoken by BQMS May at 3.00 a.m. I received orders to clear as much ammunition from the magazines at Little Hong Kong. I was to collect eight lorries, including guards and loading parties from the vehicles centre at Hong Kong University for the removal of 6-inch, 4.5-inch and 3.7-inch How shell and cartridges that were intended to replenish supplies of the remaining gun positions in the Peak area, which now numbered only four, those being the 6-inch How sites at Mount Austin and Mount Gough and the 3.7-inch How at Mount Kellett and Sanatorium plus the one 4.5-inch How at Sanatorium. I decided to reconnoitre the road in my 15-cwt accompanied by four Indian gunners to ensure that the way was clear to allow the lorries to get through, and if there was a blockage, to clear a passage. I instructed the drivers to await my return. As we approached the area in question without incident, I could hear the explosions of mortars and rifle fire coming from the areas of Brick Hill, Shouson Hill, Mount Nicholson and Mount Cameron and practically everywhere else in the vicinity.

The Indian gunners were staring intently into the darkness for any sign of the Japanese but no movement could be identified. Perhaps the Japanese were preoccupied with the fighting that was obviously occurring elsewhere. The area of the abandoned lorries was much the same as before and no serious blockage was evident. I returned to the lorries and told the drivers and loading parties that there was a clear passage on the road to the magazines and that without ammunition on board we would proceed in reasonable close formation and speed and to be aware of possible attack.

Just before the turnoff from the main road to the magazines, the whole area was lit up by the burst of mortar shells that were being directed at our defence positions. Whilst our drivers had a better view of the road, our presence was obviously noted by the Japanese, who endeavoured to redirect their fire onto the convoy. The guards in the lorries returned fire, but as it was only a short distance to the magazines, we managed to arrive unscathed, despite some near misses from the mortar shells and small arms fire. The lorries moved on for loading whilst I directed the guards to take up defensive positions in and around the magazines as ordered by a senior NCO of the Middlesex Regiment.

I reported to Maj Marsh in the concrete bunker outside the gates and I informed him that we would have to make the return journey once the lorries were loaded. I requested if he could provide covering fire from our forward lines of machine gun posts established around the surrounding hills of Mount Nicholson and Mount Cameron which overlooked the high ground of Shouson Hill and Brick Hill, having a full view of the Japanese defences along this line.

Maj Marsh contacted Sgt Bedward, who was in command of the machine guns, and ordered him to lay down a continuous barrage of fire once the lorries began the return journey to Aberdeen. Sgt Bedward had about ten machine gun posts, based around the area below Mount Nicholson. I later heard that he and the whole detachment were completely wiped out.

The lorries were loaded and we left the magazines at 5-minute intervals. The sky was again lit up by the explosion of the Japanese mortar shells. Our machine gunners provided an enormous blanket of fire, with the guards and the loading parties in the lorries opening up with their Tommy guns. This concentrated fire enabled the convoy to get through to Aberdeen without any direct hits or major casualties, although a number of our men in the lorries were wounded by splinters of shrapnel. As we passed the Queen Mary Hospital on our right, sniper fire was coming from Lamma Island on our left, but as we turned the corner to leave Aberdeen, we came under a heavy mortar attack from the high ridge overlooking this part of the road.

The first mortar hit my vehicle on the radiator, which temporarily blinded me, with the base of the shell hitting the right door of my car that jammed my right leg between the steering column and the upper part of the dashboard. I received shrapnel wounds to my right shoulder and right hand and my steel helmet was dented and knocked off my head. My relief driver on my left was 4008 Mohammed Hussain who was killed outright. One Indian gunner was severely wounded who was sitting in the rear of the vehicle and the other gunner beside him received a large piece of shrapnel to the chest.

Luckily, the attack did not impede my movement forward and in a very short time I accelerated speed moving the lorries to reasonable safety behind a high bank, which was thickly covered with trees and bushes.

Leaving the lorries in relative safety, I returned to Queen Mary Hospital only a short distance away, where I offloaded the body of Mohammed Hussain and the other gunners who were wounded. I was treated for splinter wounds and returned to the convoy where we continued on our way to reach the base of Peak Road about an hour before dawn. I instructed the drivers to make a run to reach Magazine Gap Bridge as quickly as possible before daylight, which will be out of view of the Japanese batteries on the mainland.

We were now being bombarded unmercifully hourly and the daylight bombing had increased. At this stage, I was completely exhausted, not only by the loss of sleep for such a long period, but also the strain of the past eighteen days in maintaining a continuous supply of ammunition to the defence positions on the mainland and Hong Kong Island. In addition, to make things worse, I was suffering from bleeding haemorrhoids which had been with me these past four days and not being able to treat or wash the area, or change of clothes, this caused my clothes to become stuck to the seat of the car, especially my underwear. The pain was most depressing, and the wound upon my left thigh was painful and inflamed. The shrapnel splinter on my right hand and arm had become very festered. My nose was still badly swollen, although the black eyes had disappeared.

Capt Hoyland and Lieut Vinter noticed the state I was in these past five or six days and thought it was time I reported to the hospital for treatment. I told them as soon as I had completed the disposal of the shell to the Mount Austin gun position that I would go along to the War Memorial Hospital for treatment.

The continuous artillery shelling and mortar attacks with ever-increasing low-level bombing in the Peak area made the whole of the western portion of Hong Kong one thunderous continual storm. At the present time heavy fighting is now in progress between the enemy and the British, Indian and Canadian forces, particularly around Mount Cameron, Mount Nicholson and Magazine Gap.

At about midday, a sudden haemorrhage came upon me from the haemorrhoids. BQMS May thought it best I go to hospital for treatment. I followed his advice and saw Doctor Kirk,[48] the civilian doctor in charge, he checked me over and realised the state of my condition and insisted that I enter the hospital immediately for the night where he could treat me for the septic wounds and to dress the very inflamed haemorrhoids, which at this time were severely bleeding. Doctor Kirk was flabbergasted at my run-down condition and he said, 'How long have you been like this?' I said, 'For the last five or six days.' He thought my bruised nose was infected and he gave me injections to safeguard against tetanus or other infections. I told BQMS May that what I really needed was a complete rest, to which he agreed. The doctor arranged for me to be put in to an underground and isolated room in the basement where I would be free from the heavy bombardment, which was now raging around the hospital grounds. I could hear the shells hitting the walls, which did not unduly worry me, as all I wanted was a good sleep as I was beyond caring at this stage.

Without any effort, I was asleep in seconds.

At about 9.00 p.m. I was awakened by Dr Kirk after being asleep for about five hours and I felt a little better. The haemorrhage had ceased, thank goodness. The shrapnel wounds were still painful but bearable. In the company of Dr Kirk was my friend in transport, Capt Wiseman of the vehicle centre and he informed me that I was required to make a further journey to Little Hong Kong Magazine, to withdraw 6-inch How and 3.7-inch How shell that were urgently required at the gun positions in the Peak area. Wiseman told me that I was to collect a convoy of eight lorries from Hong Kong University, with guards and loading parties.

BQMS May arranged for my car with the usual four or five Indian gunners to ride in the rear fully armed. I moved off from the hospital grounds with a wave from Dr Kirk. I arrived at Hong Kong University and collected the lorries. On my arrival at Aberdeen, I reported to Cmdr Millett and asked him if he could give me an up-to-date situation on the Japanese in the district and he told me that he did not think I would be able to get through to the magazines, as I most probably would be ambushed on the way. Despite this advice from Cmdr Millett, I felt I had to make an attempt.

It was now 10.30 p.m., fairly overcast and very dark. I got the drivers together with Sgt Tavendale in charge of the guard and I told them that I would take the convoy through the area of wrecked vehicles, but first, I would inspect the area to see if there were any Japanese and if any blockage existed and to await my return.

Once again, we had to face the awful stench from the bodies that were strewn everywhere. We found three small lorries and a car lying across the road, containing bullet-ridden bodies mown down by machine gun and rifle fire. Once again, we had to move the vehicles out of the way to create a passage for the convoy. With the Japanese having full view of this area, burial parties have never had the opportunity to bury the remains of more than one hundred bodies.

I returned to Aberdeen and told everyone that we were now ready to move. I told Sgt Tavendale to be in the first lorry and for him to take over in case anything happened to me. I left at about midnight instructing a guard in the last lorry to flag the vehicles off at five-minute intervals. On the journey, we could hear the intense noise of fighting coming from the Brick Hill area and also from Mount Nicholson and Mount Cameron. We could see the flashes of mortar shells and small arms fire, which lit up the sky. As we neared the turnoff to the magazine, we came under fire from the road that led to Repulse Bay and Shouson Hill.

I had been advised that the Japanese were in occupation of a red brick house on Shouson Hill and they were inflicting casualties to our withdrawing forces. I accelerated as much as I could peering intently into the dark night. Fortunately, the Japanese fire was not accurate so I told the Indian gunners in the rear to get as low as possible and not to return fire, as the flashes from their guns would be easily sighted. I reached the turnoff to the magazines, making all haste to find shelter behind the thick undergrowth and rocks and beyond the jungle turnoff and close to the main gates. I told the men to get out of the vehicle and take cover, also for Shahib Uddin to bring me at least half a dozen hand grenades from the supply in my vehicle. Finally the lorries arrived safely and in good time entering the magazines in all haste for loading. I ordered our guards to reinforce our defence position. The situation in our immediate vicinity was relatively quiet although in the distance the sounds of fire could be clearly heard. I glanced at my watch which showed the time just after 1 a.m. Suddenly, Sgt Tavendale said, 'Charlie, the Japs appear to be setting themselves up for an attack from the junction with the main road.' No sooner had he said this when the Japs opened fire. I ordered fire to be returned and we commenced a long barrage with machine gun and rifle. This went on for about twenty minutes after which time the Japs appeared to have withdrawn. I was informed that the lorries were now loaded and ready to move, so I waited for another 20 minutes hoping that the Japanese had disappeared. I then drove down to the junction very cautiously in the 15-cwt accompanied by the gunners telling the drivers in the lorries to wait my return. After about ten minutes I decided that the situation was reasonably safe to proceed to Aberdeen and we moved off just after 1.30 a.m. reaching our destination without incident. In my opinion I believe the Japanese are reforming for a major assault during daylight.

The fighting on Brick Hill was intensifying and in between the din of the firing, we could hear shouting and yelling particularly by the Japanese. We arrived at Aberdeen without incident, and I told all drivers to await my instructions, before continuing onwards to the Peak. I reported to Cmdr Millett who congratulated me on getting through, which at first, he did not think I would. I proceeded with the convoy to the Peak, turning at a sharp bend in the road that was covered with very high trees and near the place where we were attacked the night before, but about one hundred yards further on. Suddenly without warning, we came under a blast of mortar and artillery fire, with the result that the third lorry received a direct hit causing a terrific explosion which completely destroyed the lorry containing the 6-inch How shell, etc., with the consequence that the driver, guards and the loading party consisting of nine men were killed instantly.[49]

I directed the remainder of the vehicles to take cover behind the same high bank and trees as we did the night before. I endeavoured to establish whether or not there were any survivors at the burning lorry, but I found there were none. After a short period, we recommenced our journey, telling the drivers to keep well clear of the burning lorry and the surrounding area to avoid possible sparks and flames igniting the explosives being carried. In giving these instructions to the driver of the last lorry, a large object struck me severely on my left leg hitting me below the knee. This blow completely floored me bowling me over temporarily, but I was able to scramble onto the running board of my vehicle instructing my relief driver, Shahib Uddin, to take over.

I think the puttees I was wearing saved a lot of injury to the leg; however, the bone and muscle to the leg appeared very badly bruised causing me great pain on movement. The convoy cleared the area and we were able to arrive at Magazine Gap Bridge where we soon obtained cover from the enemy. After a short break we continued on to the Peak, arriving at approximately 5.30 a.m., and eventually unloading the ammunitions at the gun positions as ordered. Within the next half hour the Japanese opened up with a terrific bombardment of artillery and mortars on to Peak Road and area. After a lull in this bombardment, I took the opportunity to visit Dr Kirk at the hospital, which was quite near and for treatment to the injury on my left leg.

He said, 'Your leg appears to be severely bruised.' The first treatment he applied to the leg eased the pain and together with my other wounds and haemorrhoids he said I must rest as much as possible and that I should be in hospital as he considered my general health and condition was very poor. S/Sgt Gollege, who was with me said, 'Charlie, you must take the advice of Dr Kirk.'

25 December 1941

BQMS May and S/Sgt Gollege considered that I should take the advice of Dr Kirk and be admitted to hospital, which I finally agreed to, both assisting me to the underground room of the hospital. After my admission, I was visited by Dr Kirk and he said that the leg and bruises had improved, but the haemorrhoids needed an operation but this cannot be done before the inflammation of the area improves, which might take some considerable time. The pain from these was very depressing, as I had been suffering for some time, mostly caused by the strain, very little rest and also the continual use of the saturated seat of my car daily due to the unusual heavy rains we have been experiencing.

The following communiqué just received stated the following:

> The enemy made some brutal progress during the hours past midnight, despite heavy losses suffered in the eastern part of Hong Kong. Heavy fighting is in progress in the direction of Happy Valley, with our troops disputing every inch of the Japanese advance. Under strong pressure, we have successfully evacuated our forces from Repulse Bay. A further battle is in progress on the Stanley Peninsular.
>
> His Excellency the Governor has issued the following Christmas Day Message.
>
> IN PRIDE AND ADMIRATION, I SEND MY GREETINGS THIS CHRISTMAS DAY TO ALL WHO ARE FIGHTING AND TO ALL WHO ARE WORKING SO NOBLY AND SO WELL TO SUSTAIN HONG KONG AGAINST THE ASSAULT BY THE ENEMY. FIGHT ON, HOLD FAST FOR KING, COUNTRY AND EMPIRE. GOD BLESS YOU ALL IN THIS FINEST HOUR.
>
> The Pope in his Christmas message broadcast to the world gave hope for peace and said that Christ would eventually triumph and we are torn with anguish for your sufferings.

It is Christmas Day and I wonder how my darling wife and family are. She may be anxiously listening to the wireless to get news of the war and in particular the battle for Hong Kong. Fondest love to you all and to those at home in England and in India. You remember Clancy May and Gerry Gollege, as we are having a drink and wishing all our families a Merry Christmas.

The War Memorial Hospital has been continually shelled under a heavy artillery bombardment. Late this afternoon, I heard that the Governor Sir Mark Young and the GOC Major General Maltby has officially surrendered to General Sakai, the Japanese Commander, this being the most disastrous day in the history of the colony.

26 December 1941

I awoke feeling much better for the rest, although the haemorrhoids and my legs are still very painful. Since 19 December, when the haemorrhoids flared up, the agony and suffering from this complaint was unbelievable, especially under the conditions I was experiencing whilst convoying ammunition and stores, etc., from one point of the island to the other at all times of the day and night. With reference to these convoys, I must mention and recognise the brave drivers of these lorries, who were predominantly Indian and drove their vehicles loaded with shell and high explosives to all positions. They drove these lorries under nerve wracking conditions each one of them expecting to be blown up by either air attacks or artillery barrages, this also applied to the guards and loading parties.

The battle of Hong Kong ended in defeat but no one expected more. The Japanese command had reason to believe they could overrun and capture the colony within 10 days but we held out for almost double that time.

On reflection, I believe the injury to my leg was the result of being struck by debris from a mortar explosion on Christmas Eve. Dr Kirk has just visited me and said that the injury to my leg appears to be a severe bruise only, but regarding the haemorrhoids, suggests an immediate operation as soon as the inflammation subsides.

Everything now seems so peaceful after those eighteen bloody days of war. The mood of the other patients here suffering from minor wounds and for those who are seriously wounded appears to be quite cheery. The civilian doctors and nurses assisted by civilian volunteers have done splendid work during the campaign and it must have been very nerve-wracking for them when attending the wounded under the heavy bombardment of the Peak area particularly as the hospital received direct hits. I have just heard from one of the nurses, that Japanese troops can be seen from the hospital and at various other places at the Peak. There are also a number of them in front of the hospital. She also said that the Japanese officers are now inside the hospital making enquiries with Dr Kirk as to how many wounded there are. It appears that Japanese guards are already posted inside the hospital.

27 December 1941

Stocks of food appear to be low as we only received the following today:

Breakfast	1 slice bread and butter
	1 cup of tea
Lunch	1 slice of bread
	1 vegetable soup

Tea   2 cups of tea
               1 slice of bread and jam

We have sufficient food to last for about a month. These stocks are practically all tinned foods. As regards bread and flour, fresh meat, the hospital has none. The Japanese have been approached for further supplies of bread and flour. The Japanese officers and men appear to be a medical group, the officers being doctors and recognised by the wearing of Red Cross armbands. The guards that can be seen in the grounds of the hospital appear to be civilised and academic looking. They are not like the hardened type which have brutality written all over their features. I hear that all British and Indian prisoners captured in the Peak area have now been rounded up all of who are concentrated in Austin Barracks. In addition, the Peak Civilian Control Centre has now been established at the end of the hospital; the food being stacked in this part of the building is only for issue to civilians living around the Peak area, and for those civilians who have been forced up from the lower levels of the island. They have taken refuge and safety, wherever possible, in any of the unoccupied residencies.

There were families with young children in this group, who must be terrified and suffered terribly during the heavy artillery bombardments and aerial bombings that took place during the days from 13 to 25 December. The fathers and husbands, who were non-military, must now feel very guilty for not allowing their wives and children to be evacuated from Hong Kong in June 1940 as advised by the Hong Kong Government.

The hospital is full of civilians but only a very few are patients that were not engaged in combat duties. The remainder, being wounded personnel of the various units including Hong Kong Volunteers. At the end of the hospital grounds, a small cemetery has been established, where, to date eleven British and two Indian soldiers have been buried, including S/Sgt Farrier Holmes of the HK/SRA who was killed during heavy air raids upon West Administrative Pool headquarters on 21 December.

In the hospital, we have Mrs Fox, the wife of Capt Fox of 4th Medium Battery HK/SRA who was killed at Wong Nei Chong Gap headquarters on 19 December. He was killed along with Lieut Col Yale, Maj Hunt, Maj Temple, Maj Proes and Lieut Platts and others when the Japanese advanced through the Wong Nei Chong Valley. Mrs Fox is doing quite a good job in helping the nursing staff at the hospital.

28 December 1941

Dr Kirk allowed me up from my bed for a couple of hours today, where, from the veranda, I noticed quite a lot of activity amongst the Japanese troops in the front of the hospital grounds who suddenly appeared from nowhere. I have been told that the Japanese are entering and plundering all private residences in the Peak area. They are collecting and salvaging all valuable stores from the positions occupied by our troops during the siege.

The Japanese guards have suddenly become hostile to all patients, whether in their beds or out of them. They point their bayonets at us from time to time, but the Japanese doctors have curbed their hostility for the time being. Today, the first of many appalling massacres of unarmed men, who had already surrendered, started to emerge. The first victims of this barbarity were men of the 5th AA Battery of the volunteers. This Battery was a mixture of British, Eurasians, Portuguese and Chinese and had started the battle well by shooting down two Japanese aircrafts and knowing that the Japanese were heading towards them, were fully prepared to give a good account of themselves. They did not have a chance. As dawn broke on 19 December, twenty-nine men of 5th Battery found themselves completely surrounded by the Japanese and outnumbered by ten to one. A Japanese Officer called out in English, 'Surrender and we will save you.' The twenty-nine men had no choice because any further attempts to resist would have resulted in their complete liquidation. The Japanese formed a semi-circle at the entrance to the fort. The officer then shouted out an order to his men in Japanese and the soldiers stood grinning in expectancy. They nudged one another and laughed as this promised to be something to them like real sport. The officer then shouted out in English, 'Come out all you men and you will be released.' The Japanese soldiers stopped grinning and became tense and alert. Several AA gunners walked hesitantly to the entrance, but were waved back by the officer, 'One man at a time, please,' he ordered.

The first man came out and a Japanese soldier nearest to him lunged with his bayonet. The gunner let out a scream and fell clutching his stomach. This hideous procession went on until twenty-nine torn and bloodied bodies lay on the ground. Some were more fortunate than others and died almost at once. They had received thrusts through the heart or throat which had killed them almost instantly. But others were victims of more slipshod butchery and had taken the bayonet point through the lung, liver, shoulder or lower abdomen. For them, death was a long, drawn-out affair of coughing, retching, moaning and screaming.

After the gunners, some dead and some still living were thrown into a pit. Two of them later struggled from under the dead bodies and were able to survive the massacre and later were treated for their wounds after making an escape to Bowen Road Military Hospital. This was only the commencement of so many atrocities committed by the Japanese troops as they advanced through Hong Kong.[50]

After more orgies of killings, the Japanese were in need of more diversions and at St Stephen's College, Stanley, which had been hastily converted to a makeshift hospital, approximately one hundred wounded men were being treated. Two hundred Japanese troops stormed into the wards drunk with looted liquor, shooting the two doctors, Col Black and Capt Whitney, who bravely attempted to bar their way to prevent these executions, but were shot where they stood. Incidently, Capt Whitney whom I new quite well had visited my children occasionally during their sickness at Gun Club Hill Barracks. The British nurses could only stand by helplessly and watch the scene of the sickening slaughter that followed. The Japanese ripped bandaged form torn bodies and from stumps of recently amputated arms and legs as they plunged their bayonets into the bodies of the wounded men. One nurse flung her body across a wounded patient and was bayoneted along with the man in the bed. In a space of thirty minutes, fifty-six wounded men had been hacked to death. The nurses were roughly shoved into line and locked up together in a small room and during the rest of Christmas day and all Christmas night and throughout boxing day were raped by the Japanese soldiers.

One of the nurses on the staff here was the wife of Lieut Col Smith RAOC, who was raped with two others at St Stephen's College. She was shot and the other two were bayoneted.

Maj Duncan, whom I met during the retreat from Wong Nei Chong Valley, which had been overrun by the Japanese on 18/19 December told me that he had viewed through his binoculars the day before and witnessed eight British and Canadian prisoners being tied together by a Japanese patrol and were being marched to the base of Mount Cameron where they were all bayoneted to death. He, of course, could do nothing at such a distance away.

29 December 1941

New Japanese guards have been stationed at the hospital and they appear to be quite friendly for a change and I think they are third line troops.

As I am a senior NCO, they are treating me fairly well and I have been allowed to walk around the hospital grounds. The haemorrhoids are less painful and the wounds are healing well and are not so inflamed. I hope that Dr Kirk will be able to operate soon.

News has just been received to confirm that the following officers have been reported killed:

Lieut Col Yale	1st Hong Kong Regiment HK/SRA
Maj Proes	1st Hong Kong Regiment HK/SRA
Maj Hunt	1st Hong Kong Regiment HK/SRA
Maj Temple	1st Hong Kong Regiment HK/SRA
Capt Fox	1st Hong Kong Regiment HK/SRA
Maj Fielden	1st Hong Kong Regiment HK/SRA
Lieut Platts	1st Hong Kong Regiment HK/SRA
Sgt Hanger	1st Hong Kong Regiment HK/SRA

The above information was received from the Queen Mary Hospital Medical Staff.

Regarding Maj Temple, I was the last one to talk to him on the phone in the bunker when grenades were thrown into the ventilators, the blast of which nearly burst my eardrum, causing me to drop the telephone immediately. I knew this would be the last time I would speak to him.

As the numbers of Japanese increased on the island and the mainland, so did the barbaric behaviour towards unarmed prisoners captured in the fighting. More men were roped together in groups of three and used for bayonet practice. Men were beheaded and shot in cold blood. Several bodies were found, charred beyond recognition, having been roasted alive by flamethrowers. This morning, it was reported that these dreadful atrocities were now mounting in increasing numbers. Even though the Colony had surrendered, groups of men who had been forced to surrender were roped together and bayoneted.

One party of Canadians were lined up on the edge of a cliff facing the sea and then shot in the back.

Mrs Fox, the wife of Capt Fox whom I see on and off daily with other men and women in the grounds of the hospital, asks me constantly of any news of her husband, but at this stage I just cannot bring myself to tell her that he has been reported killed.

Lieut McKechnie[51] of the Winnipeg Grenadiers, which is a Canadian Regiment, is a patient in the next bed to me and a most likable chap. We agree that if we every get out of this situation we will keep in touch. He admires the photograph of my dear wife and family that I have on my table beside me.

1 January 1942

To my darling wife and children, I wish you all a happy New Year and God bless you all. I do hope we shall all be together soon. It is really cold and fresh today, but very pleasant in the sun. The Peak and surrounding hills are so clear that one can see for miles out to sea. Quite a number of ships can be seen leaving the harbour in convoy with two or three Japanese destroyers escorting. I counted twenty-three ships in this convoy.

Dr Kirk approached me today and quietly told me that the possibility of an operation of my haemorrhoids is very remote as the Japanese medical authorities are now being very awkward regarding medical treatment to prisoners of war but he will try his utmost to talk to one of the Japanese doctors and explain the position in my case. He said, 'Keep your fingers crossed.' I spotted Sir Athol McGregor, the Chief Justice of Hong Kong. He was drawing rations from the food control centre with other civilians here, who took refuge in the hospital before the fall of Hong Kong.

At the moment, the pain from the haemorrhoids has all but disappeared, thank goodness. I believe the rest has helped me and the shrapnel cuts and wounds in my leg are healing. The large piece of shrapnel that Dr Kirk removed from my left bicep is now practically healed. The Japanese officer in charge of the guards is now checking up on the wounded with a view to see what condition they are in and possibly move the fit ones to Bowen Road Military Hospital to make way for further wounded that are coming in from time to time. Bowen Road Military Hospital has been the main establishment for all Army personnel stationed either on the island or the mainland.

Reports have been received that British, Canadian and Indian troops have been assembled in the North Point area, with the view of transporting them over to Kowloon to be housed in a concentration camp somewhere in the Shamshuipo district. The civilians are expected to be interned somewhere on the Stanley Peninsula which lies to the south of Hong Kong. Quite a number of Japanese officers visited the War Memorial hospital this morning, for what reason I am not sure. My dear wife would be very interested that we have amongst us the well-known old twin sisters, the Misses Woods. These are two well-dressed ladies who lived in Mody Road, Kowloon. They are assisting in various ways in the hospital and doing a good job by helping the wives and children who should have accepted Hong Kong's advice to be evacuated in June 1940. All the families that left Hong Kong were shipped to Manila on the SS *Empress of Japan* and then to Australia on a New Zealand ship, SS *Awatea*.

2 January 1942

The female cook of the hospital has asked me and Lieut McKechnie to collect as many green vegetables from the houses nearby whose gardens are well stocked with them but not to provoke any of the sentries by doing so. The Japanese apparently understand the importance of green vegetables and did not prevent us from gathering what we could. In addition, we have also been collecting clothes left in these houses that no doubt will become useful later on.

Japanese planes have been constantly flying over Hong Kong showering the population with thousands of leaflets. These leaflets carry a message of their celebrations in the capture of Hong Kong and letting us know that they are in power.

> # To the masses in Hongkong which is closely besieged by the Japanese Army.
>
> ## Commander of the Japanese Army
>
> Now the efficient Japanese Army, Navy and Air Force tightly sieged Hongkong and Hongkong faced to the last moment. If you resist obeying orders of English Authority Hongkong Island with your lives and properties will be reduced to ashes by the efficient Japanese Army, Navy and Air Force. But if you completely give up your resistance cutting the connection with the White, Hongkong will not be reduce to ashes in vain by the Japanese Army. The only one way to protect your lives and properties is to let the White give up their resistance and abandon Hongkong. And you all in cooperation with the Japanese Army, must prevent the destruction of all means of land and sea communications, electric equipments, telephones, telegraphs, water-supplies, broadcasting stations, banks, newspaper offices, equipments of harbours and so forth in order to reestablish Hongkong for glorious Orientals. And wait for the Japanese Army. Then the Japanese Army not assure you of your lives and properties in future but also assure you of giving the suitable posts in accordance with your services.

Japanese Message

8 January 1942

As the main water supply has been cut during the bombardment of the island, the Japanese have made provision for a supply of water to the hospital twice daily. The drivers of the water tankers were selected from male nurses who were originally employed at the hospital before the outbreak of hostilities.

Dr Kirk again examined my wounds and completely removed all the dressings to allow the fresh air to finish the healing process. The inflammation to the haemorrhoids has now gone. Lieut McKechnie has been attending the eleven graves in the small cemetery at the end of the hospital grounds. It is here that the bodies of S/Sgt Farrier Holmes and twelve Indian gunners are buried who were killed during the air attacks and artillery bombardments at Sir Robert Ho Tung's residence. A number of Japanese staff officers arrived this morning and held a lengthy discussion with Dr Kirk. I understand they wanted to know if there was anyone temporarily buried in the areas of the Peak. One of the officers approached me and in perfect English asked me if I knew where any could be. I told him that about twenty-five Indian gunners were buried in the grounds of Sir Robert Ho Tung's estate. They were killed during a heavy air raid attack on 21 December 1941. They were buried in shallow graves with the intention of being re-interned in proper graves at a later date. During this discussion, the Japanese had noticed that quite a number of civilians appeared fairly fit and they suggested to Dr Kirk that they could be useful in removing some of the dead lying around the Peak area for re-internment to a cemetery agreed upon by the Japanese. It was agreed that the bodies be buried in the grounds adjacent to the one already established at the end of the hospital. I was selected to take charge of this thankless job. I was able to obtain nine volunteers to exhume and remove any dead in the district. I asked five of the civilians to prepare and dig graves for the expected newcomers. I asked Dr Kirk if he could supply picks and shovels, plus canvas sheeting to wrap the remains in a stretcher. Lieut McKechnie and myself, with four other civilians, proceeded to Sir Robert Ho Tung's estate accompanied by three Japanese sentries. When we arrived there, the large house was fully occupied by Japanese soldiers. I located the sites where 2/Lieut Parks and his party had buried the men on 21 December. I decided to use the stretcher covered with canvas sheeting laid upon the hand trolley and moved the remains of the bodies one at a time.

The bodies were recovered from shallow graves and the clothes that they were buried in assisted us to lift the decomposed remains. We of course were forced to wear covering over our faces during this operation and as we lifted the remains onto the stretcher, the Japanese sentries standing around were also heavily masked. The identity red and green discs were removed from each body, which should have been removed by Capt Hoyland on 21 December. One by one, the remains were re-interned in the hospital grounds and in the late evening when the task had been completed, I handed over the discs and other small articles to Dr Kirk. As we left the cemetery and to our great astonishment, the Japanese officers arrived and placed flowers upon each grave. Dr Kirk appreciated the work that we had done.

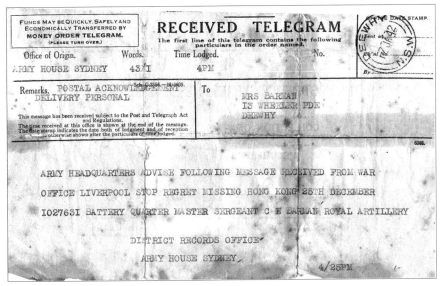

Telegram from Army House

12 January 1942

About ten lorries carrying Japanese troops arrived, the first vehicle being smaller than the remainder and marked with a huge red cross. In the front seat was a squat Japanese officer, wearing a red cross on one arm and approximately ten soldiers in the rear. The remaining lorries were carrying about twenty men per vehicle, the total number of men well in excess of one hundred. In command of these troops was another squat Japanese officer, the whole party looking battle worn and with very hard features. The troops all paraded in the grounds with the medical party heading for the main entrance to the hospital who were received by Dr Kirk.

The Japanese officer spoke fluent English and he said to Dr Kirk, 'I am here to take over the hospital and to remove all military patients to the hospital at Bowen Road at about midday, with the civilians to be transferred to Stanley at a later date.[52] The British and Indian troops will march to Bowen Road and those unable to walk will be conveyed in the small vehicle marked with a red cross.' This Japanese officer was a doctor and the men with him were the medical orderlies, all of whom were very pleasant to us but the troops paraded in the grounds were just the opposite. The remaining medical staff in the hospital was to follow later.

Finally, we were all paraded outside the hospital and Dr Kirk was instructed to inform us that we would all be leaving here at about 2.00 p.m. and everybody was to take whatever they could when we paraded at 1.30 p.m. The civilians were lined up by the lorries with the British and Indian troops nearby. Dr Kirk came to me and said, 'Q, I am afraid the operation is off, but here is some ointment for the haemorrhoids if they give you any trouble,' and he hoped something could be done for me at Bowen Road. In the group of civilians was an apparently well-known female Australian journalist whom I knew as 'Andrea'. I had several conversations with her. Her real name was Dorothy Jenner.[53] I was standing close to her when the officer in command of the remaining Japanese troops standing near her spoke some harsh language towards her and she in turn said something that the officer did not like. He turned to a senior NCO and shouted out an order to him and at the same time pointing towards me. This fellow immediately got hold of me very roughly and with his sword scabbard proceeded to belt me on the arms, back and legs. The journalist 'Andrea' responded by telling the NCO, 'Leave him alone, you yellow bastard,' and as a result of this, I received several more hard blows on my body. She said to me, 'Sorry, Charles, we will both have a drink about this episode one day, that is, if we both survive.'

We were formed up and marched off to Bowen Road Hospital. We said goodbye to everyone, particularly the doctors and nurses for their kindness under difficult conditions. The medical staff also provided us with cigarettes and as many tins of meat as they could spare.

The walking proved to be damned painful after the beating I received and continued to be painful for days afterwards, especially when we had the long march along Nathan Road to Shamshuipo Camp. I had a difficult time getting on and off the boat when crossing the harbour.

When we reached Bowen Road Hospital, Lieut McGhee[54] of the Royal Scots placed me in charge of more than thirty wounded men waiting in lorries. Near fifty fully armed Japanese soldiers were on guard. The seriously wounded men were admitted to the main wards, the remainder being accommodated in the barrack block adjacent to the hospital and within the grounds. I was allotted a bunk at the end of this building where I was fairly comfortable. The wounded Indian troops have been sent on to St Albert's Convent in Stubbs Road, which has been established as the hospital for the Indian casualties. Lieut Col Rudolf[55] of the RAMC is in charge of this hospital and was well known to the families of the military personnel when he was the medical officer in charge during the time the families were evacuated from Hong Kong to Australia via the Philippines.

I have just visited a personal friend of mine, S/Sgt Dobson of the RAVC, who was severely wounded in the back by a large piece of shell in Garden Road during an artillery bombardment on 13 December 1941. He was only just able to recognise me. The nurse told me it was only a matter of time.[56] This was number nine ward, which had some very bad cases.[57] One Canadian of the Winnipeg Grenadiers was employed as a backwoodsman in the outback before the war. He was found in a delirious condition in the jungle area to the south of Hong Kong Island. His back was completely split open and covered in maggots and was in this condition for a number of days before the surrender. The nurse was intending to clean the wound and remove the maggots but the doctor prevented her from doing so because as he said, 'Leave the maggots, only clean around the wounds as they will clear up all the gangrenous matter that had formed in the infected area,' and that with careful dressing, the maggots will eventually be removed as the outer edges of the wounds improved. Lieut Col Shackleton RAMC is in charge of Bowen Road Hospital, with a medical staff including Majs' Brown and Harrison. RSM Knightly is in charge of the medical orderlies, being assisted by RSM Bartlett. The nursing staff includes VAD nurses with Miss Dwyer being matron in charge.[58]

20 January 1942

The nurse of ward nine sent for me again to say that my friend S/Sgt Dobson was very low and that she was afraid he had only a short time to live. When I arrived at his bedside, he could not recognise me and passed away soon afterwards. After knowing him so well over the years, it upset me and within a short time they removed his body to the morgue. At least he died peacefully and will not have to face up to the hardships, which no doubt we shall all be confronted with in the future. He was buried on the high ground near the entrance gates to the hospital.

There is now a scarcity of food, so Lieut McKechnie and I have pooled what cash we have and arranged with a Chinese boy employed around the hospital to try and purchase any food he can buy on the black market outside. We hear that the Canadians have been concentrated at North Point, Hong Kong Island, and that the British troops, including Hong Kong Volunteers at Shamshuipo Camp, Kowloon. It appears that the food in both camps is mostly rice and epidemics of dysentery are now raging in both camps. The dysentery cases are arriving at the hospital in great numbers.

We are expected to be moved to one of these camps very soon, where I think we shall reside for quite some considerable time. If we are sent to Shamshuipo, it will mean crossing the harbour followed by quite a long march. The Japanese guards are now becoming aggressive and everyone is getting their usual bashings, either by rifle butts or face slapping including hard thumping to the body.

1 February 1942

From the hospital verandah we have an excellent view of the harbour and quite a number of Japanese warships and transports can be seen lying at anchor plus small Chinese craft. One can see the awful damage done to the Naval dockyards caused by the artillery bombardments and aerial bombing during the battle. Of course a lot of destruction was carried out by the defenders before surrender, to deny the Japanese making any use of them in the future, more of a burnt earth policy which was adopted by us wherever possible. The dockyard defenders completely destroyed and sank the floating dock, which was quite a loss to the Japanese Naval authorities. One could also see a number of our own ships that were scuttled or were sunk by the Japanese. Some of the ships can still be seen burning, also buildings on the lower slopes leading down to the harbour. As far as the eye could see, towards Kowloon, there appears very little activity there.

9 February 1942

Suddenly this morning, the Japanese authorities have decided to remove all of us that are accommodated in the barrack block of the hospital to the POW camps. The Canadians are to be transported to North Point and the British to be assembled there and to await further orders. This means a break of friendship that has built up since our association due to the circumstances in the final stages of the battle. I hope these friendships will continue as it did in the War Memorial Hospital and Bowen Road Hospital in the years to come. Lieut McKechnie has given me his address in Canada, where his father would employ me without hesitation should I wish to move there. I told him that I would think about it after I am reunited with my dear wife.

10 February 1942

We received orders to move at 10.00 a.m., the Canadians were first to move with Japanese guards on each lorry. I managed to say goodbye to 'Mac' wishing him the best of luck, both hoping to see each other again. I told him very quickly that I was sorry about the death of Sgt Maj Osborn.[59] He and his platoon helped me during my run with a convoy of about twenty-five lorries loaded with shell, on Repulse Bay Road between Shouson Hill and Aberdeen. I remember him shouting to his men, 'Come and scatter those yellow bastards.' During this conflict, I spotted Osborn going forward with his men using all the grenades they had, causing heavy casualties on the enemy.

The remainder of the British and Indian troops were then ordered to embark on the lorries, which were strongly guarded by Japanese sentries. The Japanese officer waved his hand to the leading lorry to proceed down towards Peak Road. We all waved to the nursing staff and civilians standing around the hospital.

Finally we arrived at the Blake Pier and embarked on various types of craft, large and small, most of which did not look very seaworthy. We were packed like sardines into boats of all sizes; the boat I was in normally carried about twenty passengers, but there were nearly sixty and all were standing. The fleet of ships containing the prisoners, numbered about fifty. After the convoy of ships had been assembled, they moved towards Kowloon. Due to the overloading and not being seaworthy, some immediately sank or capsized within a very short distance from the shore. The Japanese escorting the ships never attempted to rescue any of the men and goodness knows how many survived. Some may have been able to swim to the shores and if they did they were soon recaptured. Our boat was moving with a list of over 15 degrees and if there was any movement among us, the list increased dangerously.

When we did disembark on the wharf in Kowloon, we were confronted by a large group of well-armed Japanese troops. These appeared to be more of the brutal type in features and manner. I would say that they were front-line troops and hardened veterans with years of battle experience. It was the Blake Pier that my family and I disembarked from the SS *Rajputana* in 1936 when I was posted to the 1st Hong Kong Regiment HK/SRA, the Regiment being stationed at Gun Club Hill Barracks, Kowloon.

We all thought we would be transported to our final destination by lorries, but this was not to be. Everyone had collected what they could which would be of use to them in the camp and therefore it meant that each one would have to carry their items. I had a fair amount and hoped to hang on to it when I arrived at the camp. Whether I could manage to do so remained to be seen. Some of the men had nearly double to what I had and I'm sure they would have to discard some items before they reached the camp. It was assumed that Shamshuipo would be the camp, it being somewhere about six miles away. Not having transport, this amused the Japanese and under the circumstances, it was near impossible for some of the men to carry the amount they had. I was able to hand onto my serge suit, overcoat, and two blankets with small items in my haversack and gas mask case. After waiting nearly two hours, near the well-known Peninsula Hotel, the march commenced in column along the well-known Nathan Road with Japanese guards marching on either side of the column. There were flags everywhere, not the Union Jack but flags of the rising sun, which became known to us all as 'the poached egg'. Some of the Indian shopkeepers, not to be outdone by the anti-British activity, exploded into a rash form of nationalism and exhibited the red, white and green colours of Indian independence. During this march, we saw much of the wasteful aftermath on the sides of the road where derelict wagons, burnt-out lorries, abandoned vehicles of all types, guns, tangled equipment and dead people and horses that attracted armies of flies and ants. We saw the bombed and scuttled ships in the Causeway Bay part of the harbour and all around us was the stench of death. We saw the Japanese burning the dead and carrying small boxes bound in cloth containing the ashes. Men started to fall out of the column and were kicked and prodded back into line by bayonet points. Greatcoats and blankets were being discarded by the roadside, for at this stage of the march, only the fittest retained their possessions with which they set out. Water bottles were empty and the strong helped the weak along and there were some who sang and whistled. A senior Japanese NCO then came on the scene carrying a large sword. He looked a real nasty brute of an individual and ordered all gear that was being carried to be opened for inspection. The Japanese made us show our hands searching for rings and watches. The ring I was wearing on my little finger, which was my wedding ring, was roughly removed. This ring had been previously split by a piece of shrapnel during the mortar bombing of my car at Aberdeen.It was given to me by my dear wife many years ago. They made us open all our mouths for gold fillings which I had none. Luckily, I carried my watch inside the band of my shorts.

Charles Barman, Summer Uniform, Hong Kong, 1936

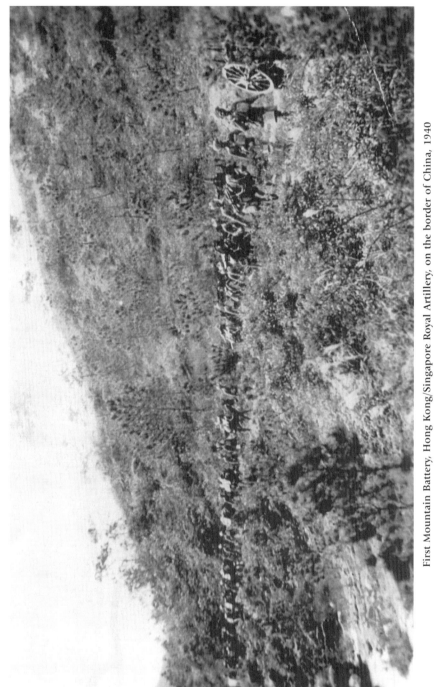

First Mountain Battery, Hong Kong/Singapore Royal Artillery, on the border of China, 1940

Colonel Tokunaga at Crimes Tribunal, who was later found guilty and hanged

The Barman family photo, 1940, kept by Charles Barman through his POW years

Fourth Medium Battery, First Hong Kong/Singapore Royal Artillery, at Gun Club Hill Barracks, Hong Kong, 1938

Hong Kong Christmas, 1936; children of the 4th Medium Battery

BESIEGED BY JAPANESE.—Special "Sun" picture shows position of Hongkong to-day, with Japanese reportedly in possession of Kowloon, chief British city on mainland opposite Hongkong Island. Photograph, taken from famed Peak residential district, shows Victoria, the capital in foreground, with Kowloon across sea three-quarters of a mile distant. Jap siege-guns are reported in Kowloon (Nine Dragon) mountain range behind Kowloon city, within easy bombarding distance of Victoria. Hongkong subterranean fortress guns are atop mountain from which photo was taken

Japanese attack

From left to right: Staff Sergeant 'Clancy' May, Charles Barman and
Staff Sergeant Gerry Gollege Gun Club Hill Barracks, 1940.

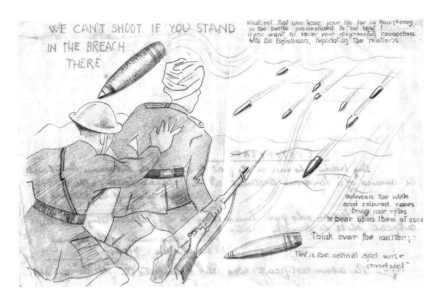

Japanese Propaganda

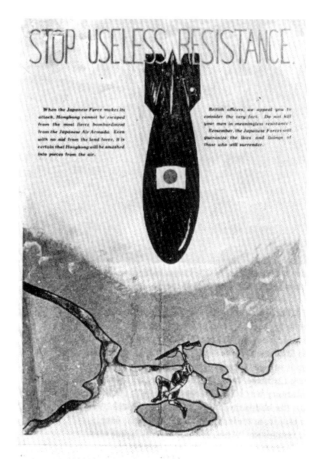

British officers and men! What do you expect in your useless resistance after having deen cornered in this small island of Hongkong? If you are waiting for the Chungking troops to stir up the Japanese rear it will only end in a fool's dream. The Malay Peninsula and the Philippines are now under the sway of Japanese forces and their fate is completely sealed.

Your comrades brought to Kowloon, have already been sent to Samchun and they are calmly enjoying a peaceful X'mas, you are at the cross-road now. It's all up to you whether you prefer death or save your life for the future.

We will give you the last chance for your reconsideration, If you surrender to us, the ultimatum ends at midnight of Dec 26th

JAPANESE ARMY COMMANDER

Japanese Propaganda

BUCKINGHAM PALACE

The Queen and I bid you a very warm welcome home.

Through all the great trials and sufferings which you have undergone at the hands of the Japanese, you and your comrades have been constantly in our thoughts. We know from the accounts we have already received how heavy those sufferings have been. We know also that these have been endured by you with the highest courage.

We mourn with you the deaths of so many of your gallant comrades.

With all our hearts, we hope that your return from captivity will bring you and your families a full measure of happiness, which you may long enjoy together.

George R.I

September 1945.

Letter from King George VI

POW men on *Formidable*, Charles Barman seated third from left

Argyle Street Officers Camp

Sketch of the Shamshuipo Camp by A. V. Skvorzov

Sun Wai Camp, 1937; Charles Barman seated next to wheel

Triumphant Entry Into Hongkong

DESPITE their much-vaunted defences, the British Garrison in Hongkong surrendered 1 he Imperial Forces two years ago today—18 days after the beginning of hostilitie Photo above shows the triumphant entry of Lieut-General Sakai, Conqueror of Hongkon and his victorious troops, which marked the formal occupation.

Triumph in Hong Kong

AUTOGRAPHS OF PERSONALITIES
IN CAMP.

RANK	NAME	AUTOGRAPHS	REMARKS.
Major General	Maltby . M.C.	*(signature)*	General Officer bomdg British Troops in China.
Brigadier	McLeod.	*(signature)*	Commanding Royal Artillery
Brigadier	Peffer O.B.E.	A. Peffers.	Brigadier i/c Administration
Brigadier	Wallis. C.	*(signature)*	Commdr. Mainland & East Infantry Bdes
Colonel	Levenham .M.C.	*(signature)*	G.S.O. I
Colonel	Clifford .O.B.E. M.C.	*(signature)*	Chief Engineer
Major	Moody	R.E. Moody	D.a.a.G
Colonel	Rose . M.C.	*(signature)* Col.	Officer Commanding Hong Kong Volunteer Defence Force.
Colonel	Andrew-Levinge	Kr. Andrew-Levinge.	Assistant Director of Supply and Transport.
Colonel	Ford	N Forde	Command Paymaster

War diary signatures 1

香港俘虏收容所

AUTOGRAPHS OF PERSONALITIES
IN CAMP.

RANK	NAME	AUTOGRAPHS	REMARKS
Colonel	Kilpatrick		Financial Adviser China Command.
Lieut Colonel	Penfold		Officer Commanding 12° Coast Regt. R.A.
Lieut Colonel	Shaw	S. Shaw	Officer Commanding 8° Coast Regt. R.A.
Lieut Colonel	Fields, M.C.	F. Field	Officer Commanding 5° A.A. Regt. R.A.
Lieut Colonel	Cadogan-Rawlinson		Officer Commanding 5/7° Rajput Regt.
Lieut Colonel	Gray		Officer Commanding 2/14° Punjabis Regt.
Lieut Colonel	White	Simon White	Officer Commanding 2nd Batt: Royal Scots.
Lieut Colonel	Stewart		Officer Commanding 1st Batt: Middlesex Regt.
Lieut Colonel	Levet	E.Levett	Chief Signal Officer China Command
Lieut Colonel	Shackleton		Royal Army Medical Corps

War diary signatures 2

香港俘虜收容所

AUTOGRAPHS OF PERSONALITIES
IN CAMP

RANK	NAME	AUTOGRAPHS	REMARKS
Lieut Colonel	Rudolf	HRudolf	R.A.M.C. O/c Combined Military Hospital Kowloon & China
Lieut Colonel	Lamb	RLamb	Commander, Fortress Engineers
Lieut Colonel	Wilson	J.B.Wilson	C.A.E. Hong Kong
Major	Crowe	JP Crowe	Officer Commanding 1st H.K. Regt. H.K.S.R.A.
Major	Duncan	JDuncan	Commanding 3rd Medium Bty H.K.S.R.A.
Major	Morgan	W.A.C.H.Morgan	Commanding 7th A.A. Bty. R.A.
Major	Temples	C.F.Templer mjr RA	Commanding 30th Heavy Bty R.A.
Major	Forrester	CForster	Commanding 965 Defence Battery RA
Major	Anderson	E.W.S Anderson	Commanding 24th Heavy Battery R.A.
Major	Mills	RMills	Commanding 26th Heavy Bty R.A. H.K.S.R.A.
Major	Heagecoe	s.z.Hedgecoe	2nd in command 1st Batt. Middlesex Regt.

War diary signatures 3

AUTOGRAPHS OF PERSONALITIES
IN CAMP

RANK	NAME	AUTOGRAPHS	REMARKS
Wing Commander	Sullivan	W.Sullivan W/Cdr.	Officer Commanding Royal Air Force in Hong Kong.
Wing Commander	Bennett	H.T. Bennett	Air H.Q. Far East.
Major	Kerr	Kerr Major	Garrison Adjutant Hong Kong.
Major	Stansfield	C. Stansfield	Officer Commanding Hong Kong Mule Corps. (I.A.S.C.).
Lieut	Simpson	Robert Kerr Simpson	Professor at Hong Kong University. Hong Kong.
Major. Lord	Merthyr	Merthyr	Commanding 20th Coast Battery R.A. Stonecutters Island Hongkong.
Captain	G.M.R. Bennett.	G.M.R. Bennett C.F.	R.A.Ch.D. Presbyterian Chaplin. (Attached R/Scots).
Surgeon Commander	Cleave. H.L.	H.L.Cleave	Royal Navy.
Captain	Woodward	Woodward Capt. Vert	Indian Medical Service
Captain	Warrack.	A.J.N Warrack.	Royal Army Medical Corp.
Captain	Strachan	W.S. Strachan	Indian Medical Service.

War diary signatures 4

1300 Ex-P.O.W.s Arrive By Aircraft Carrier

British aircraft carrier, *Formidable*, entering Sydney Harbour, October 1945

Charles Edward Barman, MM, MSM, Sydney, Remembrance Day, 11 November 1984

Internment

Shamshuipo Camp consisted of small brick huts and numbered about 50 in all. In peacetime, it was known as 'Hankow' Barracks,[60] which housed the 1st Battalion of the Middlesex Regiment. The barracks were separated by a wide tarmac road and at the end there was a large building which was used for general duties, church services, lecture hall and gymnasium. The survivors of the 1st Middlesex Regiment had occupied these barracks for three years or more. Those of the Middlesex Regiment remembered the spacious and airy rooms with each man's kit hanging smartly behind each bed. There was the dining room, where they queued for plentiful and well cooked meals, going around for a second time when the cook Sgt's back was turned. Now they all gazed upon the bleak empty shell, which was to be their home where all the fittings of each building had been removed by the Chinese residing in the district. They all looked at their new home with despair and saw themselves in a hell camp. The British WOs, S/Sgts and Sgts were mostly accommodated in 'Jubilee building' which had previously been used as married quarters prior to 1 June 1940.

Eventually, I met Lieut Col Penfold and other officers of the 1st Hong Kong Regiment HK/SRA, who were accommodated in the Jubilee building on the north side. He told me that S/Sgt Gollege, Sgt Eves and RQMS Lloyd[61] and others were in smaller rooms with about 8 or 9 men per room to the south side.

When they spotted me they all gave me a roaring welcome, as they were all under the impression that I was killed at Little Hong Kong on 24 December. The cigarettes and biscuits I had with me I shared with them and naturally they were very pleased to accept. Lloyd said to me, 'Charles, the food is bloody scanty, just rice, rice and more bloody rice.' The rice had a most uncomfortable reaction upon everyone and one becomes very bloated with this diet and tends to cause individuals to release enormous bursts of wind and to urinate excessively at all hours of the night. This of course disturbs the sleep and more so being so overcrowded in the one room. The concrete floors did not improve matters.

11 February 1942

Lieut Col Penfold sent for me this morning and told me that Major
General Maltby wanted to add any further information I may have to
the war diary, which was being prepared by him for handing into the
War Office, London, after the war. Major General Maltby wanted to know
what happened around the Peak district during the period of my entering
the War Memorial and Hospital on 25 December 1941 and our
subsequent removal to Bowen Road Hospital on 9 February 1942. Also,
information about our transfer across the harbour and the walk to
Shamshuipo on 10 February 1942. In addition, a war diary was also
being formulated by Brig T. McCleod, the officer commanding the Royal
Artillery Hong Kong, for submission to the artillery records after the
war. I commenced to inform them accordingly, stating the takeover of
the War Memorial Hospital by the Japanese, in the early hours of 26
December 1941 and of the transfer of all military personnel and others
to Bowen Road Hospital on 20 January 1942, including the removal of
all civilians to the Internee Camp at Stanley. The Indian troops were
sent to St Albert's Convent in Stubbs Road, Hong Kong. I then gave a
detailed account of our transfer across the harbour and the road to the
camp at Shamshuipo and of the very harsh treatment handed out to all
prisoners enroute.

To continue my report to Major General Maltby, I said that the
Japanese authorities insisted that, as there were a number of men
considered fit enough, they could be used as search and burial parties,
around the areas of Mt. Cameron, Mt. Nicholson and the Wong Nei
Chong Valley and also around the Peak district. The number of men
selected by the Japanese for this duty was somewhere about thirty to
thirty-five British, Canadians and members of the Hong Kong Volunteer
Defence Corps. I told Major General Maltby that on 8 January 1942, a
parade of prisoners were selected by a high-ranking Japanese Officer,
and that a senior Japanese NCO who was present carrying a sword that
appeared far larger than his dwarf-size body, with twenty sentries, hastily
and roughly grouped the men required for the job into line. The senior
NCO counted us all, not only once, but about four or five times. We
were then roughly pushed forward into groups like cattle, to embark on
the lorries waiting nearby. We were forced to stand in the lorries ringed
by sentries with their bayonets very close to each one of us. The first
battlefield area to be searched for the dead was around Mt. Cameron.
The men were offloaded from the two lorries and issued with picks and
shovels and immediately commenced digging graves. Those men on the

other lorries were detailed to search and collect the remains of bodies into old canvas sheeting and to remove them to the burial sites.

I had about ten men in my party during the search, which continued for at least a week, leaving the hospital grounds in the early morning and returning fairly late at night. We searched the battle areas where the battles were fought and where so many men of the Middlesex, Royal Scots, Canadians and Indian troops had been killed. The terrain was steep and rugged and due to our weak condition we found it difficult to keep moving. The bodies which were in a decayed and grotesque state were scattered everywhere and the sight of their bloated and blue appearance made one feel sick to the point of wanting to vomit. Open wounds were maggot-infested and bodies difficult to identify as they had been beheaded with samurai swords and their identity discs had disappeared with their heads. Other men we buried had died in various ways with bullet holes to the head and heart. Some must have also died slowly, having been shot by machine guns in the stomach and lower abdomen. Others who were roped together had died horribly from bayonet wounds.

Day after day, burial squads returned and went about this onerous task, sinking their picks and shovels into the hard soil and making crude crosses out of any wood we could find, finally placing steel helmets that were lying around on the graves. One group of men we found were of the Middlesex Regiment that we buried in a mass grave, surrounded by scrub and dying bushes that had been destroyed by shell fire. The days of this gruesome task went on and as none of us had a bible or prayer book for the burial of the dead, all we could say was 'IN YOU GO CHUM AND GOD BLESS'. After giving all the information that I could to Major General Maltby and Brig T. McLeod, I returned to my hut.

We were informed that the following would be carried out daily. Japanese roll call will be at 7.00 a.m. and 6.30 p.m. The Japanese officer in charge of all camps including the civilian internees' camp at Stanley was Col Tokunaga, known appropriately as the 'white pig'. He was fat and his complexion was much paler than the average Japanese. When he passed down the line of prisoners on the usual daily count, he snorted and belched his way around. We could smell him yards away because of his fondness for prawns and sake. His favourite pastime was to order a special parade of prisoners as separate from the daily count which lasted in the region of three to four hours in duration, often in the boiling sun with the result that men were falling down like ninepins within the ranks. We were not allowed to break ranks to assist them, and therefore they had to lay there until after the parade. The weakness amongst the men was also a great factor, plus a starvation diet that made matters worse. Dysentery and other tropical diseases were now becoming a problem and with the lack of medical advice and attention, matters will become worse.

We all knew that everyone understood 'King's Regulations' regarding escape from POW camps. While the attempt to escape was more practicable in Europe and North Africa than Hong Kong, escape from Hong Kong was something else. On the one side was the China Seas, warm, blue and hostile, and on the other side the vastness of China crawling with Japanese. Therefore, we knew that the chance of escape was slender; the Japanese knew this too, but were determined that everyone in the camps would sign a declaration that he would not escape. This signature was not binding in our eyes and it would not deter any attempts to escape, so therefore a good many signed under duress, but if the opportunity to escape did arise, we would take our chance of being caught and face the penalty of being executed without trial.

This edict caused an incident where twenty men of 'C' Company, Middlesex Regiment, which were all the men that were left of this Company after the surrender on Christmas Day 1941, refused to sign which enraged the Japanese officer. These men spent the whole day sitting tied up on the Barrack square and facing them not more than twenty yards away was a machine gun, manned by two Japanese who seemed longing to pull the firing lever. Every twenty minutes to half-hour intervals, when they were asked again, 'YOU SIGN NOW' the men all answered, 'NO'. After three to four hours, their hands were untied and the Japanese officer walked around the men with a tin of cigarettes. The men accepted the cigarettes in a cheerful manner, but their answer was still 'NO'. Their hands were tied again and even tighter. The Japanese officer said, 'YOU SIGN' and he said menacingly, 'OTHERWISE YOU ALL DIE.' '!!!! this for a lark,' said one soldier. 'What's the odds if we do sign, it does not mean a thing, because I am bloody sure I don't want to die.' CSM Soden[62] said, 'Shut your mouth.'

It was clear to the Japanese officer that his persuasions were doomed to failure. One private beckoned the Japanese officer over and said to him, 'Tell you what, mate, you can shove those cigarettes right up your arse,' with the result that he received a terrible smash to his head and face from the stick the officer was carrying. The soldier's reply was, 'You bastard,' whereby he received further bashings. A burst of fire went over the heads of the men of 'C' Company, and then the officer ordered, 'CEASE FIRE.' Once more he shouted, 'NOW YOU SIGN,' but the men shouted in harmony, 'NO, NO, NO WE WOULD RATHER DIE.' After six to seven hours of this treatment the Japanese gave up and untied the prisoners. Afterwards, the CSM told his men that it made little difference whether they signed or not, but that we had made our point.

16 February 1942

The discipline amongst the members of the Hong Kong Volunteer Defence Corps is very bad. This Corps consists of civilians recruited for defence and trained on similar lines as our Territorials in England. This unit consists of all nationalities including British, Portuguese, Chinese, and White Russians, etc., most of whom are either employed by the Hong Kong Government or hold large businesses or positions in the colony. When we are on parade or walking around the camp, we must resemble a race from the prehistoric age, having long hair, beards and wearing a mixture of clothing to make it worse.

There is no change in the food, just rice, rice and rice. The daily ration is approximately half a pound per person. The rice we do get is from time to time infested with maggots, weevils, grit and other such bodies. I cannot eat the full ration, so I leave the balance until later when I become ravenously hungry. Everyone has their eyes on the cookhouse for any rice that might be left over, but I always find that if there is any left it is distributed to those in need.

18 February 1942

Another weakness amongst some of the men was the bartering of clothes for cigarettes, these being mostly obtained through the Portuguese, Chinese and other members of the Hong Kong Volunteers who have wives and relations living outside the camp and send in parcels to them which come through the main gates. The Japanese guards thoroughly inspect the contents, before being issued to those to which they are intended. This privilege of parcels being allowed inside the camp is authorised by the Camp Commandant, Col Tokunaga. The parcels are allowed one per week which, of course, is naturally the envy of all those that are not so fortunate to receive any. It was ordered by Major General Maltby that the bartering of clothing, food, etc., for cigarettes would cease forthwith, but I am sure this order was ignored by a good many. I saw a pair of khaki shorts traded for five cigarettes and a towel for cigarettes. This practice of course was a surprise to me after all my years of service and therefore I could see the motto was 'every man for himself'. I never let this attitude gain control of me at any time, even though a smoke did ease the pangs of hunger. When a cigarette was available, we started a habit of sharing one between six of us, but we soon gave that away, because it was one way of transmitting diseases. We even used dried-out Chinese tea-leaves for cigarettes.

The rice is just as bad and issues appear to be getting less every day, although today we were issued with green vegetables of sorts which are very rare. Today, we had our first taste of whale meat and it was very delicious and it went down very well with the rice.

Working parties are still being detailed for various jobs outside the camp. One party is engaged at Kai Tak Aerodrome, in clearing rubble caused by the bombing. Another group is being put to work removing a huge rock weighing about five tonnes on Tai Po Road, whilst another working party was clearing a landslide; a huge rock was dislodged killing an NCO of the Middlesex Regiment and injuring three others. The dead NCO was immediately taken away for burial in the cemetery adjacent to the Central British School in Argyle Street. Burials are now becoming very common and are becoming daily. The Japanese guards in attendance at these funerals appear to be non-combat troops and seem to be quite easy to get along with and far better than those in the camp.

7 March 1942

We have been getting a certain amount of news into the camp, regarding world affairs and the progress of the war. No doubt some of the news may be authentic and yet some may be just rumours. It's possible that some of this news we get could be through a secretly hidden wireless set, built from parts smuggled into camp. This news, whether authentic or rumours, keeps the morale up amongst the men. The Japanese have become very suspicious in recent days and this morning the camp was paraded whilst the Japanese carried out a thorough inspection of the whole camp. The search was carried out by the Japanese Military Police who were looking for a wireless set that they thought could be secretly hidden. During the search, they confiscated many items such as binoculars, compasses and cameras, which had been smuggled into the camp by the prisoners after capture. Sgt Eves had his camera confiscated. This inspection lasted four hours and we were very thankful when we were dismissed, as I for one was so tired that I passed off to sleep immediately once my head hit the pillow. Most of us of course had no beds, just the bare concrete floor to sleep upon, and with so little covering to lay on, one could feel the dampness coming from underneath. After a time, I managed to put together a type of bed made from bits of wood and wire netting that I had collected whilst on a working party at Kai Tak Aerodrome. I made sure I gained permission from a Japanese NCO to take the material; otherwise, one could receive an awful bashing. It is now often a daily routine to search all clothes for lice as we are now becoming lousy with these little creatures.

9 March 1942

It is noted of late that the Japanese have become more aggressive towards us and are inflicting bashings by rifle butt and face slapping whenever possible upon the unfortunates who are unlucky to be in their vicinity. We did not hide our loathing and hatred of the Japanese after collecting slaps, punches and kicks that were increasing day by day. One can see that all the roads leading to and from the main street of Shamshuipo are empty, and patrols of Japanese troops can be seen searching the houses in the vicinity. Relatives and friends of the Hong Kong Volunteer Defence Corps and lady friends connected with some of the regulars can be seen on the other side of the road that runs parallel with the camp. None of them are allowed to approach the camp perimeter wire or to speak, and no signals of any description are allowed between them. I am attached to the survivors of the 12th Coast Regiment, Royal Artillery, of which Lieut Col Penfold is in command and he is also in charge of the remaining officers and NCOs of the 1st Hong Kong Regiment HK/SRA.

13 March 1942

During my usual walk around the camp this morning, I noticed the body of an Indian soldier floating in the water face downwards, who no doubt was killed during the attacks by the Japanese on Stonecutters Island. This island is only a very short distance from the camp, which is separated by a channel of water. The island appears to have been taken over by the Japanese Naval Authorities, and viewing from the camp one can see in the distance quite a lot of activity from the Japanese Navy Personnel. Incidentally, before the war, my family would often visit Stonecutters Island on a Sunday, particularly in the summer, which was a lovely place for swimming and playing on the beach. From the seaward side of the camp, we have seen quite a large number of Japanese warships arriving and leaving the harbour using the entrance from Green Island direction. Presumably this route is being used because the main entrance to the harbour, which is via the Lei Yu Mun Channel, was blocked by ships, and sunk by us during the attack upon Hong Kong Island. It will take some time for the Japanese to remove the craft sunk there.

Everyone feels the pangs of hunger due to the large gap between the early morning and evening meals. Rice is only satisfying for approximately half an hour and when cooked, becomes very bulky and is too much to accept in the early morning, so I save the remainder for the midday meal. I am suffering daily with awful indigestion, but one has to overcome this. There are always complaints, which is to be expected from hungry men, particularly from the younger ones. The current issue of rice from the Japanese is very dirty, and mixed in with quite a lot of it are the sweepings from the storage depot floors, which contains bits of glass and grit. It is not advisable to wash the rice because it removes the husks, which are most important to retain because they contain vitamin B, which helps to prevent the disease beriberi. Weevils and rice maggots are very common in the cooked rice but one has to eat it to survive or die.

Looking through the perimeter wire, we are witnessing terrible treatment to Chinese men, women and children by the Japanese troops who are attacking them with bamboo sticks and rifle butts. The agony and screaming from these poor unfortunates is very depressing, particularly as we are all helpless to prevent or intervene in these cruel atrocities taking place. Later that day, I saw the Japanese cruel treatment to a Chinese coolie. One of the sentries used the butt of his rifle on this poor devil's back and finally when they had him on the ground, screaming in terrible agony, they secured his hands behind his back and caused him to kneel with his back to the sun for six hours. I heard later during the day that they marched him on to Shamshuipo Pier where they shot him, his body falling into the harbour.

The build-up of Japanese aircraft appears to be on the increase and it gives one the impression that it is becoming the main base to supply their forces in their thrust southwards in the Pacific region towards Indonesia and Australia. The Japanese continue to use their planes for the releasing of propaganda leaflets over the colony, China and across other foreign borders. The leaflets report their victories in other areas in the Pacific. I have in my possession a few of these leaflets, which are printed in English, Chinese and other foreign languages which read as follows:

Leniency will be given to whoever surrenders, but those who resist the Imperial Japanese Forces, no mercy will be shown, etc., etc.

17 March 1942

Escapes from the camp were becoming very active, but the odds of getting away were very remote, and it was generally agreed that it would take strength and endurance to undergo the many miles trek to friendly territory in the mainland of China. Furthermore, our diet of rice these past three months would make it more difficult as no one was really fit enough to undertake such an attempt. There was a better chance of success for men to escape in groups rather than individually. Some individuals that escaped were either caught and executed, or had died in their attempt where they had disappeared completely without trace. I had planned to escape in early January, advising Lieut Col Penfold of my intentions; however, he later warned me to postpone my attempt as another one was to be made within the next few days. Later I heard that three officers and a Chinese made a successful escape to free China in early January. They were Lieut Col Ride (HKVDC), Lieut Morley and Sub Lieut Davies (HKRNVR) and L/Cpl Lee (HKVDC).[63]

For the last few days I was planning to make my attempt to escape, despite the odds, and this night was most suitable, being very dark and no moon. I slid down a monsoon drain, under the inner electrical wire and the outer perimeter barbed wire fencing, where I landed into a swamp of mud and slush, which had accumulated from the recent rains. I only just managed to clear under the inner electrified fence by about three inches.

With saturated legs and mud, I proceeded towards the area of Lai Chi Kok, where I turned right in the direction of the village of Shatin and the railway station, which was about ten miles from the camp and the village of Tai Po about the same distance further on. I rested up in thick bush close to Shatin as it was getting close to daylight and ate a small portion of my meagre rations, washed down with water from my water bottle. I chanced my luck and resumed my journey before it became dark and was making steady progress. However, I accidentally came upon a Chinese lady doing her toilet in the long grass. She, of course in fright, gave out a shriek that was heard by other Chinese who were working on the clearance of devastated buildings, which had been demolished by our troops during their retreat. The Chinese were being supervised in this work by a Japanese officer, one NCO who was armed with a large sword and approximately thirty troops. Very quickly I was recaptured, the officer immediately ordering me to be flogged. I was manhandled very roughly into an upright position and received several bashings with a large bamboo stick badly bruising my back, limbs and face, finishing up with a black eye which was bloody painful. I thought that I would be executed, but due to my courageous attempt to escape, the Japanese appeared to admire my effort and to my astonishment I was given a meal of rice and meat of sorts, which was very tasty indeed. The Japanese officer, who spoke fluent English with an Oxford accent, I think, saved me from being executed.

He and his men were not front-line troops and not so brutal-looking as the sentries within the camp. Finally, they took me back to the camp, where I was handed over to the guard commander of the camp. After the conversation that took place between the officer and the guard commander, surprisingly I was allowed to return to my hut without any further ill treatment, which I am sure the Japanese officer prevented. I reported to Lieut Col Penfold and other officers who congratulated me on my attempted escape and that I was very lucky not to be executed. Penfold told me that he and other officers had plans to escape at a later date and asked me if I would like to be included and naturally my reply was yes.

18 March 1942

As the extreme summer of Hong Kong approached, a new garment put in an appearance, which had never been listed in the clothing of a British soldier. It was not exactly a jock strap, a panty brief, a G-string, or a baby's napkin, but something like a combination of all four. The Japanese call it a 'fundoshi' and on the wearer, it looks as unattractive as its name. Its basic materials were a wide strip of cloth with strings at one end. The Japanese issued these fundoshis two per man. This item of clothing could be easily washed and thereby saved our scarce amount of clothing in our possession. The fundoshi was fitted by tying the strings in a bow acting as a belt, with the cloth at the back, the material then hauled between the legs and lapped onto the string, thus partially covering the posterior and genital organs.

Our footwear was a problem, as almost everyone's soles of the boot had parted from the uppers and laces had quickly rotted. Men in possession of gym shoes found that their toes were forced through the thin canvas and many men went barefoot, the soles of their feet gradually becoming hard and calloused like aged leather. Wooden clogs were being made out of old pieces of wood and worn by those whose feet were very tender, due to malnutrition. This primitive footwear was very hard to accept at first but we soon got used to keeping the clogs on our feet by a shuffling action.

Later this morning, three men in a depressed mood or sudden desperation attempted an escape but met with terrible retribution at the hands of the Japanese. They were recaptured and confined in a small dark cell for fourteen days. On the fifteenth day they were released and each issued with a spade, then in front of everyone, they dug their own graves, were shot and buried. Two others also made an attempt to escape but were never seen again; their bodies were never recovered and the Japanese interpreter, Nimori, when asked what had happened to them, he replied, 'They tried to escape, they will not try again.' Their identity disks were handed to a British officer.

These attempted escapes meant that all prisoners were counted and recounted often as many as twenty times a day when we were paraded in the main square and made to stand to attention for anything up to four hours at a time, often in blistering sunshine or pouring rain. These escapes and other incidents, which annoyed the Japanese, meant the deprivation of private parcels to the members of the Hong Kong Volunteers. In addition, there was a reduction in the rice ration, more beatings and kicks, and longer hours for working parties outside the camp. One can see, through the perimeter wire, large Japanese troop movements proceeding along the Castle Peak and Tai Po Highways. These movements may be the withdrawal of surplus combat troops to other theatres of war.

19 March 1942

The physical condition of the men is starting to show even though it is not quite three months since surrender. Due to our loss of weight we have aged considerably even the younger men, and facial features were becoming haggard with cheek bones prominent, eyes sunken and mouths losing their firmness. The loss of weight has caused our bodies to look frail, with shoulder bones, arms and ribs prominent, resembling us to look like skeletons with our skin appearing like weathered parchment.

Many of the men's mentality has changed and they are challenged by out-of-character behaviour, causing friendship to be strained. Punch-ups occurred for no apparent reason. The abnormalities amongst my men were drawn from all services such as the Army, Navy and Hong Kong Volunteers, the latter being of a mixed race consisting of British, Portuguese, Chinese and Indian, some of which were well-known businessmen, that their abnormal behaviour you would not see under normal conditions. I controlled these men with strict discipline in the most tactful manner, but I had to be very firm with my orders regarding the issue of meals and the duties in and outside the camp. In particular, it was necessary for the men to maintain cleanliness so as to avoid possible epidemics. I found that I had to be more severe towards the members of various nationalities who were not trained as combat troops and neither were they expected to serve under such unforeseen conditions.

20 March 1942

Time passes slowly; the days seem weeks, the weeks like months and the months like years. It is hard not to become discouraged and I spend a lot of time trying to keep up morale.

It is now bitterly cold and many of us are in working shorts. In the huts, I try to prevent the men from lying down even if they do get bashed about. Every day, one, two, three or more faint from sheer weakness and exposure. The rice has been about one half the usual rations for at least ten days, sometimes only a small teacup full. We just cannot exist this way for much longer. God, when will the end of all this be in sight? Men are wondering what the end will be like if and when it comes. Still, we can only live from day to day and never lose hope of heart.

Japanese discipline was harsh. On meeting a guard, prisoners had to snap to attention and bow; a slow or sloppy bow drew an immediate slap and punches. Every three weeks, a change of guards brought a fresh wave of beatings until the novelty wore off. Some prisoners had teeth knocked out.

21 March 1942

Another typical day in store:-
    Bright gleaming bayonets, screaming guards, men getting beaten up
        for no apparent reason.
    7.00 a.m. Roll call, standing for at least half an hour and all counted,
        then dismissed.

7.30 a.m. Breakfast of boiled rice and barley, green boiled leaves and sometimes vegetables of sorts.

8.00 a.m. Working parties out, medical staff to tend to the sick until midday.

12.30 p.m. Dinner as per breakfast.

1.30 p.m. Medical staff returned to hospital to attend the sick.

6.00 p.m. Dinner as per breakfast.

6.30 p.m. Roll call, standing for at least half an hour and all counted, then dismissed.

8.30 p.m. Lights out.

Sentries come through the huts all night and outside the floodlights are on. It is hard to get a sound sleep on the bamboo mats. The bashings are so severe that only by the grace of god have we escaped broken limbs so far.

The hospital is merely a hut, with no drugs, no equipment, not even a bedpan. A great number of men are always jammed into this tiny space and 150 or so report for sick parade every day. Some are losing sensation in their hands and feet, a symptom of beriberi, a nerve inflammation caused by vitamin deficiency. Some developed metatarsalgia, a bone ailment, marked by intense burning of the feet. A lot of men are suffering from what is called 'shotgun diarrhoea'.

This morning, sick parade was rather larger than average, but all cases were genuine. A Japanese appeared, absolutely white with rage, screaming at everyone, and lined them up and shouted at them in Japanese. Then he gave each man a good slapping with a long wooden roller. One man was picked out; he was suffering from acute gastritis and he struck him continually until he collapsed. The whole sick parade were then lined up in the midday sun without hats. One officer collapsed with a very high temperature.

The sick men's food allowance was cut by one-third and for those that could not work, the Japanese considered they did not deserve normal privileges. The other prisoners simply shared with the sick, on the sly. Everything was shared even the very little medicine, the food and even the ground where one was buried. There was no talk of women and no need to; the sex urge had gone long ago. As far as we were concerned the first thing was food, food, always food and the hope of survival. Some of the prisoners had jungle ulcers that could quickly turn gangrenous and these were seared with a hot poker, which was almost a painful for the doctor as for the patients, but scores of men were cured. A pneumonia patient had an accumulation of pus in the chest cavity.

The doctor made a small incision with a razor blade scalpel without anaesthetic and drained the pus with a catheter made from the rubber valve tube of an old bicycle tyre. The patient recovered, thank goodness. Once every two weeks on average, a burial party trudged to the hillside cemetery with a body in a blanket. The Japanese, in keeping with custom, issued gifts of fruit and rice biscuits to accompany the bodies of the men who died.

Later, the living prisoners swiftly shared the food. Burials had to be quick; sometimes the bodies were disintegrating in the heat. The graves were on stony ground and were constantly being washed open by rain. With each burial, the work party had the grizzly task of recovering older graves. To many, death was welcome.

Roughly half the men in camp were infested with round worms and often vomited them up or they passed through the bowels. A small room for the sickest of the men was set aside where thirteen men died there in one month. It became known as the death hut. Enormous round worms from the bowels were drawn out by a piece of string tied to the end of its body.

The GOC Major General Maltby has told us that bread and a canteen may be allowed soon, but he could not say when as the Japanese have given many promises which have yet to be fulfilled, anyway, it's a start and this will be a godsend and would be a welcomed relief from rice. The proposed site and the construction of the bakery is now well under way.

25 March 1942

This morning, 100 men and myself were detailed as a working party to clear rubble and debris from the main road near the railway station at Shatin and the highway leading to the fishing village of Tai Po. The working party were moved to the sites by lorry and well guarded all the way. It was during this period, whilst everybody was engaged in removing and clearing the highway, that two NCOs and I took the opportunity to reconnoitre the area for possible escape from Shamshuipo. Upon our return to camp that evening we discussed the possibility and decided to wait until the weather changed to a very overcast night.

The route to be taken was to follow as near as possible the railway line from Shatin station via Tai Po village and then onwards to Shing Mun River. The idea at the moment was only a preliminary discussion because we had to prepare sufficient food to carry to our final destination, that being over the border into Mainland China. From Shatin, I estimated it to be 70–80 miles where we would hope to make contact with the Chinese guerrillas. My compatriots in this venture were S/Sgt McGrady of the RAOC and WO2 Jock Henderson of the Middlesex Regiment.[64] If only I had been in the camp when Major Munro and others made their escape in late January. I wonder if they made good their escape.[65]

29 March 1942

The Japanese sentries now in control of the camp appear to be new and very young-looking. I would say none of them have had battle experience. Last night, some fool of an officer thought he would play a joke on a sentry patrolling the water at the edge of the camp and near the Jubilee building. This officer threw a comparatively large stone into the sea from the verandah of the building and the sentry on hearing the splash naturally thought that someone had dived from the block in an attempt to escape.

The result of this action was an immediate midnight roll call of all prisoners by the Japanese, which took more than two hours to complete on a very chilly and unpleasant night. After this incident, orders were issued by Major General Maltby that actions of this sort were to cease forthwith, otherwise the Japanese would impose restrictions upon the whole camp which could result in denial of the recent improvements and better relations with the Camp Commandant, Col Tokunaga.

3 April 1942

Today is Good Friday, and I attended Holy Communion at 11.00 a.m., the service being conducted by Capt Bennett,[66] the Presbyterian Minister who is the Chaplain of the 2nd Battalion Royal Scots Regiment. During the service, I thought of my dear wife and family and prayed that they were all safe and well.

We have been promised an issue of bread in a few days' time. It is understood that we can count on one slice of bread and half a pound of rice per day, served together with two meals of soup. The soup consisted of whatever vegetable that was available and recently we have been lucky as it has been Chinese radish or the green tops of sweet potato, but never the potatoes themselves. Now and again we get some dried fish, or animal bone, but what kind of animal we never know. We are all wondering how long the bread issue will last, as the stocks they are using must be from the remaining sacks of flour that was in store at the various RASC Depots throughout the island. We all rapidly discovered that the new Japanese sentries were well supplied with cigarettes and we also noted that they had a great weakness for watches, fountain pens, rings, cigarette lighters and jewellery in any shape or form.

The Japanese who have fear of epidemics and disease in general noted that the ordinary fly was increasing in plague formations and was causing them quite a lot of concern. The Japanese adopted a method of reducing their numbers, by offering anyone ten cigarettes for every hundred caught, which were to be handed over to the interpreter.

5 April 1942

Today is Easter Sunday. Everyone received a most pleasant surprise this morning, this being an issue of 1/2 lb. of bread per man, hopefully this being a regular handout in the future. The bread was rather doughy due to insufficient yeast, but we hope it will improve as time goes on. How nice it was to get your teeth into a piece of bread, which was quite a change from rice. This ration of bread will probably last for only a short time, as the flour will probably run out.

There have been quite a lot of activities to and from Japanese headquarters by the most hated of all Japanese interpreters in the camp, who is Lieut Hideo Wada (known as 'rat face') and the remaining interpreters Lieut Tanaka ('deadly nightshade') and ('bollock chops') whose name escapes me. With all these activities, we are wondering what they have on their minds.

It's not often that some delicacy, besides the usual rice, comes out of the cooking pot, but this incident which the men talked about for many months afterwards concerns the slaughter of twenty saddleback pigs and this episode goes as follows.

It was about four hours since our last meal and the next meal was a good seven hours away. Late this morning, a lorry entered the camp and naturally the men in close proximity eyed this vehicle with interest and even more so, when inside the back of the lorry, came the unmistakable squealing of pigs. The prisoners, all with empty stomachs, listened to this commotion with envious thoughts. Standing beside me was an RASC qualified Army butcher, who was known to us all as 'butch', who said, 'Listen, chaps, if I could get my hands on them, I will surely oblige you all and with great pleasure, prepare them for the cooking pot.' As he said this, the engine of the lorry suddenly stalled, causing it to come to an abrupt halt, and at the same time caused the tailboard to drop. Inside the back of the lorry was a solitary Jap soldier who was promptly upended by the stampede of about 25 to 30 pigs.

As the tailboard of the lorry faced the entrance gate to the camp, a few of the pigs fled towards the buildings outside, with the remainder scattering towards the huts within the camp. With wild shouts of joy from the prisoners, who took off in pursuit of the pigs which were scattering in all directions between the huts, tripped them up, tackled them rugby style, and grabbed them by their ears, tails, and hind trotters.

In about fifteen to twenty minutes there was not a living pig to be seen in the camp and within the hour, everyone was being served a nice portion of roast pork. The cooking oil that we had was put to full advantage. We saw the Japanese searching for the pigs outside the camp, where they thought they had escaped in the direction of the Chinese residential area. 'Butch', the executioner, carried out his job expertly and swiftly and had the pigs cut up and ready for the huge rice kongs with a capacity near on fifty gallons and was soon cooking the issue for the next two hours.

Dogs also were not safe in the camp. A large mongrel, which appeared to be a cross between a chow and a Labrador retriever, straying into the camp one morning and was slaughtered for the pot, skinned, boiled and was quickly eaten by the men, but they said that the taste was too sweet, nevertheless, it went down with the boiled rice. Some of those men that were told it was dog that they had eaten became violently sick at the thought. Not long ago a dachshund waddled swankily into the camp and met the same fate. Rats were pursued relentlessly, caught and killed by 'butch', but found to be rather tough. Cats that strayed into the camp suffered the same fate and when skinned, appeared to resemble a rabbit, but not so tasty. As the hunger became worse, anything edible was not safe.

Cases of beriberi had reached a peak and 50 of the most serious cases were admitted to the primitive hospital in the camp.

15 April 1942

The Japanese gave orders this morning that all prisoners would have their hair cut to close crop. I had already cut my hair and completely shaved off the remainder to be bald-headed. I have also removed all the hair from under the armpits and crutch, so as to avoid a possible outbreak of typhus where these type of germs breed.

As beriberi is on the increase, a daily dose of yeast is being issued to everyone in the camp, which is being produced by the Japanese. The first issue of yeast was at 3.00 p.m. and it is hoped it will improve the vitamin deficiencies that is widespread throughout the prisoners at this time.

16 April 1942

During the night, three officers and one OR escaped. The Japanese made an extensive search of the whole camp, during which two roll call parades were ordered, which lasted between three and four hours. All areas of the electrified wire fence and barbed wire fence were checked and thoroughly inspected during the time we were all on the parade ground. They endeavoured to locate the areas from which they escaped, looking for any damage, but without success. The escape was no doubt carefully planned by using one of the manholes that runs into the sea close by and enters somewhere near Lai Chi Kok from where they may have headed for the jungle and across the highway leading to Castle Peak, and then onwards to the Fanling and Tai Po Highway and swim along Shing Mun River and eventually reach Waichow which is situated on the Chinese mainland with a hope of contacting Chinese guerrillas who are expected to be in this area not occupied by Japanese troops. With contact from the Chinese, who have received orders to assist any escaped prisoners arriving from Hong Kong, I later found out that the escape party comprised of British Officers Clague, White and Pearce of the RA and Sgt Bosanquet of the HKVDC. Later, Lieut Pearce's brother and his batman L/Bdr Robinson,[67] who lived in the same building, were taken out of the camp for questioning by the Japanese. They were both under severe interrogation for quite a considerable time, but the Japanese could not get any information from them.

17 April 1942

As the escape of the officers was well planned, the Japanese were very concerned as to how they accomplished a breakout not detected by the sentries. We established that they must have used one of the existing manholes situated around the camp that allows the surplus water to run into the sea that surrounds the area. Japanese headquarters concluded that the manholes were the only way to escape and therefore have ordered that they are to be completely filled in. Due to this escape, Col Tokunaga, universally known as 'The White Pig', has ordered reprisals to be imposed upon the whole camp; this most likely will be a reduction in rations for a period, plus the restrictions and loss of freedom of walking around the camp. It is likely that the sentries will also be strengthened. We all hope that the officers will be able to make good their escape and be able to give the outside world the information about the conditions to which we are being subjected.

18 April 1942

The Japanese have done their utmost to undermine the morale of the prisoners, but realised they had opposition from the officers within the camp and therefore decided to transfer all the officers to another camp, that being at Argyle Street, with the exception of one senior officer and a small number of junior officers to control those prisoners being left in Shamshuipo Camp. The senior officer appointed by the Japanese was a disaster and he eventually became known 'Major Disaster' and sometimes referred to as 'Major Ballsup'.

The camp in Argyle Street was made up of huts that had been used to house Chinese refugees, who fled over the border from mainland China during the Japanese occupation in 1937. The Japanese allowed 113 other ranks plus myself to act as batman to the officers, plus other duties within the camp. Lieut Colonel Penfold whom I served with for years sent for me and pointed out that I had been asked by the artillery officers to join them in this move and that I would be required to take charge of all the other ranks. At the time I was not very keen, but after consulting S/Sgt Gollege and other senior NCOs, they encouraged me to accept this position, therefore I did accept. At this time, RQMS Tom Lloyd of 12th Coast Regiment RA[68] had been appointed to take charge of the main cookhouse in Shamshuipo and was hoping for me to assist him, but I explained my position advising him that it was essential that the other ranks that were to be transferred to Argyle Street required supervision. Major General Maltby GOC Hong Kong Command held a conference with all officers informing them that the Japanese authorities had decided to transfer most of the officers to another camp and that one batman for every five officers would be allowed to be taken. These batmen would be used for general cleaning of the whole camp and other duties as required. A senior NCO would be allowed to take charge of the men and this duty will be my responsibility. I realised in accepting this position that I would have the great responsibility in controlling these men under abnormal conditions, where I would have to use a great amount of tact and firm discipline where it may be required.

The following was written by one of the officers in the camp:

The British and Indian forces made their stand
On the Island of Hong Kong, a foreign land
Waiting for help that did not come
Doing all that could be done
While in retreat across Hong Kong Harbour in a valiant fight

Craft of all types with beleaguered troops and guns carrying her crew to a watery grave
An honoured crypt for the lives they gave

These men first met as prisoners of war
Not knowing what fate they would have in store
Beaten and starved, tortured and ill
Months became years as our world stood still

Hell ships and jungles, 'Railway of Death'
Forced to work till our dying breath
The cemeteries filled, as the days wore on
Still faith remained when strength was gone
Ten thousand British, Indian and volunteers
Died waiting for ships, planes and tanks for years
Now they lie in peace 'neath eastern soil
Free from starvation, disease and toil

Though their bodies remain, their sole departs
Their names cherished forever in our hearts
On gods great earth you'll never find
Better men than those we left behind

WRITTEN IN THEIR HONOUR

The Japanese soldier had the tendency to take pleasure in cruelty, with some appearing to be mentally unstable. They are very callous and do not share with Christians, Moslems, or Jews, etc., the feeling of preciousness of individual life. Their own military discipline is harsh and brutal, based on the casual beatings they inflict for trivial infringements of regulations. Naturally, they treat prisoners of war in the same way. I received the butt of a rifle on my toes for not saluting and bowing. For routine beatings Corporals and below used their rifle butts, which was more painful than the flat side of a sword scabbard used by Sergeants and Officers. Torture was a different matter and this was inflicted deliberately by the 'Kampei', the Japanese Military Police, to further whatever investigation that they happened to be pursuing, such as:

Who are the prisoners in touch with the Chinese Communists?
Where was the camp radio hidden?
What is radar?

The procedure was simple and effective. The Lieutenant or Sergeant carrying out the enquiry would ask the prisoners questions. If not satisfied with the answers, or replies, two privates would hold the prisoners head under water until he lost consciousness and then revived and continue to repeat this treatment until they were satisfied with the answers. The Kampei realised that the prisoners were in a poor state of health and would not survive too many drownings in a day and normally they limited themselves to five or six. Up to the present, I have yet to suffer any torture to that degree, only physical abuse such as I received in my attempted escape.

The Japanese front-line troops including Koreans and Formosans have become more brutal to everyone, not only to prisoners of war, but to the Chinese as well, including other nationalities residing in Hong Kong or Kowloon. This ill treatment to the Chinese was a regular daily occurrence, carried out by the sentries if any of the Chinese were unlucky to fall into their hands. Only yesterday, a Japanese on duty in the pill box indicated by touching the machine gun at his side to all those standing near the perimeter wire, to move away to deny us viewing the inhuman treatment. The Japanese soldiers had a natural instinct to be cruel towards the enemy and became more aggressive with the further training they received from German army instructors that had been attached to them for quite a number of years prior to 1939.

19 April 1942

After the Japanese count of prisoners this morning, the interpreter, Namori Genichiro, known in the camp as 'Panama Pete', informed Brig Peffers to form a party of men of about 200–250, to parade for work outside the camp. Within the hour, this group was formed and marched out of the main gate, where they were taken over by a Japanese guard consisting of about 50 men fully armed with machine guns. We were all ordered to board a convoy of lorries, which eventually moved off arriving at Kai Tak Aerodrome about ten miles away. We noticed that the Japanese guard did not appear as brutal as those within the camp and looked like a batch of third-line troops, who at a glance were fairly young and some of them were quite pleasant. We were given axes, picks and shovels, including bamboo poles of about eight feet in length and three to four inches in diameter for carrying small baskets attached to each end for removing earth or rubbish from one site to another. By making stoppers to the end of the bamboo poles, one could fill them up with rice. By this method, we were able to smuggle enough rice and other food items to feed about six men. At times I smuggled in my pole small fish known as 'white bait', that I had managed to remove from the Japanese supply lorries.

We received instructions from a Japanese officer through an interpreter; the officer appeared to be some sort of an engineer. The job was to complete a drainage system at the airport that had been commenced by our Royal Engineers before the war. The drainage and expansion was necessary to receive more Japanese aircraft into Hong Kong, which was increasing daily. The officers and senior NCOs were hardy individuals similar to those we have in the camp. The sentries, who were more pleasant, spoke very good English and I would say they were recruited from Japanese colleges and universities for duties behind the lines. As the day wore on, they became friendlier and when the officers and senior NCOs were not watching, they offered us cigarettes from time to time. It was to our advantage, to try and get out of these working parties, so anyone with concealed valuables, such as watches, rings, etc., would barter for items of food and drugs from the Japanese sentries and Chinese overseers on the project. I had a couple of dollars on me and an old watch, for which I received three small packets of soybeans and some sugar to spread over the rice.

22 April 1942

What a surprise for us all today, as everyone in the camp received a nice piece of stewed meat, which went down well with the rice. For the last two to three days, the Japanese have been supplying a small amount of green vegetables, this being turnip tops and a few onions. Today, we also received a meal of soybeans and Chinese dates. This is a wonderful surprise, but how long will it last. The dates are apparently grown in north China and are lovely in taste and very sweet when boiled. I wonder how long the Japanese will keep up this change in our diet. Perhaps they realise that the health of the prisoners have deteriorated to a very low ebb. Starvation is the main problem facing us and at the moment we have less than a third of the required amount of food.

A group of us known as the 'thieves of Shamshuipo' stole supplies from the Japanese ration stores after dark, carrying away foodstuff which was shared around to supplement the daily diet. We suffered the risk of fearful beatings and possible executions if caught. Today, I stole a small octopus that I took from a Japanese supply lorry, which I hid in the crutch of the fundoshi and managed to escape the attention of the sentries but one sentry did notice one of the octopus tentacles protruding down the side of my leg, and he smiled, I assumed he must have thought me deformed. We raided the Japanese supply lorries in the most efficient manner that would make a first-class robber sit up. To improve our miserable diet of soggy rice, commodities such as cooking fat, peanut oil, sugar and any fish that may be seen would be quickly removed.

24 April 1942

The Japanese Tenko (meaning 'Roll Call') sometimes varied; as of late it was at 9.00 a.m. and 7.30 p.m. daily and this took them nearly an hour to complete the count of the prisoners in the camp, where the long standing caused quite a number of men to faint and fall flat upon their faces, mostly due to weakness and malnutrition conditions, plus those that were suffering from diseases. I began to feel very shaky on my legs having to stand for such long periods. The Japanese insisted that all sick would attend the count daily and we had men on parade with temperatures of 104 degrees or worse and at times we had to carry them onto the parade ground.

25 April 1942

An inspection of the camp and all prisoners was carried out today by the Japanese Governor of Hong Kong. He marched on to the parade ground with a full complement of about twenty officers and a bodyguard of about forty men fully armed with machine guns. We were all kept standing on the parade ground for well over two hours, during which men could be seen falling flat on their faces and no one was allowed to help them until after the inspection.

We noticed that the Japanese have a real fear of epidemics, as most of them can be seen walking around heavily masked. The Japanese are still making the offer of ten cigarettes for every hundred flies caught. The standard Japanese brand of cigarette was 'Kooas' and their taste was similar to Camel and Embassy cigarettes. Nimori Genichiro, civilian interpreter and right-hand man of Col Tokunaga, the 'white pig', wielded as much power. Nimori had been educated at Cornell College, Mount Vernon, Iowa, USA and had spent 21 years in that country. His English was almost perfect with an American accent and expressions that included such sayings as 'Come on baby, etc.'. At the first sight of him, he appeared to be full of fun and was universally known to us as 'Panama Pete'. But Nimori's idea of fun was the infliction of physical pain onto any unfortunate individual who displeased him. He would slash the air or a prisoner with his stick, which he always carried, and he always had on hand three Japanese sergeants named 'Shagnasty', 'Bollock Chops', and 'Strawberry Balls'. The Geneva Convention did not mean a thing to the Japanese regarding the treatment of prisoners of war. Article 2 of the convention states: 'Prisoners of war are at all times to be humanely treated particularly against acts of violence, insults and reprisals.' Article 10 states: 'Adequate clothing and housing is to be provided with quarters similar to those provided for depot troops.' A Japanese answer to this was the misery of Shamshuipo and North Point Camps.

As for Article 11, which covers food, I need say no more.

The medical officers in the camp cannot do much for the sick because of the lack of drugs, which are not expected to be supplied by the Japanese. All they can do is to give advice. Major General Maltby has approached the Japanese on the question of medical supplies, also an improvement in the diet and an increase in the rice ration per man. At the moment the rice ration is half a pound per man per day, but it should be at least one pound plus the importance of the supply of green vegetables.

A few days later, the Japanese introduced meagre supplies into the camp such as iodine, aspirin, chloroform, magnesium, sulphate and carbonate of soda, the latter being the old-fashioned boon for the overeater. There were never enough of these supplies, but the iodine helped in many of the septic conditions and could be dabbed on any form of open wound or any such skin diseases. For the dysentery patients, the doctors could do little or nothing. One room, set aside for a latrine, was always full to capacity. This ramshackled hut had been allocated as a hospital, where two medical officers are doing their level best to treat the worst cases of dysentery. Under the most trying conditions and the

presence of Dr Saito makes the problems even worse and he will have a
lot to answer for when the war is over. I had a very bad infected finger
that had turned septic and to remove the pus, Capt Warrack[69] RAMC
had to remove the pus by incision of a razor blade. This was damn
painful and more so when I soaked it in salt water, which was worse
than the razor blade. The diseases were rampant and if not treated, death
was the ultimate end. Out of 12,000 men in all camps, all are suffering
from some form of diet deficiencies and the death rate will continue to
rise until we all finally fade out in a couple of years.

28 April 1942

This morning, all officers and other ranks were inspected and searched
thoroughly before leaving Shamshuipo.

The new camp selected by the Japanese authorities was in Argyle
Street, Kowloon, and was to be known as 'Officers Camp N'. This site
was approximately six miles from Shamshuipo, which was quite a fair
walk. The move of the officers and other ranks was to be done in two
batches; the first move would be about 11.30 a.m. and the second about
4.00 p.m. Each group would travel to the new camp via Prince Edward
Road, moving in the direction of Kowloon City and Kai Tak airport.
During the second batch at 4.00 p.m., some of the men were collapsing
due to their weak condition and were assisted whenever possible provided
that the Japanese sentries allowed us to do so. My party consisted of
men from Royal Scots, Middlesex and Hong Kong Volunteer Regiments,
who were moved to the rear of the column by the Japanese guards, for
what reason I was not sure. I noticed a number of men pilfering the kits
belonging to those officers in the first batch, when being halted at
intervals along the road. I was unable to prevent this from happening
because the sentries would not allow me to interfere. These men were
endeavouring to locate cigarettes and tinned food that they knew the
officers had collected. As these men were selected by the officers whose
baggage they were carrying, I simply had to turn a blind eye.

I have to mention that the Japanese had persuaded a certain number
of Indian troops to turn over to them and this was noticed during our
march from Shamshuipo, where we observed quite a number of them
being employed in the reinforcement of the barbed wire fence around
the camp. I also noticed that Indian Officers and senior NCOs were
equipped with Japanese swords. Their numbers totalled about one-third
of the 1st Regiment HK/SRA, some of these men were from my own

battery. The guards spread along the column were a mixture of Japanese and Indian troops, some of whom I recognised who just simply ignored me, probably for their own safety, where they had no option. During the occasional halts along Prince Edward Road, the Indian sentries appeared to be well stocked with cigarettes but no offer of a cigarette was made to us by any of them. I even spotted my own Battery Clerk L/ Naik Ilan Din who was only about four yards from me and whom I thought may have slipped a packet to me, but he simply ignored my presence. I don't think we should blame the majority of the Indian troops that have turned over to the Japanese, as they probably would have been forced into the situation to serve under them, or be tortured, followed by complete ill treatment and starvation. It has been reported that the Indian troops refusing to serve under the Japanese have received terrible torturing, and quite a number have died due to this ill treatment, and therefore we cannot judge them too harshly nor condemn them for their actions. It is known of course that the Japanese are trying to encourage the Indian Government to press for independence from Britain. For some time there has been friction between Gandhi and the British Government on the question of independence.

It was not an ideal day for the move as it was extremely cold and wet and it was not a pleasant thought to look forward to sleeping on concrete floors. It was not so bad for the officers because there were beds of sorts in the huts they were to occupy, which were presumably left by the Chinese refugees who occupied this camp from 1937 to 1939. The other ranks had bare concrete floors. The 93 Army and Navy batmen plus nineteen NCOs and myself have been accommodated in two huts, which mean about 56 men to each hut, where we shall be packed in like sardines. As the senior NCO, I have taken charge of the batmen and in the morning I will arrange for their duties such as cleaning around the camp and providing staff for cooking, etc. I dismissed the cooks immediately to arrange for our first meal of the evening, and the cooking arrangements and staff will be taken over by Sgt Bullimore, originally employed by the Naval dockyards. The food stores will be under the charge of Lieut Pontin[70] of the RASC, who will be in direct contact with the Japanese Supply Dept for the issues of supplies to the camp.

29 April 1942

Due to insufficient blankets, I had to put on my heavy overcoat to sleep in due to the cold and damp concrete floor and it took me ages before I could get to sleep. When I awoke in the morning, all my body was terribly stiff. The Hong Kong winters can be damn cold, especially when the winds sweep across the New Territories. On the whole, the morale of the British prisoners was good in the circumstances, having developed an inner toughness and discipline under adversity.

The following batmen were detailed for employment in the cookhouse:

Sgt Bullimore	Dockyard Defence Corps	(OIC)
Sgt Simpson	Dockyard Defence Corps	
L/Cpl Bushell	Corps of Military Police	
AB Felsted	Royal Navy	
L/Bdr Birkinshaw	12th Coast Regiment RA	
Gnr Cumming	12th Coast Regiment RA	
Mne Kenworthy	Royal Marines	
Spr James	Royal Engineers	
Spr Price	Royal Engineers	
Pte Jones	1st Middlesex Regiment	
Pte Bradley	1st Middlesex Regiment	
Pte Prince	1st Middlesex Regiment	
Pte Hastings	RASC	
Pte Prata	HKVDC	
Pte Lam	HKVDC	
Pte Kaluzhany	HKVDC	

Maj Hedgecow[71] of the 1st Bat. Middlesex Regiment was detailed as messing officer for the camp and in charge of the cookhouse and the above staff. This officer, in my opinion, is the right man in the right place for a situation like this.

Sleeping on these concrete floors is not going to improve our health very much, and the GOC Major General Maltby has already approached the Japanese for the provision of beds, but whether we shall get them remains to be seen.

The food is simply awful and we are getting rice only, plus a very small quantity of vegetables. We cannot expect too much of anything and no doubt the poor food is part of the punishment imposed upon us for the recent escape of prisoners.

Col Tokunaga is a real bastard and his life will not be worth a cent if ever he is caught after the war. It is now understood that he is going to put us all on a forced parole, which will bind us by oath that we will not try to escape from this camp and if the oath is broken by any person, collective punishment will be imposed. I fancy that Tokunaga must have

received very severe orders on this from Tokyo over the escape of so
many prisoners from Shamshuipo during the past months of December,
January and March. The escapes have caused him to take firm measures
in preventing any further breakouts.

Starvation is our main problem and as time goes on we are deprived
of further rations, which have been imposed upon us as punishment, or
because of corruption, or inefficiency of the Japanese supply services.

30 April 1942

Major General Maltby has organised the administrative staff within the
camp as follows:

Major General Maltby	OIC of Officers Camp
Brig Peffers	OIC of Administration
Brig McCleod	OIC of Sports
Brig Clifford	OIC of Entertainment
Maj Hedgecow	OIC of Messing and Cookhouse
Maj Moody	OIC of Camp Officers and Orders
Maj Marsh	OIC of Gardening
Cmdr Warner	OIC of Hot Water Boilers
Capt Davies	OIC of Sanitation
Capt Warrack (RAMC)	OIC of Medical Room
Lieut Almada	OIC of Camp Library

L/Cpl Earnshaw,[72] who was suffering from dysentery, was admitted
to the Indian hospital outside the camp this morning. Dysentery has
been raging in both Shamshuipo and Argyle Street prisoner-of-war camps
for quite some considerable time now, and the only treatment that can
be given for this is the continual purging of salts. Recently, one of the
officers here had a very bad attack of piles (haemorrhoids). To ease the
pain, all the medical officer could do was to make an incision with a
razor blade. There are quite a number of officers and men suffering
septic wounds and sores, which will not heal. Skin problems are very
bad indeed and some have got terrible leg ulcers that will not heal unless
their diet improves.

Everyone is now on the scrounge for spare bits of wood and nails in
an attempt to make beds, small tables and stools, etc. Most of the huts
have long planks of timber fitted in the roof and extend the full length.
We have decided to remove some of the planking and cut it up into bed
lengths and issue it to the men for the making of beds. Out of some of

the wood leftover, I was able to make myself a pair of clogs, which I needed because my boots are beginning to become beyond repair.

1 May 1942

A good many of us are beginning to feel the strains of diet and the cases of malnutrition plus the other diseases are increasing. We have managed to obtain from an outside source 'thiamine' which contains vitamin B for the treatment of deficiency diseases and is given by injection.

The batmen have a beastly job in batting for the officers and those that were selected by the officers, I feel wished that they had not. They wash clothes, utensils, collect meals when necessary, make beds, etc., and have to accept the moods of those they bat for and sometimes the officers can be bloody nasty. Anyway, that is camp life and no one can do anything about it. The situation gets on everybody's nerves at times, particularly having to live so close to each other and is so depressing when everyone is suffering in some way or form.

No supply of rice or any such rations have been supplied to the camp today by the Japanese and I am beginning to wonder when our next meal will be, but late in the afternoon the supply lorry arrived with a few bags of rice, but no green vegetables, which everyone needs so badly.

Due to the excessive wax in my ears, I am completely deaf and arrangements are being made for them to be syringed. How? I don't know because as far as I am aware, there are no syringes in the camp, so I will just have to wait and see. Through this temporary deafness, I can see the men calling me everything under the sun, and no doubt they will continue to do so without my knowledge.

2 May 1942

No letters at all for me and I am so concerned for my dear wife and family. The Japanese are holding a certain amount of mail and, due to their bloody mindedness, will not deliver it to the camp. There may not be any for me, but I am hoping that some letters will be delivered to the camp shortly. I have not received one letter since my captivity. Major General Maltby has repeatedly requested that all letters should be delivered to the camp, but his requests have been a continual waste of time. I am so impatient hearing that there is mail lying around in Japanese headquarters.

3 May 1942

Bridge, crib, and chess tournaments are being organised in the camp and are expected to commence in a few days' time. I am not interested in chess, but I will probably get a partner for the bridge games, not that I am a very good player, but will get better with a little practice.

Our headquarters in the camp have been the centre of trouble amongst the men, as somehow or other they have been able to obtain cigarettes. Maj Kerr,[73] who can speak Japanese, had obtained these cigarettes from sentries. I know that Maj Kerr has given orders that all empty cigarette packets must be burnt to prevent the Col Commandant from knowing that they are arriving in the camp in an unofficial way.

We have had terrible weather for the last week or so and there has been exceptional heavy rain. The majority of the batmen do their daily jobs half naked in the rain, as the humidity had been very uncomfortable.[74]

4 May 1942

Capt Belton[75] of the York and Lancaster Regiment was detailed by Brigade headquarters of the camp (Brig Peffers), to take over the duties of Hut officer of batman for Hut No. 2 and Cmdr Selby of the Royal Navy was ordered to take over Hut No. 5 of the Naval Batmen. Capt Belton and myself allocated the Army batmen to their respective huts and as near as possible to the officers for whom they were batting. Over and above their batting duties, they are responsible within the camp for the following duties:

1. Removal and stacking of wood on arrival by Japanese lorry, which is delivered once per fortnight working in conjunction with the batmen in Hut 5.
2. Flushing of the three main drains daily alternating with the batmen in Hut 5.
3. Camp working parties for inside and outside the camp as required by the Japanese authorities.
4. Sullage fatigues to be done by the Naval batmen.
5. Sanitary fatigues to be done by the Army batmen.

Duty rosters for the above that affect my hut have been drawn up.

The following batmen were detailed to report to Capt R. Davis in charge of sanitation duties:

L/Bdr Roche	12th Coast Reg
L/Bdr Holland	8th Coast Reg
Gnr Brain	8th Coast Reg
Pte Sprague	HKVDC
Pte McDougall	Royal Scots Reg

Food is conveyed and carried in all types of improvised containers from the cookhouse to the various messes in each hut, this being the duty of the batmen and supervised by the messing officer detailed for each hut. In the case of my hut, I have taken on the duty myself. The feeding times are mornings and evenings and at times the issue of certain green vegetables are made during the day. Measures for the issue of rice and vegetables are distributed in old tins with any leftovers being equally given to each man as fair as possible. There is quite a lot of bickering going on in other huts over the food issues, although the men in my hut are satisfied with the arrangements and also I will not allow any complaints because that is all we get so no one can say very much, and in any case I have arranged with Sgt Bullimore, in charge of the cookhouse, that if there is anything left after the share, it would be given to me for distribution. We even get burnt rice that invariably is stuck to the 'Kongs', this receptacle being used to cook the rice. This burnt rice is distributed fairly around to everyone in the hut. Quite a number of electrical cooking appliances have been improvised for the purpose of cooking pilfered food. The additional power required may cause a breakdown in power throughout the camp. This use of power is taken off the electric light supply and therefore a breakdown is possible. Everyone has been warned to be lenient in this method of cooking as any breakdown in power may cause the Japanese authorities to take some form of reprisals. How interesting, the officers in Hut No. 7 cannot agree to the division of the sugar ration that the Japanese issued to the camp and they have now decided to allow the batmen to allocate a fair issue amongst the various huts used by the officers.

6 May 1942

Pte Pedersen, a Dane by birth and a member of the HKVDC, gave a very interesting lecture on China today to the batmen of No. 2 and No. 5 Huts. He has resided in China for the last 35 years and was present at the 'Shamian Incident' of 1927, 'Shamian' being the foreign residential island off Canton.

It is rumoured that the Russians have invaded Norway in collaboration with Britain?

During the afternoon we received the first consignment of double-tier beds, which were collected by a party of 80 of our men from the old Chinese refugee camp. Debugging was carried out immediately on these beds and believe me, we found hundreds of them. At the time we were on the job of collecting the beds, I managed to scrounge a cigarette from a Japanese interpreter who was not a bad chap. We called him 'Cardiff Joe' because of the number of years he spent in Wales where he held interests in a large firm. Cardiff Joe appeared to be sorry that we were at war with Japan and he knew full well that Japan will be the losers in the long run. He was in Japan at the outbreak of war and naturally was called up to serve his country, but his thoughts were of his family who were in Cardiff.[76]

Cardiff Joe has approached the Japanese Commandant in a very tactful manner to allow the prisoners to write letters and he pursued any mail stored in headquarters to be delivered to the camps.

9 May 1942

The diet and climate is now beginning to affect a good many of the men. I do not feel at all well myself, and with all the batting supervision and other jobs that I do, I continually keep on having spasms of weakness which depress me and I find them extremely hard to overcome. It is only the thoughts of my dear wife and family that keep me going and I hope for our release from this awful existence. I believe that prisoners of the Pacific War are far worse off than any other prisoners in the world as not only do they have the oriental mind to contend with but the diseases that are associated with the tropics. That is the luck of the draw and nothing can be done about it. My main concern at this point of time is that the comradeship in the camp is lacking amongst practically everyone and it takes most of my time to sustain morale. One other thing that I must mention is the number of persons receiving weekly parcels from outside the camp which does cause discontent, more so as we do not get the regular Red Cross parcels that prisoners of war in Europe receive. It would be nice if some system could be adopted and we could pool our resources and obtain parcels from the outside, the contents of which could be issued by the messing officer. However, we cannot assess the situation from those people providing the parcels from the outside, which most likely could be in extremely dangerous circumstances.

14 May 1942

Today is my 41st birthday, this being my first since being a prisoner of war. I am sure my dear wife and children are all thinking of me on this day and also my people at home and in India. I wonder if they have received any news of my whereabouts or the card that I sent them from the War Memorial Hospital. I wonder if I will be here on my next birthday.

We received out first issue of bread from Shamshuipo Camp today, with the result that the Japanese have reduced our rice ration by 50%.

We are having terrible weather and the rain has been exceptionally heavy, and the batmen have been struggling to maintain their duties.

20 May 1942

We have heard that there is some sort of communications going on between the Chinese communists operating along the border, these communications being built up by the prisoners who have managed to escape in the early days of being confined at Shamshuipo. It is understood that these bases have been established along the border and Waichow being the most likely site for this purpose. I must mention that on the order from headquarters to surrender on 25 December, it was decided between Maj Munro and myself that we would attempt to escape within a short period of time after being captured, but due to me being in hospital at the War Memorial and subsequently moved to Bowen Military Hospital late in January 1942, I did not arrive at Shamshuipo Camp until 4 February. Maj Munro took the opportunity to escape with two others on 1 February 1942; this of course upset my plan to join them. I am sure he made good his escape with his two comrades and no doubt by now is suggesting plans with the communists for a massed escape of all prisoners in Kowloon.

26 May 1942

The following news has infiltrated into the camp, presumably hidden in parcels approved for entry by the Japanese to those of the HKVDC who are very fortunate to receive them. The news being received is that the death rate amongst the Chinese living in Hong Kong is steadily rising due to starvation. It says that thousands are dying, but although this may be an exaggeration, this nevertheless is close to the truth. Apparently from the informers' personal observations, great numbers of unburied bodies are lying around the districts; the worst feature is cannibalism where human flesh is sold at $5 a plate. Apparently parents leave their children at certain recognised points, where they are seized and butchered by human flesh vendors.

1 June 1942

We received an issue of cucumbers today with a result that many of the men are suffering from acute indigestion. The supply of Chinese dates are gradually dwindling, perhaps they are going out of season. A number of eggplants have arrived as a substitute for the dates and these will be served tomorrow with rice.

Fourteen officers arrived from Bowen Road Hospital today and in this number was Professor R. K. M. Simpson[77] of my battery who was wounded at the Mount Kellett OP during the early stages of the attack upon Hong Kong Island.

5 June 1942

Concerts are getting under way which Cmdr Grenham[78] of the Royal Navy and Lieut Suttcliffe of the RAOC are producing. Pte Prince of the Middlesex Regiment who is an accomplished accordionist will play during the concerts.

I have met a very cheerful lad, Pte Francomb of the Middlesex Regiment, and he has a real cockney personality. I think he comes from Bermondsey in the south of London. He has been given the nickname of 'chunky' which he is called by everyone in the camp. He originally came from Dagenham in Essex and with his cockney accent he is very amusing to listen to and causes laughter for everyone. He has been up to all manner of tricks to obtain cigarettes, one source being from the Japanese sentries near the latrines where he is able to obtain them with gently persuasion through the lavatory windows. It is also very amusing to watch Pte Sprague[79] hunting the parade ground and other places for cigarette ends for his pipe and he finds quite a number of them near the Japanese guardroom during his sanitation duties of that area. There is still a scarcity of cigarettes in the camp, which there always has been, but some officers had quite a few which arrived in the weekly parcels.

10 June 1942

Major General Maltby was approached today by the Japanese regarding the question of individual signatures from the men in exchange for certain privileges. The Major General, W/Cmdr Bennett,[80] and the Commodore of the Royal Navy were taken to Japanese headquarters for the purpose of reference to a parole system. Major General Maltby and the other officers returned from the conference and advised everybody to sign and once this is completed, the Japanese have promised that we will be allowed to write letters. It appears that the Japanese Camp Commandant must have received direct orders from Tokyo to the effect that this parole must be signed by all prisoners forthwith. The parole is still being discussed but none of us as yet have signed. I believe there is a certain amount of snags in such a declaration and the decision by all of us to ponder this situation is holding up a final outcome. The Japanese apparently signed some kind of parole during the Russia/Japanese war of 1904, in which the Japanese prisoners were allowed freedom and gave their word that they would not take up arms. I cannot see the Japanese giving us that privilege even if we all sign the document, and in any case, it is the duty of every prisoner to attempt escape if he has the opportunity. We shall probably hear more about this matter in the near future.

16 June 1942

The first supply of peanut oil was issued in the camp today and a certain amount of meat, sugar and vegetables also arrived. It is unusual to see so many commodities of food arriving at once. However, soap is getting very scarce and everyone has to wash the best way he can.

During the afternoon, the whole camp was summoned on parade. The Japanese Camp Commandant gave orders to the effect that 'we having surrendered unconditionally in December 1941 were now prisoners of war and subject to the orders of Japanese Military Authorities'. He gave this order to us in Japanese with a Japanese interpreter repeating the order in English. He then gave us an order in Japanese to sign the declaration to the effect that we would not attempt to escape whilst we were prisoners. The Navy Personnel completed the signing of the declaration by that evening with the Army commencing at 9.00 a.m. the following morning.

22 June 1942

The Army carried out the signing of the declaration which was delayed; that lasted practically the whole day and the declaration we signed was worded as follows:

I hereby swear that I will not attempt to escape whilst a prisoner of the Imperial Japanese Army.

We were forced to salute the Camp Commandant before and after the signature.

That evening brought us all good news:

(a) Rations of bread were immediately issued.
(b) We were told that we could write letters monthly to Australia and England in the first batch.

That night, I commenced writing my first letter to my darling wife but was only allowed 200 words. This is not many, but better than none at all. The rules for writing letters are as follows:

1. Use one side of one sheet of paper only.
2. Only English language is permitted.
3. Words must be written in block letters or typewritten.
4. Do not use code or secret marks.
5. Use simple words and phrases only.
6. Matters pertaining to military, political, commercial, or industrial matters are not acceptable.

I expect the above rules will also apply to anyone writing to us.

25 June 1942

Since we have signed the parole conditions, the camps have improved and this morning, to our surprise, we all received an issue of fried fish cooked in peanut oil and with the rice it tasted very nice. The Japanese have promised writing paper, ink and pens to write the letters that have been promised, but none as yet have arrived. I have my draft of letter ready to write to my dear wife and children, so I am anxious to get this letter away.

The Japanese have indicated that a canteen would be allowed in the camp with the goods being supplied by them. Items for sale have yet to be decided, but I would say goods such as cigarettes, sugar and a certain amount of tin supplies of a Japanese brand may be on offer. Anyway, we shall all wait and see. The Japanese also indicated that soap would be available in due course.

27 June 1942

The canteen has arrived which brought in a free issue of soap and toothpaste, which everyone needed. In addition, a certain amount of cigarettes were for sale to anyone who had the cash. Everyone enjoyed their first cigarette in comfort, not having to fiddle for or scrounge.

The Japanese authorities also appear to be abiding by some of the rules of the Geneva Convention regarding treatment of prisoners of war and they have also decided to make a small monetary allowance to officers only, not other ranks. With this allowance the officers will be able to purchase what is available at the canteen and it is hoped that the officers will provide some financial assistance to the batmen to buy items from the canteen.

The Camp Commandant has ordered that the number of hymns that can be sung during church services would in future be limited to two and that also 'God Save the King' will not be allowed to be sung.

30 June 1942

Bad news has developed once again; the Japanese have stopped the bread ration we receive from Shamshuipo. We have a certain amount of flour in stock here, but no means of baking it for bread. Dumplings have been suggested in lieu of bread and cooked with a vegetable stew, which will be issued in the next meal.

All letters that were written by everyone have been returned for re-writing as the majority contains more than 200 words. Also the Japanese pointed out that no reference is to be made of our comrades, whom I for one did mention many. We were also told not to make any remarks regarding the food we were receiving. This morning, a naval officer was called out on parade and dealt with severely for making some remark in his letter about the Japanese, the result of which a Japanese Sgt Maj who looked a real pig of a man beat him up. He was also thrown to the ground, kicked and his ears savagely bashed which caused blood to flow freely from the ears and nose and on the following morning, he was completely deaf. How this officer managed to control his feelings at the time was beyond me. Had he attempted to retaliate he would have immediately been shot without trial. This Japanese Sgt Maj who was from the 'Gestapo' and an interpreter produced the evidence to the Camp Commandant who listened to the charges against the officer in question. The officer was handed over to the Japanese NCO who finally applied more punishment; all this took place in front of everyone on parade. Apparently, the officer described the Japanese in his letter as either 'nips' or 'Japs'.

It looks to me that Lieut Col Penfold had written something in his letters, which was not approved of by the Japanese censorship committee and has now been called out from the evening parade. He did not receive the same treatment as the previous officer, but was made to stand to attention in front of the guardroom for about four hours. Eventually he was released in a state of near collapse in the dreadful heat where the mosquitoes had bitten all the uncovered portions of his legs and arms. Apparently, the Japanese disapproved of him referring to them as 'nips'.

5 July 1942

A site within the camp has been suggested for the bakery and the Camp Commandant has approved of the area, but this depends on his moods as to whether or not we have a bakery.

Orders have been given by the Japanese that when lights are extinguished at night they would not be put on again under any circumstances. Also, the sentries patrolling outside the perimeter wire have received orders to shoot anyone outside of their hut after lights out. Last night, some of the men were outside due to the very hot and humid weather and one was shot and severely wounded.

A certain amount of dhal (Indian corn) has been issued to the camp store and the messing officer has decided to produce some kind of pea soup for us which will be a nice change to our daily ration.

8 July 1942

Escape still occupied the minds of the men, but the odds of success have increased tremendously. Not only had the Japanese tightened up on security due to the previous escapes from Shamshuipo Camp, but the location of Argyle Street Camp made this much more difficult and dangerous. Furthermore, our physical condition has deteriorated somewhat and with limited food provisions, it would take a supreme effort to negotiate the 900 or so miles journey to Kunming or Chungking unless, of course, contact could be made with the Chinese Guerrillas or British lines. Any escape plan by prisoner(s) was first required to be submitted to the escape committee, who would only approve it if there was a good chance of success. Some proposals were completely reckless and weak that they were immediately abandoned whilst others were well thought out.

Lieut R. Goodwin, a New Zealander in the RNVR, was wounded whilst serving on one of the MTBs and spent some time in the Queen Mary Hospital near Aberdeen before being imprisoned in North Point Camp. He was then transferred to Argyle St Camp in April 1942. From the very first day as a prisoner, he thought of nothing else but escape, planning ways and means of achieving this goal. He was forever gazing at the electrified fence and distant hills beyond, and spoke incessantly of breaking out. Most of the men viewed their confinement with apathy, resigned to their predicament. Thoughts of escape were not on their minds, just survival. Some of the men got bored with Goodwin's obsession while others admired his determination to succeed. He did not care about the opinions of others, as he was going anyway when the opportunity presented itself and in any case, nobody would know.

9 July 1942

As the wood situation improved, we are able to get the primitive hot water boiler for use once a day for the whole camp. The boiler contains approximately six hundred pints, which is practically the strength of the officers' camp and although the batmen are not so fortunate to have tea, some of the officers do look after the batmen, but some are mighty mean; this I will most likely talk about in the years to come.

Due to the very hot and humid weather, four officers collapsed on the parade ground this morning. After the parade I arranged for some of the batmen to carry them back to their quarters.

The brand of cigarettes the Japanese troops are receiving are called 'pirates' and 'ruby queen', which I well remember the Chinese smoked before the outbreak of war and I often refused to accept one when I was in their company as they were terrible.

12 July 1942

Capt Davis of the HKVDC is trying to control the outbreak of disease. He, with the men at his disposal, is responsible for the cleaning of all drains that surround the camp. This includes all toilets whether built or improvised, the latter mostly used for dysentery cases where the latrine buckets are installed. Due to the short supply of disinfectants, block salt is being melted down to flush out the lavatories, latrine buckets and drains, etc., at least twice per day.

More timber has arrived in the camp so as to enable us to build up improved beds and thereby get as many people off the concrete floors as soon as possible.

19 July 1942

We have been getting heavy rains these past few weeks caused by the tail end of typhoons that have hit the mainland recently. The huts have fairly rocked with strong gusts of wind, which are disastrous, and normally happen during typhoons. If we had a typhoon that I experienced in 1937, this camp would be completely flattened and if this did happen, we would all be rounded up like rats in a trap with sentries prodding us with bayonets together with rifle bashings. As far as we know, the Japanese have not prepared or arranged for an alternative site if this should happen. They have supplied each hut with eight large struts for the purpose of strengthening and preventing them from swaying during the fierce heavy gusts of winds.

20 July 1942

The International Red Cross representatives visited the camp today, but the Japanese authorities ensured that no conversations took place between the Red Cross and the prisoners during the tour. We noticed that the Japanese supply lorry purposely unloaded a lot of green vegetables near the cookhouse and in view of the Red Cross, but the vegetables were quickly removed after the inspection. The Red Cross recognised the fact that conditions within the camp were not good and as much as the Japanese Commandant tried to cover up wherever possible to give a good impression that the conditions were very good, it was not convincing.

4 August 1942

The Japanese have informed us that there is no more meat available in the colony and further supplies are not expected in the near future. We have been expecting this after the International Red Cross Inspectors were informed that meat was issued to all the prisoners in the camp.

Cpl Mattison[81] of the RASC is suffering from severe ulcers of the left leg of about 2 inches in diameter and has a very high temperature, but at this time nothing can be done for him. A Japanese Medical Officer arrived at the camp this morning to inspect him and has now prescribed M and B tablets, which may help to bring his temperature and his condition under some degree of control.

11 August 1942

Lieut Gutteries, an officer of the Portuguese Company of the HKVDC, died today. He was dying before he left camp for Bowen Road Military Hospital and he was buried in the late evening in the spare ground adjacent to the CBS building, which is situated in front of our camp in Argyle Street. Directly to the east of the CBS School lies the Indian cemetery, allotted to them by the Japanese, and on the opposite side of the British cemetery, burials are taking place at the rate of two to three per day. I heard that BQMS Pettit and BSM Morley lie in this section. They were both great friends of mine in the past.[82] Close to these cemeteries, the Japanese conduct their daily cremations and it is noticed that they are using the CBS building and La Salle College as hospitals for the troops which appear to be arriving from the New Territories in great numbers.

18 August 1942

The men have been reduced to a shadow of their former selves due to hunger, illness and being worked to death by the Japanese, but they are not being subdued or unyielding and in return for their efforts, receive punishment either physical or a reduction in their daily rations, which is decided upon by the English-speaking interpreters. This has left a mark on the men and our main concern is the increase in the cases of disease exacerbated by the foul and disgusting conditions in which we are expected to live. Nearly all of the men in Shamshuipo and Argyle Street were afflicted with some form of disease, be it scurvy, beriberi, pellagra, amoebic dysentery, malaria, or diphtheria. The latter, being the worst of all, was caused by acute malnutrition, and with the lack of preventative drugs and proper diet, this caused intensive suffering. Many of the men suffered from beriberi and pellagra which is caused by the lack of vitamin B. Beriberi is also rife and is a crippling disease, particularly in the legs. These diseases are completely foreign to most of the men. Pellagra causes sores to develop on the skin and ulcers became evident in the mouth, lips and tongue. Advanced stages of this disease, affects the throat and some men find it difficult to consume their meagre diet. It also causes genitals and the inside of the thighs to become inflamed, red raw and extremely chafed and is commonly called 'rice' or 'strawberry' balls. Scurvy was very bad and is caused by the lack of green vegetables and as we don't get any, goodness knows how we can get treated for this complaint. The dysentery patients we could do little for, with one room set aside as a latrine that was always full to capacity, with 10 large-sized crude wooden seats set out in a semi-circle, where men endlessly squatted often for hours at a time. Many dysentery patients visited the buckets as many as 40 times a day.[83]

The instances of death amongst the Canadians, particularly the French element of the Royal Rifles of Canada, are alarmingly high compared to the British soldiers. This steady rate of death has been occurring for no apparent reason and shows the lack of will to live. Conversely, the British soldier possesses greater discipline, hygiene, mental and physical ability plus the will and perseverance to survive in these wretched conditions and under severe duress. Nevertheless, men of all nationalities are dying as a result of this miserable existence. The Japanese are not making any issues of medical supplies to meet these problems and the medical officers are doing their level best to treat and overcome these diseases. Some medical supplies are infiltrating into the camp by unknown sources that are helping to treat the critically ill people. The Japanese are allowing a certain number of very bad cases to be taken to St Theresa's Hospital in Prince Edward Road, Kowloon, which had foreign medical staff including Japanese. Deaths were occurring at a steady rate and the so-called hospital which looked as sick as its patients had a leaking roof with no windows and was always full to overflowing, where men died when doctors' or orderlies' backs were turned for a moment.

On a bare hill opposite the Argyle St POW Camp is a cemetery for those who died in captivity. The burials of six men took place this morning; the bodies were placed into sacks and lowered into the graves dug by the batmen. I was in charge of this burial party but I could not remember or even know little of the bible or prayer book; however, I had a set oration for each body. 'In you go chum and God bless.' The guards during burials did not show any ill feeling towards us at the actual burial, but it was just the opposite when digging and preparing graves for future burials and then it was the usual rifle butt bashing and prodding with bayonets.

The poem below was written in August 1942 by S/Sgt Cole[84] of the HKVDC, when the great diphtheria epidemic was raging at Shamshuipo Camp and every day brought a funeral, sometimes three or four.

Obsequy

Standing behind the wire,
We see the slow procession climb the hill,
The bearers straining at their task, until,
They reach the wasting edge of scrub and sand,
Granted by strangers in a conquered land,
To those called from us,
Who must wait in sleep,
For that infallible appointment we all must keep.

Quietly the party stands,
The solemn message to the earth confers,
Its own and mortal dust made spiritless refers,
To dust terrestrial one more fleshy seed
Sown to allay the unrequited greed
Of this bare hill for grim fertility
Inexorably to be satisfied by deaths ubiquity.

The mourners move away, under their escorts' eyes, their duty done,
Our tongues must speak and we say 'well one more gone'
But not our thoughts, unwilling to confide
Within this little world, though wire deprived
Us our rightful liberty, we are alive.

20 August 1942

Today, we all received forms from the Japanese authorities to complete as soon as possible. Each form required us to state our qualifications, trades and other particulars, which we assumed were a prelude for a further shipment of prisoners to Japan or Japanese occupied territories. On the bottom of the form it stated if we were prepared to work for

Japan. Major General Maltby advised us all to ignore this paragraph, which everyone did. We did not receive any further information in this respect.

21 August 1942

The camp is infested with bugs again, particularly in the primitively made wooden beds, and it is very amusing to watch everyone debugging their beds daily by holding lighted paper to all the cracks and walls in which they breed. One can hear the eggs cracking due to the heat of the flames. We also use boiling water, which also has some destructive effect. Kerosene oil would be ideal if we could get some, which of course is out of the question, as this would not be supplied by the Japanese. These bugs naturally bite one at nights and suck the blood from one's body in the process, and when you kill or crush a bug it smells terrible. This causes awful itching and continual scratching that tends to keep one awake at night. We all hope that when the cool weather occurs this will cause them to disappear.

22 August 1942

Doctor Saito, the Japanese medical representative for all the camps and the one person most hated by everyone, including his own troops, who has remained steadfastly indifferent to the state of the health of the prisoners, suddenly became interested in our physical condition in Shamshuipo and Argyle St Camps and instructed his underlings that we must be subjected to the most rigorous examination. Those men selected from Argyle St were then taken by lorry to Shamshuipo Camp.

The fittest men were singled out even though they were only fit enough to carry out work of a light nature, but to Saito they represented potential dockers, miners and factory workers. A body of men were selected including myself and every man in this draft was vaccinated with needles, which rapidly became blunt. The Japanese developed a mania for stool tests and we were called upon to produce specimens at frequent intervals, which were not difficult, as scarcely a man did not have bowels that were not functioning.

The medical examination of the rectum was by injecting an enormous glass tube which was forced into the back passage so rough that the pain was unbearable. I said to Sgt Sutherland, 'Sandy, what the hell are they looking for up there?' The interpreter, whom I did not notice, fully understood my remark, came over and gave me a hard whack with a stick he was carrying, following by a few hard punches to the face and he said, 'You understand why Dr Saito is carrying out these tests.' What happened to the specimens we never knew, but the ritual was carried out with solemn precision; however, this did not unduly upset us. We took the view that if you are going to shit six times or more in a day, it did not make much difference who eventually got it and if the Japanese want it, then they can bloody well have it because there is plenty more from where it came from.

One of the men of the 2nd Battalion of the Royal Scots had tattoos on each buttock and were in the form of two large eyes and under each one was tattooed, 'eye see you and you see me', strange to say this amused the interpreter and instead of receiving a whack he received a pat. Finally, we were all photographed and a numbered draft card was pinned on each man's shirt and we were then isolated from the rest in the camp. Suddenly, for some unknown reason, I was withdrawn by a sentry from the group and returned to those looking on in the distance.

The 'hard men' as they came to be known were then isolated to wait orders to embark on a transport ship presumably for Japan. The Japanese interpreter called out names including mine, informing us that we were not required for this draft and would be returned to camp. I am being sent to Argyle St to take over the batmen once again with some of the others, the remainder to remain at Shamshuipo from which they originally came.

28 August 1942

Farming has commenced by voluntary officers. The Japanese have given us a piece of ground in front of the camp, which was a Chinese farm originally. Maj Marsh of the Middlesex Regiment is in charge of this farming and with his knowledge we shall no doubt be able to get some decent vegetables for the camp. I have gone out in the evenings to assist in the watering of the various plants, but we find that it is not long before we get tired.

4 September 1942

Lieut Woods of the RASC refused to pull his weight as regards fatigues detailed by the Hut Commander. To remedy this, the officers of the hut gave him a good dip in the 'pig trough' after which he still refused to do anything. This case was sent forward to Brig Peffers, who decided that he should be issued his daily ration raw and to cook his food for himself

5 September 1942

Lieut Woods received his first issue of raw rations with firewood. I wonder how long he will keep up the daily cooking of his own food. I give him two more days.

7 September 1942

Lieut Woods has given up the idea of cooking his own food and has gladly offered his services to do his full share of fatigues of the hut.

Several people of the HKVDC and also regular troops have received postcards from Macau, Amoy and Shanghai. The Chinese personnel of the Hong Kong Volunteers are being released as prisoners of war by the Japanese and have removed them from Shamshuipo to St Theresa's Hospital pending their release. As the hospital is quite near our camp, we can see the Chinese volunteers quite plainly, but no signal of any description are allowed between us. Pte Lam[85] is the only Chinese in this camp and he appears quite happy about their release.

8 September 1942

Presently, I have eighteen boils on my body, the majority of which are under the armpits. Capt Warrack of the RAMC believes in the lancing method but he is not so gentle about it and the small-improvised knife he has been using is not very sharp and I am sure he could find a way of getting a finer edge. A razor blade would be far better than the knife.

We have received another type of Chinese vegetable, that is called the 'taro', but how this will be cooked we don't know.

We have eaten the taros, which tasted quite nice after all and they have a taste more like ordinary potatoes.

Maj Dewar[86] of the RASC who was nearly blind due to malnutrition was today sent to Bowen Road Hospital.

14 September 1942

My hut has produced an excellent concert, which commenced last night and finishes today. It is known as the 'Batmen's Review' and believe me the lads did really well and put in a lot of spirit. The officers of the camp showed their appreciation with a reward of cigarettes and they were given these after last night's concert. I expect they shall also receive something after today's performance.

21 September 1942

Four officers had their faces viciously slapped by the Japanese today for going behind the canteen building which is situated near the perimeter fencing. These officers were at fault because orders were issued that everyone is to keep at least ten yards from the perimeter fence.

There are rumours that British troops have infiltrated Norway, for what reason we do not know.

The officers and batmen are now being detailed by the Japanese to cut the grass around and under the perimeter fences. What an awkward job this is, working under the barbed wire without cutting yourself.

25 September 1942

This morning, everyone was woken at 4.00 a.m. Breakfast of rice and a small piece of fish and two small rice loaves were issued to each man as our ration for the day. By 6.00 a.m., the men were seated upon the parade ground and were still there at 11.30 a.m. waiting for Col Tokunaga. By midday, all the food had been eaten and once again hunger took over. At 12.20 p.m., a shriek from a Jap Sgt Maj brought all the prisoners to attention as a staff car containing the 'white pig' and his cronies drove onto the parade ground. Tokunaga stepped from the car, stumbled and all but fell over, whereupon there were comments from the ranks, which finally exploded into very loud laughter. 'Go on,' encourages one of the men from the ranks, 'break your xxxxxx neck.' 'Silence,' bawled out the interpreter Nimori, and Japanese guards immediately strode up and down the ranks jabbering in their language. Faces were slapped; shins were kicked, which was not unusual on the parade ground.

Col Tokunaga, who could not speak English, addressed the parade with Nimori interpreting. His opening speech to everyone was, 'You prisoners of war are going to Japan. His Majesty the Emperor has saved your lives for which in return, you must work hard for the benefit and prosperity of Japan.' He glared fiercely around him, alert for any disrespect and then turned on his heel and waddled back to his car. Lieut Hideo Wada, who also gave an address, took the Colonel's place. He said, 'The delights of Japan are awaiting you and also they will safeguard your health at all times. You will remember my face in the future as all of you will be seeing a lot of me.' From the ranks, I could hear this comment, 'Seeing you once is enough for me and as for your face, I would love to change it.' 'Silence,' shouted Nimori.

Before the draft left Hong Kong, Major General Maltby addressed the forty-three officers. 'Wherever you go, be as bloody-minded as you can,' he said to them. 'Remember one thing always; these people cannot win the war.'

In the afternoon, we all saw in the distance lighters pull out with their human cargoes from the Hong Kong waterfront for the *Lisbon Maru*. Some lighters appeared to be listing due probably to overloading of the prisoners. At the first sight of the ship, she appeared to promise a medium amount of comfort, but later I found out that any such thoughts were speedily dispelled when the prisoners saw the accommodation allotted to them.

27 September 1942

On 27 September, just as dawn was breaking, the *Lisbon Maru* dropped her moorings, raised her anchors and headed for the open sea for her destination, Japan.

30 September 1942

Able Seaman Laurence of the Royal Navy was operated on today for appendicitis, the operation being very successful. Spr Moore[87] is suffering from a severely sore heel and it looks as though he might need an operation to find out the cause.

Our camp library is gradually getting better and today we received more books from the International Red Cross who have been visiting Hong Kong at this present time. We are now in possession of a camp magazine and it is produced by six or seven officers in the camp and is called *Within*. We have another magazine being published and it is being called *Prisoners' Pie*. Both are very interesting indeed.

It was proposed at the weekly mess meeting, that all types of fish heads brought into the camp by the Japanese supply lorry be boiled and issued as fish soup. We had our first taste of this today and believe me it will be the last for some time to come, as everybody was terribly sick as a result.

1 October 1942

We could see in the distance the 'Number 7 Typhoon' signal being hoisted, being the warning that one is on the way and with the weather conditions being close, dark and overcast and the air still; it looks like it could strike at any moment. The typhoon struck about midnight and the force of the wind caused the huts to sway dangerously and in the early hours of the next morning, it increased in intensity but abated about midday.

Some of the huts required additional support with wooden struts particularly to Huts No. 7, 10, 12 and 15 but no casualties were reported.

We have heard that the *Gypsholm*, a Norwegian ship, chartered by the International Red Cross, is carrying 1,000 tons of Red Cross parcels, but whether we get them remains to be seen. If they are distributed throughout the camps, they will be the first that we have received. I am sure the contents of each parcel will be very welcome and will boost the morale of everyone here, particularly healthwise.

5 October 1942

Lieut Blaker of the Dockyard Defence Corps was suddenly removed to the hospital erected temporarily within the camp and found to be suffering from that dreaded disease, cholera.[88] Everyone that has the symptoms of diarrhoea has been told to remain on parade after dismissal. Eighty remained on the parade ground and they were immediately removed to the spare hut, which is hut number three which automatically became the isolation hut for the outbreak. The daily disinfecting and spraying of the inside of all huts was ordered by the Japanese, the spraying machine, etc., being supplied by them. As a result of the outbreak of cholera, the Japanese medical squad took rectum swabs of everyone in the camp, this taking about four hours. I dreaded the use of the glass tubular swab, which was very painful on insertion, particularly as I had haemorrhoids.

9 October 1942

More rectum swabs were taken today on a certain number of men. With this outbreak of cholera and for those that are isolated, it is unusual to see each other wearing masks that were issued by the Japanese. We heard today that the Pope had forwarded 6,000 pounds for the prisoners of war in Hong Kong, but whether we get any of it remains to be seen. It depends on the mood of the Japanese.

An attempt was made by the bakery staff to produce bread composed partly of flour and rice, but this experiment was not successful.

14 October 1942

The isolation period for suspected cholera cases lapsed today and everyone is very pleased. We all hope that there will be no further outbreaks.

20 October 1942

The whole camp was shocked to hear that the Japanese ship *Lisbon Maru*, carrying British prisoners from Hong Kong to Japan, had been sunk by an American submarine in the China Seas with a terrible loss of life, so we had been told. A service of all denominations was immediately held to hear this dreadful news. No doubt the world must have heard of this terrible tragedy and the loss of so many men. This means much sorrow to those throughout the world particularly Australia. I am wondering whether Gerry Gollege, Alfred Lloyd or Johnny Eves were on the boat. I understand that Capt Knowles of the 12th Coast Regiment Royal Artillery is not one of the survivors and I believe Lieut Woodcock of the Royal Engineers is reported missing.[89] This news is terrible.

25 October 1942

Another group of Japanese officers and other men visited the camp today, for what reason, no one knows, but there may be more reprisals, which always crop up after such visits.

Eye cases are becoming very serious amongst some of us now, with the consequence that some fellows are gradually becoming blind, which is caused mostly by deficiencies in the diet.

What a surprise we all had today. Allied planes raided Hong Kong and Kowloon at about 1.15 p.m. Immediately, the Japanese dispersed everyone into their huts at bayonet point, with threats that anyone seen outside the huts would be shot. From the hut, I viewed about twenty planes in the raid and they appeared to be bombing the docks area and Kai Tak Aerodrome. Japanese AA Batteries opened up from many positions, but whether they were able to down any of the Fortress bombers could not be determined. The main thing is that it really boosted up the morale. The excitement amongst us all was tremendous, all of whom expected that there would be more raids in the future. Further excitement then took place at about 4.30 p.m., with another raid taking place and there were explosions from bombs being dropped somewhere in the vicinity of Whitfield Barracks in Nathan Road and the Kowloon Docks. Well, prospects are sure looking up now, but we all expect some sort of reprisals over this bombing and no doubt it will be in the form of a ration reduction. Our rice ration may be cut in half once again and will probably last for a week or more. The Japanese may restrict our movements around the camp and most probably keep us in the huts as much as possible. There will be the usual bashings from the sentries that appear to have been doubled.

27 October 1942

Today is the 24th anniversary with the Royal Artillery, for which I have served 18 years overseas, 10 of those in India and eight years in Hong Kong. I am proud to say that I am the oldest soldier serving in the 1st HK/SRA.

28 October 1942

During the morning, another air raid took place with about 25 allied planes taking part. I had a better chance of observing this raid and saw the force of planes split up into two groups, one group heading for an attack upon Kai Tak Aerodrome and the other bombing shipping lying in the harbour. They then formed into one group and made a combined attack upon Hong Kong and Kowloon Docks. This raid lasted for well over an hour and could have been supported by further flights from what we think are aircraft carriers lying somewhere in the China Seas.

30 October 1942

One man received a letter from England, this being the first letter to arrive in the camp since we became prisoners of war. I wonder if I shall be lucky and get a letter in the near future, as I am so anxious to hear from my loved ones in Australia.

There are more health problems in the camp, as a case of diphtheria has been confirmed and found in hut number six and this has caused the hut with its occupants to be completely isolated. All precautions are being taken to prevent the disease from spreading and orders have been issued that everyone will sleep in the huts by head to toe.

There was a rumour today that Canton was raided and retaken by Chinese forces but I think this rumour is one of wishful thinking.

31 October 1942

Compulsory gargling and spraying of huts daily since the reported outbreak of diphtheria has been ordered and anyone suffering from sore throats or colds is to report to the sick bay immediately. Masks are to be worn at all times, either when sleeping or in groups during the day. The Japanese authorities are to see that their orders have been carried out in order to prevent the disease from spreading and will inspect the huts.

Every time we see Japanese fighters leave the Kai Tak Aerodrome, we all wonder whether they have gone up to intercept a flight of American planes bent on raiding Japanese installations and defences in and around Hong Kong and the New Territories. On the last raid it was reported that two American planes were brought down and their pilots were buried by the Japanese in the British cemetery near our camp.

9 November 1942

The Japanese authorities carried out an officer's technical examination this morning, our hut being used for this purpose. The object of the examination is not clear, but I imagine it is something to do with the officers being employed on specialised jobs in Japanese occupied territories, whereabouts is anyone's guess.

During the day, a parade was ordered and everyone was drawn out in pairs, and then photographed in pairs by the Japanese. It appears that this was done for identification purposes and for general use when on working parties or for escaped prisoners. I was snapped with a New Zealander by the name of Franklin. I wonder whether any of these photographs will be published in our newspapers through the International Red Cross. If this did occur, I would really look an awful specimen with my close-cropped haircut, which gives me the appearance of an escaped convict.

I have really turned native now, as I have at last thrown my old boots away and have adapted to wearing wooden sandals made by me and which I am hoping if all goes well, bring them home with me as a memento, plus the fundoshi that I wear practically all the time. This keeps the washing of clothes to the minimum and is most comfortable in hot and humid weather. What with wearing this type of rig-out with close cropped hair, I really do look like a native and all I have to do is to get thoroughly brown in the sun and I shall definitely look the part.

13 November 1942

We have been banned from using the four- to five-feet diameter concrete pipe monsoon drain for showers as all kinds of rubbish flows in the water and being so high off the ground, one cannot see what is coming out of the mouth of the pipe. It has been banned temporarily because it is thought that the diphtheria germ could be located in the storm water.

Further swabs of the rectum were taken of the whole camp due to the outbreak of diphtheria.

Skin trouble is common in the camp at this present time and quite a number of men are suffering from severe face rashes.

Power blackouts are getting quite frequent of late which is probably due to the air raids being made on Hong Kong, Kowloon and outlying districts even over the border into China. These blackouts make one feel very uncomfortable as movements outside the huts to the toilets, etc., could result in one being shot by very nervous sentries.

17 November 1942

We were all overjoyed to hear some unofficial news that Rommel is now on the run in North Africa.

Strange to say, that an unusual supply of a small amount of fish and vegetables were delivered to the camp today. This arrival of food is a real change of heart by the Japanese. I wonder why?

Whilst on parade this evening, for the usual count of all prisoners, the Japanese interpreter suddenly ordered us to disperse immediately to the huts. We thought this might be due to an expected air raid by the allied forces. We were all confined to our huts for about an hour but nothing happened. During this period of confinement, Japanese sentries threatened to shoot anyone found moving outside and the situation got that bad that they would not even allow us to proceed to the toilets.

26 November 1942

An air raid warning was sounded but within a very short time, the all-clear was given. The Japanese supplied a small amount of peanut oil, which soon was used for various ways of cooking, and they also supplied a small amount of fish with the peanut oil being used to fry the fish; a small amount of about two square inches was issued to each man, which tasted quite nice with the rice.

28 November 1942

What excitement we all had today, as this morning, a Japanese lorry arrived at the camp carrying 480 Red Cross parcels, followed within a very short time, further lorries containing bully beef, cocoa and dried fruit. During the afternoon, one more lorry arrived with sugar of which was issued five pounds per man. The majority of the Red Cross parcels contained sixteen items and they were as follows:

1. Tinned butter	7. tinned cheese
2. Tinned bacon	8. tinned biscuits
3. Tinned puddings	9. tinned jam
4. Tinned sugar	10. tinned treacle
5. Tinned meat pudding	11. tinned soap
6. Tinned meat rolls	12. packets of chocolate

(There were other items to make up the tally of sixteen.)

We all arranged amongst those in the hut, to attempt to provide a Christmas meal with various items of food being confiscated by us from the supply lorries from time to time, assisted by a certain amount of items obtained from the recently provided canteen that was authorised by the Japanese. The only question remaining was the payment of cash for these items and the only way to get some was from the officers who were paid a certain amount, which was very little but with some luck we hope to receive a donation from them to get the items of food necessary. However, with the arrival of the Red Cross parcels, we have decided to pool some of the food items towards our Christmas dinner.

2 December 1942

The Japanese have become quite generous today, as this morning a lorry arrived into the camp with 100 blankets for the batmen, which are greatly needed in this very cold weather. They will replace the use of rice sacks for sleeping in, with the corners cut out to allow one's arms in and a hole in the centre to allow one's head to fit through. I have been using a rice sack to sleep in on the very cold nights for some time.

The camp was inspected by a high-ranking Japanese officer, who even shook hands with Major General Maltby, the GOC Troops, Hong Kong Command. As far as I could see, this senior Japanese officer was wearing British decorations from World War I, these were confirmed later as being the General Service and Victory Medal, which was very unusual to us being that the Japanese were now our enemies.

The Japanese have offered to supply pork for Christmas through the canteen at three yen per lb. One can also order cakes for the internees at Stanley, where some prisoners have dependants. The Japanese will ensure that delivery of these items will be arranged. This consideration from the Japanese has been a complete change in their mood and we are all wondering why this is the case, but believe that this will only be temporary.

7 December 1942

Today is the first anniversary of the bombing of Pearl Harbor.

The Japanese have supplied flour, which must have been obtained from the stocks left in our depots. We will endeavour to make some bread, which will be a change from rice. The flour appears to be in fairly good condition, despite being in our stores for the last 12 months; however, we would not be surprised to find quite a few weevils in the flour.

We have heard bad news from the camp at Shamshuipo, where disease is rife amongst the prisoners and this suffering can only continue, as there are no medical supplies available.

Everyone is being frugal with the contents of their Red Cross parcel with some of the prisoners saving this food in the event of emergency or where escape may be considered.

The Japanese are getting very strict regarding the distance we must keep from the perimeter wire that runs parallel with the main roadway. The distance of 10 yards from the fence has been indicated on the ground. This has been done to stop any prisoners attracting or making any form of signals to the Chinese or other nationalities on the outside. Any infringement of this rule, the sentries have been ordered to shoot without hesitation.

10 December 1942

Some mail has arrived in the camp, but as usual, there was no mail for me.

The Japanese sentries suddenly raided all huts within the camp this morning and confiscated all improvised cookers, which had been constructed by individuals for private cooking. The temporary Camp Commandant apparently had ordered this, as he feared that an outbreak of fire would occur. He promised an area for cooking in the near future and until this was approved, no further cooking is allowed.

If the chaplains' duties during battle were a burden, in captivity, they became infinitely more so. There were men in the camps who were losing faith, losing hair, losing eyesight, losing manhood and losing reason. There were men dying every day and it was a proud boast from the clergy that every man where possible who died was given a Christian burial. The four chaplains in the camps whose task was to administer the last rights to men choking on diphtheria, brought comfort to very sick men in dysentery wards in frightful condition, whose lifeblood was gradually draining away. There are only a very few men who can in all honesty claim to have received spiritual advice from those who are engaged on man's most humble mission. The chaplains were:

Reverend Lewis Davies, Padre of the Middlesex Regiment
Gordon Bennett, Padre of the Royal Scots Regiment
Reverend Charles Strong of the Royal Navy
Father Green, Roman Catholic Priest

16 December 1942

All the batmen are now very busy in their spare time, as they have been drawing up all kinds of Christmas cards for the officers and other men, and what I have seen of them, they look very good indeed. Japanese papers of sorts have been obtained from various sources for this exercise.

Major General Maltby, the Commodore and the three Brigadiers were suddenly taken out to dine with the Japanese Colonel Commandant late this evening.

During the day, some other officers have arrived from Bowen Road Military Hospital and they have informed us that the conditions in Shamshuipo Camp have improved.

21 December 1942

Extra large parcels arrived today for those in the Hong Kong Volunteer Defence Corps, from their relations and friends who resided in Hong Kong and the New Territories. Before the war these prisoners who were a mixture of English, Chinese and other nationalities had businesses in Hong Kong or worked for Government Departments.

The Swiss Nationals, who are representatives of the International Red Cross, visited the camp this morning. To prevent any of us having direct contact with any of them, we were all confined to our huts. Very little conversation was allowed between Major General Maltby, his staff officers and the Red Cross officials. I believe one question was allowed to be put to the Red Cross and this was in regard to letters being delivered to the camp. The Senior Red Cross representative replied by saying, 'The chance of receiving regular mail is very remote.' That reply did not exactly raise our expectations.

24 December 1942

The Japanese have sent us a few Christmas trees, which will help us to celebrate Christmas. This was quite a surprise to everyone.

The cooks have produced a new dish, which we call, 'bubble and squeak', which is made out of vegetables and peanut oil. It was a welcome change from the continual rice.

Well, it's Christmas Eve once again and I know my dear wife and family will be thinking of me. God bless them all and I hope I shall be with them on the next one.

25 December 1942

Best wishes to my darling wife and family on this Christmas day. Please God keep them in good health and free from the dangers of this world. I attended the Christmas service and carols at 11.30 a.m. this morning.

Some mail was received today, but not for me. The following is our menu for the day: rice and scalded cabbage and tea.

27 December 1942

Brig Peffers has advised that a rest has been approved for all in the camp. Our lunch today consisted of bully beef and stewed yams. The bully beef was pooled by everyone from the Red Cross parcels we had received recently. This was followed by a pudding of dried fruit and raisins also from the Red Cross parcels. Major General Maltby made an excellent speech, which was followed by a Royal toast to King George VI and an impromptu concert. The General's speech was very cheery and he finished by saying that he hoped we would be released next year.

31 December 1942

There was an optimistic feeling on this New Year's Eve and we are hoping that we shall be out of this camp this coming year.

I wonder if my dear wife and family have enjoyed this Christmas. I am hoping that they are still in Australia and have not returned to England where the conditions must be simply terrible with the country being bombed continuously.

8 January 1943

The Japanese have allowed us to establish a library in the camp which consisted of books that we assume were obtained from libraries in Hong Kong. A few of the officers have volunteered to run the library and this morning a lorry arrived in the camp loaded with books of all sorts which at the moment are being categorised.

Flight Officer Thomson[90] arrived in the camp today from Bowen Road Hospital and he informed Major General Maltby that another draft of prisoners have been formed for shipment to Japan. Whoever is on the draft, I am sure that I will know them all.

16 January 1943

I had to charge Gnr Elsworth[91] of the 5th AA Regiment for insubordination and insolence. Capt Flood gave him a suspended sentence and fined him ten yen, which will become operable if brought forward on any further charges. Some of the chaps are very trying at times and I have had to put my foot down on various occasions.

We were paid thirty yen today, twenty yen being from the camp funds and ten yen from the International Red Cross. The thirty yen was a figure decided upon by a committee to assist us and junior officers in the camp to buy basic diet items from the canteen, which the committee considered were essential for the health of everyone. This caused quite an amount of friction amongst the senior officers. It took some days for the GOC to impress on the senior officers who did not approve of this payment, how necessary this thirty yen was to the batmen and junior officers. Eventually he managed to obtain our first payment, which no doubt he stressed as vital in view of the present scale of rations we receive from the Japanese. Major General Maltby, in my mind, is a fine example of the British Officer, intelligent, fair-minded, frank and sincere. His tenacity of purpose and indomitable spirit, physical and moral courage, were reflected in his personality.

20 January 1943

During the morning parade, the Camp Commandant gave orders on camp discipline. The Japanese interpreter who was standing by his side relayed these orders to us. He pointed out that he would do everything possible to improve conditions within the camp and to assist us to overcome any grievances we might have. He stated that everyone should take care of his health as sickness and deaths of the past and present were mostly due to our own faults which he knew fully well was not the case. He promised recreation hours outside the camp, hot showers where possible and better lighting arrangements inside the huts. He also said that a daily newspaper would be issued in the camp which no doubt would only produce Japanese propaganda.

30 January 1943

What a surprise today, as a film in an open-air cinema was shown to us this evening, which was about the Japanese version of the attack upon Pearl Harbor. The whole attack shown to us was a miniature affair showing dummy ships and buildings, which they tried to portray as the real thing. Naturally, during the filming, our feelings and comments got out of control with raspberries and coarse language came from everyone from all directions. The Japanese Naval and air attacks, no doubt, caused huge damage on the American fleet lying in the harbour, but not as it were shown to us. The film also showed scenes of Naval and Air Force recruits during training. Some of the batmen made rude comments and gestures, which finally caused the Japanese soldiers who were armed to the teeth to lose their tempers and they quickly infiltrated the lines where they administered the usual bashings. As senior NCO in charge of the batmen, I was personally singled out receiving several heavy blows to the head and body, causing me to collapse to the ground. The Japanese finally closed down the film and dispersed us to our huts. I was carried to my bed where Capt Strachan[92] treated me, bandaging the cut to my head and strapping my chest for suspected fractured ribs.

31 January 1943

This morning, I can hardly move being in a fair degree of pain.

A certain number of officers in the camp were asked by the Japanese to submit essays on last night's film. Anyway, the elected officers' comments must have been restrained as no one was beaten up and no reprisals were forthcoming.

I submitted a request for the supply of warm clothing and blankets for the batmen for the forthcoming winter. This request was submitted to the Japanese authorities; however, whilst there may be a chance to get some additional clothing, I do not expect that the blankets will be forthcoming. Footwear amongst the batmen is also a real problem, whereas the majority of the officers appear fairly well off in boots and shoes.

The Japanese are bent on making Kai Tak a large airport; the expansion of which we can see is well under way; where we are labouring in working parties at the airport daily, we can see hundreds of coolies also employed on this work in the far distance. Apparently, the whole of Kowloon city and villages close by are being demolished in this project. We have been continually filling in large craters caused by the American bombers who are gradually increasing their bombing raids over Hong Kong. The runways are completely pitted with huge craters and being in an exposed position we have to take cover wherever possible, usually in one of the craters.

2 February 1943

Suddenly the camp was struck by a frightening illness similar to cholera and one of the victims was a member of the HKVDC. His sudden illness saw him stretcher borne to the sick bay. The Japanese took immediate action and the stretcher carriers were isolated, white-gowned and masked. The Japanese had all of us paraded for rectum swabs, which was rather undignified for the senior officers. There were no fresh cases of this illness, but hundreds of Chinese in Hong Kong were dying of cholera.

7 February 1943

Groups of fifty prisoners are now allowed to leave the camp daily for recreation purposes between the hours of 2.00 p.m. and 4.00 p.m., accompanied of course by a great number of well armed sentries. The recreation sites allotted are within about one hundred yards from the outer perimeter of the camp and are overlooked by Kowloon Hospital and La Salle College, which runs parallel with Prince Edward Road. The sentries keep a close watch upon us to ensure that no signals are made between us and the occupants of the hospital and college. Various Indian guards employed by the Japanese pass to and fro near these buildings, some of whom I recognise and who, in turn, greet me the best way they can when the Japanese sentries are not present or are not looking. Some of them appear uneasy and in my opinion are embarrassed by my presence.

14 February 1943

We received another consignment of sugar from the Red Cross, which is a bonus to our previous issue from them. The sugar will help to make the rice more palatable and also for those that have sugar with their tea.

More letters were received by the Japanese at their headquarters for distribution amongst the men, but there was none for me. I suppose I must get some news eventually particularly from my dear wife and family.

3 April 1943

I have been unable to add to this diary for well over two weeks. The Japanese have been carrying out inspections of the huts and the surrounding areas frequently, and I have to be extremely careful that this diary I secrete in the latrines is not found, because if it was, I would be immediately executed.

5 April 1943

We have heard that the Japanese has received further mail and again I hope there will be one for me. It was some time about the latter part of November or the first week in December 1941, that I last received news of my family, who were then in Australia. They are constantly in my thoughts, more so since we all fear of an invasion of Australia by the Japanese. However, we now understand that the allied forces operating in the Pacific area has prevented this from happening. It would be a great relief for me to know of their whereabouts and that they are all in good health. My girls, Winifred and Pamela, must be grown into ladies since I last saw them and the boys, Richard, Derek and Raymond, must be growing up also.

Once a month, the prisoners were permitted to print in block letters one postcard not exceeding fifty words, which was later reduced to twenty-five to make the Japanese censor's job easier. These letters had to follow a standard format, which must not convey any information on our physical condition, sickness or other adverse circumstances. The batch of incoming mail was delivered in December 1942, but since then letters have arrived infrequently. Those lucky enough to receive letters reacted with excitement, but many had not received any, including myself.

Prisoners of war found it difficult to divert their attention from food for long, thereby the following poem was written by Roger Rothwell of the Middlesex Regiment.

A Prisoner's Prayer

You know Lord, how one must strive
At Shamshuipo to keep alive
And how there isn't much to eat
Just rice and greens at Argyle Street

It's not much God, when dinner comes
To find it's just chrysanthemums
Nor can I stick at any price
The soft white maggots in the rice
Nor yet those little hard, black weevils
The lumps of grit and other evils

I know Lord, I shouldn't grumble
And please don't think that I'm not humble
When I most thankfully recall
My luck to be alive at all

But Lord, I think that even you
Would soon get tired of ersatz stew
So what I really want to say
Is if we soon don't get away
From Shamshuipo and Argyle St
Then please Lord, could we have some meat

A luscious, fragrant, heaped up plateful
And also Lord, we would be grateful
If you would send a living boon
And send some Red Cross parcels soon.

It has been reported by the Japanese that HMS *Medway*, the submarine parent ship whom we all know very well and have seen in the harbour of Hong Kong, has been sunk in the Mediterranean.

7 April 1943

For a change, I volunteered to go outside the camp and assist Lieut Colonel White[93] of the 2nd Royal Scots Regiment in the poultry farm. Up until now, camp funds have been used to purchase the whole of the poultry we have, and there are somewhere about 100 fowls now. The eggs from these fowls are not very plentiful at present, but we hope they will be in the near future. The eggs that we are getting are supplied to the patients in the hospital.

10 April 1943

We have received unofficial news that the New Zealand liner, *Awatea*, has been sunk in the Mediterranean Sea. This ship was the one used to evacuate the families of servicemen from the Philippines to Australia in the late 1940, which included my dear wife and family.

Lieut Col Penfold[94] received a postcard from Mrs Pat Fox of Stanley Internee camp, who was enquiring if he could confirm whether her husband, Capt J. Fox, was alive or dead. Penfold replied to say he was sorry to inform her that he was definitely killed in action. I forgot to mention in the diary before that all civilians including women and children are interned at Stanley, which is situated in the southeast of Hong Kong Island.

Brig McCleod, the CRA, has just received news that his son has been killed in action, in what theatre of war it is not known.

Gnr Snell, one of my batmen, received news by postcard from England today. Everyone's nerves are now becoming strained, and I often have to intervene to avoid confrontation between the prisoners. It took me at least two to three minutes to stop a fight between Sgt Sutherland of the Royal Scots and L/Bdr Holland[95] of the Royal Artillery.

11 April 1943

The Japanese ordered a sudden inspection of the whole of the camp this morning and all prisoners were paraded for this purpose, as the Japanese were suspicious that an underground communication network was in existence, through which the prisoners had been in contact with the outside world. It was also thought that certain information had been leaking out of the camp to people outside the wire to wives and relations of the HKVDC, who resided in Kowloon, Hong Kong Island and other areas. Some had been caught passing messages and other information, the result of which was very harsh reprisals taken against the whole camp. Rations were cut to half and brutal punishment was handed out to anyone caught or suspected of passing messages to the outsiders or sending signals whatsoever from within the camp. Those who were unfortunately seen in the act of passing information were severely interrogated and tortured, and many who underwent this treatment finally died. The circumstances have changed completely in the camp, where the sentries are watching you all the time. They were walking, carrying large bamboo sticks like swords and if you were not working hard enough you received some harsh physical abuse. One fellow was treated this way; he was made to stand outside the Japanese guardroom and had his eye knocked clean out of its socket. Lieut Col Penfold and I were unjustly beaten even though we were not guilty of any offence and we were made to stand to attention for five hours or more, being completely bitten alive with mosquitoes. Finally, I was dealt terrific blows on the back with the bamboo stick, which left me with awful welts. I was then dismissed. Some men were more unfortunate to be placed in a wooden cage built only about two feet off the ground, the roof being too low for them to stand upright. They were treated like caged animals. They received no water for the first three days and on the third night the Japanese forced them to drink until they were sick. After days in this confinement, they were given no food or a wash and when finally released they were covered in lice and scabies.

16 April 1943

Sig Howell[96] of the Royal Corps of Signals received a letter from England today.

Capt Atkinson of the 1st Regiment, HK/SRA, received a letter from Col Tayleur, who was residing in England and was previously in command of the 1st Regiment HK/SRA from 1937 to 1939. In his letter, he said that Lieut Nicholson who was in the same regiment has been killed in action, somewhere in the Middle East. He also informed Capt Atkinson that he had passed on to Mrs Temple of her husband's death during the battle of Hong Kong.

At present, I am suffering from severe malnutrition, beriberi, etc., and my legs and feet are very swollen and it is extremely painful to walk.

17 April 1943

Letters were received from England for the following men:

L/Cpl Hobbs	Gnr Dinner
Pte Francomb	Gnr Blazey
Pte Hale	Gnr Webber

20 April 1943

Lieut Col Penfold told me that he received a letter from his wife in England. He said that all the family are well and that the 'Nanny', Olive Maple, is now being employed by the NAAFI. Olive had been the Penfold's governess and nursemaid to the children whilst they were in India and Hong Kong and they were of course evacuated to Australia with my wife and family in 1940.

More letters arrived in the camp today, but as usual I did not receive any. Most of the letters received have, in the majority, been for the officers and a number have been forwarded to Shamshuipo camp.

The following are representations that were laid before the Japanese on 20 April 1943 and were discussed with the Camp Commandant.

Food

A letter putting a case for improvement of the diet was submitted together with a suggested newly daily ration scale.[97] It was pointed out that the prevalence of beriberi and eye cases were directly due and attributable to a diet which over a period of a year has been deficient in essentials and food values. The Camp Commandant stated that the existing diet scale was laid down by the Governor of Hong Kong and our letters and recommendations would be referred to him. Throughout our sojourn in camp, the need to improve the diet has been constantly referred to the Japanese authorities by letter, conferences and interviews. Efforts have also been made to acquaint the International Red Cross with our position and needs, which of course has never reached them.

Eye Cases

A letter requesting the removal of 17 eye cases to Bowen Road Hospital was submitted. Other suggestions were brought forward, such as repairs to the camp, etc.

30 April 1943

It is rumoured that Tunisia has fallen to the British and if this is correct, it's about time.

During our recreation period this afternoon, we saw quite a number of Japanese nurses going to and from Kowloon Hospital and La Salle

College. The latter being used by the Japanese as a hospital. I can see Kowloon Hospital from the hut where I sleep and it brings memories back for me, when I used to visit my dear wife and family who were admitted there on occasions for illnesses during our stay in Hong Kong.

Pte Pederson of the HKVDC kindly gave me an egg which I appreciated very much indeed. His fiancé sends him a parcel every week when the Japanese allow her to do so. He is of Danish nationality, although he has practically lived in China all his life and held quite a responsible position in a well-known import and export firm based in Hong Kong. I like him very much and he is not like some of the civilians, whom I have known and have come in contact with prior to the outbreak of hostilities.

1 May 1943

We have all noticed that for the past three weeks the Japanese have been interested in cleaning up all of the cemeteries which contain the bodies of British and Indian people, including soldiers. The men in the working parties have been supplied with the necessary tools to clear the long grass and other undergrowth surrounding the graves. This sudden change came after working upon wharves, air fields, or removing rubble from devastated buildings caused by the recent bombings by the US Army Air Force, upon the installations manned by the Japanese defences. The Red Cross representatives on their recent inspection might have pointed out this cleaning up of graves, which were in a dreadful condition.

According to information just received this morning, a certain amount of mail has been delivered to Japanese headquarters situated below the camp and I was hoping that I might get a letter from my dear wife and family, but as it turned out, I had no such luck.

2 May 1943

The following is an extract from our magazine, *Viewpoint*, which has been introduced in the camp periodically and is censored by the Japanese before circulation. A question in the magazine that was put to all officers and ORs who wished to take part stated as follows:

What course the War in Europe will take, is a question of special interest to all of us at the present time. In order to help us answer, we have

asked representatives of the Army, Navy, RAF and members of the
HKVDC Units, stating their rank and to give their opinions. It is realised
that they will be handicapped by the fact that information is limited
and that lack of space will prevent them from giving their reasons
comprehensively. In spite of this, it is believed that their views will be
of considerable interest to the rest of the camp. All forecasts were to be
written before April 1943.

Some of the responses were as follows:

Major General C. M. Maltby MC GOC
Gives no opinion as to when the European situation will collapse.

L/Cpl Sawyer RAVC
The same opinion as Major General Maltby.

Lieut Col Cardogan-Rawlinson 5th/7th Rajputs
Does not form an opinion.

Capt Belton York and Lancashire Regiment
Does not form an opinion.

Lieut Pike RA
States, October may well see the first appeals for an armistice and all
resistance to the allies concluded by Xmas 1943.

Maj Mills RA
This officer has suggested the following timetable:
End of April 1943
Liquidation of the North African Campaign with the Germans
commandeering the Italian Navy in a suicidal attempt to cover the
evacuation of Rommel's forces from Tunis and Bizerta.
Early May
Turkey declares war and marches into Bulgaria. British forces land on
western shores of the Black Sea. Russians capture Smolensk.
Late May
Turks capture Ploesti oil fields and Romania capitulates. Germans
withdraw from Greece and Yugoslavia and British land in Sardinia.
Early June
Italy capitulates. British and Turks attack Livew. Russians capture Minsk.
July
Serious disturbances in Czech-Slovakia, Hungary, France. Japan declares
war on Russia.
August
Russians enter into East Prussia. Britain and Turkey enter Germany.
British bombing of Germany increasing in intensity. Parachute landings
in Berlin.

September
Germany revolts and Army asks for peace. British, Russians and Turks enter Berlin simultaneously. Peace in Europe.

Brig Peffers
Forms no opinion.

As regards my personal opinion, it's always been, wait and see.

5 May 1943

Received 2nd injection for dysentery and cholera. These were fairly large doses and therefore I may have some after-effects.

We have five dogs in the camp and they are fairly fit considering the very small diet they get. Their names and owners are as follows:

Sheila	Has travelled quite a lot around Gun Club Hill Barracks where she was well known in the officers' mess there. She is about 12 years old. Owned by Lieut Col Penfold RA.
Geney	A dog that loves to play and very amusing to watch playing with a ball. She is a thoroughbred bullterrier. The owner, Lieut Col White, looks after her as if it was his own child and even sleeps on his bed.
Judy	Is the famous 'ratter' of the camp, to which she holds 200 rats and mice to her name since we have been here. She hates the sight of the Japanese and her owner, Capt Flood of 1st Middlesex Regiment, has to keep her constantly on a lead.
Bosun	This is a pure bred 'mongrel' that was brought to the camp as a puppy by Mne Handsley[98] from Hong Kong Island.

7 May 1943

This morning, myself and two other ranks went outside the camp to water the graves of the Indian soldiers buried in their cemetery. I managed to take note of the following names buried there that were in my regiment. I had to be very careful when recording these names because the Japanese sentries are not very keen on us seeing those who had died, whether Indian or British.[99]

During the time I was recording the above names and watering the graves, I took the opportunity of approaching the interpreters to establish the true situation regarding letters for the prisoners of war in the camp. He told me that there were no more letters remaining in Japanese headquarters. I relayed this information to the prisoners, which was very disheartening for everyone; however, whether one can believe these bastards is questionable. Anyway, I still live in hope of getting news of my dear wife and family and it is now well over 16 months since I have heard from them.

Conference Notes of 5 May 1943

The following points were raised at the conference with the Camp Commandant:-

1. The question of sending cables to relatives through the International Red Cross is still under discussion.
2. The Camp Commandant states that internees at Shanghai were receiving more financial assistance than the internees at Stanley Camp on Hong Kong Island. Each internee of the latter place is said to be in receipt of an average of 25 yen per month, this amount depending on monies received from the International Red Cross.
3. The Camp Commandant is to arrange shortly for the transfer of Father Green from Shamshuipo to Argyle St.
4. Bed mats are to be issued in a day or two.
5. There is still a delay in transferring prisoners with eye problems to Bowen Road Hospital. The Camp Commandant said he would make representation to the medical authorities for their need to be transferred. It was suggested that if removal of eye cases were delayed much longer, the specialist at Bowen Road Hospital, Maj Fraser,[100] should be permitted to come here to advise and administer treatment.

8 May 1943

I took an hour's recreation outside the camp this afternoon and found Lieut Col Penfold's dog, Sheila, who went missing from the camp for some time. The condition of the dog was not good and we wonder how she survived; however, she recognised Penfold immediately, which seemed to make her feel a lot better.

14 May 1943

I am 42 today and am wondering if I will be here on my next birthday. Two of my men, both in the Royal Scots, who had enlisted together and were occupying beds side by side, suddenly found themselves charged with fighting of extreme intensity and although the fight was initially entertaining, it was soon apparent that this particular contest was beyond a laughing matter. I finally separated them, grabbing them both by the scruff of the neck and asked one of them what the fight was about. I received a bewildering answer from him, 'I just didnae like the look of the bastard.' This incident proved again that some of the men were getting on each other's nerves, which I will have to curtail at the first sign of aggravation.

It is rumoured that the prisoners in Shamshuipo Camp are expecting to receive an issue of Red Cross parcels, this will be their second. We have received one only and that was six months ago. We can only hope that we will receive another issue as well.

Blackout precautions is taking place throughout Hong Kong Island and Kowloon. I think the Japanese are expecting night raids by the American Air Force.

17 May 1943

On Easter Sunday, I attended Holy Communion at 8.00 a.m., which is one hour before the Japanese count of all prisoners. The GOC and most of the other officers attended the service.

The weather is still very humid, but far better than the great amounts of rain we have been experiencing. The rain has been clogging up the drains around the camp which we are forever cleaning to avoid blockages.

A Japanese sentry approached me today and told me that the Germans were successful in the North African Campaign and that Japan had invaded Australia. I did not tell him that his comments were ludicrous.

There was another blackout tonight, which lasted for about four hours. During this blackout, there was quite a lot of punching, rifle butting and face slapping from the Japanese sentries, who appeared to be quite edgy during this period. It was noticed that the sentries had been doubled and that machine guns situated at the corners of the camp had been increased. The Japanese sentries continued on their violent rampage throughout the huts inflicting the same type of treatment. These vicious blows by the sentries were so severe that one of the officers suffered a badly cut mouth with the loss of several teeth. Gnr Elsworth and L/Bdr Roche[101] were badly beaten and so was I for intervening. I received heavy blows to the arms, shoulder and back from a rifle causing enormous lumps and bruising. Major General Maltby obtained full information of these incidents and will lodge a protest to the Camp Commandant in the morning.

The protests against the above incidents were lodged by the GOC to the Camp Commandant this morning. From what I hear, he objected strongly to the unnecessary treatment of officers and men by the Japanese guards and we were all glad that the GOC was very firm about this.

After 16 months of prison life, there was scarcely an ounce of fat on anybody. Ribs and hipbones were clearly visible and arms and legs were coming to resemble brittle sticks. The faces in every man in the camp had become haggard, eyes had become sunken, cheekbones were prominent and mouths were losing their firmness and beginning to turn down at the corners.

Another blackout tonight, this being the fourth night in a row. One can see from the camp, night convoys of Japanese lorries proceeding along Customs Pass Road with the headlights of all vehicles on. The Japanese are probably moving their troops and supplies to another location in an effort to avoid being bombed.

23 May 1943

This morning, the prisoners in the camp had inoculations for dysentery and cholera, the second time in about ten days.

We had some very good news this morning. Maj Robinson[102] informed us that Red Cross parcels could be expected shortly. Apparently this news came out of the conference this afternoon between the GOC and the Camp Commandant. In the meantime, the Japanese sent in 40 sacks of Atta flour, which is an Indian commodity to boost our diet.

I heard that the incident between the Japanese sentries and our officers and other ranks on 17 May was dealt with today and a full apology was received from the Camp Commandant.

Tonight, I feel rather off colour, which no doubt is due to today's inoculations.

The Japanese have stated that they will try and get permission to allow us to send cables to our families and relations wherever they may be. Naturally we would be delighted if this were possible.

26 May 1943

According to the Japanese newspaper, there was a large-scale landing of American troops on Attu Island in the Aleutians, which shows that the offensive in the Pacific is now well under way. We also hear that we were victorious in the North African Campaign.

The camp was suddenly inspected today by a high-ranking Japanese officer and it was noticed that he made no attempt to shake hands with the GOC on arrival or when leaving.

2 June 1943

The *Hong Kong News* shows us that the Japanese have admitted to the loss of Attu Island in the Aleutians and this is good news.

Pte Gardner of the HKVDC was operated on this afternoon for appendicitis; the operating instruments as usual were the sterilised razor blade and a pair of scissors. I am pleased to say that the operation was successful under primitive conditions.

I submitted a cable to my dear wife and children in accordance with Japanese instructions. Whether it will ever leave here is anyone's guess. My cable was worded as follows:

MY DARLING WIFE AND CHILDREN. I AM QUITE FIT AND WELL.
NO NEWS YET, PLEASE REPLY.
GOD BLESS YOU
LOVE CHARLES

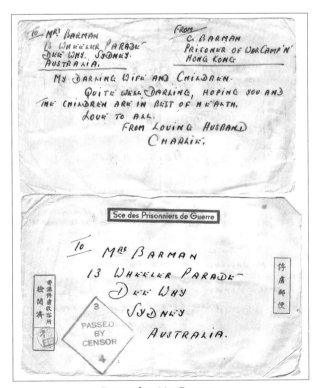

Postcard to Mrs Barman

8 June 1943

It has been 18 months now since hostilities broke out in Hong Kong. The Camp Commandant informed the GOC that Red Cross parcels were expected tomorrow, but did not mention the nature of these supplies. Letters were received today from England for L/Cpl Hobbs and Pte Hastings.[103]

Quite a lot of excitement was caused this afternoon when the following Red Cross supplies arrived in the camp:

1. Atta flour   50 sacks
2. Sugar   19 sacks (approx 2 1/2 lb. per man)
3. Meat and Veg.   980 tins
4. Meat 8 oz.   1296 tins
5. Dried pears   450 lb.
6. Cocoa   111 lb.
7. Tea   1000 lb.
8. Red Cross parcels   135 (109 complete and 26 incomplete)

11 June 1943

Conference Notes

1. The Camp Commandant was unable to attend the conference; therefore the following points were discussed with the interpreter.
2. Rations
    Red rice, rice polishings and barley are not available as part of the ration. The question of meat issue is still under consideration.
    The provision of Chinese dates was requested.
3. Lists of prisoners of war over 60 years of age who are sick be recommended for repatriation.
4. Issue of toilet paper was requested.
5. Requests for camp entertainment approved.
6. Permission for music practice in the morning not granted.
7. Request was made for issue of Red Cross clothing.
8. Negotiations for the provision of fresh meat is still not resolved
9. The GOC Major General Maltby pointed out that according to officers who had come from Shamshuipo Camp, all the personnel there were receiving Red Cross parcels containing meat and a double ration of rice. The GOC went on to express dissatisfaction with the scale of quantity of rations here in Argyle St. Unless there was an

improvement, the health of the camp would deteriorate rapidly. This question had been raised some time ago, but there was no improvement, in fact it was worse than ever and Col Tokunaga knew very well of the differing scales between Shamshuipo and Argyle St Camps. Col Tokunaga repeated that he did not know about the differing scales, but would personally go to Shamshuipo to satisfy himself regarding the extra items issued there.

10. Col Tokunaga was then taken to the kitchen and shown our evening meal. He was given a copy of the diet sheets for the last fortnight. If the situation does not improve, the GOC will request another interview with the Camp Commandant.

11. Cables
Only urgent cables are to be sent by the Japanese authorities. The most urgent as decided by the Japanese are to be handed in as soon as possible. Cables for the Philippines will be sent, as steps have already been taken by the Japanese to enquire after families of prisoners who may be there.

12. All personnel who have not received any letters or other communications from their families or relatives would hand in their names immediately. This I have done right away.

Miscellaneous

The following items were submitted:-

(a) Lime for latrine buckets. A new isolated latrine area to be erected for serious dysentery cases.

(b) A supply of creosote for the destruction of bugs.

(c) A supply of timber required for the making of wooden clogs.

As American air attacks appear to be increasing around Hong Kong, the Japanese have ordered that during blackouts, no smoking or lighting of matches are permitted. Another death this afternoon from beriberi: CSM Gales of the RE's. Pte McDougall of the Royal Scots suddenly collapsed and was taken to hospital. I think he is suffering from malaria.

L/Bdr Roche and Pte Haughey[104] were charged with insolence to Maj Parsons of the RE's and received a warning from Lieut Col White of the Royal Scots that they would be severely dealt with if this occurred again.

A certain amount of Red Cross parcels were issued, but due to the fact that there were insufficient parcels for one each, the contents were pooled and equal proportions was issued to each hut. I have detailed six men to stand by in readiness for distribution.

I sent my usual monthly letter today to my dear wife and children, mentioning the cable that I have sent to them and wondering if they have received it.

Reference was made about the British Empire in today's Hong Kong newspaper, stating a figure of 514,993 service personnel have been killed, wounded, missing or are POWs. These included service people from Britain, India, Canada, Australia, New Zealand, South Africa and other colonies.

Batmen's Daily Routine

7.00 a.m.	Rise and collect hot water for tea.
7.15 a.m.	Clean officers' footwear.
7.30 a.m.	Sweep and clean own bed space.
7.35 a.m.	Clean drains around batmen's and officers' huts and drains surrounding whole camp.
8.00 a.m.	Proceed to officers' hut to make beds, sweep floors and wash utensils.
9.00 a.m.	Parade for Japanese count.
9.15 a.m.	Draw food from the cookhouse in containers for the officers.
9.45 a.m.	Wash dishes and utensils of officers.
10.00 a.m.	Further sweeping of officers' huts and camp area. Other fatigues as detailed by me.
11.00 a.m.	Sullage fatigues and washing officers' clothes.
11.30 a.m.	Supply wood ready for cutting to be used in the cookhouse.
1.00 p.m.	Collect food from the cookhouse for officers.
1.15 p.m.	Collect own food from the cookhouse.
1.30 p.m.	Washing dishes and utensils of the officers.
2.00 p.m.	Grass cutting around camp, rice washing or cleaning and chicken farm fatigues.
3.00 p.m.	Washing clothes if not on other fatigues.
4.15 p.m.	Collect your own daily issue of yeast.
4.20 p.m.	Take a shower.
5.00 p.m.	Parade for Japanese count.
5.15 p.m.	Collect food in containers for officers.
5.30 p.m.	Consume own food.
5.45 p.m.	Washing dishes and utensils of the officers.
6.00 p.m.	Make your own bed.
7.15 p.m.	Collect boiling water for making tea.
8.00 p.m.	If one can hear the US bombers, it will probably result in a blackout, which means you may as well go to bed. However, before everybody does, I give out the orders for the following day's duties.

12 June 1943

The Japanese gave orders yesterday that the whole camp was to be grouped into parties of ten, commanded by a group commander.[105] This commander would be held responsible for discipline and any escape of prisoners under his charge. Why this system has suddenly been adopted we don't know, but it might mean that the Japanese are expecting trouble in the camp, which may be due to the present state of food, and it has been very poor indeed. All we have been getting for some time is rice and 6 oz. of bread. There have been practically no vegetables at all.

14 June 1943

The blackout is still in force as it has been for the last five nights; we are also getting lovely moonlight nights, which are ideal for air raids. The Japanese sentries appear to be very jittery which tends to put them in a bad mood resulting in bashings.

At present, I have two large blisters on my left arm, which look fairly angry. I have had them dressed and during the dressing, Capt Warrack asked me how long I have had them, and I replied, 'Two or three days.' He asked me to show him my tongue, which I did and he said it looks fairly OK, although I was not satisfied. So later on, I saw the medical orderly Pte Loncraine[106] and he thought it was a touch of pellagra, which is an awful disease to have and for which nothing can be done on our present diet and limited medical supplies.

21 June 1943

L/Cpl Fowler[107] and I played a friendly game of bridge against Lieut Col White and Maj Browning, in which we won by 1,500 points, but later we played against Maj Perry and Capt Glasgow and we lost by 500 points.

The numerous sores I have over my body and legs are due to diet deficiencies, but at the moment they are not at the ulcer stage like some of the men in the camp.

At present I am enjoying a piece of bread that is most satisfying, however the rice we are getting now have quite a number of maggots and a number of the fellows cannot turn a blind eye and therefore cannot eat them, so they pass their rice on to me which I do eat and I do not dislike them because they have a nutty flavour.

I hear some of the men sometimes referring to me saying, 'Give that maggot-infested rice to the old warhorse, he will make short work of it.'

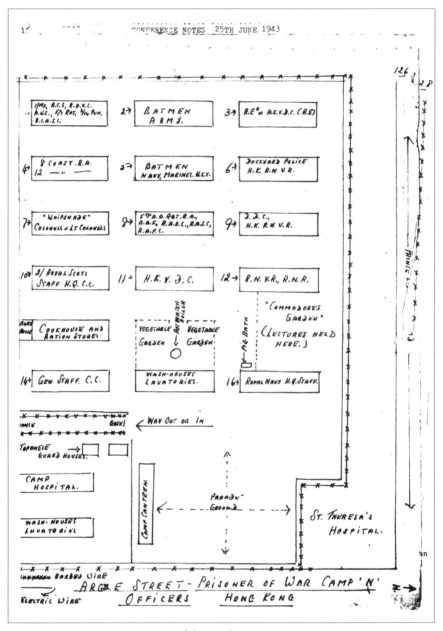

Layout of the Argyle Street Camp

26 June 1943

This morning, we all noticed about fifty Japanese new soldiers dressed in ragged and ill-fitting clothes outside the guardroom near the entrance to the camp. We ourselves must have looked a forlorn mob, with our clothes in shreds, our straw hats almost disintegrated and some with old boots flapping on their feet. These newly arrived Japanese soldiers were full of jibes and taunts when they saw us and like 'cocks of the roost', they acted as if they were veterans. We soon got used to it and knew how to deal with them, for they were the greenest, rawest rookies we had seen. All Japanese privates wore pointed stars on the collars of their tunic depicting their length of service. They were some one-star privates, indicating that the recruits had completed six months' service. There were of course the odd two and three-star privates who assumed command in the absence of an NCO. When a recruit has completed his first 6-month service he was entitled to one star, but this group had scarcely a star amongst them. We would stare at them hard, indicating to them that if there were no stars on the collar of their tunics, we would say 'baby soldier'. We would at the same time illustrate our point by gently rocking the arms in a cradling motion. These antics never failed and there were howls of rage followed by a few hectic minutes of everybody being pushed and slapped around. These baby soldiers, as we called them, were most deflated. We would watch them marching through the gates in their shoddy uniforms, cheap and ill-fitting, their rifles being carried at all angles, with some on one shoulder and some on the other shoulder. Their cloth-looking toupees were bouncing on the back of their necks and they were untidy and slovenly, small in stature which somehow made their goose-stepping comical and pathetic, like a lot of jerking puppets. Someone said, 'Just look at those poor little bastards, they look as if they have been doped.' However, in each face was a blind fanatical obsession to fight and kill and their slit eyes were filled with hate against us.

27 June 1943

We have received news that the Commandant Col Tokunaga is inspecting the whole camp tomorrow, which is very unusual because he has been avoiding inspections and has only attended the morning and evening counts of prisoners. It may have been a pre-inspection prior to the attendance of a much senior Japanese officer, or the GOC has requested an interview with him over the present food problem.

The present rainy weather we are getting is very depressing and we are confined to our huts. As a result, some of the men are getting on each other's nerves, although I must say that after fourteen months in this place, the men have taken it very calmly. When I hear a certain amount of petty bickering, I soon step in and prevent further confrontation.

Today's orders for the officers have called their attention to King's Regulations that the wearing of beards will not be permitted forthwith. Some two dozen officers' faces will emerge from behind huge masses of hair and we shall be able to recognise them as long lost friends.

28 June 1943

This morning, I had a confrontation with the most hated Japanese interpreter, Lieut Hideo Wada ('rat face'), who became very hostile towards me because one man in my group was late on parade for the morning count of prisoners. These counts are held at 9.00 a.m. and 5.00 p.m. daily. With an aggressive manner he gave me a nasty bash across the face with his sword scabbard and said to me, 'If this happens again, you will get further punishment.' I told him to piss off, resulting in me receiving a heavy blow across my back with his sword scabbard. Sandy Sutherland, my number one in the front rank and in hearing distance said, 'Charles, take it easy or you will receive some hours in the "box".' I have mentioned this box before but not in detail.

It was a wooden framed construction, about four square yards and about three feet high with two feet of it buried in the ground with the roof and walls blocked out to prevent any light entering the area. When in use the prisoner would drop to the floor and when the door was closed on the roof, one was in complete pitch darkness. The floor was mud and the smell inside was hard to accept, as it was not only the body odour of prisoners but also the urine that had been drained onto the floor. The stench of all this was unbearable. There was also a certain amount of excreta in the dark interior, and as for cockroaches, the place was alive with them and one could feel them crawling all over you. I had been interned in this box before and it was a most unpleasant experience.

The other Japanese military interpreters were not as aggressive as 'rat face', although the Japanese Sgt Maj could also be very nasty. His name escapes me, but we all knew him as 'bollock chops'. The other two interpreters were Lieut Tanaka whom we called 'deadly nightshade' and the other interpreter's name escapes me.

The Japanese ration officer suddenly came into the camp this evening and told the Brigadier and us that the following two items of food would be reduced: rice to be reduced from 440 grams to 384, and flour to be reduced from 120 grams to 104.

The food situation must be getting bad and according to what we hear, we shall all be lucky in the near future if we get 100 grams of rice a day, let alone any flour. I noted that the GOC Major General Maltby had quite a long and sometimes heated discussion with the Camp Commandant, Col Tokunaga. As a result, we are unable to obtain rice yet.

30 June 1943

Due to some irregularity in the camp office today, Capt Robertson was ordered out of the office and relieved of his job there by the GOC. I have yet to find out the reason for this. Fistfights amongst the officers in the camp are getting quite regular now. There were two fights today and the combatants were as follows:

Lieut Col White	v.	Maj Browning
Capt Egal	v.	Lieut Palmer

The recent intake of Japanese recruits have now taken over the duties as camp guards from those who have been here since we moved into this camp. The old guard is now on parade awaiting instructions for transfer to other duties, which I presume, are on the Chinese frontier about eighty miles away. The new sentries have been feeling their feet already, and have accosted quite a few of us to test our metal.

Mail was received from England today, the letters being dated July 1942 for the following personnel:

Sgt Tupper	1 letter
L/Bdr Birkinshaw	1 letter
Pte Normandale	2 letters
Gnr York	2 letters
Gnr Hannington	1 letter
Gnr Webber	1 letter

I heard that three letters received at camp headquarters were dated October 1942, which means that another Red Cross boat must have arrived in the Colony. It has now been 18 months without mail for me, and I do hope that my wife and children are all well. It is very depressing for me when you cannot get any news of your loved ones and I constantly pray that we shall be together soon, although at times the end of this war seems so far away.

Just after midday, a gloom suddenly came over the camp when Lieut Haddock and Pte Prata[108] were taken out of the camp by the Japanese whom they suspected of being the recipients of news from the outside.[109]

We were all informed immediately when the two unfortunates were taken out of the camp. Col Newnham GSOI informed everyone to take the necessary precautions in case any of us were taken out for questioning, those precautions being:

(a) if we were asked whether there was a bulletin produced within the camp, our reply was to be, 'I know nothing.'

(b) If we were asked what became of the trap message, our reply was to be, 'I know nothing.'

It is feared that these poor chaps will be severely dealt with by the Japanese third degree methods, which are drastic. Pte Prata, whose wife and parents reside in Hong Kong, no doubt will suffer at the hands of the Japanese if he does not disclose the information they require, and if he does spill the beans, I don't think we can blame him. Prata is a Portuguese by nationality and became a Hong Kong Volunteer before hostilities. As regards Lieut Haddock, we are fairly sure he will not reveal any information, as he has no family ties in the colony as far as we know. Haddock is in the Royal Navy Reserve.

We are all now wondering what reprisals will be on in the camp if the case is proved that we have been receiving news of the outside world, etc., by the various pre-arranged methods and it will go bad for those who have assisted.

Doctor Selwyn-Clarke, who was originally the Chief Government Medical Advisor of the Colony before the war, was released by the Japanese with his assistant about a month after surrender for the purpose of assisting them in the health of the Hong Kong and the Mainland Japanese personnel. A few days ago, we heard that Selwyn-Clarke and his staff had been rounded up at the French Hospital for disclosing information of the present world situation to prisoner-of-war camps and other such places. We also believe he was caught in possession of a wireless set as well. I hear that he and his staff are now in Stanley prison in Hong Kong and will be lucky if they ever get out alive.[110]

It is now believed that the root of the trouble was caused over the Selwyn-Clarke affair and the Japanese have ordered that until further notice, no further parcels from wives or relatives will be allowed to be delivered to the internees at Stanley. It looks as if they were caught in the same way as we were here at Shamshuipo and Argyle St. We don't expect to see either Haddock or Prata again.

As we were caught using improvised instruments for communication purposes, everyone in the camp has accepted the warning to destroy all references to the camp by burying or burning, the latter being the safer decision. I have decided to continue to bury mine in two old biscuit tins which have been containing my diary in the earth under a latrine bucket in the isolated latrines used for dysentery cases. The Japanese sentries avoid the place because of their fear of disease, more so since the serious outbreak of suspected diphtheria. The Japanese sentries and staff can be seen wearing thick masks. I completed the burying of all information last night, well sealed in the tins.

2 July 1943

Lieut Haddock and Pte Prata are still out of the camp and the Japanese have instructed that the kits of these men are to be packed ready in case they are required. This evening, an incident happened involving the camp sullage party when moving rubbish for burying outside the camp. Apparently, a local Chinese was seen by a Japanese sentry talking to Spr Moore of the RE's and Pte Hale[111] of the Middlesex Regiment, whilst they were waiting on the road to enter camp after the completion of the sullage fatigue. Capt Davies, who was in charge of this party, was not on the scene at the time, as he was ensuring that the sullage pit was properly filled in.

The Chinese was brought to the Japanese guardroom and questioned and finally Capt Davis, Moore and Hale, were sent for and taken to the Japanese Headquarters for further questioning. They returned to the camp about an hour later and Pte Hale told me that they were all asked if the Chinese did speak and quite rightly they all said 'no', but according to the sentry, he still maintains that they did. Therefore, it remains to be seen whether they accept their word or the sentry's. The Japanese have been constantly checking all Chinese using the road in front of the camp. All of them have been thoroughly searched. It looks as if the Japanese are having a lot of trouble with the Chinese.

3 July 1943

Conference Notes 1 July 1943

As we feel that the Japanese are now realising that the war is going against them, and also with the successes of the Allies in Western Europe, we have put the following points for discussion with the Camp Commandant with the hope that they will endeavour to improve the rations.

Rations
(a) Negotiations are in progress to produce meat from the unoccupied Territories. If the negotiations are successful, it is hoped to provide a meat ration once a week.
(b) The need for fats was emphasised. The Camp Commandant stated that no further supplies of Ghee were available. It was not possible to increase rations of peanut oil or to provide milk for the whole camp.
(c) It was suggested that the fish ration should be increased.
(d) 2,800 eggs to be brought in through the canteen.
(e) It was suggested that a list of our urgent requirements should be given to a representative of the International Red Cross. The Camp Commandant agreed to discuss the matters with the Red Cross authorities. Meanwhile, a list of these urgent requirements is being prepared and will be handed to the Camp Commandant.

Huts
An effort to be made to provide repair materials for the huts as soon as possible.

Letters
The Camp Commandant stated that one mailbag of letters for Stanley, Shamshuipo and Argyle St camps had arrived last week and it was now at Stanley where the letters would be sorted. He stated that June postcards would be forthcoming shortly from Stanley. It was suggested that officers might be useful in helping to sort out the mail for prisoners of war.
The Camp Commandant noted the following points that require urgent action:
(a) The provision of heavy oil, flit and flit guns, brooms, baking tins and disinfectants.
(b) Removal of tins from the rubbish dump.

(c) Repair of showers recently installed since the non-use of the broken down monsoon drain.

(d) Improvement of lighting in the huts.

(e) Provision of additional wooden beds to replace those that are now falling apart.

4 July 1943

Our spirits were lifted today when all of a sudden we each received a Red Cross parcel, which contained fifteen items. We all reacted like a bunch of kids at a Christmas party. We were amazed to receive this shipment of foodstuffs. There was bully beef, jam, meat, vegetables, cocoa, dried fruit, sugar, cigarettes and clothing. This changed the whole picture and we now had reason to believe that we might survive our internment. The Camp Commandant decided that he and some of his guards should have their share of Red Cross parcels, even though they had sufficient food already.

I have written another letter to my wife and family. I am extremely anxious because it has been twenty months without any news. Private parcels were again delivered to the camp from wives and relatives residing in Hong Kong or Kowloon. The weather is now terribly hot and the months of July and August are the worst especially under these conditions.

We hear that the guerrillas have been giving the Japanese quite a bit of trouble lately and have blown up a bridge at Lowu, attacking Japanese guards at Sha Tau Kok and Tai Po. They have also attacked the installations at Lei Yu Mun. Quite a number of casualties were inflicted upon the Japanese during these raids and it is also nice to hear that our people have been operating with the guerrilla forces.

Lieut Col Cadogan-Rawlinson[112] said that in his opinion, the European situation would be over within six months. Well, I hope his statement becomes true.

8 July 1943

The bed bugs are appearing again as it is the season for them. This means a daily routine of debugging the beds with burning paper so as to avoid being bitten alive all night. They are like leaches, sucking the blood from one's body and causing annoying irritation with the lumps they leave. When one is killed, its body is full of blood with an awful smell following. They have an enormous number of legs and fangs and they breed in concealed joints of the wood. My ankles are covered with an irritating rash, which is getting on my nerves.

The officers in Argyle St Camp come from a multitude of pre-war professions and there are many odd characters. One officer in the RASC received a message from England that he had inherited a fortune of 89,000 pounds from a relative. However, when he heard that Singapore had fallen he turned his head to the wall, ate nothing and died of starvation, weighing less than four stone when he was buried.

It was 19 months ago today when the Japanese attacked Hong Kong.

9 July 1943

There has been quite a lot of aerial activity lately by the Japanese taking off from Kai Tak Aerodrome, obviously for exercises. Their planes appear to be in good shape, but I wonder how they perform in combat.

Lieut Haddock and Pte Prata are still out of the camp, but the Japanese sent in men to collect their clothing. I am afraid that they are undergoing some form of torture at the Japanese headquarters and I believe that if they live, they will eventually be moved to Stanley prison on the Island.

According to the Japanese newspaper this morning, the following areas have been renamed:

Current Name	New Name
Prince Edward Road	Kashima
Kowloon City	Motoku
Nathan Road	Katori

This morning, we had a real tasty change in the breakfast, thanks to the cooks. They produced for us a meal of fish and rice, and believe me, with the addition of a small portion of soya sauce it was delicious. The soya sauce came in a gallon jar, which I stole from a Japanese supply lorry a few weeks ago with the help of some of the men. As I passed the vehicle, the men distracted the Japanese, whereupon I confiscated the jar and immediately headed for the dysentery latrine area about 20 yards away and hid the jar behind one of the buckets. This was my usual hiding place for whatever I had the opportunity to steal from the supplies. I was nearly caught once when a sentry came up to the green canvas surrounding the latrine, but luckily I heard his guttural voice before he reached the screen. I had a cloth bag that contained about four pounds of rice, which I discarded into the latrine bucket. Fortunately, it did not contain any excreta. When the sentry disappeared, I retrieved the bag, which appeared to be no worse for wear.

We are hoping that the US forces have landed upon Rendova Island in the Solomon's group as the Japanese newspaper has stated that the Americans have attacked this place on 5 July. According to this information, we don't appear to be moving in the Pacific as quickly as we would like. We are hoping of course that the war in the Pacific is progressing much better than what we read in the Japanese newspaper.

The Camp Commandant called for five batmen this morning to remove a piano and carry it up three flights of stairs to his residence near the Japanese headquarters, but due to their physical condition they only just managed to complete the removal after a long struggle and upon their return to the hut, they just collapsed on their beds. There is no doubt that our physical condition is at a very low state and we cannot undertake any heavy work whatsoever. Goodness knows what some of us will be like if we ever get out of this place.[113]

<u>10 July 1943</u>

Last night I dreamt that I received eight letters from my wife and this morning. I heard that 200 letters had arrived at the Japanese headquarters, of which fifty were being delivered to the camp this evening. I do hope there is one for me.

The Japanese have once again made a raid upon the camp, ordering everyone out of the huts. They were looking for any material, which referred to the communications that had been uncovered in the camp, and any other such material that might have been maintained by POWs such as diaries. Any such material that may be found may be used against those prisoners that were removed from the camp and who no doubt are being tortured. At the first opportunity, I will have to unearth my diary to check its condition, although the tins are quite well sealed and I may have to rethink a hiding place.

Well, well, I have just received a letter, not from my dear wife but from her sister, Sybil at Colaba, India. However, I was very pleased to receive one anyway and she tells me that Peg and the family are well. The letter was dated 6 July 1942, just over a year to get here. I heard that some more letters are arriving tomorrow and I hope one is for me.

Col Newnham GS0I is still out of the camp and no doubt is going under severe punishment from the Japanese.

At noon today, I had to intervene to prevent a fistfight between Gnr Elsworth and Sgt Sutherland of the Royal Scots. I think Elsworth objected to the remark that Sutherland made towards him, which said that he had part-Negro blood. I said to Sutherland, 'You should have known better than throwing his colour at him.' Eventually they became quite friendly again and I think Sandy Sutherland realised that he had made a mistake.

I heard yesterday that Lieut Allanson of the 8th Coast Regiment RA[114] was one of the unfortunates to go down when the *Lisbon Maru* was sunk last year, he was an excellent officer. The following were very lucky to receive mail today: Pte Hale, Pte Francomb, Spr Price, L/Bdr Holland, L/Cpl Hobbs, Pte Woods, L/Cpl Pickles, L/Bdr Birkinshaw, Pte Jones, Gnr Cumming, Pte Smart, Pte Bradley, and L/Cpl Earnshaw.

Pte Hale received 5 letters.

12 July 1943

According to the *Hong Kong News*, the allies have invaded Italy at two points with the support of 2,500 planes. This is good news and lifts the morale of everyone.

L/Cpl Fowler of the Royal Scots and myself were knocked out of the bridge game. We both started off well but finished off rather badly.

The Japanese have called for a statement showing those not in possession of mess tins, blankets, water bottles, etc. Whether this means that a possible move from the camp to some other area such as Japan we shall just have to wait and see. I have a feeling that we may be moved suddenly from here.

The GOC Major General Maltby was interviewed by the Japanese press, followed by photographs being taken of him and the senior officers of the Japanese headquarters staff. No doubt this will be used for propaganda purposes.

16 July 1943

The following officers and batmen are leaving the camp tomorrow and are being temporarily isolated in the hospital compound before their expected departure to an unknown destination in about ten days.

Officers	Batmen
Major General Maltby MC	L/Cpl Earnshaw
Brig Peffers	AB Fairburn
Brig Wallis	Pte Smith
Brig McLeod	Pte Winkworth
Col Clifford	Pte Hastings
Col Simpson	Mne Rogers
Col Rose	Two Naval Batmen
Col Andrew-Levinge	
Col Kilpatrick	
Col Hopkins	
Commodore Collinson	

Their destination will probably be Formosa, or maybe even Japan. We will all be sorry to see the GOC and staff leave the camp. They have done everything they could to make things as pleasant as possible where we are concerned. The following letter signed by all batmen was forwarded to the GOC today showing their appreciation.

To
Major General C M Maltby MC
Prisoner of War Camp 'N'
Argyle St
Kowloon HONG KONG

16 July 1943

Sir,

A further turn of the wheel brings your departure from this camp and we, the batmen, desire to acquaint you of our deep appreciation and thanks for the interest you have shown in our welfare during our internment which interest has found tangible expression in spite of difficult circumstances.

Good luck to you, sir, to you and your staff and in happier times to which we confidently look forward and expect to be there to serve again.

Yours sincerely

C E Barman BQMS
4th Medium Battery HK/SRA

17 July 1943

I arranged for the removal of all baggage, etc., of the GOC and staff to the hospital compound this morning. I shook hands with the GOC and he thanked me personally for my cooperation and good work here and during the war. I also received the same remarks from Brigadiers' Wallis, McLeod and Peffers. Lieut Col Field of the 5th AA Regiment RA is now in charge of the camp. Lieut Col White of the Royal Scots has been removed to the hospital.

18 July 1943

Privates Chainey and Randle,[115] who left here for Bowen Road Hospital a few weeks ago, have now been returned to Shamshuipo Camp and it looks as if they will be kept there. I am still suffering from a severe throat infection and have been isolated for a few days now in a room close to the camp hospital, probably in case I may have diphtheria.

26 July 1943

I was removed from the isolation hut as I have now been cleared of suspected diphtheria. But I was admitted to the camp hospital as I am suffering from a diet deficiency disease, which appears to be beriberi.

28 July 1943

In a small room in the hospital, my bedmates are Lieut Pike, Lieut Stoker, Pte Cheeseborough and Pte Smart.[116] In the other room we have Wng Cmdr Bennett and Lieut Col Cadogan-Rawlinson. Our medical orderlies are Lieut Ferguson and Pte Robertson, both of the HKVDC. I have lost about forty pounds in weight since being a POW, which is not good.

I forgot to mention before that all the red buses of the Kowloon bus company have been converted into transport lorries by the Japanese. When I see them passing, I think of my dear wife and family and the times we have travelled on them. I also think of my daughters, Winfred and Pamela, who used to run to catch one of them to school in the mornings.

We have just heard that the GOC and his staff are expected to leave their place of isolation tomorrow. This may mean our removal of the

personnel in the temporary hospital to the hospital compound, which
will be much nicer than where we are now.

According to the *Hong Kong News* there has been a complete reshuffle
of the Italian cabinet and the resignation of Benito Mussolini, which is
good news. The allies appear to be doing very well in the attack upon
Sicily and in the very near future they may be on the mainland of Italy.

Our forces at 14.45 p.m. have once again raided the colony of Hong
Kong. The force consisted of six bombers and two fighters. They came
from the west and dropped bombs on the harbour and installations.

29 July 1943

What a lovely surprise this morning, I had a boiled egg and a glass of
milk, which I understand was a gift from a Chinese Hong Kong Volunteer,
Hon Lee, who receives a parcel of goods once a week from his relatives
residing in Hong Kong or Kowloon. Quite a number of Chinese
volunteers in the camp have also been able to obtain small quantities of
drugs which they share whenever possible amongst those in the hospital.

This afternoon, we saw the return of Capt Campbell from Bowen
Road Hospital and he is now in isolation with the GOC and staff, all of
whom have had their departure postponed for five days. From my
window, I can see the GOC and staff taking exercise in the compound.

30 July 1943

I have just spotted a Japanese interpreter passing with a bundle of letters
under his arm; I wonder if there will be one for me. About three quarters
of the camp have all received mail and in some cases, individuals have
received five to six letters. The departure of the GOC and staff has been
further delayed for another week, and I think the problem is to do with
the availability of a ship.

31 July 1943

It is a very hot day and beautiful weather for an air raid.

I feel very depressed today and these fits of depression are becoming
hard to fight off. One of the patients here with me is an officer in one of
the Indian Regiments and he informs me that he was in Mhow, India,

before arriving in Hong Kong. Mhow is of great sentimental interest to me as it was there that Peg and I were married and where three of our children — Winifred, Pamela and Richard — were born. Naturally, I asked him quite a lot about the place, more so because he was there years after me. He and his Regiment were stationed well down the 'Indore' Road, which is well past the area where Peg lived. I can still see the huge bungalow set well back in spacious grounds, which was situated on this road and where Peg and I rode our horses through the jungle nearby.

3 August 1943

Today I was discharged from hospital and returned to the camp.

A consignment of vitamin 'A' caramels were supplied to the camp by the Red Cross. We received our issue of four per man this afternoon with instructions only to eat one a day, but due to the very hot weather, I have eaten the whole of my issue.

The kits and belongings of the GOC and staff were thoroughly searched before their departure, which is scheduled for tomorrow morning at 7.30 a.m. We have no knowledge of their final destination, but presume it will be 'Formosa'.

4 August 1943

The GOC and staff left camp this morning at 7.30 a.m. in closed lorries. Practically the whole camp turned out to wish them the best of luck. The Camp Commandant turned up at the camp at 7 a.m. in full war kit to conduct the party to its destination. The following officers and batmen were in the party:

Major General Maltby	GOC	
Brig Peffers		
Brig Wallis		
Brig McLeod	CRA	
Brig Clifford		
Lieut Col Simpson		
Lieut Col Andrew-Levinge		
Col Ford		
2 Naval Officers		
Pte Winkworth	1st Middlesex Regiment]	
Pte Hartman	12 Company RASC]	Batmen
Two other Naval Batmen		

5 August 1943

According to the paper, we see that the Japanese have given the 'Burmese' their independence. Burma of course immediately declared war on Great Britain and America.

Maj Prasad 2/14 Punjabis was taken out of the camp this afternoon by the Japanese authorities for some special purpose. Probably as he is an Indian officer holding a King's Commission, they will try and coax him to turn over to the Indian National Army, which has been formed by the well-known Chandra Bose. Anyway, Prasad was returned later this evening, so they could not have been successful in their intentions. I believe they asked him various questions about Indian troops and he said they did endeavour to try and persuade him to turn over to them, but as he said, he did not play along with any of the questions they put toward him.

6 August 1943

Due to a shortage of rice and vegetables, we have had very little food today. There is also a shortage of fuel, which is a regular thing these days. The Camp Commandant stated the fuel was extremely difficult to transport from the New Territories as the lorries were being constantly ambushed by guerrilla forces that have been operating in that area for the last few months. This, of course, is good news for us as there may be a chance of being relieved by them one of these days, but this is only wishful thinking on my part.

10 August 1943

Due to an exceptionally heavy thunderstorm today, the lightning struck and fused the electric lights and upset the power used for electrifying the wire around the camp. Tropical storms are normally bad but this is the worst one I have experienced since I have been in the Far East.

According to the paper today, we see that the Russians have taken 'Orel' also. It was a German conference consisting of Generals, Admirals, and other noted politicians that was held at Hitler's headquarters.

16 August 1943

The Japanese authorities have allowed the Chinese and Japanese editions of newspapers into the camp.

The Camp Commandant returned today and told us that the GOC and staff arrived at their destination without incident. I am of the opinion that they went to Formosa as it is rumoured that they made the trip in quite a small vessel.

The paper tells us today that our forces raided Rome and will visit the Pope. Approximately fourteen senior Canadian officers arrived in camp today from Shamshuipo.

21 August 1943

Once again, we hear of Japanese supply lorries being ambushed by guerrillas operating in the New Territories. We heard machine gun fire during the night and it appeared to have come from the direction of Lion Rock, Kowloon, which lies practically due north from here and can be seen quite plainly from the camp. I wonder if there is any real activity between here and Canton.

25 August 1943

There were two air raids today, one at 9.30 a.m. and the other at 6.00 p.m. In the first raid, our force consisted of eight bombers and six fighter planes that dropped heavy bombs near the CBS building, near the Kowloon Railway workshops and Kowloon Docks. In the second raid, our force consisted of seven bombers and three fighter planes, which dropped bombs at Port Helter, Kai Tak Aerodrome and Lei Yu Mun. During the afternoon, one of our reconnaissance planes flew over the colony. On both of these air raids, Japanese AA fire appeared very poor and the sentries posted in and around the camp were in a state of extreme panic.

26 August 1943

We received five air raid warnings today and on four occasions, nothing happened, but on the fifth one our force of fourteen bombers with fighter escorts raided the colony and passed straight over the camp. Everone ducked during the bombing of the Kowloon Railway and the Kowloon Docks. As these targets are so near the camp for accurate bombing, I fancy there was an error on the part of the airmen. God forbid! We could have had a few bombs in the camp that would have been disastrous. The swish of the bombs dropping gave one the impression that they were going to drop on the camp. During the raid they also bombed Tai Koo Docks at Hong Kong and other installations. No one is allowed outside during air raids and if anyone is caught outside their hut they are liable to be shot by the sentries.

Lieut Burgess was caught once leaving his hut and he received a few face slaps from the guard commander. I must say this was a good day for us.

27 August 1943

We read in the newspaper of the German evacuation of Kharkov, which is good news.

Two air raid warnings today, the first at about 2.30 p.m., when we saw four Japanese planes, and the second at 4.20 p.m. But absolutely nothing appeared in the sky. We presumed our forces were raiding Canton or some other Japanese positions in the New Territories.

29 August 1943

An air raid warning at 3.00 p.m. and another at 6.00 p.m. Nothing happened on both occasions. We did see four Japanese zero planes but there was no aerial activity. We can only assume that the Americans were again raiding Canton or other Japanese defences.

31 August 1943

Broadcasting cables of thirty words were allotted to those men who had not received any mail since being a prisoner of war. As I was one of them, I managed to get a cable away to my darling wife and hope it would reach her. Apparently the Japanese will only allow five cables from the camp per month and as it was, I was fortunate enough to be one of those five. I am still looking for a letter from my dear wife but have yet to receive one.

We heard quite a number of planes above the camp this afternoon, but as they were flying so high that we could not distinguish whether they were Japanese or ours. No air raid siren was sounded so I should imagine that the planes must have been Japanese.

During the evening, certain officers returned from Bowen Road Hospital and stated that in the last big raid, they saw two of our bombers bomb two ships near Stonecutters Island setting fire to both of them.

1 September 1943

There has been quite a lot of Japanese aerial activity today.

I was walking past one of the huts when I smelt some form of cooking. I put my head in and came face to face with four Chinese volunteers, the first being Cpl Hon Lee, then Kunfoo, Ling Chang and finally Sun Yet Sun. I said to them, 'That smells good, what is it?' Their reply was, 'Boiled snails in salt water.' Hon Lee asked me to try one, whereby he broke the shell and out came the snail. It tasted real good and similar to one of the winkles caught and cooked on the beach at Whitstable, Kent, in England. They produced a small amount of cooked rice and placed four or five of these snails on the side of the dish. The snails tasted very good with the rice. The cooking was done upon a piece of coiled wire attached to a lead, which was plugged into an electric light globe socket with a circular lid of a biscuit tin being used as the cooking plate. I asked Lee where he got the snails from and he said from the vegetation at the rear of the latrines where we farm them. I told him that I would like to see them in the morning.

Next day we proceeded to the scrub area and woe betide, there were hundreds of snails feeding off the leaves of the vegetation. I asked him how long they lived and he said, 'As long as the vegetation lasts, which is about four or five months.' 'How about the sentries?' I said, and he replied, 'We use a whistle as a type of alarm. The sentries just accept us as working some form of garden and when the supply of snails finally disappears, we fall back on the nest of cockroaches in a covered hole about ten yards further on, which we cover after feeding the cockroaches with bits of rice daily.' When he lifted the circular metal lid covering the hole, there were hundreds of cockroaches moving around. 'Do you eat these?' I said, and he replied, 'Yes, when the snails fade out, would you like to have some tonight?' I hesitated for a moment and agreed. Lee said to me, 'You have to pluck the wings off first, then fry them in some form of vegetable oil which I am able to get. It is important to remove the wings otherwise the cockroach will stick in your throat.' That evening we prepared the cockroaches for frying on the biscuit tin lid and after removing the wings placed them in the pan with the vegetable oil and commenced to fry. At first glance, seeing them in the pan did not look very appetising, but they smelt good. Lee produced a small amount of rice and placed the cockroaches on the edge of a plate, which I was very reluctant to taste, but after mustering up some courage, I tasted the first one, which appeared very nice indeed and similar to fried meat. After completing the meal, I returned to my hut, but after a short while, I felt a bit uneasy in the stomach and slightly sick. This feeling wore off and in the morning I spoke to Lee and jokingly said that the cockroaches were quite nice but obviously the oil needs changing. Anyway, a couple of nights later, I had another feed of cockroaches and eventually took quite a liking for them. However, we eventually went back on the snails because the scrub area was overrunning with them.

We had quite a bit of excitement this evening when six heavy bombers with escorting fighters flew over the colony. Of course, the Japanese AA Batteries came into action immediately without obtaining any results. I think this flight was here to see what likely targets were in the harbour, or they might have been just returning from another Japanese target.

2 September 1943

Quite a number of US heavy bombers visited Hong Kong this morning, which took the Japanese by surprise. They arrived just a few minutes after the morning count of prisoners. The planes took cover in the low-lying clouds, but after a few minutes they appeared and circled overhead in the direction of Aberdeen and Stonecutters Island. Shortly after, we heard the explosions of bombs. The air raid alarm was heard, but by then the raid was over. The Japanese guards appeared enraged and rushed through the camp using their rifle butts on the prisoners.

At approximately 1.30 p.m., a force of fifteen bombers escorted by fighters raided the Lai Chi Kok oil dumps, etc., setting fire to four or five large petrol tanks. The blaze and heavy fumes from the tanks were enormous and, with the assistance of the wind, enveloped the whole of Shamshuipo and Stonecutters Island. The planes definitely hit the targets and, in my opinion, this fire will last for days. I also suspect it rather upset the Japanese oil supply.

3 September 1943

I see that we have made a landing in Italy according to the morning's newspaper. The paper also quotes that all buses and lorry services have been suspended in Hong Kong and Kowloon until further orders. This order was enforced and I suspect it was due to the disastrous raid of yesterday. The flames and heavy volumes of smoke are still pouring from Lai Chi Kok and it looks to me that it will take some time to die down. Rickshaws and tricycles are being used for the conveyance of the public in Hong Kong and Kowloon. We have noticed as well that they are using carts pulled by two ponies along Prince Edward Road.

It looks to me that everything is at a standstill in Hong Kong. According to one of the officers who recently arrived from Bowen Road Hospital, none of the trams are running and the Peak tramway is definitely not being used.

4 September 1943

The shrapnel wounds on my arms and legs appear to be surfacing once again and those on my right arm and left thigh will have to be treated. Capt Warrack of the RAMC is going to remove them by razor blade incision tomorrow morning as he did previously twelve months ago.

The batmen received 24 yen today from the International Red Cross, which was very welcome indeed. I bought the following out of this amount, which will help to keep me going: eggs, tinned beans, soya sauce, tinned sardines, cigarettes, tinned tomatoes, sugar cubes, tinned milk, and chocolate milk powder.

5 September 1943

Capt Warrack carried out the removal of the shrapnel today and it was very painful. Later in the day my temperature went up to 100f, which could have been a reaction to the removal of the shrapnel.

The Japanese provided an issue of whale meat and it tasted quite good. It looked like beef, but naturally it had a fishy taste.

12 September 1943

A typhoon struck the colony this morning. As a result, a good many huts were flooded out in the camp. The batmen's hut was the worst and was washed right out altogether. All you could hear during the night was bad language and the moving of beds to dodge leaks from the roof. All my clothes and bedding got drenched and as that was all I had, it meant no sleep for me. Goodness knows how I am going to get them dried. The Camp Commandant inspected all huts and allowed some of the batmen to be accommodated in other buildings, but as for the repair of them, he never mentioned a word.

We later found that some of the barbed wire from the perimeter fence had been dislodged and was strewn right across the parade ground. We were confined to our huts and warned by the Japanese that anyone would be shot if they left the hut. Later, a party of men were detailed by the Japanese to clear the mess up and repair the fence.

14 September 1943

Our air forces raided the colony at 4.15 p.m. the planes coming in from a direction of Customs Pass. There were in this force twelve 'P38 Lightnings' and their objective according to what we could see was Kowloon Bay and Kai Tak Aerodrome. We were unable to see what damage was done during these raids as we were confined to our huts for one thing and also that the surrounding hills cut off our view at times. Some POW's were able to get a better view of these raids as their huts were situated in a better position. There was no newspaper today, I wonder why.

15 September 1943

Well, this is what we like to read. The newspaper says that Italy capitulated today and that part of her fleet has been turned over to us. This is good news.

The US Army Air Force raided Hong Kong and Kowloon again at 4.15 p.m.; the force consisted of about 20 bombers coming in from the direction of Customs Pass. Their objective, from what we could see, was Kai Tak Aerodrome and ships in Kowloon Bay, but we were unable to see what damage had been done as we were immediately confined to our huts.

21 September 1943

A sudden search of the whole camp was immediately made after the parade by the Japanese authorities this morning. What took us by surprise was when a troop of Japanese soldiers suddenly surrounded us on the parade ground. We thought at first that some of us were going to be shot. We could not understand what this was all about, but as soon as the Japanese gendarmerie arrived, we knew they were after something in the wireless line, which they finally located in the naval officer's hut which was number 14. This search lasted from 9.00 a.m. to 12.45 p.m. and, believe me, we all felt rather weak without anything in our stomachs. As a reaction of this search, the Japanese came back in the evening when the following officers were arrested from the hut where the wireless was located: Lieut Cmdr Young, Lieut Cmdr Chaddick, Pay Cmdr Burton, Cmdr Craven, and Lieut Dixon.

22 September 1943

Lieut Col Levett and Lieut Col Field were taken out of camp today by the Japanese. We think it had something to do with the wireless affair.

28 September 1943

We read of the German evacuation from Smolensk in the newspaper today. Also according to the newspaper, Goebels stated in a speech that Germany was now having a period in which she had to fight for her life. Naples, we also read, is about to fall.

4 October 1943

We read in today's newspaper that Naples has fallen to our troops. What good news.

An unknown plane flew over the camp today and let out a smoke sign in the form of a 'V' which was meant to encourage us.

We had an air raid warning at midday, but nothing happened.

10 October 1943

We heard of the shelling of Wake Island by the American forces, obviously by their Navy.

All the batmen were detailed today to carry out repair work at Kai Tak Aerodrome, probably to fill in bomb craters. We were transported by lorry and received the usual rough treatment by the Japanese guards. No sooner had we commenced work when a force of American bombers arrived circling over the aerodrome, but no bombs were dropped as they must have recognised the groups of prisoners working on the strip and they quickly departed the scene.

13 October 1943

A most unusual event occurred this morning. A Japanese naval officer visited the camp. For what reason we are not sure, but it may be something to do with the sending of another boatload of prisoners to Japan. I have another medical complaint, which is known as 'Avitaminosis', which makes me feel very depressed and quite ill after eating.

There were two air raid warnings today, one at 2.00 p.m. and the other at 4.15 p.m. On both occasions nothing happened.

This morning we received a TAB inoculation.

16 October 1943

About a year ago, approximately 2,000 yen of Red Cross writing pads, ink, pens and envelopes were sent into the camp and charged for by the Japanese authorities. For some reason, they refunded the amount of 2,000 yen.

I have just been told that I am being sent to Bowen Road Hospital due to this recent complaint. This move is not yet definite so I will just have to wait and see, but my concern is the safety of my diary.

The Russian news is extremely good today and the German situation on the Russian front is described as critical according to a 'Stockholm' message. The news appears good for us in all theatres of war.

There is very little mail these days and I hear now that the Japanese have started the idea of 'smoking' all letters and postcards to see if there is any traces of 'blue ink'.

19 October 1943

Received an injection for cholera this morning.

There appears to be fighting between Chungking and Japanese troops on the Burma/Yunnan border according to this morning's newspaper.

We read of sweeping advances in Italy. The following officers returned to camp today: Lieut Col Field, Lieut Col Levett, Capt Woodward, Lieut Cmdr Burton, and Lieut Cmdr Chaddick.

The officers looked just like coolies and very down in health, but cheerful. They were instructed by the Camp Commandant not to disclose any information of their confinement, or any trials or tribulations they went through during their period of absence from the camp. So you can guess that they must have experienced some terrible punishment and lived under some awful conditions, which were not fit for the remainder of us to know about; otherwise, the Japanese would not have put them under oath as they did. However, all these things and other atrocities will eventually become known and those responsible punished.

22 October 1943

The Camp Commandant ordered that the five dogs in the camp were to be accommodated outside the camp in the chicken farm. This, I think, is caused by the new Japanese sergeant (Harada) who recently returned (nicknamed 'Napoleon'). He no doubt objected to the animals being here and may of course be in his orders that no dogs are allowed in prisoner-of-war camps, and this he reported to the Camp Commandant. As usual, Harada struts about brandishing his sword.

The names of the dogs and owners are as follows:

Geney	Lieut Col White
Sheila	Lieut Col Penfold
Judy	Capt Flood
Chow	Maj Paterson (who was GOC of dogs before he left camp)
Bosun	Mne Handsley

We read of the 'Moscow' conference in today's newspaper.

Three or four officers were detailed to collect eggs from the chicken farm and take them to the hospital for the very sick men there.

Sandy Sutherland of the Royal Scots and I were heading for the parade ground when in the distance we spotted an old face, this being the Japanese NCO whom we nicknamed 'strawberry balls'. He was in charge of the guard room but has been away on duty somewhere else for some months. Sandy said to me, 'Ease up, Charlie, and go along if he expects you to salute; otherwise it will mean another bashing for you and probably for me as well.' As we met him he made guttural sounds towards me with awful hatred in his face, but as I turned to face him, for some reason he turned away and just walked on. Sandy said to me, 'Thank Christ, I thought you were going to blow up Charles. He seemed very edgy with that sword of his.' This was the first time I had seen him with a sword, so he must have been promoted.

26 October 1943

Quite a lot of Japanese activities commenced around the camp in the early hours of this morning. The Japanese authorities informed us that they were holding exercises, I wonder! Everyone was confined to their huts during the so-called exercises.

We were also told by the Japanese that the flour received today would be the last issue to the camp. It means after the current supply has gone, there will be no more bread. This morning's newspaper informs us of the heavy raid our forces carried out on Vienna. This, I think, is the first raid that they have had and are getting nearer to the heart of Germany.

It has been noticed by all here that since the supposed exercises, the Japanese guards have been doubled.

28 October 1943

We read in the newspaper of Japanese operations in Yunnan province and in the area of the 'Salween River' against Chungking forces. I wonder if this is the so-much-talked-of Burma operations by Lord Mountbatten.

One or two of the batmen have started to keep mantises for pets and very interesting pets they are. These mantises are a very large grasshopper type, which are very common in the East.

1 November 1943

My darling daughter Winnie's birthday today, 'God bless her'. I can remember the birthday months of my remaining children but I am not sure of the dates. I have even forgotten my dear wife's birthday as well. My memory is bad these days.

The Japanese have stopped all public meetings in the camp and no more than five persons are allowed to be grouped together, either inside or outside the huts, with the exception of church services only.

Peanuts are 11 yen per lb. shelled and 6 yen per lb. unshelled. What a price to pay as compared with the price in peacetime. The conditions amongst the Chinese outside must be terrible, especially amongst the coolie class whom we see pass the camp daily. I cannot see Hong Kong coming back to its normal way of life for years to come.

We had an air raid warning at 11.00 a.m. but nothing happened, although about an hour later, Japanese bombers escorted by fighters flew over the colony. Some of the fighters gave a few aerial acrobatics on the way, which no doubt was for the eyes of the Chinese.

How extremely happy I am, as I have just received my first letter from my darling wife, God bless her. Her letter was dated 10 July 1942, which took over twelve months to arrive. During the reading of this loving letter, tears came into my eyes which caused me to leave the hut for a while. I was so pleased to hear that the family had been evacuated from Sydney to the country and that they were all away from the horrors of war. I do hope that she has received some of my letters by now which I addressed to 'C/- Mr Bayliss' at 13 Wheeler Pde Dee Why, Sydney. I can imagine how dear Peg was when she heard of my safety and also how upset she must have been during the months of anxious waiting for news of me.

I thank God for my safety from the 'battle of Hong Kong' and with his assistance, I hope to be safely brought out of this miserable existence soon and be happily re-united with my family.

3 November 1943

It is rumoured that Rome is in our hands. If this is correct, it is great news.

Lieut Taylor of 5th AA Regiment RA was removed suddenly to hospital last night with severe stomach pains and it was found that an immediate operation was necessary. Good luck to our Surgeon Cmdr Cleeve and his assistants in this operation, which I hope will be as successful as your previous ones under such awful conditions and the poorest of surgical instruments.

5 November 1943

There is very little news from the Japanese newspaper. A large force of planes flew over the colony this morning, but there was no action all day. The Japanese troops have been very busy these last three weeks, building barricades around sentry posts, the entrance to the camp and to the Japanese headquarters.

The Japanese authorities instructed that no more letters will be written in the future, but we will be allowed to write one postcard of 25 words every two months. We may as well not write at all under these orders.

7 November 1943

The Japanese have ordered that the five dogs from the camp are to be destroyed, which I am sorry to hear. We shall miss them all very much, especially 'Judy', the camp's champion ratter. Maj Simpson of the RAVC is using some painless and quick killing stuff that he was able to save from the battle for future use. Lieut Col White has obtained a reprieve for Geney and is being accommodated permanently in the chicken farm. This morning's paper gives us the Japanese version of the first battle of Bougainville in the S.W. Pacific. Who, do you think, would believe them? Well, I don't for one.

11 November 1943

Well, Armistice Day for WWI is here again and nothing has happened of interest this day. I wonder if my dear wife can tell me where we were on Armistice Day 1928. We were in the Indian Ocean returning to India from leave in England. The boat was the SS *California*.

The news in general is good as apparently the Russians have captured Kiev.

Approximately 300 letters have arrived in camp, of which about 100 are local. I wonder if there will be any for me.

The Japanese once again gave two versions of the battle of Bougainville in the newspaper this morning but I think their claims are rather fantastic. There were no letters for me, better luck next time.

13 November 1943

We read of more claims from the Japanese of their victory over our fleets in the S.W. Pacific and according to their reports, over the period of the last fortnight, we cannot have any fleet and planes left at all. But for all their reports, I notice that General MacArthur is still advancing on the whole front of the S.W. Pacific and our fleets are still moving.

14 November 1943

According to the newspaper of this morning, we read of the Russian attack on 'Kherson' and of the street fighting in Rome. There are more claims by the Japanese in the third battle of Bougainville in the S.W. Pacific.

15 November 1943

We had quite a lot of excitement tonight when our air force made a moonlight raid on the colony at 10.45 p.m. The blast of the bombs that were dropped in the vicinity of the docks and other places could be felt in the camp. I felt a terrific blast of the last bomb in the centre doorway of our hut and at the time I really thought it had dropped in the camp, but apparently it was in the area of the police station near Kai Tak Aerodrome. When these loads of bombs were dropped, everyone ducked under their beds and the planes flew practically right over the camp. Strange that the sirens did not give a warning until the raid was over.

16 November 1943

The senior Japanese supply officer visited the camp today, but I don't think we will get any change out of him where an increase or a change in variety of food is concerned. The food does need improvement as it has been awful the last few months. However, it has never been this bad since we became prisoners of war. The following dogs were destroyed and buried in the hospital compound: Sheila, Judy, Chow, Bosun.

'Geney' has been reprieved by the Japanese and will be accommodated permanently in the chicken farm. L/Cpl Sawyer of the RAVC assisted Maj Simpson in the destruction of these dogs. Our planes raided the colony today and an eyewitness who had a good view from the bakery told me that he saw our planes bomb ships in the harbour, one of which had a direct hit.

Another camp committee was held today to discuss the question of batmen's pay and to decide whether they should receive 35 yen or 40 yen. There is always trouble about this pay amongst the officers in the camp. Never have I seen such looks before on the officer's faces and it opened my eyes after all my years of service.

We read of the Japanese version of the fourth battle of Bougainville and of their fantastic claims! There was no news of Europe.

They also gave an account of the operations that appear to be going on between Chungking forces and themselves between here and Canton. I wonder how large a scale these operations are! The Russians still seem to be going strong on the eastern front.

22 November 1943

We had a sudden drop in temperature this morning and didn't we feel it. The thermometer registered 52 degrees compared to 82 degrees yesterday. The sudden change got everyone down.

L/Cpl Bushell, Pte Francomb, Marines Chamberlain and Sanderson, and Stoker Hodgson[117] are all working very hard on the Xmas decorations, which are being produced out of old May blossom cigarette covers and old ginger jars, etc. The ginger jars are for use as table lamps, fitted with paper shades and are neatly decorated with little works of art. All this is being done to make Christmas to us as near as possible under the conditions.

All the batmen are contributing the sum of four yen each towards the Xmas fare in which every effort is being made by the elected hut committee to give us all the best Christmas dinner possible with the Japanese rations. Sgt Bullimore who is in charge of the cookhouse is doing the catering for this and I know he will do the best and make the meals out of 'nothing', as you might say for our Xmas dinner.

A concert is being produced by our famous producer L/Cpl Sawyer of the RAVC and the talent being found from the Army, Navy and Air Force Batmen assisted by the camp band. Permission has been asked for from the Japanese for rehearsals to be carried out in the cookhouse. This was granted, but rehearsal parties will not exceed twelve persons at any one time. So far, these rehearsals have not been disturbed by the Japanese as from previous experience. They are apt to suddenly stop any form of entertainment, even when they have given permission.

23 November 1943

The following clothing was brought into camp today and looks like a Red Cross issue. Believe me, we need it as it is getting extremely cold now.

Singlets	1 per man
Khaki serge jackets	2 per man
Khaki drill shorts	1 per man

My spectacular first fight with L/Cpl Bushell of the Corps of the Military Police. I would not have done this in normal time of course, as I would probably have my rank reduced by court martial. This chap, Bushell, was inclined to be rather of the bullying type and could afford to be so with his height and weight. He was gifted with the gab, which made some people rather afraid of him. I personally had no trouble with him until today, when he did something I did not like and I let him have it. He was as surprised as was those in the hut to see me at my age battling a fellow of his stamp and I don't mind saying I was surprised myself. The remainder of the hut approved of my ability to subdue this fellow and believe me, I did. However, I gave him one thing to his credit; after the fight, he immediately came up and shook my hand. My punishment out of this was a bleeding nose, but his was a black eye with a nasty cut over the other eye.

24 November 1943

I managed to scrounge some extra rice and onions this morning and was able to produce for myself a reasonable tasty meal for midday by cooking this on a small fire. Practically, a third of the camp of which mostly are officers cook their midday meals in the area allotted by the Japanese. It's quite amusing to see the various improvised small fires of all sizes being used. These fires have been made out of old tins of all shapes and sizes. The fuel for these small fires is partly scrounged from the woodpile and also from old stocks of wood collected over a period of time from the gardeners, etc. Even Lieut Col Penfold gets down to his small fire daily and if I have any extra food I can spare, I often pass it over to him. He is not the only one. Maj Duncan, Maj Crowe, Maj Squires, Lieut Hoskins[118] and other officers of the 1st HK/SRA Regiment have only recently got into the cooking habit because you must do something to enable yourself to live as the diet is so bad these days.

I myself am feeling weaker daily, which can be expected now after so many months of poor food. Goodness knows how much longer it will be now, and I feel the cold very much.

We read of more news in today's paper about the Kowloon and Canton fighting. This must be quite a large-scale operation. Our forces have attacked the Gilbert Islands and two landings have been made on the Islands of Makin and Tarawa. This is good news and shows that the continual claims by the Japanese of sinking our fleets are completely false.

26 November 1943

An air raid warning was sounded at 1.30 p.m. but nothing happened. The all-clear was sounded at 2.00 p.m.

According to the Camp Commandant there will be no more bread after the 28th of this month, as all stocks of flour in the colony are now exhausted. There may be some flour imported but that seems unlikely. As regards the increase of rice in lieu of flour, the Japanese have mentioned nothing. Unless there is some increase in the present ration, we may starve.

The Camp Commandant stated that another bunch of letters will be arriving at the camp in two or three days' time, I do hope that I will receive one.

27 November 1943

I find that the batmen duties are getting very boring and my nerves are also bad. I am responsible for arranging the batting duties for the following officers: Lieut Col Penfold RA, Lieut Col Galpin (financial staff), Maj Crowe RA, Lieut Hoskins RA, and Lieut Vinter RA.

There has been a sudden outbreak of dysentery in the camp in the last four days. There have been 32 cases admitted to the hospital, which is now out of bounds for visiting. The medical authorities in the camp urge the cleanliness of utensils and of killing as many flies as possible. For the last week, the camp has been infested with flies. Colds are very common at the present time and many of us are fairly low. You are liable to catch the least little thing.

28 November 1943

This is the last day for the issue of bread, which we shall all miss very much. Lieut Col Field has approached the Japanese for an increase of rice, but whether this will be forthcoming remains to be seen.

After so many months, I am now suffering from an attack of piles and believe me, I am feeling bad.

We are now in our twenty-fourth month of captivity and I wonder how many more months it will be. One of our reconnaissance planes was over today, so an air raid is expected. The rice has been increased from 13 and a half oz. to 15 oz. per man.

2 December 1943

We had two exciting air raids today, one at 3.30 p.m. and the other at 5.15 p.m. At the 3.30 p.m. raid, our force consisted of fourteen bombers with fighter escorts which heavily raided the harbour and other installations. At 5.15 p.m., nine of our planes which looked like B25s (Mitchells) came in suddenly from the direction of Lei Yu Mun at a very low altitude and they machine-gunned the harbour. I thought this was a very daring raid and we spotted them coming immediately after our dismissal from evening parade. At first we thought them to be Japanese planes, but as soon as we heard A.A. fire, etc., we all dived for cover. It's not quite clear whether the damage was done, but I would imagine they came in to finish their objectives of the first raid by firing cannons and incendiary bullets.

I hear that such places as Whitfield Barracks, Water Police Station, Docks and other military objectives were badly hit during these raids. Three lorry loads of Indian troops were wounded and seen passing the camp. From the camp, you can see graves being prepared by the Japanese, presumably for the Indians killed in today's raids, as the graves were being dug in the Indian cemetery.

3 December 1943

Even though the wood situation is still very bad in the camp, it is essential for cooking our food. The Japanese sentries still continue to take dry wood from our cookhouse and they demand it too. We have reported this from time to time to the Camp Commandant, but nothing seems to have been done about it. Often we have had to go without food because of the shortage of wood and the Japanese appear to be very reluctant in giving us our correct amount of fuel.

There was quite a surprise today when we saw twenty bags of flour arrive, so we shall have a few more days of bread after all.

The whole of my thoughts were centred on my darling wife this morning and I was thinking of what they were doing for the Xmas preparations. How I wish I could spend the forthcoming one with them. God bless them all and I hope I shall be with them next Christmas. In a few days' time we shall have been prisoners of war for two years.

We are having rather cold weather now; it has lasted for two or three days. I feel the cold weather very much.

8 December 1943

Well, it's exactly two years today when the Pacific war commenced and these years have gone very quickly for me. The Japanese are celebrating the occasion by posting their national flags at the entrance to the camp and on other such buildings occupied by them. You can see the flags on Kowloon British School, La Salle College and Kowloon Hospital. All these places are being used by the Japanese as hospitals. I wonder if our people will celebrate by bombing Hong Kong today. Something did happen today which was not expected. The Japanese selected fifty batmen from the camp and transferred them to Shamshuipo Camp, thus leaving the strength of batmen here to fifty-three to carry out batting duties. We presume this is being taken to complete a draft at Shamshuipo for Japan or Formosa. As this was all so sudden, it really impacted on our Xmas preparations and we also have to be parted from comrades. The Camp Commandant and Capt Saito (recently promoted), who is also the medical officer, selected the draft as the batmen marched around the square in single file, from which Saito called out those he considered unfit. At first I thought I was considered for the draft, but I was told to fall out. As soon as the required number was picked, they were ordered to pack their kits as soon as possible and to be ready to leave camp immediately. This order was followed by the arrival of two lorries for their conveyance to Shamshuipo. Finally, they all fell in on the square and away they went amid our cheers and a hearty send-off.

10 December 1943

Owing to the strength of batmen being reduced by the recent draft, we find that practically all our talent has gone and somewhat upset our plans for the Xmas concert. This morning we held a meeting about this and have found sufficient entertainers to produce an impromptu show on 27 December, which is the day being allotted to the batmen as their Christmas day. Lieut Col Field has approved this.

The remaining batmen of Hut 2 have now been transferred to Hut 5, which is the hut housing all batmen. We all find ourselves from all services and from all nationalities such as Irish, Chinese, Russian, Danish, Portuguese, New Zealand, Scots, and of course English. What a cosmopolitan crowd and I am in charge of them all.[119]

15 December 1943

Mne Chamberlain, who has now taken over the decorations for Christmas, which is to be held in Hut 2, is now working hard to complete this task with the help of other volunteers. He hopes to have the whole of the hut finally decorated by Christmas Eve.

We have been ordered to prepare for a Red Cross inspection of the camp tomorrow. The Camp Commandant and his staff carried out a preliminary inspection of huts and men this evening. I don't suppose we shall get any satisfaction from the Red Cross delegate by having this inspection, although we realise their hands are tied to a certain extent. A Red Cross parcel for Christmas would be welcome and would greatly improve our health.

It has been extremely hot today, but I expect it will very cold tonight. That's the climate in Hong Kong.

18 December 1943

An air raid warning was sounded at 9.00 a.m., followed by the all-clear at 9.30 a.m. There was no action.

We are all ready for the Red Cross inspection, supposedly due to be held at 10.00 a.m.

An air raid warning was again sounded at 4.45 p.m. There was no action although there were quite a number of Japanese planes in the air.

It is now just over a week before Christmas and I hope this will be the last one as a prisoner of war.

There was another air raid warning this afternoon, but again the all-clear was given after half an hour as it did not eventuate. We did see a number of Japanese planes take to the air.

20 December 1943

Quite a number of batmen are very busy decorating Hut 2 for Xmas and rehearsals for the Christmas concert and the New Year play are well under way. In the New Year play we have the following artists taking part: Maj Duncan RA, Capt Warrack RAMC, Capt Jones R/Scots (Potato), Capt Burch HKVDC, and W/Cdr. Sullivan RAF.

I saw about fifty letters passed to Lieut Col Field this evening by the Japanese interpreter. I wonder if there will be any for me.

It was rumoured today that Turkey was in the war, but I think that is wishful thinking by someone.

I was lucky after all as I received a loving letter from my dear old dad.

According to the letter, he is still in hospital but I hope he will soon be out and in good health once again. You are right, dad, this existence needs some sticking, and it is easier said than done, but I am keeping my chin up to the best of my ability and I am sure with God's help, I shall make it alright.

Dad's letter was dated 4 December 1942, which was over twelve months ago. This is my third letter from dear old dad; a grand old fellow and God bless him. I am hoping to hear from my darling wife soon.

22 December 1943

Mne Chamberlain and his gang are now very busy decorating Hut 2 and from what I have seen so far, the decorations look jolly good and bring back memories to me of the preparations I did in decorating our house for my dear wife and family, and I am sure my darling Peg remembers that so well. Carol singing practice was carried out this afternoon and was very nice to hear.

I received some bad news today. Lieut Col Penfold informed me that three British officers had been executed a few days ago, following the investigation by the Japanese into the wireless affair, etc. They were

Col Newnham of the Middlesex Regiment, Capt Ford of the 2nd Royal Scots and Flt Lieut Gray of the RAF. Prior to this, an officer of the 5th/7th Rajputs, a Capt Ansari, was also executed for a similar offence.

This has certainly dampened our Christmas spirits considerably.

23 December 1943

Mne Chamberlain and his gang completed the decorating of Hut 2 this evening and they have made a damn fine job of it too.

The food is still awfully bad and today's menu has been onion, lettuce and, of course, the usual rice.

All the lights were suddenly switched off in Hong Kong at 9.00 p.m. this evening and we were given five minutes to prepare our beds as it was understood that it might affect Kowloon as well. I wonder why this was done.

The officers in Hut 8 have decorated their hut for Xmas and it looks very good. Lieuts Wardle and Sutcliffe have apparently done all the decorating.

24 December 1943

At about 7.00 p.m. I had a meal of beans and rice which was not bad, but it made me think of the good dishes I should be having if I was out of this place. Anyhow, there it is and all I can hope for is that I shall be present with my loved ones at Christmas 1944.

Well, it's now Xmas eve and the time is 8.00 p.m. I am lying on my bed and listening to the carol singing in the next hut and I am having loving thoughts of my wife and family, also dear old dad and mum, George and Mabel, Dick and family, Elsie and family, Sybil, Ernest, Dorothy and June. I know they are thinking of me at the present time and God bless them all with all my wishes for a happy Xmas in which I shall be with you all in spirit even under these trying conditions. How the carols bring back memories of my young days at Holy Cross church and St Peter's Church in Canterbury. They are now singing the carol, 'Hark! The Herald Angels Sing', which is a great favourite of mine. I am attending Holy Communion tomorrow morning at the 8.00 a.m. service if possible.

There was some doubt as to whether we should have any food tomorrow because of the shortage of wood, but the situation was saved when a lorry load of wood arrived at the camp.

I weighed myself today and found that I am 114 lb., which is not bad under these conditions, but I am afraid everyone would get a shock if they could see me now.

25 December 1943

Christmas day is here once again. I attended the 8.00 a.m. Holy Communion service in Hut 2, where I prayed for my loved ones in Australia, England and India. For breakfast atta and barley porridge with rice. At 11 a.m., there was a lottery draw and I was not fortunate enough to draw a winning number, but I did buy a book of tickets. The prizes were as follows:

1st Prize	1 Xmas hamper
2nd prize	10 yen
3rd prize	5 yen

One-third of the proceeds of the lottery were dedicated for the widows and orphans at Stanley concentration camp.

The Xmas dinner was chow fan produced out of vegetables, peanut oil and rice.

Just before the midday meal we had an air raid warning. At the time of this warning, I was out on the parade ground having a chat to a friend of mine, Lieut Spearey.[120] I said to him casually, 'Well, it's a beautiful day for a raid.' No sooner had those words left my mouth than the siren went. However, there was no action over the colony and the all-clear was sounded about half an hour later. During the afternoon I had a fairly comfortable sleep for about two hours. At about 7.30 p.m. we had a salmon fish pie, which was very well done but had little taste, although I am sorry to say I could not eat much of it as I have lost my appetite.

Later in the evening, I attended a singsong in Hut 8, which was beautifully decorated out of all kinds of rubbish.

Just before the singsong, paper hats were sold at five yen each, the proceeds of which were given to assist the widows' fund. The collection for this being 113 yen.

The following carols and songs into which everyone put their hearts and souls were sung during the evening:

Carols	Songs
While Shepherds Watched	Annie Laurie
Noel	Drink to me only
Hark! The Herald Angels Sing	Jingle Bells
It came Upon the Midnight Clear	Loch Lomond
Christians Awake	Loves Old Sweet Song
Holy Night, Silent Night	Men of Harlech
O Come All Ye Faithful	It's a Long Way to Tipperary
Once in Royal David's City	Pack Up Your Troubles
	Tramp, Tramp, Tramp
	Land of Hope and Glory
	Auld Lang Syne

Finally, my last loving thoughts of my darling wife and family and then I went to bed.

26 December 1943

This morning's meal was fried rice only. The weather is beautiful and is far too good for one to stay inside. There has been little news in the Japanese newspapers of late, but I am sure things are progressing favourably for us. I received a six-yen Xmas box from the officer in my hut and was also presented with cigarettes from the following officers: 10 Pkts from Maj Crowe RA, 3 Pkts from Capt Robinson RAMC, and 2 Pkts from Maj Duncan RA.

Lieut Col Penfold RA also gave me a khaki shirt. All these items were very acceptable.

The batmen are looking forward to our Xmas show tomorrow, and I am sure Sgt Bullimore will prepare the best meal possible under the conditions.

27 December 1943

In this morning's newspaper we read of the heavy bombing raid carried out by our forces on Berlin on Christmas Eve, in which 1500 tons were dropped. What a Xmas box for the Germans.

We had our Xmas dinner today and the tables were laid with decorations, etc., and looked jolly good. It shows what can be done in the conditions. The dinner was scheduled for 5.30 p.m. and the menu is as follows:

Chow Fan
Vegetable soup
Treacle pudding
Tea

As I am the oldest soldier and of course the senior NCO, I was asked to propose a Royal toast on the arrival of Lieut Col Field. The dinner was excellent and the officers of the camp all said what a damn good show. During the presence of Lieut Col Field, I proposed the following toasts:

1. Gentlemen, I will now propose a royal toast — The King.
2. Gentlemen, I will now propose to drink to the health of Major General Maltby, the staff officers and other ranks that have left the camp.
3. Gentlemen, to the health of the GOC and others.
4. Gentlemen, I now propose to drink to the health of Lieut Col Field and other officers in the camp.
5. Gentlemen, to the health of Lieut Col Field and officers.
6. Speaking on behalf of you all, I wish to pass a vote of thanks to the committee, some of whom left us recently for the spirit and hard work they have shown to make this party of ours possible.

Lieut Col Field then said a few words of praise and was pleased to see that the spirit was still there amongst us after two years of miserable existence.

In the evening, we produced our impromptu concert to many people in the camp and considering that we had only a short while to prepare for the show, it went down wonderfully well. Everyone said that the show was excellent. L/Bdr Holland and L/Sea. Coleman played their parts well and so did Bartlett, Moulton, Price, Chamberlain, Bullimore, Harveson, Smith, Burch, Sprague, Skinner, and Cheeseborough. Maj Colquhoun, L/Sgt Walker, Pte Prince and Capt Cartwright-Taylor gave us all a good turn with the piano, accordion, bass and drums.

I hear that the officers have asked for an extra night for our concert and therefore we will run it again tomorrow night.

I have been feeling very uncomfortable in the stomach since our Xmas dinner and probably the treacle pudding has caused that. It goes to show you that our stomachs cannot take to a large meal after being on a rice diet for such a long time. I expect our stomachs have shrunk to a very small size and we shall have to be very careful about how much we eat when we leave this place.

28 December 1943

The concert is being shown again tonight.

Lieut Col Penfold and Capt Hammett[121] were cooking a meal at the small fires today. The Col had arranged a share for me and I was looking forward to it. The meal was very tasty and I enjoyed it very much.

This afternoon, the camp band has been playing one of my favourite marches, that being Colonel Bogey.

There is one thing we do know and that is of the Russian successes on the eastern front and they are now within thirty kilometres of the Polish border.

31 December 1943

Within a few more hours, the old year will be out and I wonder what the New Year will bring. Hope it will see us away from this place and the whole world at peace once again. I know at the present time, thoughts are with my dear wife and family, so God bless them and I wish them all a happy new year.

So far, we have not had any food today, as there is no fuel to cook it with. The Camp Commandant has been approached, but it doesn't look as if we shall get much change from him.

According to the newspaper today, we read that 150,000 bags of rice have arrived in the colony from Thailand and according to my guess on the present population, the rice would last for approximately 60 days.

We do know that the food problem is very serious here and no doubt our submarines are causing problems with the Japanese shipping.

A small amount of wood has arrived at the camp, but it is only sufficient to last for two days at the most. Anyway, this will enable us to have our first meal today.

This evening at about 7.00 p.m. there will be a singsong in Hut 2 which will brighten us on the last day of the year. Five or six of the Canadian officers are giving us a few hillbilly songs sung in the real Canadian way, and if they sing them as well as they did at rehearsals, it will be very nice to hear.

1 January 1944

It is New Year's Day and according to what I can see, we shall be lucky if we get any food today. There is not a bit of fuel in the camp and as it is a Japanese holiday, I cannot see them doing anything about it. All we can do is to hope for the best.

I am getting awful aches and pains in my legs these days, which I suppose are due to a vitamin deficiency; in fact, I feel properly run-down.

The concert went off extremely well last night, especially the hillbilly boys which I enjoyed very much.

I wonder what this year will bring us. I do hope we shall see the world at peace again.

The newspaper gives us an account of the sinking of the German battleship *Scharnhorst*, which is good news. It looks to me that our navy trapped her when they were escorting a large convoy to Murmansk. Our new battleship *Duke of York* caught them napping.

15 January 1944

The rice has increased from 13 and a half oz. to 15 and a half oz. per day according to today's orders.

We hear of good news this afternoon, that being of the evacuation of Zhitomir by the Germans. This shows that the Russians are doing very well. Although we do not know the real news, I think that if we only knew what the real situation was, we would all be surprised.

This life is getting so boring to us all and I feel very low in health and so depressed.

Russians are doing well on all parts of the eastern front according to the newspapers and if they go on as they are, they will soon be in Poland and Romania.

The problem is how to get kindling wood for the small fires. Lieut Speary, who is a friend of mine and who is employed in the garden, managed to strike an old Chinese coffin during the process of digging a well, so we used this for cooking our midday meal. Gruesome, I know, but in times like this, you burn anything to get some kind of a meal.

16 January 1944

A day to remember.

During the morning, whilst forming my men on parade for the Japanese early count, I commenced to bleed severely from the back passage. This was caused by a rupture to an old wound I received by a Japanese bayonet during a fight at the Little Hong Kong Magazine on the night of 22 December 1941, coupled with bleeding haemorrhoids. On 23 December 1941, at the War Memorial Hospital, Dr Kirk was attempting to treat both the wound and the haemorrhoids, but this treatment was not completed due to the lack of time and that I was required to revisit the Magazines at Little Hong Kong that night to obtain more ammunition for the guns in the western half of the Island. Apparently, the rupture which burst the wounds was caused by severe strain that happened on a working party the previous day, that being 15 January 1944. After the parade, the continual flow of blood was temporarily stopped by Capt Strachan who was one of our medical officers. I was removed to the camp hospital, which resembled a large shack and where numerous patients suffering from various wounds and diseases were laid out and looked just like skeletons. Capt Strachan, Capt Eves and others laid me out on a bed of mats to prepare me for an operation. Pte Schiller sterilized the makeshift scalpel which comprised of a piece of wood with a razor blade embedded at one end, and some scissors in an improvised pot of boiling water, with a recess at the base for a small fire of wood chips.

Capt Strachan had already made a request to the Japanese medical officer, Capt Saito, for a supply of anaesthetic for the operation. This was provided, being a liquid for spinal operations. Capt Strachan said the serum he was given was way out of date, so he advised me that it could be ineffective and therefore I could suffer enormous pain during the operation. He also said that he would try to prevent any significant loss of blood in an effort to save my life. What choice did I have? I had to accept the situation as it was. I was then placed on a crude, improvised operating table. It was about midday when I was given the needle at the base of the spine, which subsequently proved virtually ineffective. Capt Strachan and others then rolled me on my back and my legs were spread. Capt Strachan or somebody obviously with both hands forced my anus to the widest possible position to perform the operation. Apparently, he commenced to strangle the main vein within which was necessary. Suddenly, as I felt the razor blade penetrating the flesh with subsequent excruciating pain, I could hear the engines of a formation of planes approaching in the distance, which no doubt were American. They were obviously about to commence a bombing raid. This could not have occurred at a worse time, particularly for me. Shortly, I could hear the whistle of bombs followed by tremendous explosions and shocking vibrations which appeared close to the camp. This experience was completely nerve-wracking, as I was left on the table from time to time when it was impossible to continue the operation with the medical staff taking cover. I thought it was only a matter of time before a string of bombs would hit the camp and there was not a bloody thing I could do about it. The building shook violently and I clung to the table grimly, suffering terrible pain. After some minutes, which felt like hours, there was a short lull in the bombing and Capt Strachan and the medical staff completed the operation in the least possible time and finally I was laid to rest on a primitive bed.

The aid raid continued around the clock and the noise was unbearable. Being at a low ebb, I didn't care whether I lived or died. I later heard that an amount of shrapnel that fell into the camp caused casualties amongst the prisoners. Fortunately, my only wound was from the operation. Someone was certainly watching over me.

17 January 1944

We have been ordered by the Japanese to write essays on (a) a description of a battle you fought in and your impressions of the Japanese troops during this campaign and after, and (b) give your impressions of being a prisoner of war. This, you can see, is required for their use as propaganda in which all we can see in their newspapers these days.

My essay on the Battle of Hong Kong was as follows: I did not disclose any incident or battle in which I took part as I was not prepared for the Japanese to splash my name across any of their newspapers and make a good story out of it. This, of course, was the object of everyone here when they prepared their essays. As you can see, they could not get very much out of my essays.

As Battery Quartermaster Sergeant, I cannot give a description of any particular battle that was fought during the campaign, as my duties were in the nature of conveying ammunition, rations and other such supplies to the various gun positions of my unit, which was scattered at all parts of the Island and the mainland. Accordingly, my mind was occupied in carrying out orders I received from my superior officers, such orders being unexceptional in that they are usual.

Our Air Force made a heavy bombing raid on Hong Kong today at 4.40 p.m. and believe me, it was a massive load of bombs which really shook our huts. The targets appeared to be Kai Tak Aerodrome, Lai Chi Kok, Stonecutters Island and other installations in Hong Kong. I would imagine the casualties must have been very high as a result of the raid. It was noted that the Japanese planes at Kai Tak scattered as soon as the air raid alarm sounded. Whether or not their intention was to intercept our bombers, I do not know, but I think they took to the air for evasive purposes.

22 January 1944

As of this date, the names of the occupants of the huts at Officer Camp 'N', Argyle St, are as follows (see Appendix 10).

26 January 1944

We read of the landing in Italy by the American 5th Army in the paper, which is good news; probably Rome has now fallen.

The days are getting so depressing and it looks as if there is going to be no ending. All our nerves are on edge, which you can expect after being a prisoner all this time and being confined in the one place. Our captors, of course, make life more uncomfortable with brutal treatment of the prisoners.

7 February 1944

It has been 26 months tomorrow since the colony of Hong Kong fell to the Japanese and the time has gone very quick for me. When we were first taken as prisoners, I never realised that the time would have gone so quickly. I do hope that we are more than half way towards our release, as the men are really getting very depressed.

The weather has been very cold these last few days, and we feel it so, particularly in our present run-down and half-starved condition. Somehow, I think that I shall find it very trying during the cold weather when I go home to England, especially after being here in Hong Kong for the last eight years. I somehow feel that I would like to stay in the Far East, as I have been stationed here for 18 years. But on the other hand, I would prefer to see my old dad, brothers and sister once again in the old town of Canterbury, my birthplace. I have been offered a job in the colony after the war by Lieut Dawson RA as warehouse manager at the approximate salary of $500 per month. I have also been offered another job in Jersey in the Channel Islands by Capt Simon,[122] for the position of head man over his estate. The job appeals to me very much and I think it would also appeal to my dear wife. However, one cannot forecast anything in our current circumstances.

11 February 1944

There was an air raid at 4.00 p.m. Our force consisted of twelve bombers and three fighters and they dropped bombs again in the vicinity of Kai Tak Aerodrome and Lai Chi Kok. In the Kai Tak area, the Amoy Tinning factory, which lies on the waterfront of Kowloon Bay, was badly hit. From one of the windows of my hut, I observed a parachute coming to earth, but I could not see whether there was an airman on the end of it. I fancy there was not as the parachute looked too small to be used by an airman for bailing out. I fancy it was the type of parachute for carrying leaflets although it was impossible for me to see any leaflets coming down due to the long distance and the bright sunlight. The Japanese said that there was an unarmed airman attached to the parachute and taken to Hong Kong, but personally, I don't believe a word of their story. According to recent information, the Japanese stated that the parachutist will be coming into this camp on Monday, so we will wait and see if he arrives. The Japanese also stated that one of our planes was brought down near Shamshuipo Bay. I think that this may be true because I heard what appeared to be a plane crashing to earth. The whistles of the bombs and the roar of the AA fire were quite nerve-wracking, especially when our planes were flying over this camp. The weather we are having now is ideal for bombing and I expect these raids will increase.

13 February 1944

During a game of bridge this evening and at about 9.00 p.m., the air raid sirens were sounded. Whether or not this was for practice, I don't know. If an air raid was expected over the colony, this would be unlikely because of the very high winds and heavy clouds. Perhaps Canton was to be attacked as the weather might have been more suitable for bombing.

We are having a very lean time now and have had no food since midday. If wood does not come soon, we shall not have any food tomorrow.

14 February 1944

I feel lousy this morning due mostly to no food and still no wood has arrived. The Camp Commandant was told of our plight and of the wood shortage, so all we can do is to wait and hope.

A load of wood arrived this afternoon at about 2.00 p.m., so we shall be able to prepare a meal. Three of the men in the camp are being operated on this morning for piles and believe me, it is going to be rough for them due to the very crude instruments that are being used. There is no anaesthetic and the physical condition of the men concerned is poor. Cmdr Cleeve RN[123] is doing the operation and I take my hat off to him as he has done excellent work in the camp.

18 February 1944

It was terribly cold last night and I had very little sleep as a result. I think of the hardships we are going through and have already gone through these last two years, and the men feel so depressed, particularly in their physical condition. I do hope this existence will not last much longer.

Sub Lieut Fraser[124] of the RNVR was operated on for a gastric ulcer and twisted stomach at about 1.00 a.m. this morning. No assistance was given as regards permission for the operation to be carried out by Dr Saito, so Cmdr Cleeve took the law into his own hands and operated immediately, the operating room being a deserted bunk at the end of the hospital. Apparently, there is a fairly decent operating theatre in the Indian camp which is about half a mile from here. There is also St Theresa's Hospital next to the camp, but the Japanese will not allow any of these places to be used for any urgent operations, so it just shows you how the Japanese are treating us and confirms what we read in the Japanese newspapers of Anthony Edens' lashing remarks about the treatment of war prisoners in Japanese hands.

An air raid warning was sounded early in the morning and the all-clear was sounded half an hour later. We subsequently found out that the raid was on Canton again.

6 March 1944

Received a loving letter from my dear sister Elsie, the letter dated 14 September 1942, which was quite a long time ago. Have had to take over the task of camp storeman because so many of the batmen are ill. Whether I shall be fit enough to do the work remains to be seen; it is fairly heavy work for a man of my age.

8 March 1944

Today the Japanese suddenly ordered that there will be no more small fires allowed in the camp and that all small fire apparatus was to be handed in immediately to the Japanese for disposal by the Japanese headquarters. When this order was issued, Lieut Col Field requested that all kindling wood in possession throughout the camp was to be handed in to the store. The collection of the kindling wood amounted to approximately 500 lb. and it was suggested that it be sent to the hospital for cooking purposes if approved by the Japanese.

11 March 1944

We had a visit from our air force tonight. The air raid sirens were sounded at 10.20 p.m. with one force arriving at about 11.00 p.m. They came from all directions to bomb their respective targets. As far as I could make out, one heavy load of bombs were dropped on Whitfield Barracks and Canton Road. With anti-aircraft fire and dog-fights that could be seen in the bright moonlit night, we had to take cover. A siren was again sounded about one hour after our forces had left and once again at about 2.00 a.m. we assumed that they were bombing other places nearby.

17 March 1944

We were all suddenly ordered to take all our clothes and our bedding out for inspection by 10.30 a.m. The senior Japanese supply officer of Hong Kong carried out inspection. After the inspection he was satisfied that some prisoners had sufficient amount of clothing, but some had very little, he said he would endeavour to make up the shortfall if possible.

19 March 1944

I was suddenly attacked with severe stomach pains early in the morning. The pains increased during the day, which finally led me to being sent to the camp hospital where I received three tablets and a dose of caster oil. This treatment cleared me out to a certain extent by I still feel damned lousy. By the end of the day I had got over the attack of colic and came out of hospital although feeling rather weak and I have a large boil on the back of my neck. Received another loving letter from dear sister Elsie today, she says that everyone is well. This is the fifth letter that I have received since being a prisoner of war.

29 March 1944

The rations have been reduced to real starvation diet, which I have been expecting for some time. We are hungry all day long now and getting weaker. Received a postcard from Mrs Wilson at Stanley internment camp asking if I can inform her of the whereabouts of her husband, S/Sgt Wilson. I suggested that she apply to the Red Cross for this information as although I know he is probably in Japan, I dare not mention that in the postcard I send to her, or I shall probably be up in front of the Japanese who would want to know where I got this information, even when it's only a guess on my part. With these people, you have to be so careful of what you write or say because if they think anything is wrong they apply drastic punishment, no matter how trivial it is. I have to be particularly careful that they do not find out about this diary. I dread to think what would happen to me if they knew.

Mrs Wilson told me that her baby (Wendy) is doing fine.

6 April 1944

How happy I was when I saw that there was a letter from my darling wife dated 19 September 1943, which was good going under the circumstances. I wonder where those letters are between the first one received on 6 July 1942 and this one. I expect they will arrive some time; some in the camp have had as many as fourteen letters from Australia. I see according to the letter that it only contains 25 words, which is all that is allowed. I heard that Capt Hubbard received a letter from his wife who lives in Melbourne; it stated the sad news of those who were drowned on the *Lisbon Maru*. All wives whose husbands were on board the ship were also notified. What a tragedy for us prisoners of war.

7 April 1944

Well, it is Good Friday once again, and my loving thoughts go to my dear wife and family on this day. God bless them all and also to those in England.

I have had this year, how I wish I could get rid of all these beastly things and these conditions and poor food that makes matters worse. I have been subjected to boils and carbuncles since being in Hong Kong and I don't suppose they will leave me until I leave this place. I have been in the East far too long, that's the trouble.

The weather has been simply awful, nothing but rain for the past fourteen days and this is making everyone miserable, especially in such a confined area where we have been for the last two years. Anyway, the news appears to be very good from what we can read between the lines of the Japanese newspapers, but when the war will end, we cannot say. I hope it will not be long now.

9 April 1944

I missed the Holy Communion this morning being Easter Sunday so I attended the Church of Scotland for this service instead. I was surprised how they conducted the Communion service; you receive the bread and wine where you sit, not as we do in the Church of England where one kneels at the alter. I must admit the service was very nice indeed and being a new member, I was enrolled in the book maintained by the Church of Scotland padre who, by the way, conducts the Church of England service in the camp.

10 April 1944

The Japanese sent in some supplies today; they are:
1. Shark liver oil
2. Bran
3. Peanut oil and butter
4. Brown sugar

There are only small amounts of the above, but they are very welcome and help us to keep going. Items 2 and 3 have been issued individually in the camp. The shark liver oil is being retained for hospital purposes and is useful for those suffering from eye trouble.

10 May 1944

A draft of 140 officers left the camp this morning for an unknown destination, but we think it may be Shamshuipo Camp. The draft was detailed immediately after the morning's parade and they were given half an hour to pack their kits, etc. The following officers proceeded with this draft; this of course breaks my connection with Lieut Col Penfold, who shook hands with me before he left and said that we might meet again in the near future.

Lieut Col Penfold	Capt Jones
Lieut Col Shaw	Capt Camp
Maj Merthyr (Lord)	Capt Bramble
Maj Anderson	Lieut Dawson
Maj Mills	Lieut Challinor
Maj Duncan	Lieut Trapman
	Lieut Burgess

After a lot of trouble in the movement of kits, etc., they all finally left the camp in the best of spirits and we actually gave them a good send-off. To see all their kits and bedding on the square ready for moving, you would have thought it was just a heap of refuse waiting to be burnt.

At the evening parade, 200 officers and four batmen were detailed to be ready with kits at 8.30 in the morning for removal to another camp. I am included in this draft and I believe that we need a change.

11 May 1944

The move commenced at 8.30 a.m. and was completed by 12.00 noon. Our destination was Shamshuipo Camp, as I expected, and it is of course where we met up with the first draft that left on 10 May.

We were warned that there were a certain number of spies operating in the next camp whom we have known to be traitors for some considerable time. Personally, I don't think anyone can really say that they are traitors until after the war, as a lot of these stories that we have been told about these people regarding their movements, etc., may be very far-fetched. It is not always the case of rumours that do go around this camp. I know two of these supposed traitors fairly well. Both of these men are married to Chinese women. However, as these men may be out to cause trouble and could be in the pay of the Japs, we have been warned not to make any attempt to either converse or make any signals to anyone else in the other camp. Both camps are divided by barbed wire at a distance of a neutral barrier between the camps of approximately fifty yards. Apparently some recognition must have been made between members of the camp and those in the next, because within a few hours, a party in the next camp were placing additional barbed wire around our camp. To my surprise, I saw Paddy Wellwood who appeared to be in charge of the party. Sentries were with the party to prevent any conversation from going on between the party and us, although I had quite a number of chances when Paddy was passing the windows of my hut during the time he was placing the barbed wire. When the sentries were not looking, we took the opportunity and chatted quite freely. He looked quite fit and told me that old Joe Henson was still OK but very weak. I asked him if there were any of the HK/SRA in his camp and he said they had all gone to either Formosa or Japan.

Immediately after we arrived here, we were all paraded and given a lecture by the Japanese Commander (Lt. Gen Tanaka) in Japanese. The Japanese interpreter then explained it to us in English. He told us that he had more power to do things for us provided that we gave no unnecessary trouble and insisted on close co-operation from everybody.

The accommodation here is extremely bad. It is so overcrowded in the huts that if something is not done about it, we shall have some form of epidemic breaking out. I cannot see the Japanese doing anything for our comfort; they have always had their knives into us and would continue to do so until the end of the war. However, we shall get our own back one of these days.

The sanitary conditions are also very bad and we have only fourteen latrine buckets amongst 470 men. They are totally inadequate and above all, not at all healthy.

14 May 1944

Once again it is my birthday and I am 43 years old. I wonder where I shall be for my next. I am sure there are loving thoughts from my darling wife and family in Australia and from home. I cannot say how I celebrated this birthday because I have nothing to celebrate with. A birthday meal is out of the question, as you cannot do much with rice or boiled greens.

17 May 1944

Seen in the other camp were the following personnel: QMS Nichols (RAOC), S/Sgt Hunter (RAOC), S/Sgt Bashford (RAOC), QMS Cullimore

(AEC), SM Woods (RA), SM Lobham (RA), RQMS Lord (RA), QMS Williams (RASC), QMS Hutchens (RASC), QMS Cole (RASC), QMS Wellwood (RE), Sgt Toole (RAOC), Sgt Lewis (HK/SRA), and Joe Henson.

We were not allowed to make contact with these people.

22 May 1944

The third and last batch of officers and batmen arrived here from Argyle St this morning and they told me that it was very hard work in the general clean-up of the camp, which took a number of days to do. I believe the hot water boiler was going all day long as there was so much rubbish that had to be burnt.

1 June 1944

Well, we are now into the other half of the year and I wonder what the next half will bring us.

The Japanese authorities notified us today that we are now allowed 50 words in all future letters that we write instead of the previous number of 25.

According to the Japanese newspaper it looks that Rome will fall into our hands at any moment now.

A certain amount of local Red Cross supplies were received today and consisted of the following: peanut oil, peanut butter, soya bean milk, bran, soya beans, shark liver oil, and brown sugar.

Owing to the bad sanitary conditions, the Camp Commandant was approached for an additional supply of latrine buckets and he replied by saying that the cost of these were 75 yen each and did not offer to supply any. We asked if we could buy a number of these buckets out of camp funds. Whether the Camp Commandant will authorise this remains to be seen. The seating accommodation in the latrines is of metal piping run through the walls of the latrine spaces and this is not only awkward to perch upon but is also very cold.

We have only eight showers and three basins in the camp and you are lucky if you are able to get a shower once a day and a face wash once a week. This condition can be improved as only minor alteration to provide additional water piping and taps is necessary.

6 June 1944

Lieut Llewellyn[125] of Hong Kong Mule Corps told me today that his wife mentioned in one of her letters that Mrs Searle had been notified that her husband was on the *Lisbon Maru*. I was very sorry to hear that dear old 'Badgy Searle' and so many others had gone under and also how many more we know so well that died. It must have been a terrible disaster. We had an air raid during the night; the warning was sounded at 11.00 p.m. and the all-clear at 1.00 a.m. There were no bombs nor air action here and I fancy our forces were raiding Canton. A siren sounded from the Shamshuipo police station near the entrance to the camp and it made an awful noise.

7 June 1944

The Japanese suddenly ordered a muster parade of the whole camp this evening. The parade was required for identification purposes and the Japanese gendarmerie identified and took the following officers out of the camp: Maj Smith and Capt Bothello.

No reason has been given for the removal of these officers, but I think that Smith and Bothello might have attempted to get some information out of the camp through the source of a sentry; that of course is only speculation on my part.

9 June 1944

The long-awaited day has arrived as we read in the Japanese newspaper of the imminent invasion of Europe, which sent quite a wave of joy throughout the camp. This, of course, put morale up tremendously. I expect the world is now centred on France to see how the invasion goes. It looks to me as if we have got our feet well in. We hope that this is the right opportune moment for invading France with the sole object of causing an early end to this war. Believe me, I shall be damned glad to see it all over.

What a surprise I had today, with the receipt of nine letters! Goodness me, what has happened? This is excellent. This has made me very happy. There were three from George (brother), four from dad and two from my darling wife and cheerfully written they are. I am so proud of George in noting that he is a lieutenant, something that none of our family has ever been, as far as I can remember. Just think of that rude lot who resided opposite our house in St Peter's Lane, Canterbury. Well, I think we have now definitely put them in the shade. Their name was Prebble; I wonder what happened to the two boys of this family I knew in my schoolboy days.

12 June 1944

The whole camp was inspected by the Camp Commandant today. He took quite a long time and, in my opinion, was interested in our comfort to a certain extent. Anyway, he did pay more attention, which he had never done before.

Lieut Simpson and Capt Bird were taken out of the camp today. This also has something to do with the identification parade on 7 June last.

13 June 1944

Capt Bird was brought back into the camp today for a short period and the hut in which he is accommodated was thoroughly inspected for some reason by the Japanese Gendarmerie. We have no idea why these officers were taken out of the camp. Capt Bird was taken away out of the camp after the inspection of this hut.

Chinese and Japanese vernacular newspapers have been suspended and this may be due to Capt Bird being removed by the gendarmerie as he was in charge of the camp news service, which was taken from these two newspapers and also from the *Hong Kong News*. The Chinese and Japanese newspapers were our best information for news of the outside world; they always gave a more accurate account of the various communiqués issued from the theatres of war. I think the Japanese, after such a long time, realised that the news in these papers were far too much for us to hear. well, if it is, it's taken them a long time to find out.

A vote was called for amongst the officers for those who were in favour of the batmen's pay still being 40 yen per month. The vote was carried in favour of this allowance still to be paid to the batmen.

Two air raid warnings were sounded during the night but there was no action. A number of men heard faint sound of planes in the distance.

15 June 1944

For quite a considerable time we have produced a voluntary party of officers in improving the cemetery and, according to what I hear, roads and paths have been built in and around the cemetery and all graves have been decently restored as well. The completion of this good work has now been handed over to the other camp and the Camp Commandant Col Tokunaga personally passed a vote of thanks to the volunteer party for such excellent work through the Japanese interpreter, which we never expected from him. In the cemetery there are 273 graves and these were the deaths practically for the 12 to 18 months of being prisoners of war. As I have said previously, men are being buried at approximately the rate of eight per week.

17 June 1944

We read of a raid by our forces on the Mariana Islands in the Pacific. The Americans, no doubt, are moving damned fast. Keep going, the Yanks. We have the newspapers but we don't get much out of the news they present. The war may be nearly over as far as we know.

We hear of an American landing at Saipan and of an air raid on Japan which, I bet, shook up the Japs. I can foresee the Japanese being raided daily in the near future and I personally think that they will not hold their positions much longer. Roosevelt said that he was out to strike at the heart of Japan and I believe he is not far off doing that.

We all received a further injection of TAB and cholera, which is welcome in Hong Kong at the present time.

The Red Cross sent into the camp ten pairs of boots and fifty pairs of dark glasses. The boots were immediately given to the batmen who were very badly off for footwear. There was another air raid warning at 10.00 p.m. but no action eventuated.

19 June 1944

I recognised 'Jumbo' Smith in the next camp this morning and he does not look at all well. He left Argyle St on 8 December 1943 for draft to Japan, but for some reason was detained in Shamshuipo owing to sickness. He was a sick man when he left us.

Today, I finally stopped smoking as I found the poor quality Chinese cigarettes were affecting my general health. Today we received Red Cross supplies. They are local of course and are as follows: lard, soya beans, sugar, bran, and soya sauce.

This all helps to keep us going, especially the beans which have improved the health of the camp considerably.

We are very short of soap and the Japanese say they cannot supply any. All we can do is the best we can. I am using 'lye' for the washing of my clothes and you cannot use too much as it rots the clothes. I did not know what 'lye' was until I became a prisoner of war and I don't think many do. 'Lye' is produced from ashes, which are soaked in water and allowed to drain off into a bucket. It can be used as a disinfectant and is very effective too and I am sure that 'Lye' is often used in the manufacture and production of soaps and disinfectants.

20 June 1944

Col Mitchell and Lieut Shrigley[126] were taken out of the camp by the Japanese authorities. For what reason we don't know and they were returned in the evening. For those that have left the camp, some have returned and some have not, but all are bound in oath by the Japanese that they will not disclose any information referring to any of their experiences in the hands of the Japanese. Those that returned have shown the awful physical treatment they experienced. All have been admitted to hospital after their return. I was weighed today and found that I am 125 lb., which is very light for my size, but an improvement since I last weighed myself.

21 June 1944

We received a peanut oil ration for twenty days and I have taken a real liking to this oil and enjoy it on rice.

Persons wishing to trade watches, rings or any other valuables may do so through the Japanese and Red Cross delegates. This doesn't affect me, as I have no valuables. I wish I did have because the cash would be very welcome now as goods are so expensive. The going price for the average watch is 1,000 yen. But I noticed that one watch fetched 2,500 yen. This trading is not allowed officially. We have been able to obtain medical supplies, which have been essential in the camp with the money.

We all received further inoculations of TAB and cholera. The Japanese authorities approached Lieut Col White today and asked him what he thought the camp would like to have as hobbies. I will be surprised if the Japanese send us anything anyway.

24 June 1944

The Red Cross gave us money for the batmen at the rate of seventeen yen per head. This of course is not much and this amount was deducted from our monthly allowance anyway, which is 40 yen. The Japanese returned Lieut Simpson, Capt Bird and Lieut Col Field to the camp this morning and what a disgusting state they looked. The poor fellows had to be admitted to hospital right away.

The Japanese interpreter told the headquarters staff that he thought Germany was finished.

1 July 1944

Col Tokunaga appeared very pleased and pleasant on his inspection of the camp. Never have I seen him smiling so much.

We were allowed to write our usual periodical postcards. I wrote to my darling wife and was allowed 50 words instead of the usual 25.

Lieut Col Fredericks sold his cigarette case to a Japanese for the sum of 3,700 yen.

Pte Smith of the Hong Kong HKVDC was operated on for appendicitis. The cause of the trouble was a bean trapped in the appendix. His condition is satisfactory.

It has been four years today since our wives and children were evacuated from Hong Kong and how well I remember that sad day. The faces of my family I last saw when they boarded the ship *Empress of Japan*. I do hope that by July next year we shall be together again.

During the night two air raid warnings were sounded but no bombs or AA fire was heard. A lone plane was heard later during the night, which was definitely one of ours.

We received more Red Cross supplies, which were soya beans, sugar, peanut butter, lard, bran and another fifty pairs of dark glasses.

5 July 1944

It is rumoured that Paris has fallen to the allies.

Received another letter from my dear brother George, which was dated 20 June 1943. How welcome this letter was.

There was another inspection of the whole camp by Col Tokunaga today. He was still in an exceptionally pleasant mood, showing quite an interest in various things around the camp.

The Japanese have ordered that all books in possession of individuals in the camp are to be inspected and censored by the Camp Commandant. Those that are approved will be officially stamped by him and those that are not will be destroyed.

We hear that communications between Canton and Hong Kong have been cut, but this is only a rumour.

Another air raid warning was sounded during the night but there was no action.

10 July 1944

Due to the low fuel situation in Hong Kong, we are down to two meals per day. However, it does not make much difference to us as we save some of our breakfast for the midday meal.

An issue of one pair of clogs per officer was made today. These were asked for nearly 18 months ago. Quite a number are not suitable to some officers as their feet were far too big. I had a job to wear them myself. The latest rumour is that the war will be over in a week. We can only hope.

Maj Bailey of the Canadians is very ill with malaria and at present it is touch and go whether he will survive. During the night a message was sent to Sgt Maj Honda for brandy and glucose, but only the latter could be supplied, so all we can do is to trust in god that he will pull through.

17 July 1944

Maj Bailey's condition has improved, thank goodness, and we hope that he will improve further.

Today was quite an eventful one, Lieut R. Goodwin of the RNVR escaped during the night. This was the first attempt since March 1942 when quite a number escaped in batches. In one of these batches, Maj Munro escaped. He was adjutant of the 1st HK/SRA Regiment before taking up the post of Brigade Maj to headquarters, China Command. The escape of Goodwin was noted by the hut commander of Hut 6 (Lieut Col Smith RAOC) on parade this morning, which was finally found out by the Japanese during the count. As we all have to sign under duress a form of declaration not to escape at Argyle St, we are all now wondering what form of punishment will be imposed and whether this form of punishment will be individual or collective. If it is individual, I'm afraid that those who were sleeping on either side of Goodwin or the hut commander may expect a very hard time before them. Due to the escape, we were kept waiting on parade for four and a half hours and, believe me, the strain of standing without any food became unbearable and I was glad when the search by the Japanese was over. During the wait on the parade ground, three unlucky unfortunates were called out for interrogation by the Japanese Gendarmerie and they were Lieut Col Smith RAOC (hut commander), Lieut Willcocks 12th Coastal Regiment (bed associate), and Sub-Lieut Chand HKRNVR (bed associate).

These officers were questioned individually behind closed doors, where they were all severely beaten by various Japanese personnel. I believe the well-known Japanese interpreter (Komura) was present to inflict any punishment he could which he has been so well known for since he has been with us. He is on the top of the list for trial when we get out of here; there are also quite a number of other Japanese on the same list. The unfortunate officers were not taken out of the camp, so therefore I think we shall all have to undergo some form of collective punishment. What form of punishment it will be, I do not know, but I can think of two of them, that being the cancellation of cigarettes and parcels to the camp and most likely they will also stop the newspaper. Anyhow, whatever the punishments are, we can take them. It is for a good cause and good luck to Goodwin and we hope he makes it. Since our dismissal from the parade ground, we have been confined to our huts. We were informed that the Japanese Camp Commandant has ordered that sentries supplied by us will work in conjunction with the Japanese sentries and guard all huts.

P.O.W. Camp "N",
9th June, 1944.

Sir,

I beg to request that the Japanese Authorities be asked if I may be allowed to substitute for Major James Smith to serve any punishment he may have been given for any insorbordination or breach of regulations. Major Smith is a very old friend of my family; he is an old man and does not enjoy good health. It is for this latter reason particularly that I make this request, and feel sure that Colonel Tokunaga, being first and foremost a soldier and gentleman, will understand and appreciate my position and motive.

I have the honour to be,
Sir,
Your obedient Servant,

W. Stoker

W.Stoker,
Lieutenant, HKVDC.

Lt.-Col S. White,

Stoker's Letter

19 July 1944

The Camp Commandant has now ordered that all the batmen will guard the huts in the camp, at four men every hour from 10 p.m. to 7 a.m. These men will be under the supervision of the Japanese sentries.

The following protest letter was submitted to the Japanese by Lieut Col White in regards to batmen being employed for guarding prisoners of war. Copy of protest as follows:

To. Col Tokunaga
Camp Commandant
Shamshuipo Camp   18th July 1944
Hong Kong

Sir,

1. With reference to administrative regulations for the
    prisoners of war, the prisoner of war camp — Hong Kong
    article 27. This article explains that prisoner night watchmen
    shall watch to prevent fire, theft, and decampment and give
    special attention to sanitation. I respectfully have to inform
    you that the hut commanders and myself and all officers
    of the camp have unanimously agreed that we cannot accept
    or share with the Japanese military authorities any
    responsibility for guarding prisoners of war. Any other
    attitude we feel would be completely contrary to our code
    of ethics as British subjects.

2. In confirmation of your verbal orders that in future batmen
    were to be nightwatchmen on the officer's huts, I have to
    report that it is the unanimous opinion of the officers in
    the camp that batmen should not be asked to look after
    the personal welfare of officers. Should you insist on the
    batmen carrying out this task, I have to inform you that
    the officers have volunteered to perform this duty with the
    batmen.

3. The question of nightwatchmen being used solely for the
    welfare of prisoners of war would appear unnecessary as
    for the past two years, individual officers have been held
    personally responsible for taking elementary hygiene
    precautions, such as keeping their stomachs covered at night
    etc. This has proved completely satisfactory to date.

    I respectfully submit the foregoing points for your
    consideration.

                                    I have the honour to be Sir,
                                    Your obedient servant
                                    C White Lieut Colonel.

20 July 1944

The Japanese informed us today that the issues of newspapers to the
camp have been discontinued, whether this in part is the expected
punishment or whether it is because of the present world situation, which
they do not want us to see, we don't know.

Each hut is finding its own guard; the Japanese have therefore
accepted our protest of the 18 July last. The duty is of one-hour watches
and done by everyone in the huts, less the hut commander, and as I am
a hut commander, I am excused.

21 July 1944

The Japanese on the whole have not taken the escape too badly; it may
be due to the present world situation! If the escape had happened twelve
months ago, I think the Japanese would have taken a far more serious
view by taking greater drastic reprisals.

There has been a sudden change for the worse in the treatment of
officers and men by the Japanese sentries. Continually throughout the
night, sentries are heard and seen bashing officers throughout the camp.
Their attacks with rifle butts and kicking have increased in volume.
Protests for these nasty incidents have been submitted to the Japanese
authorities, but no replies have yet been received. No doubt the protests
get no further than Sgt Harada who probably sits on them or more
likely tears them up. These acts of violence take place for any form of
dislikes that may happen between the sentry and prisoner. I think the
most of the ill treatment of prisoners by sentries is either caused by the
hatred they have for us, or the fears they have of the Japanese NCOs
who unmercifully beat up the sentries for the least thing. This, of course,
is due to the fact that all the sentries are 'Formosans' and not Japanese.
This face-slapping procedure of theirs is of course a very common thing
in Japan and amongst their troops, and believe me, some of the slapping
is very severe. Some of the sentries are extremely pleasant and this is
due to the fact that they have been brought up in mission schools from
which you will find that these types are fairly well educated and speak
English fluently. There is no question about it that the guards, who were
responsible for Goodwin, received some form of severe of punishment
at the hands of their Japanese superiors and no doubt some of them
who came on guard a few days later had it in their minds to beat every
one of us for any minor pretext they could find.

29 July 1944

Immediately after parade this morning, the Japanese authorities ordered a thorough search of the whole camp. Kits and bedding, etc., were all thoroughly searched by groups of Formosan troops supervised by Japanese interpreters and Japanese NCOs. They confiscated all written material, maps, a certain amount of food and Hong Kong dollars that were found to be hoarded by a certain member of the camp. Odds and ends of web equipment and private tools were also taken. Lieut Andrews lost forty tins of food and 450 Hong Kong dollars! Serves him right.

I haven't really found much difference since I stopped smoking. I must say though, that my digestion has improved considerably since I gave up.

2 August 1944

During the night the colony was raided by our heavy bombers who dropped their cargo on Tai Koo as far as we can ascertain. The raid apparently took place at about 11.45 p.m., and because the explosions were so near the camp, it took us by surprise, as most of us were asleep at the time. We heard the sentries shouting and rushing about immediately after the raid and appeared to be very nervous since the escape of Goodwin. We appear to be under punishment as there are no signs of newspapers or cigarettes at the canteen. Some people are of the opinion that the newspapers were stopped due to the world news being so good in favour of the allies.

6 August 1944

The members of the camp who had received parcels from the outside were very disappointed, as none had arrived; therefore it looks as if this is another penalty for the recent escape.

A night raid was carried out by our air forces between 12.00 and 1.00 this morning. Japanese AA fire was extremely heavy and we could hear the large explosions of bombs in the far distance. It could be that Kai Tak Aerodrome, Lei Yu Mun and Mount Davis appear to be their objectives. The sentries are extremely nervous and one has to be so careful because the least little incident may mean a bayonet or a bullet.

The night duty on huts is such a bore and we are continually disturbed during the night by the sentries checking up the strength in the huts. It is so hard to make them understand if they happen to find somebody absent from their bed, the absence is caused by the individual being at the latrines in all cases. If you are challenged by any one of the sentries when proceeding to the latrines, the password is 'benjo'. So if it happens that someone is absent from the hut, we say 'benjo' to the sentries. It seems to work all right and they leave the hut satisfied.

It is also very awkward to count the men in the hut by torchlight as everyone is so closely confined with such small bedspace. The sentries are not particular on how they swing their rifles and bayonets around and one is liable to get struck in the body.

Sgt Harada carried out a preliminary inspection of the whole camp today. As the kits and bedding in officers' huts were not laid out for inspection satisfactorily, he commenced the usual thing of slapping faces here and there and using his boots on people whenever he had the chance. According to Lieut Owen, who is the camp interpreter, Sgt Harada was quite satisfied with the batmen's hut and stated that it was the best hut in the camp. Finally the camp was inspected by Lieut Tanaka who was satisfied with everything. He stated to Lieut Col White that a similar inspection would be held for the Commandant, Col Tokunaga, tomorrow and will be accompanied by a Red Cross Delegate. In other words, it will be the usual half-yearly Red Cross inspection.

10 August 1944

The inspection of the camp by the Red Cross was very short and sharp. This was due to a nasty incident that happened in Number 1 Hut. The Red Cross Delegate and the Commandant were passing through the hut and just when they arrived at the bedspace of Capt Barnett of the HKVDC, Barnett suddenly shouted in three languages that they were half starved. Komura, the Japanese interpreter, immediately attempted to beat Barnett in front of the Red Cross Delegate and the Japanese staff, but the Commandant Col Tokunaga frustrated the attempt. As soon as the Red Cross delegate passed towards the end of the hut, a scuffle took place between Barnett and two Japanese NCOs, which he must have heard. Barnett was then finally thrown into a small hut opposite where he was, placed under lock and key with a guard and two sentries. After this, the inspection came to a sudden end and as a result, a very small portion of the camp was seen. But after all that, I think the Red Cross Delegate had the knowledge that something was wrong in the camp and I hope he notifies our government that conditions are not very good. Believe me, the conditions have never been any good and are simply awful.

The OIC of the camp, Lieut Col White, has asked the Camp Commandant twice for an interview with the Red Cross, but the Camp Commandant said, 'They were all now proceeding for lunch to the other camp, but he would return this afternoon with the Red Cross Delegate.' This reply was, of course, only said to put us off. However, Lieut Col White sent a message during the afternoon to the Camp Commandant requesting that he see the Commandant on business of an urgent nature. The business is, of course, the 'Barnett' affair. Lieut Col White received a reply saying that the Camp Commandant would be here at 3.00 p.m. The Camp Commandant never arrived as promised of course, but sent his apologies to Lieut Col White via Sgt Maj Honda, saying that he was unable to attend because he had to go to Hong Kong on urgent business. In my opinion, this was of course bloody bunkum.

As soon as the inspection was over, we witnessed a terrible bashing of Barnett by Sgt Harada who unmercifully beat him with a large-sized piece of timber. The first two blows were aimed at the head, which caused Barnett to collapse into unconsciousness. Harada still continued to beat the unconscious body and finally broke the stick into two pieces. Afterwards, he used his boot on Barnett's stomach with an attempt to revive him but we found that water was the only thing for that. As soon as Barnett came to his senses, he was marched out of the camp between two sentries with Harada following in the rear.

During the whole of this awful affair one dare not intervene, as I am sure Harada would have decapitated anyone attempting to stop him from beating Barnett. We all wanted to intervene, but if a group of us made any attempt to interfere, the Japanese authorities would no doubt take this as mutiny. We would be made to stand against a wall and be shot. A protest over the affair has been prepared and will be given to the Camp Commandant at the first opportunity. In the protest, we have asked for the return of Capt Barnett who, we consider, has not committed any crime against international law. We have also stated that there was no order published by the Japanese that no one would not speak out in the presence of the Red Cross. Also, we have asked for the removal of Sgt Harada.

After the inspection, Zindel discussed with Col Tokunaga his concern over the obvious inadequate diet, which the POWs were receiving. Tokunaga became furious and shouted at him that if he mentioned one word of his views to Geneva, he would immediately stop parcels to all the camps. It was obvious to Zindel that malnutrition was rife and conditions were deplorable.

I heard today that Maj Brooks died in Bowen Road Military Hospital, the day and date I am not sure about. I was very sorry to hear this because he was such a nice chap. My dear wife will remember him and his wife when they were in quarters at 'Gun Club Hill Barracks', Kowloon.

16 August 1944

I think we have gained a moral victory over the Japanese, as they have agreed to remove Sgt Harada and replace Lieut Tanaka with Lieut Wada as soon as the latter officer is fit for duty. A new sergeant by the name of Kamatzu has arrived this evening to take over the duties from Harada. He looks quite a pleasant and sincere chap and is more after the style of Sgt Maj Honda who has, as far as we know, never forced any harsh treatment on any of the prisoners. I wonder why the Japanese appear to be trying to create a good impression.

Barnett was returned to camp and looks very ill indeed. He has been admitted to the camp hospital.

For the last three days, it has rained continuously and everyone feels so depressed and has to be confined to the huts.

My dear Winnie suddenly crept into my thoughts this morning and I was thinking of the awful scare she gave me when she swallowed a boiled sweet, which lodged in her throat. At that time we were staying in quarters at 'Fenham Barracks', Newcastle-upon-Tyne. I remember her going blue in the face and how she bit my finger when I attempted to dislodge the sweet in her throat. I finally wrapped her in a blanket and ran as hard as I could to the doctor in the medical inspection room. When I arrived and uncovered her little face in the blanket, she was laughing in my face. What a scare she did give me. My dear wife will remember that incident very well.

18 August 1944

Parades for the Japanese head count have now been changed to 7.45 a.m. and 8.00 p.m.

The 'fall in' will be signalled by the bugle from the other camp.

Thank goodness, we have at last received some soup from the Japanese. The issue is one box to four men, which is not a bad issue, but how long will it be before we get another?

We received from the Japanese authorities a copy of a programme of a play that took place at Rosary Hill Red Cross Home on 12 August 1944.

Sgt Maj Honda asked what the condition was of the food containers in the camp and has offered to try and exchange any that are in a bad condition.

The houses around the camp, which are not occupied, are collapsing daily due to the heavy rains. The condition of buildings in Kowloon and Hong Kong must also be very bad, especially those that have not been in use since December 1941. You can see that the Japanese have removed all windows, doors and ironwork from the buildings. We can see from the camp that the all the buildings look ruined.

21 August 1944

The 'Pheasant Stew' was damn fine and five ducks and five chickens were taken from the camp farm to make it a real tasty meal.

The Japanese authorities have ordered that there will be no electric light power in Hong Kong or Kowloon until further notice. This was expected as they have been putting restrictions on the use of electric lights for the last six months. I expect this measure was taken because of the fuel shortage. We are informed by the Camp Commandant that this will only be for a short period. It is going to be unpleasant for us without lights.

25 August 1944

Today we heard of Red Cross supplies from home.

The following is a rough text of the conversation between Capt Saito and Capt Strachan RAMC which I consider is the finest news we have heard in the camp and proves to me that we have the Japanese where we want them.

Capt Saito stated that the news from the Western Front was very good for the allies. He also stated that the news from Germany was also very good for the allies. These statements were made on his own initiative and not in reply to questions. Capt Saito was unusually polite throughout the conversation and seemed anxious to create a good impression.

The medical officer Capt Strachan took advantage of this attitude and immediately stressed our need for more food, emphasizing the general loss of weight and the increase in pellagra. Capt Saito accepted these points and enquired of Capt Strachan if he had received any food parcels. He hoped we would receive more Red Cross supplies.

Air raid warnings were sounded during the night and on one occasion one of our heavy bombers flew very low over Hong Kong and Kowloon. He dropped no bombs anyway. This lone plane has been making regular night trips for the last week. Two nights ago it came in very bad thunderstorm and it appears that this climate does not worry our Air Force.

26 August 1944

We received more pheasants and partridges, also boxes of large fish instead of the usual small ones we have had for the last six months. What has come over the Japanese!

Well, this is the best news of all. Red Cross parcels are being issued to the camp and there will be four per man. On top of all these, we are receiving the local Red Cross supplies as well. There is so much excitement around the camp that one cannot sleep.

The contents of each parcel are as follows: one tin of butter, one packet of biscuits, one tin of bully beef, one tin of sausages, one tin of milk, one tin of marmalade or jam, one packet of sugar, one packet of tea or coffee, one cake of soap, one bar of chocolate, one packet of raisins, and one packet of prunes.

My first dip into the parcel was the milk and sugar from which I had a nice cup of hot milk. How lovely it was. Everyone is now extremely happy throughout the camp.

This change of food makes one feel rather off colour, which is only natural of course.

29 August 1944

The Japanese authorities appear to be very cheerful these days and it must be for some reason for this marked change in their attitude. I personally think that it has some bearing on the news outside as I am firmly convinced that the European situation is now coming to an end and also the Japanese are beginning to feel the strain in the Pacific. If the news had been all on their side, you could bet your life we would not be receiving parcels, pheasants or partridges.

Received a loving letter from dear George and Mabel today; the letter was dated 12 March 1944. Glad to hear that they, Peg and family and everyone at home are keeping fairly well.

1 September 1944

Well, what is coming over the Japanese? They have just delivered thirty ox tongues. First it was pheasants, then partridges and now ox tongues. I wonder what we shall get next, maybe a side of beef. We must be winning the war.

We received Red Cross medical supplies, which are most welcome in the camp. There are sufficient vitamins in each box to last 100 persons for six months. This afternoon I received 500 capsules for issue to all the batmen at two per day.

3 September 1944

Today is the fifth anniversary of the European war and I wonder how much longer it will last.

Received a lovely letter from my dear sister Elsie, god bless her. The date of the letter was 20 December 1943.

I shall be glad when I can receive more news of my dear wife and family. I have had only three letters from them.

5 September 1944

Received more letters from dear George and Mabel, god bless them. The letters were dated 11 December 1943 and 26 January 1944.

We read of Finland's breaking off with Germany and her acceptance of Russia's peace terms.

We are still without electric light and it is so depressing in the huts without them. To pass the dark evenings I generally talk and walk between the huts with one of the officers, although I cannot walk too far these days. I am far too weak for that.

Practically every day we hear the reconnaissance plane of ours. I have seen the plane at times, but it is difficult to pick out due to the great height it flies. To see it in the air, you would think it was just a six-penny toy plane from Woolworths.

7 September 1944

Our reconnaissance plane flew over once again and three of the Japanese planes have just gone up from Kai Tak Aerodrome but I don't think they have an earthly chance to intercept her as she is flying at great altitude and also great speed.

Practically every night, air raid warnings are sounded and last night we had a visit from our forces in which they heavily bombed the hills overlooking Lai Chi Kok. I should imagine the Japanese must have some defences along there, which no doubt was spotted by our reconnaissance plane.

Goodness me, we have now received some liver, that's a nice change. I believe we are going to fry it. The liver was lovely and with potatoes made a jolly fine meal. All this game, tongue and liver will help tremendously if they keep it up, but I fancy that as there is no electric power, the dairy farm cold storage is out of action, and therefore, all of the meat must be held in cold storage as soon as possible. I wonder why they are making such an attempt to feed us well.

18 September 1944

I was weighed by the Japanese today and was 137 lb., damn good as I have gone up 12 lb. since the last weighing.

Our reconnaissance plane flew over today and I spotted it flying at a tremendous height.

More liver was issued to the camp today, so we can expect a decent meal this evening.

The food from the Red Cross parcels is going along fine and I have really dipped into my issue. All the cheese, sugar and chocolate have gone. Lately I have had trouble with my stomach, probably due to the change in the food and I am not at all well in myself. I was admitted to hospital this evening and I hope it is not dysentery. My stomach is awful and I feel terrible.

19 September 1944

The news we have received in the last few weeks has been excellent and our people have gone through France into Germany very quickly. If only we could get the real news of the world situation, we should no doubt be sitting right on top of the world. We only get the news from the Japanese angle, but reading between the lines, they give themselves away every time in their newspapers. This evening's newspaper gives us more good news and that is, we have landed parachute troops in Holland. Keep it up, boys. The Dutch officer we have here (Sub Lieut Huidekoper) is quite bucked up to hear of this news. We all know roughly where our forces are in Germany and I expect they are hanging their washing on the Siegfried line by now. I am sure that Germany cannot last much longer.

21 September 1944

The newspapers say that our troops are now at a point just twenty miles from Cologne! Good work, boys and keep going. The whole ring round Germany is gradually tightening. We also appear to be going forward in the Pacific and I fancy the Americans have already landed in the Philippines. Things at the present time do not look at all healthy for Japan.

For the last week we have been having gramophone recitals. The gramophone and records were sent by the Red Cross. Lieut Col Penfold told me of the death of the lady who was supplying the private parcels to him from Hong Kong. She was apparently the secretary to Lieut Challinor of the 3rd Medium Battery HK/SRA who was employed here by the ICI Company before the war. Lieut Col Penfold gave me the newspaper showing her death on 3 September 1944. I was very sorry to hear of her passing.

According to the *Hong Kong News* of the 20th, we read of transports being sunk with American prisoners on board, they said that 750 Americans as well as the Japanese crew were lost when the transport was sunk by an allied submarine on 7 September. Also, 180 prisoners were killed when another Japanese transport was sunk by an allied submarine off Sumatra on 26 June last; there was 720 prisoners on board and 540 were saved.

22 September 1944

My stomach is still out of order; however, I don't think its dysentery despite the fact that I am not feeling well at all.

Excellent news in the newspaper today, as we read that Hitler has taken over supreme command of the Germans. The Western Front looks as if his generals have deserted him.

23 September 1944

I was told there was an air raid last night, just before 10.00 p.m. I must have been very tired because I was well asleep at that time and never heard anything. Apparently our friend, the reconnaissance plane, was around and although it doesn't drop any bombs it came under a fierce barrage of AA fire. The new moon came up a couple of nights ago, so we may expect a few exciting nights in the near future, as the moon gets larger.

Capt Glasgow of the 2nd Royal Scots, who was acting as medical orderly in the camp hospital, gave his first injection this morning. I was the first individual to be practised on by him with a needle and believe me, he was rough. I really felt that needle entering my arm, but nevertheless someone has got to do these things.

We read the following in the newspaper today. All firms and private residences must hoist the Japanese national flag as a mark of respect to Syuki-Korei-Sai, by the Chinese representatives Co-operative Councils yesterday.

Electric light will be allowed from 7.30 p.m. to 9.30 p.m. from tomorrow, which is Sunday. This will be a change from sitting in the dark during the late evenings, which is so boring.

24 September 1944

Another visit was made last night by our friend, the lone raider. The sirens were sounded, but no AA fire or bombs were heard. The visit of course was in the nature of reconnaissance.

I am still in the camp hospital, but feel a lot better in myself.

Quite interesting news today, the newspaper tells us of the heavy raids in the Philippines and it stated that 440 planes took part in the last raid. It also mentioned of the American raids on Japan. Keep going, Yankees. I wonder if we shall be relieved by a force of our people. No one can forecast how we can get out of here. There is, of course, still the possibility of the Japanese moving us either to Formosa or Japan; one cannot forecast what they may do.

25 September 1944

Today brings us to the 33rd month as prisoners of war. It was terribly hot during the night and I had no sleep at all. This morning the humidity is really unbearable.

There was no European news today, but good news from the Philippines. Manila was raided again with 500 carrier-based planes and a task force has been sighted heading for a landing somewhere in the Philippines. After the heavy raid on Manila, the 'Philippine Government' immediately declared war on America and Britain. This action of course was expected and no doubt the result of Japanese pressure. Personally, I think the Americans are already on Philippine soil.

26 September 1944

There is a shortage of cigarettes in the colony and also in the camp. All you can hear in the camp is 'any spare cigarettes' or 'give me a draw, fellow'. Thank goodness, I don't smoke now.

We had an awful thunderstorm last night and the dysentery ward almost got flooded out. Cmdr Millett who sleeps on my right had to move about ten times during the night away from leakages and I had to do the same. Even though it was an awful night, our air force still paid their usual visit and bombs were dropped during the thunderstorm. I never thought our people would attempt a raid on such a night.

This afternoon I have been reading the only four letters I have left from my darling wife written to me before hostilities broke out. These were all the letters I could salvage out of the heap of rubble of Sir Robert Ho Tung's home after the terrible bombing it had received during the battle of Hong Kong. Due to the recent good news, there is a sweep of optimism throughout the camp that Germany will collapse in a few weeks' time!

28 September 1944

Air raid sirens were sounded at about 3.00 a.m. this morning, but our lone raider did not turn up this time, probably had another area to visit.

Received a loving letter from my dear old dad, god bless him. The letter was dated 14 December 1942. The old chap told me to keep my pecker up, which I am doing. He also mentions the fall of Hong Kong.

How well they remember that awful news and he hopes to have the colony shortly back under British rule. Some of the people in England have received postcards from Stanley and he states in his letter that quite a number of civilians have died there. I noted that the letter from dad is nearly two years old.

The reconnaissance plane of ours went over a few minutes ago and I spotted him flying at a great height. The Japanese planes immediately went up from Kai Tak Aerodrome, but I don't know why, because they have not an earthly chance of catching him.

30 September 1944

There is a rumour that a draft of 200 officers and 400 other ranks are leaving Shamshuipo shortly. If this takes place I am ready, even though the theatre of war is gradually getting closer to Hong Kong, and if we are to be torpedoed, I can say it is just bad luck.

The following officers returned from Bowen Road Hospital this afternoon:

Lieut Potts	RN
Lieut Plummer	RA
Lieut Heath	RA
W/Cmdr Bennett	RAF
Lieut Bryden	HKVDC
Capt Atkinson	HK/SRA
AB Laurence	RN (Batman)

We had an air raid warning last night at about 8.30 p.m., but there was no action. The all-clear was sounded at 9.10 p.m. Probably our forces were raiding somewhere in the area of Canton.

My treatment in hospital has been 'enema' twice a day and 2 cc injections daily. I have finished that and they are now going to give me 'thiamine' and 'nicotinic acid' (niacin) injections twice a day. My stomach is a lot better now, but I find my eyes are giving me trouble these days, and either I need glasses for reading or it may be caused by some vitamin deficiency. I suffer terrible headaches at times, which appear to commence after a short time of reading.

The men returning from hospital today say that a Japanese sloop blew up in the harbour yesterday, so that must have been the cause of the two explosions we heard at 8.00 p.m.

Lieut Poltock was taken to Bowen Road Hospital this afternoon and 2/Lieut Joyce was brought into camp hospital today with suspected appendicitis.

I was thinking this afternoon of the places I would so much like to visit. I should very much like to see Mhow once again, and other places in India. Naturally I would want to see my home town of Canterbury in England and my mother and father, then Reading in Berkshire where my wife's relations live. I would then go north to Leicester to see my bosom pal, Jack Nicholls, whom I went to school with before he settled into a business in that city. I well remember his first employment in Leicester and that was working for Harvey Earnshaw, photographer, at New Walk. I would also like to see Fenham Barracks in Newcastle-Upon-Tyne, which is well known to me as I clearly remember landing at that city from India in December 1931. I can still feel the snow underfoot and remember dear Peg crying at the condition of our quarters when we arrived. We were also billeted in disgusting quarters at Aldershot just prior to our leaving for Hong Kong in 1936. Of course, all of these travels would not be complete without my darling wife and family.

I am afraid I have not very much food left out of my Red Cross parcels; my stock at present is as follows: one tin of butter, one tin of bully beef, one tin of milk, one tin of sausage meat, one lb. of raisins, and one packet of biscuits.

1 October 1944

The lone raider visited us again in the early hours of this morning and surprisingly was flying very low. Anti-aircraft fire was heard from the area of Mount Davis. The siren was being sounded when he was actually over the colony. The plane was a large bomber and the engines made a terrific noise. I think these night visits are for mine laying the harbour as well as reconnaissance work and for bombing of targets as necessary.

We have two Canadian officers here in the ward, both suffering from some form of dysentery. They are both from the Winnipeg Grenadiers and their names are Maj Baird and Maj Hook. Both of these officers are veterans of WWI.

W/Cmdr Bennett of the RAF, who returned from Bowen Road Hospital yesterday, is now again in hospital, suffering from some form of stomach complaint.

If ever it is possible, I should love to take my wife and family to see the following:

1 February   The King opening Parliament
2 March   The famous Oxford versus Cambridge boat race on the Thames
3 April   Chelsea Hospital and its old soldiers

4 May	The Royal Tournament at Olympia
5 June	Epsom Derby
14 June	Trooping the Colour at Horse Guards Parade
6 August	St Paul's Cathedral
	Explore the Tower of London
	Regent's Park zoo
	Changing of the Guard at St James's Palace
	The Royal Mews
7 November	The Lord Mayors Show
11 November	Remembrance Day service at the Cenotaph Whitehall
December	Pantomime plays

2 October 1944

I came out of hospital today and did not feel so bad. The air raid siren sounded at 1.30 a.m. but there was no action.

I heard that S/Sgt Hunter of the RAOC, who once resided in married quarters No. 11 at Gun Club Hill, was taken to Bowen Road Hospital suffering from a broken leg, which he received during fatigues at Kai Tak Aerodrome.[127]

Col Tokunaga carried out an inspection of the camp at 1.00 p.m.

9 October 1944

I attended the Church of Scotland at midday today and received Holy Communion. Padre Bennett officiated.

There was not any European news in the newspapers of 8 or 9 October 1944. I wonder if Germany has finally surrendered!

14 October 1944

I was admitted to hospital this evening with some form of stomach problem, possibly pellagra.

We read of the heavy air raids on Formosa in the morning newspaper where over 1,100 planes of ours took part. This is excellent news as Formosa is approximately 200 miles from here.

Our usual reconnaissance plane has been very active over Hong Kong for the last few days. I think it is due to the unusual amount of shipping in the harbour.

16 October 1944

The heaviest raid on Hong Kong and Kowloon took place at 3.00 p.m. and it was estimated that our force consisted of thirty-five heavy bombers, with six fighter escorts. They heavily bombed shipping and other installations in and around the harbour and also dive-bombed their targets with shell and machine gun fire. During the raid, other planes carried out low-level attacks in which one of them machine-gunned the Japanese sentries outside the camp. Japanese pom-poms came into action from a direction of the harbour and two of their shells pierced the roof of Hut 11, seriously injuring Lieut Eardley of the HKRNVR and slightly wounding two others. Eardley was immediately operated upon and is now lying comfortably in the ward. I thought our numbers were up when the planes dive-bombed in the area of the camp and I can say that everyone hugged the floor very closely. One of the Jap pom-pom shells landed on Maj Kerr's bed of No. 4 hut, but luckily he was not near the bed or in the hut at that time.

17 October 1944

According to the morning's newspaper, the Japanese claim that two bombers were brought down during yesterday's raid.

Lieut Eardley is progressing very well and is quite chirpy. He is expected to be moved to Bowen Road Hospital shortly according to Capt Saito. When I spoke to him this morning, Lieut Eardley was quite cheerful.

Our friend, the reconnaissance plane, was over this morning so we may expect another raid today.

The air raid warning has just been sounded, and it is now 3.30 p.m. Up to the present, no planes can be heard. Maybe they have some other target in view today, but if they do intend to visit us, I hope the shells and bullets keep clear of the camp this time.

The all-clear has been sounded so our planes must have visited some other place.

18 October 1944

We had a very disturbing night due to so much aerial activity and the continued sounding of the air raid warnings. We heard quite heavy explosions during the night as a result of the aerial activity. Things are surely warming up and I think that there must be quite a lot of ships lying in and outside the harbour, which have arrived here daily for shelter since our attacks on the Philippines and Formosa. If we are in possession of these places, particularly the latter, then retreat to Japan is simply cut off.

We read in today's newspaper of the death of Field-Marshal Rommell who was apparently struck by bomb splinters when inspecting the German troops on the Western Front. If this is true, I think that Germany has lost their finest general of recent years and no doubt he kept us very worried in the battles of North Africa.

The ants are terrible at present and you cannot walk without treading on them and also they crawl all over your bed and makes one feel so uncomfortable that one cannot get a proper night's rest. The bed and wall bugs, whatever they may be, are still an awful nuisance and when they bite me, I receive awful irritation.

Quite a number of men in the camp are suffering from septic sores of the feet. This may be due to the lack of green vegetables.

The Camp Commandant asked Lieut Col White to submit a letter of protest to General Stillwell, the American Commander in China, to instruct his air forces to be careful in future when bombing Hong Kong as there was a number of casualties in the last raid of 16 October 1944, when their planes were supposed to have fired shell and bullets into the camp. This of course is totally incorrect as the shellfire was from Japanese pom-poms. The bullets from our planes were being directed at Stonecutters Island. Anyway, I thought this suggestion by the Camp Commandant was a huge joke and he must have thought that all of us are a lot of damn fools to make any attempt to submit a letter of that description to Stillwell, even if our forces did accidentally drop any bombs on this camp. We all realize that this is war and if we are unlucky to receive any bombs, etc., well, it is just bad luck and we do expect to be under fire one of these days and maybe soon.

I hear that there were 100 planes in the raid of 16 October last instead of 35. They apparently came in from all directions and the casualties in the raid must have been very heavy, possibly as many as 5,000 killed.

19 October 1944

The cigarette problem is very acute in Hong Kong and also in the camp. The Japanese have told the prisoners of war that cigarettes will be issued to officers at the rate of five per day and for ORs three cigarettes per day. This does not concern me, as I do not smoke. The price of cigarettes in the colony is exorbitant; 'Mayflower' cigarettes, which used to be 10 cents a packet, are now $1.80 and 'Pirate' cigarettes are 2.50 yen.

According to the people who recently returned from Bowen Road Hospital, the conditions there are not very good and the treatment here in the camp is far better. I think that also applies to the food as well.

21 October 1944

We read of good news in the newspaper and it looks as if we are moving fast in the Pacific. Having landed in the Philippines and Formosa, British troops have invaded the Nicobar and Andaman Islands. This is the first news from the Indian Ocean for quite some considerable time.

The Japanese are quite generous today as they have issued an extra postcard which may be sent anywhere with the exception of Stanley in Hong Kong. I have therefore written to dear old dad for the first time since being a prisoner of war. Of course, it was not possible before as we were only allowed one postcard per month and naturally I have always used it to write to Peg and the family.

We have received a certain amount of Red Cross clothing and I believe it consists of the following: jerkins, socks, towels, trousers, overcoats, jackets, etc. One was given to each man.

Apparently, there are 700 articles that will be issued and distribution will be by the drawing of playing cards. I have drawn the jack of hearts and will wait for the article that corresponds with this card.

The Japanese has severely criticised the Americans for the bombing of Chinese civilians in the closely populated area of 'Whampoa Docks' in Kowloon.

26 October 1944

Well, all I got out of the Red Cross clothing was a towel, but it was a damn good one, which I needed badly. The clothing was American issue and of very good quality.

To be on the safe side and with the hope of being able to take this complete diary with me, I shall have to get ready and have it safely packed away, because sooner or later, things are going to happen fairly quickly and when the British and the Americans arrive, I think the fight will be short and sharp.

Today marks for my 25 years' service and I really feel quite an old soldier.

The Japanese suddenly made a free issue of five cigarettes per officer and OR this afternoon. They were of Japanese make. This is very unusual, especially that the cigarette supply is not so good in Hong Kong.

The electric power is off throughout Hong Kong again and it is so miserable without light. If only we knew of the real news from the outside at the present time we should no doubt be sitting on top of the world. The propaganda we get in the newspaper is terrible, but we all know by reading between the lines that this is just an attempt by the Japanese to cover things up. We believe we are moving very fast in the Pacific and in Europe; I am convinced that the British and the Americans will be arriving in Hong Kong in the near future.

Lieut Spearey of the HKVDC took a bad turn with malaria this afternoon and the hospital staff have been working very hard to get his temperature down. I believe they have succeeded in doing just that a few minutes ago. They have been sponging him down with cold water for the last hour.

Another two months will find us at Christmas again and I often wonder whether we shall be spending it as prisoners of war. I think we shall, but one never knows of course.

Last night everyone in camp received a further inoculation to combat dysentery and cholera, and this morning I felt the effects of these inoculations. It is not very often that we have injections for 'Rat Plague'; this makes one feel really bad and I experienced this before during the plague of 1921 in 'Nowshera' on the Northwest Frontier in India.

I definitely think that the policy of the Japanese, as far as treatment of prisoners of war are concerned, has changed for the better. Probably this is the result of direct orders from Tokyo and maybe due to the present situation in the Pacific and I am sure that they are feeling rather bad now. It might be that Lieut Goodwin, who escaped from here about four months ago, did manage to reach our troops somewhere in China and therefore he might have told the world of our treatment and the conditions that we have been living under. Somehow I feel Goodwin has made it.

2 November 1944

I received a letter from my dear wife dated August 1942.

Information was given to us today that a further inspection of the camp by Col Tokunaga will take place either on the 5th or 7th of this month.

Practically everyone has eaten the contents of their Red Cross parcels and we are all hoping that there will be another issue in the near future.

The Japanese authorities have once again warned the camp that trading is not to be done with the sentries and if anyone is caught, they will be severely punished. What annoys me and is so disgusting is that some men who received Red Cross clothing recently have already started to dispose of them by selling it to the sentries. All I can say is that those who have done this did not really need the clothing and could have given this clothing to those who are in dire need, me in particular. They call themselves officers. Lieut Col White has issued an order that there will be an inspection of the recent issue of Red Cross clothing and that hut commanders must take a record of these issues in their respective huts. Those culprits who have disposed of their clothing will be found out. Another aspect to look at in the clothing question is that if the Red Cross delegate in Hong Kong finds out that the clothing is being sold, he will naturally give up the idea of sending any more to the camp. I am sure that the Japanese authorities will inform him of these incidents with delight.

17 November 1944

At about 11 p.m., the air raid sirens sounded, which woke everyone. At the same time, one could hear the rumble of aircraft engines approaching. Instinctively, we all took cover under our beds as a whistle of falling bombs could be heard, followed by enormous explosions which appeared to be coming from Kai Tak Aerodrome and dockyard areas. One string of bombs exploded not too far from the camp, with subsequent blasts shaking our huts violently. I made a quick glance through the window openings, but all the huts appeared to be undamaged. The raid lasted about twenty minutes. We had heard that the Americans were not all that accurate at bombing, particularly on night raids. I dare not go outside, as I would attract immediate fire if spotted by the Japanese guards. I could hear and see Japanese anti-aircraft fire light up the sky.

During the raid one pom-pom shell came through the roof of the batmen's hut. It passed over my head and narrowly missed Pte Cheeseborough.

18 November 1944

The Japanese guards were quite agitated and in a foul mood this morning. Several of the men were bashed for no apparent reason whilst going on parade. I received several blows myself and believe all this brutality had something to do with last night's air raid. Two of my men fainted on parade and I requested that they be taken to the hospital. This enraged Sgt Kamatzu and he said they stayed where they were until the parade was over.

8 December 1944

The latest news is that the American Navy have engaged the Japanese Navy in the Pacific off the Philippines coast and that American troops have landed on several south Philippine islands. It would appear that the prospects of an early end to the war is not far away, and this is good news.

Today is the fourth anniversary of the fall of Hong Kong and shortly our fourth Christmas will be upon us. Many of the men are in terrible physical condition through years of neglect and brutal treatment. I keep telling them that the allies are going well in both Europe and in the Pacific region and that the war will shortly be over.

Some of the men received letters from loved ones which will boost morale and will make their Christmas more bearable. Unfortunately, there is no letter for me. I hope my wife and children are well and wonder if they know I am still alive.

25 December 1944

Another Christmas day. My thoughts of course were with my dear wife and family. I attended Holy Communion at 8 a.m. before the usual parade. The weather was cold and miserable and keeping warm was a problem as our clothes were literally in rags. Some men were better off than others and many draped blankets over their shoulders to keep warm. For Christmas dinner, each of the batmen managed to contribute something from what they had remaining of their Red Cross parcels. This was to supplement the ration from the Japanese, which was very little and comprised as usual of rice with a small piece of whale meat. Later in the day we sang some old favourites and a few carols. We discussed the war situation and were of the opinion that the Japanese cannot last much longer. I went to bed with positive thoughts and believe the men did also.

The pain I am getting in the legs is getting worse and is known as 'electric feet'. Many of the men suffer the same, some worse than others, but there is little that can be done. Requests by our medical staff for essential vitamins would help to relieve the situation if they were forthcoming. I also find it extremely difficult to maintain the diary on a regular basis due to the difficulty in unearthing it, adding notes before burying it again. To do this is now taking more time and therefore in greater danger of being caught by the Japanese, which would mean probable execution.

15 January 1945

Whilst on parade for the morning count, we could hear the droning of a great number of planes. We were immediately dismissed just as the air raid sirens sounded, and we made our way back to our respective huts. Within a short period of time, I could see a great number of aircraft dotting the sky. There must have been 80 to 100 coming in from the east, flying over the island with the majority of them turning to head north. They comprised of B25 Mitchells accompanied by P38 Lightnings. They fanned out into several groups and started to drop bombs in all directions. One group headed straight over our camp and we all laid flat to the floor under the beds or wherever one could find some sort of cover. Explosions were deafening and the sound of AA fire could be heard. One string of bombs must have landed close to the camp, causing vibrations which shook our hut violently. During a lull in the bombing, I took a quick look through one of the windows but could see no damage in the camp. Neither were the guards visible although I could hear them jabbering away as if in a state of panic. I could see large plumes of smoke rising from what appeared to be the dockside area, Kai Tak and on the island. The raid continued for about one hour and after that they withdrew. I could not see if any of our planes were downed.

16 January 1945

This morning's parade was cancelled when the air raid siren sounded as the drone of a great number of planes could be heard. Their numbers were much greater than those of yesterday and continued for about three hours. The aerial activity was amazing to see, but became more dangerous for us than yesterday. There appeared to be more Lightning P38s and it looked as though they were going to operate separately at a much lower altitude than the Mitchells. A string of bombs impacted just a short distance from the camp throwing debris and shrapnel into our area. We were all laid flat to the floor as we were yesterday. One could hear machine gun bullets rattling various structures. Whilst no one was hit in our hut, we later found out that unfortunately, some of the men in other huts were hit by shrapnel. Compared to yesterday, I saw little of the action and some of the men were quietly cheering. I do not know how many of our planes were downed, but later I was told by the Japanese guards that American pilots were captured and executed, which we thought was disgusting and against all conventions of war and treatment of prisoners. Later, the Japanese were quite agitated and in a panic over the raid, jabbering away in their guttural tones. They became more hostile than usual towards us and more face slapping, rifle bashing and bayonet prodding appeared to be the order of the day. The look on some of their faces indicated that they feel the end of the war is near.

During the raid, Lt Richards (RASC) and Maj Stansfield (RIASC) were wounded in their huts by pom-pom shells that penetrated the roof and were subsequently treated for their wounds.

28 January 1945

The Pacific War was going well for the allies, with the Americans landing in Luzon. The food situation has again deteriorated with a reduction in our rice ration. The Japanese blame this on the loss of their shipping, but we believe there is plenty of rice available in Hong Kong and China. Capt Strachan has again made a request for medicines and vitamins, but this has fallen of deaf ears. This afternoon, I had to restrain one of the men who started to lose control of his mind, which is understandable in this wretched situation. With the assistance of others, we managed to calm him down. The general attitude of the men is somewhat sombre, after the air raids of nearly two weeks ago when hopes for an end to this war appeared close.

8 February 1945

With the ever-increasing incidents of allied air raids, we have noted that the Japanese have relocated and increased their air defences close to the camp and no doubt close to other camps for obvious reasons. They know full well that the allies are aware of the location of all these camps and that the risk of casualties to the prisoners would be greatly increased if their defences were attacked. However, our men, I believe, are quite willing to take that risk if only to shorten the war.

3 March 1945

Today is my dear wife's birthday. She will be 35 years old. God bless her and all my children. Winifred must now be 18, Pamela 16, Richard 14, Derek 12 and Raymond 9. I do hope that they are all well. Once again, as so often the case has been recently, the morning count was cancelled due to bombing raids. We have noticed that some of the Japanese guards, particularly the Formosans, are wearing civilian clothes under their uniform, which to me is a sure sign that the end of the war is getting closer.

I visited Sgt Tupper of 12th Coast Regiment. He is not well and his spirits are down, made worse by his poor physical condition.[128] We talked about his home town in England, that being Chichester and of his family there. He knew I came from Canterbury in Kent. The talk, I believe, made both of us feel a little better.

25 March 1945

It is no secret that the war is going well for the allies in both Europe and the Pacific. There is continual news of this and try as they might, the Japanese are unable to suppress this information.

16 April 1945

Due to the bombing raids, electric power has again been cut, meaning that we shall be without light in the evenings. During the night, some of the men took the opportunity to trade through the wire with some of the Chinese, despite the warnings by the Japanese not to do so.

28 April 1945

Deaths are still occurring at a steady rate. Today the burial took place of an able seaman. Despite seeing burials so many times, one cannot but be emotional and saddened by this scene and we wonder who will be next. I for one am determined to stick it out, God willing. The number of empty beds in the huts is testimony to the men who have died and our hut is no exception. Surely it cannot be much longer before there is an end to this wretched existence.

10 May 1945

Wonderful news. The war in Europe is over; Germany has been defeated. The Japanese appear to be devastated by this news, which means that most of the allied resources can now be concentrated on the Pacific War. Despite this, the Japanese authorities have issued a statement saying that Japan will fight on. The mood in the camp is one of jubilation; however, the senior British officer in the camp, Lieut Col White, has issued instructions to all the prisoners to refrain from showing any emotion that may upset the Japanese. However, there is no denying that the spirits of the prisoners have now been well and truly lifted.

14 May 1945

Today is my 44th birthday.
    More good news. The Island of Iwo Jima has fallen to the Americans and Burma has been regained by the allies. The mood amongst the Japanese troops is varied. Most guards are quite subdued as they feel the end is near, whilst others still appear to be belligerent and hateful and one wonders what they might do if the situation becomes desperate.

25 May 1945

Sgt Kamatzu was in a foul mood this morning. Shortly after the morning parade, I heard a commotion behind me. On turning around, I could see the prostrate figure of Gnr Dinner on the ground with blood coming from a wound on his forehead. As I approached, Kamatzu, who was standing over Dinner, shouted at me, 'British prisoners must have respect for Japanese soldier. You are the responsible officer.' He placed his sword on my shoulder and was about to say something else when he was summoned by a guard, cutting short the confrontation. He about turned and marched off. Gnr Elsworth was close by and I signalled him to give me a hand. With a bit of a struggle we managed to get Dinner to his feet and half carried him back to his bed laying him down. I told Elsworth to get a medical orderly from the hospital to treat the wound, Dinner was fully conscious and I asked him what happened, he said, 'It's my back, sir, I couldn't bow,' enough said.[129]

28 June 1945

Col Tokunaga made a surprise visit to the camp this morning, accompanied by the medical officer, Capt Saito. He was met by our Senior Officer Lieut Col White. They conversed for about fifteen minutes and after that the Japanese departed. I later found out that the Japanese said that more medical supplies would be delivered to the camp shortly. If forthcoming, they would be a bonus. However, essential food supplies are what we also need to combat the effects of malnutrition and assist in overcoming diseases. I will believe this when I see the delivery.

4 July 1945

News has just been received that Okinawa has fallen to the Americans. This is wonderful news and means that Japan itself will be the next to be attacked in force. I believe that the war is all but over and that we shall all be liberated from this wretched existence shortly. The Japanese guards look absolutely devastated by this news.

Some medical supplies have been delivered, but with the assistance of the International Red Cross which does not surprise me. This must have been with the approval of the Japanese who we think are back-peddling in view of the current military situation.

29 July 1945

Three or four news outlets, including the Hong Kong newspaper, which is an English printed paper controlled by the Japanese, have reported a meeting between Britain, America and Russia in which they have issued a communiqué to the Japanese government, to surrender unconditionally or see their homeland destroyed. Later, I found out that the ultimatum was rejected as an impudent threat.

7 August 1945

A message was delivered by a food truck driver, which stated that a new type of bomb has been dropped on a Japanese city with devastating effect. Just in case this news is true, orders were issued by one of our senior officers that emotions should not be shown by the men lest it should infuriate the Japanese.

10 August 1945

Everyone is full of anticipation that the Japanese will capitulate. We have just heard that a second bomb has devastated the city of Nagasaki.[130]

14 August 1945

I was prevented from getting any real sleep during the night due to the pain in my legs, particularly below the knees. It must be the effects of the beriberi that I am suffering from and there is nothing that can really be done about it, due to the lack of medical supplies and the poor food. The latter is becoming worse every day.

At about 2 a.m., there was what appeared to be a confrontation of sorts, coming from outside the camp. Scuffling was occurring with an exchange of Japanese and Chinese language. I could hear the burst of fire from a machine gun, which I assume was Japanese. By this time, everyone in the hut was awake. I did not get up to investigate for two reasons, one being, getting on my feet was difficult and two, there was a possibility of me being shot.

I was extremely tired by the time of the morning count, which fortunately was not drawn out. About midday, we could hear the drone of planes. The air raid siren did not operate. Nevertheless, we all took cover. The planes sounded like they were coming from the north and in a short matter of time about six to eight appeared and they were not at a great height. There were a mixture of bombers and fighters, flying directly over the camp. However, instead of the usual bombs, I could see the glistening of bits of paper floating down. We waited until the planes disappeared and I promptly went out and gathered one leaflet from the ground. It was a message signed by A. C. Wedemeyer, Lieut General, USE, Commanding, which read as follows:

Allied Prisoners of War and Civilian Internees, these are your orders and/or instructions in case there is a capitulation of the Japanese forces.

(1) You are to remain in your camp area until you receive further instructions from this headquarters

(2) Law and order to be maintained in the camp area.

(3) In case of a Japanese surrender, there will be allied occupational forces sent into your camp to care for your needs and eventual evacuation to your homes.

(4) You must help by remaining in the area in which you are now. Your camp leaders we charge with these responsibilities.

(5) The end is near; do not be disheartened, we are thinking of you. Plans are underway to assist you at the earliest possible moment.

Signed A C Wedemeyer
Lt General USE Commanding

15 August 1945

Today is a day for which we have all been waiting. We heard from our underground network that the Japanese has surrendered, this has yet to be confirmed. The news spread very quickly throughout the camp and the feeling amongst the men was a mixture of numbness, excitement and sheer exhilaration. We could hear chanting from outside the camp, 'It's all over.' The Japanese guards were congregated at the guard room, jabbering away as if not knowing what to do next and some of them appeared to be disconsolate, indicating to me, that the war is really over. I had an incredible feeling of relief. We were ordered to retire to our huts by the Senior Officer Lieut Col White which I believe was to avoid any confrontation with the Japanese.

16 August 1945

The Hong Kong newspaper headlines stated today that Japan has surrendered and accepted unconditionally the peace accord conditions set out by Britain, America, Russia and China. The paper further stated that a cease fire would come into effect immediately.

The Camp Commandant, Col Tokunaga, arrived for the morning count but none of us were lined up as per usual. Lieut Col White approached Tokunaga and told him in no uncertain terms that the war was over and that there would be no count this morning or at any other time. Tokunaga said that he had not heard of any surrender, upon which Lieut Col White produced the Hong Kong newspaper. Tokunaga stood stone-faced for some moments, and then promptly left the camp only to return a short time later to confirm the surrender. One could feel the tension in the air, but this soon abated when the Japanese guards were ordered to withdraw to the guard room. A delegation of officers approached the Japanese and demanded that food be delivered to the camp by noon and if this was not forthcoming, then they would go out and get it themselves. Later the Japanese guards withdrew from the camp completely. A detail of men later left the camp by lorry to obtain food from Japanese supplies.

Lieut Col White issued orders that duty rosters were to be prepared to maintain order and discipline whilst awaiting relief forces.

17 August 1945

On 15 August, rumours of Japan's surrender began to filter through into the camp. The Japanese camp administration withheld all information until today. All prisoners whether able, crippled or blind, assembled on the parade ground, and those who could not walk crawled, assisted by the able bodied men. A party of four men with shovels, proceeded to the '.22' range in the camp, where the first man died and was buried there. He was a S/Sgt of the RAOC. A Union Jack and White Ensign was smuggled into the camp in the first week of captivity, covered in a piece of anti-gas material and finally placed at the feet of this S/Sgt when he was being buried. This of course was carried out without the knowledge of the Japanese, who were present at the burial. The party of men with shovels, as previously mentioned, were detailed to dig the grave and retrieve the two flags from the base of the feet of the skeletons. The condition of the flags were slightly eaten by some form of insects, but quite serviceable to be flown once again. Finally, the Union Jack was affixed and raised to the top of the mast followed by an outburst of 'GOD SAVE THE KING'. What an emotional gathering and one I shall never forget. An end to a wonderful and exciting day. The spirit and mood amongst the men had lifted considerably, even to those in the hospital. My thoughts dwelt particularly on my family, who by now must be aware of the good news.

18 August 1945

This morning on the island, a Union Jack was hoisted at Victoria Peak, it could be clearly seen from the mainland where our camp is, and what a magnificent sight for all to see. Several other flags have also been hoisted in the camp, acknowledging the various nationalities in the ranks, amongst who are Dutch, Portuguese, Chinese, Russian and others. The men are getting a bit anxious about the lack of progress in relieving their situation, particularly in the area of medical supplies and food, and more importantly, they just want to get out of this bloody camp and go home.

Some of the prisoners have family at Stanley civilian camp, particularly those from the HKVDC and they are anxious to reunite with them. The Colonial Secretary, F. C. Gimson, was instrumental in arranging a reunion and several are to be transported from Shamshuipo to Stanley by launch whilst others will use the roads and ferries.

Tomorrow, Lieut Col White of the 2nd Royal Scots and Lieut Col Field of the Royal Artillery have arranged to meet Mr Gimson; for what purposes I am not sure, but no doubt rehabilitation operations will be on the agenda.

I visited the Japanese guardroom and store shortly after their surrender and confiscated approximately 200 sheets of plain white paper, for the purpose of rewriting the diary which I had written in pencil. This is because the diary is now fading and discolouring and therefore it is essential that this work is preserved. These plain sheets were issued to the prisoners for writing correspondence during imprisonment, for in the top right hand corner of each page is a 1 3/4"x 3/8" rectangular block, within which were seven Chinese characters. When translated, they mean, 'Hong Kong Prisoner of War Detainee or Hostage'.

The Chinese Block

23 August 1945

I was talking to Maj Crowe when a lorry entered the camp which contained food and other supplies. One of the items were cigarettes and when offered some packets, I foolishly took them, bearing in mind that it has been well over 12 months since I stopped smoking. I lit one up, inhaled and within a matter of seconds had to grab hold of a pole as the whole camp was spinning. Needless to say, I did not continue to smoke the cigarette. The last few days, starving Chinese were outside the perimeter fence begging for food, but there was very little we could offer them from our meagre rations. This situation was most depressing. A number of Indian troops from Mau Tau Chung Camp visited us and many handshakes and gentle backslapping were the order of the day. Some of the officers and surprisingly myself included were lifted up on their shoulders and marched around. I particularly found that a humbling experience.

29 August 1945

Lieut Cols White and Field left the camp this morning by car driven by a L/Cpl, for what reason we are not sure. Later they returned to report that there was a large British Naval task force to the east of the island. The fleet comprised of two aircraft carriers, one battleship, three cruisers and several auxiliary ships under the command of Rear-Admiral C. H. G. Harcourt. I assume it will not be long before a contingent of men led by the Rear-Admiral will enter the harbour and take control of the situation.

2 September 1945

A contingent of Royal Marines entered the camp, partly as a Public Relations exercise and we were extremely happy to see them. Although some of the more urgent medical cases had been removed to better surroundings and care, we must have looked a real sight. Moves are under way; to move all of us out of the camp with repatriation to England is on most everyone's mind. Many of us will of course want to be reunited with our families in Australia, where they were evacuated before the war, then on to England. Slowly but surely, my health is improving. However, the food I have eaten has not been accepted by my system kindly, which is understandable. I have packed most of my personal belongings particularly this diary.

14 September 1945

Today, I boarded the troop ship *Empress of Australia* near the Star Ferry Terminal in Kowloon that will be sailing to Manila in the Philippines where I shall remain for a time, awaiting a ship to transfer us to Australia.

The official surrender of the Japanese is yet to be finalised but I understand that this will take place in a couple of days' time.

10 October 1945

These past four weeks, the British ex-POWs, along with many Australians, who were POWs, transhipped to Manila from various areas in the Pacific where we were cared for by the Americans and damn well at that. I cannot speak too highly of the care we received from them but their generosity was extraordinary. Naturally my health has improved somewhat, although in due course I will need continued treatment and probably operations to rectify the injuries and disease I still suffer. My legs are still giving me pain, particularly to my ankles and feet.

Today, a small contingent of British ex-POWs, whose families had been evacuated to Australia, together with a large contingent of Australian ex POWs, were meant to embark on the British aircraft carrier, *Formidable*, for Australia, which we were supposed to do on the 8th, but a severe typhoon prevented us from doing so. Even today we had to embark via landing barges as the carrier was unable to berth due to the rough conditions. During the voyage, seventeen ex-POWs died due to their poor health and physical condition. All were buried at sea with full military honours. The welcome accorded to the men when the *Formidable* arrived at Woolloomooloo in Sydney Harbour along with another British aircraft carrier *Indefatigable* on 13 October was wonderful. I was reunited with my wife and children, but it was a sad day for the relatives of the men that had died at sea.

Postscript

Charles Barman's wife and family had spent the war years — like most service families from Hong Kong — in Australia.

The Senior NCOs and their children in Hong Kong's pre-war garrison had been great friends. During evacuation from Hong Kong on the *Awatea*, and in Australia itself, the Barmans teamed up with the Gollege family, Greta Gollege, daughter Pat and son Gerry. They lived in the same suburb in Sydney and later in Moree in the north of New South Wales.[131]

After the war, the Barman family had to wait for Charles in Hargrave Park Army Camp at Warwick Farm some fifteen miles southwest of Sydney. They were not allowed on HMS *Formidable*; instead, the British ex-POWs were transported to this camp by double decker buses. The reunion was emotional, but due to his physical condition Charles was unable to pick his children up. From there they all went back to Moree for a short time, and then moved to a hotel in the heart of Sydney where they stayed for a number of weeks waiting for a passage back to the UK on one of the several liners that entered the harbour. Finally, they were given passage in March 1946 on a South African Union Castle liner, *Stirling Castle*, making it to England in a little over a month via Suez. They stayed at Southampton for some four weeks, before travelling to Dover by train. Charles was still serving, but his physical condition remained unsatisfactory. He was experiencing considerable trouble with his legs, particularly the feet (a problem which stayed with him for the rest of his life), and he had chest, abdomen and bowel problems. Eventually, this resulted in a long stint in a military hospital at Orpington in Kent, where he also spent some time in rehabilitation.

His thoughts then turned to retirement from the Army. One option was to become a Beefeater at the Tower, a position usually reserved for distinguished former Senior NCOs, but as accommodation was not available with the position, he declined.

He was finally discharged from the army on 24 November 1950. But this break from uniform was short-lived. Due to cold war tensions, the authorities decided they required an experienced man to control the gun sites (including AA) in and around London. Charles was the pick and accepted, being re-engaged at the rank of WO1.

He started at Bushy Heath to the north of London, and then moved to Keston in Kent for about eighteen months. It was here that a sixth child, Carol, was born, perhaps because he had missed out on his other children growing up. However, he settled for the remaining time at a more central location at Dulwich which was situated high on a hill and overlooked the city, being only six miles from Whitehall. The gunsite was very secluded — it was like living in the country, as the majority of Dulwich was owned by Dulwich College — and security was paramount. It was also surrounded on two sides by woods and on the other two by a golf course. Barman mainly wore civilian clothes or fatigues and the family resided in the large old converted officer's mess. The gunsite housed 5.25-inch automatic self-loading and rotating guns, which could be virtually operated by one man. They were heavily fortified in thick concrete; only the barrels could be seen.

Charles retired from this position in 1956 and immigrated to Australia as the English weather was not kind to his ailments. He obtained a position in Sydney with a large shipping company controlling all inwards and outwards stock — perfect employment for an ex-Quartermaster. He finally retired in the late 1960s, enjoying life with his wife in a two-bedroom place on the harbour foreshores at Manly, Sydney. In retirement, the couple also travelled back to their old haunts, visiting Hong Kong, Singapore, India and England.

They maintained contact with Crowe, Penfold, Major Duncan, Lieut Col Field and others for many years.

Charles Barman passed away in 1987, his wife having predeceased him in 1981.

Charles Barman is acknowledged in the *Royal Artillery Commemoration Book* and the *Royal Artillery War Diary* for his gallantry and leadership in the Battle of Hong Kong.

Excerpt from the *Royal Artillery Commemoration Book, 1939–1945*:

> The only magazine remaining was at Little Hong Kong, and that was surrounded by the Japs. BQMS Barman of 4th Medium Battery HK/SRA on the last five nights of the siege fought his way in and out of the magazine with a convoy of lorries to get ammunition for the guns in the western half.

Excerpt from the *Royal Artillery War Diary (The Second World War 1939–1945)*:

Almost every evening since the commencement of hostilities convoys were first run to Lye Mun magazine and after that had fallen to the enemy to Little Hong Kong magazine to draw ammunition for the various equipments. These attempts were rendered hazardous by the reason of the fact that the enemy had the roads approaching the magazine under controlled fire assisted by fifth columnists. Most nights the efforts of these parties were crowned with success, but on other nights had to admit defeat. Outstanding amongst the personnel of these parties for his gallantry, devotion to duty and the inspiration of the men under him was BQMS C E Barman of 25 Medium Battery HK/SRA. [Charles Barman was actually in the 4th Medium Battery.] Night after night he proceeded with these parties and during the day distributed the ammunition to the various gun positions.

Appendices

Appendix 1: Bowen Road Hospital Patients, 12 January 1942

Some of the men that were in the hospital including myself were as follows:

Lieut McKechnie
Lieut Campbell
Pte Clark
Pte Albert
Pte Moffat   (Winnipeg Grenadiers Canada)
Pte Olafson
Pte Novak
Pte Charboyer
Pte Sartey

Lieut McGhee
Sgt Whippy
Cpl Butterworth
Cpl Blackie
L/Cpl Burns
L/Cpl Kirkpatrick   (2nd Royal Scots)
Pte Quinn
Pte Gordon
Pte McNally

Sig Squires   (Royal Canadian Corps of Signals)

Pte Tartleton   (Royal Army Service Corps)

Cpl Jenkins   (Royal Corps of Signals)
Cpl Hodge

L/Bdr Stanton
Gnr Griffiths   (8th Coast Regiment RA)
Gnr Davis A.
Gnr Davis J.

Gnr Coombes   (5th AA Regiment RA)

L/Cpl Tubbs   (Royal Engineers)
Spr Sarsfield

QMS Haynes   (Royal Army Ordnance Corps)

Cpl Coulson
Pte Clemo
Pte De Roza   (Hong Kong Volunteer Defence Corps)
Pte Didsbury
Pte Prish

Appendix 2: Roll of Army and Navy Batmen in Order of Rank

Rank	Name	Unit	Address
BQMS	Barman	1st Reg HK/SRA	353 Sturry Rd Canterbury Kent Eng
Sgt	Tupper	12th Coast Reg RA	159 Orchard St Chichester Sussex Eng
Sgt	Sutherland	2nd Royal Scots Reg	C/- Royal Scots Assoc Edinburgh Scot
Sgt	Bullimore	Dockyard Defence Corps	SEE Depot Portsmouth Naval Yard Portsmouth Hampshire Eng
Sgt	Simpson	Dockyard Defence Corps	SCE Rosyth Naval Dockyard Scotland
Sgt	Kernaghan	Dockyard Police Dockyard Defence Corps	15 Mayfair St Old Park Rd Belfast Northern Ireland
Cpl	Holden	12th Coy RAOC	C/- OIC Records Deptford Kent Eng
Cpl	Mattison	12th Coy RAOC	'Colinton' Great Berry Rd Crown Hill Nr Plymouth Devon Eng
L/Bdr	Birkinshaw	12th Coast Reg RA	90 Cross Lane Royston Nr Barnsley Yorkshire Eng
L/Bdr	Holland	8th Coast Reg RA	9 Vincent Cresc Shoeburyness Essex Eng
L/Bdr	Robinson	5th AA Reg RA	20 Gordon Rd Canterbury Kent Eng
L/Bdr	Roche	8th Coast Reg RA	28 Cedar Rd Beddington Surrey Eng
L/Cpl	Bushell	Corp of Military Police	C/- Mrs C M Bushell 43 Leslie Grove East Croydon Surrey Eng
L/Cpl	Earnshaw	RAPC	'St Aubins' Long Lane Dalton Huddersfield Yorkshire Eng
L/Cpl	Fowler	2nd Royal Scots Reg	Albion House Main St Thorn Hill Stirling Scotland
L/Cpl	Hobbs	12th Coy RASC	C/- H Castdood High Lanes Grovesnor Rd Godalming Surrey Eng

L/Cpl	Pickles	6th Sect RAOC	25 Heidelburg Rd Totter Lane Bradford Yorkshire Eng
L/Cpl	Sawyer	RAVC	60 Arlington Ave Islington London Eng
L/Cpl	Taylor	Royal Engineers	59 South Meadow Lane Preston Lancs Eng
Spr	James	Royal Engineers	The College Garage Higher Heath Whitchurch Shropshire Eng
Spr	Price	Royal Engineers	16 Bradford Tce Birches Head Hanley Stoke-On-Trent Staffs Eng
Spr	Richmond	Royal Engineers	56 Deepdale Ave Grove Hill Middlesborough Yorkshire Eng
Spr	Moore	Royal Engineers	14 Rignell Rd Great Misseden Bucks Eng
Spr	Black	Royal Engineers	26 Fair St Drogheda Louth Ireland
Spr	Lee	HKVDC	C/- Chan and Lee Architects 51 Cumberland Rd Kowloon Tong HK
Spr	Bhumgara	HKVDC	Address unknown
Spr	McMasters	HKVDC	C/- Hong Kong Whampoa Docks Kowloon Hong Kong
Gnr	Blazey	5AA Reg RA	30 St Johns Rd Seven Kings Essex Eng
Gnr	Brain	8th Coast Reg RA	Church St Little Dean Gloucester Eng
Gnr	Cumming	12th Coast Reg RA	4 Whitley St Garston Liverpool Lanc Eng
Gnr	Dinner	12th Coast Reg RA	Cross Parks Holsworthy Devon Eng
Gnr	Elsworth	5th AA Reg RA	Bostcot Waldwon Bournemouth Hampshire Eng
Gnr	Hannington	5th AA Reg RA	68 Devonshire Rd Southall Middlesex Eng
Gnr	Eastwood	8th Coast Reg RA	Kings Arms Hotel Silsden Nr Keighley Yorkshire Eng
Gnr	Webber	8th Coast Reg RA	148 Emlyn Ave Ebbew Vale Monmouthshire Wales
Gnr	York	12th Coast Reg RA	14 Pembroke Rd Southwell Bristol Gloucestershire Eng
Gnr	Snell	12th Coast Reg RA	42 Mount Gould Rd Plymouth Devon Eng
Gnr	Skinner	HKVDC	C/- Hong Kong Shanghai Bank HK Or London Eng
Gnr	O'Grady	HKVDC	British American Tobacco Coy Westminster House Milbank London Eng
Gnr	Pedersen	HKVDC	C/- Jebson and Coy Hong Kong
Pte	Albiston	RAMC	323 Leith Walk Edinburgh Scotland

Pte	Franklin A E	RAMC	8 Redcliffe Rd Chelmsford Essex Eng
Pte	Cheeseborough	RAMC	Address unknown
Pte	Smith FW	12th Coy RASC	8 Rue de L'Assomption Paris 16 France
Pte	Smith C	12th Coy RASC	42 Brockenhurst Way Norbury London SW16 Eng
Pte	Smart	12th Coy RASC	Wood Dene Woodlands Rd Hockley Essex Eng
Pte	Tanner	12th Coy RASC	5 Wellington Hill West Henleage Bristol Somerset Eng
Pte	Hastings	12th Coy RASC	4 Doric Ave Lower Bradbury Stockport Cheshire Eng
Pte	Winkworth	1st Middlesex Reg	13 Burlington Gardens Acton London W3 Eng
Pte	Woods	1st Middlesex Reg	4 Park Rd Edmonton London Eng
Pte	Bradley	1st Middlesex Reg	Edenwall Coleford Gloucester Eng
Pte	Francomb	1st Middlesex Reg	26 Manning Rd Heathway Dagenham Essex Eng
Pte	Normandale	1st Middlesex Reg	43 Argyle Rd Ilford Essex Eng
Pte	Hale	1st Middlesex Reg	7 Park Lane Chudwell Heath Romford Essex Eng
Pte	Jones	1st Middlesex Reg	16 Turner St Hereford Herefordshire Eng
Pte	Chainey	6th Section RAOC	Address unknown
Pte	Haughey	2nd Royal Scots Reg	Derry Hassanmore Downimp Co Donegal Ireland
Pte	McDougall	2nd Royal Scots Reg	Kingsmore Cottages Slateford Edinburgh Scotland
Pte	McMillan	2nd Royal Scots Reg	145 Broughton Rd Edinburgh Scotland
Pte	McKay	2nd Royal Scots Reg	29 Cheyne St Stockbridge Edinburgh Scotland
Pte	Howe	RAMC	'Marine View' Nr Annan Dumphries Scotland
Pte	Kaluzhany	HKVDC	C/- Hong Kong or Shanghai Hotels Hong Kong
Pte	Loncraine	HKVDC	'Berk Lodge' Beaconsfield Bucks Eng
Pte	Lam	HKVDC	Released from camp August 1942 Address Unknown
Pte	Novikiou	HKVDC	C/- Gilman and Co Ltd Hong Kong
Pte	Prata	HKVDC	C/- Hong Kong and Shanghai Hotels Hong Kong
Pte	Pinna	HKVDC	Address unknown
Pte	Robertson	HKVDC	Pure Cane Mattress Coy Hong Kong Or United Mattress Coy Bush House Aldwich London Eng
Pte	Randle	HKVDC	Address Unknown

Pte	Alltree	HKVDC	C/- Supreme Court Hong Kong
Pte	Gardner	HKVDC	Address Unknown
Pte	Clibborn	HKVDC	C/- Imperial Chemical Industries Ltd Millbank London Eng
Pte	Schiller	HKVDC	1173 Bubbling Well Rd Appt 18 Shanghai China
Pte	Burch	HKVDC	227 Prince Edward Rd Kowloon Hong Kong or C/- HK Government
Pte	White	HKVDC	China Power Light Coy Kowloon Hong Kong
Pte	Miller	Dockyard Defence Corps	E.M.D.O Depot Chatham Naval Dockyard Chatham Kent Eng
Pte	Tull	Dockyard Defence Corps	C/- Messrs Mears Bros 157 Sydenham Rd London SE26 Eng
Pte	Evans	RAPC	Evans Bros Alltgoch Quarries Cwrtnewydd Llanybyther Carmarthenshire South Wales
Sig	Latter	Royal Corps of Signals	5 Diamond Villas Paddock Wood Kent Eng
Sig	Howell	Royal Corps of Signals	Celyn House Whitfield Rd Hollywell Flintshire Nth Wales
Sig	Smith N L	HKVDC	5 Village Rd Happy Valley Hong Kong Colonial Secretary Hong Kong Govt.
Lead Sea	Coleman	Royal Navy	C/- 79 Grosvenor Rd Romford Essex Eng Or C/- RN Barracks Portsmouth Hampshire Eng
Lead Sea	Harveson	Royal Navy	Address Unknown
Able Sea	Bartlett	Royal Navy	32 Poppy Rd Bassett Green Southampton Hampshire Eng
Able Sea	Barnes	Royal Navy	23 Conniston Drive Kentwood Estate Ticehurst Berkshire Eng
Able Sea	Coite	Royal Navy	4 Staddon Close Heath Farm Plympton Nr Plymouth Devon Eng
Able Sea	Felstead	Royal Navy	73 Libra Rd Bow London E1 Eng
Able Sea	Fairburn	Royal Navy	8 Hargraves St Grimsby Lincolnshire Eng
Able Sea	Glover	Royal Navy	New Mills Newcastle-On-Tyne Eng
Able Sea	Hooker	Royal Navy	15 Council Houses Phoenix Green Hartley Wintney Hampshire Eng
Able Sea	James	Royal Navy	37 Rectory Ave Prestwich Manchester Lancashire Eng
Able Sea	Laurence	Royal Navy	Calle Farmiento 25 Curdad Buenos Aires Argentina or 59 Broadlords Rd Swaythling Hampton Park Southampton Hampshire Eng

Able Sea	McCall	Royal Navy	Address Unkown
Able Sea	Williams	Royal Navy	47 Fore Street St Columb Major Cornwall Eng
Able Sea	Hodgson	Royal Navy	56 Oswald Rd Lupset Wakefield Yorkshire Eng
Teleg	Bell	Royal Navy	3 Westgate St Hevingham Norwich Norfolk Eng
Teleg	Franklin	Royal Navy	Gordon Rd Northcote Auckland N.Z. or C/- Claude Neolights of New Zealand Hobson St Auckland New Zealand
Teleg	Goodwin	Royal Navy	12 King St Sutton Bridge Holbeach Lincolnshire Eng
Teleg	Walker	Royal Navy	15 Fancott Rd Northfield Birmingham Warwickshire Eng
Mne	Chamberlain	Royal Marines	27 Preston Ave Wymondham Norfolk Eng
Mne	Glover	Royal Marines	Trelights Port Isaac Cornwall Eng Or R M Barracks Plymouth Devon. Eng
Mne	Hamer	Royal Marines	6 Osmund Ave Breighmet Bolton Lancashire Eng
Mne	Hancock	Royal Marines	62 Manstone Ave Sidmouth Devon Eng or R M Barracks Plymouth Devon Eng
Mne	Hulme	Royal Marines	Address Unknown
Mne	Handsley	Royal Marines	4 Mount Hedgecumbe Terrace Devonport Devon Eng or 10 High St Gainsborough Lincolnshire Eng
Mne	Kilroy	Royal Marines	8 Union Terrace Chapel- Allerton Leeds Yorkshire Eng
Mne	Kenworthy	Royal Marines	Address Unknown
Mne	Pearce	Royal Marines	175 Westfield Rd Southsea Hampshire Eng
Mne	Rogerson	Royal Marines	104 Oak Ave Newton-Le-Willows Lancashire Eng
Mne	Rogers	Royal Marines	'Huffley Farm' Broad Oak Nr Shrewsbury Shropshire Eng
Mne	Sanderson	Royal Marines	C/- 'G' Coy Royal Marine Barracks Plymouth Eng
Mne	Sutherland	Royal Marines	10 Holmside Place Newcastle-On-Tyne Northumberland Eng or RN Barracks Plymouth Devon Eng
Bug	Rogers	Royal Marines	Royal Marines Stone House Plymouth Devon Eng

Appendix: 3 Major General C. M. Maltby, MC

Major General Maltby is easily approachable, difficult to interview and to the Japanese, Special Prisoner No. 1. Unlike most successful soldiers, he is allergic to the personal pronoun, intolerant of fools and the possessor of a shrewd sense of humour. Born within the sound of 'Bow Bells', London, on Friday 13 January 1890 ('a bad combination, he'll never be weaned,' said his mother), he regards himself as a true cockney, with the traditional hardiness of a Londoner — perhaps with good reason, for he weathered the first winter when the Thames froze and a whole ox was roasted on the ice. He was taken to Travencore, India, while still a baby, his father being a Yorkshireman and a member of the Indian Civil Service. His only recollection of this early period was the excitement he felt when he witnessed his first execution of a sheep.

Educated at Kings School, Canterbury and Bedford School he told me 'he learned nothing', showed little aptitude for games, collected second colours only, but earned some distinction as a long distance runner. Over a year absent from school, he maintained a discreet and stubborn silence about this aspect. Rumour has it that he ran away and joined the Army as a trooper, but however, he insists he first donned His Majesty's uniform as a school cadet in 1902. He attended the Coronation and funeral of Edward VII, the former event as a chorister and the latter as one of the cadets lining the streets. He went to the 'Shop' in 1909 and was commissioned from there in September 1910 as a 2/Lieut attached to the Royal Sussex Regiment in Rawalpindi, India. He transferred to the Indian Army of Russell's Infantry and Jat Regiment in 1911, in time to attend the Delhi Durbar of that year in company with Indian Mutiny Veterans. He saw his first active service in 1913–1914 in the Persian Gulf Arms Traffic blockade and is one of the very few Army officers with the Naval General Service Medal, which is worn next to his Military Cross and has long proved an object of curiosity to most of us. From 1914–1920, he got all the fighting and change of scenery he wanted, being in Mesopotamia (twice), Egypt, Salonika, Turkey, South Russia (with Denniken) and the North West Frontier of India, winning the Military Cross at Mesopotamia and five times mentioned in despatches, being wounded in the leg at the Battle of Hanna, finishing the war with a Brevt Majority. Further war services include Wasiristan in 1923 and 1937.

Equally varied peacetime soldiering includes, in order of appointments, Instructor of Musketry, Staff College Quetta, India, RAF Staff College, GSO2 Army headquarters India, Instructor GS01 Staff College Quetta, India (a job which has been held by many famous Commanders), and GS01 Baluchistan District. He later commanded the 3rd Jhelum Calcutta Area, 19th Infantry Brigade and finally, Deccan District previous to his present appointment. Though loving India, he considers himself an unfortunate exile from the land of his birth and will never forgive 'Hitler' for upsetting all his arrangements to retire to his comfortable Somerset home at the beginning of 1940.

So much for the soldier, and of the man there is little he will tell us, and in his own words, 'I'm pretty useless at games, finding no pleasure in chasing small balls except for exercise' and that in the face of our personal experience of him on the 'Flagstaff House' tennis courts. His other pastimes are shooting, hunting, pig sticking and bird photography. Regarding indoor sports, he just said 'a limited liking for pink gins and beer'. As for languages, he was fluent in Urdu, Pushto and Persian plus 'Billingsgate'. He has a wife in India and two beautiful daughters at school near Taunton, Somerset, England, who of course he believes, take after him. We know him neither for 'red tabs' nor the conventional irascibility that a Major General can conceal. A devoted family man and a 'Sahib' in the best sense of the word.

Appendix 4: Nominal Roll of British and Indian Prisoners of 1st HK/SRA Regiment at Shamshuipo Camp as of 21 March 1942

Rank	Name		Army No.	Rank	Name	Army No.
Maj	Duncan			S/Maj	Maghar Singh	2590
Maj	Crowe			Jem	Dost Mohammad	3031
Capt	Hoyland			Jem	Dadan Kahn	2332
Lieut	Vinter			Jem	Kishen Singh	2561
Lieut	Dawson			Jem	Lal Khan	3136
Lieut	Trapman			Jem	Samund Singh	3284
Lieut	Allanson			Jem	Farzand Ali	2717
Lieut	Parkes			Hav	Chanan Singh	2934
Lieut	Walkden			Hav	Tara Singh	2847
Lieut	Hoskins			Hav	Hazara Singh	2591
BQMS	Barman	(d)	1027631	Hav	Gurdial Singh	7741
BQMS	May		1070149	Hav	Dilbagh Singh	2848
BQMS	Yearling		809823	Hav	Boton Khan	3196
BQMS	Johns	(a)	1416983	Hav	Wilayat Khan	3125
BQMS	Searle	(b)	1043916	Hav	Jagir Singh	3251
BQMS	Adamson	(c)	1424392	Hav	Tara Singh	2731
S/Sgt	Gollege	(#)	1415975	Hav	Mohammad Amir Khan	3089
Sgt	Waterhouse		847044	Hav	Saghar Khan	3035
Sgt	Phillips	(#)	–	Hav	Mohammad Anwar	5039
Sgt	Holberry		–	Hav	Mohammad Akbar	3211
Sgt	Buckett		819844	Hav	Farman Ali	3356
Sgt	Wilson	(*)	809818	Hav	Ahmad Khan	2935
				Hav/M	Hur Mohammad	2942
L/Sgt	Gordon	(#)	1069565	Naik	Dalip Singh	3250
L/Sgt	Bromley	(#)	1425948	Naik	Bachan Singh	3042
L/Sgt	Williams	(#)	1065679	Naik	Chanan Singh	3683
L/Sgt	Musto	(##)	1069779	Naik	Ghulam Martaza	3200
				Naik	Wais Mohammad	3073
				Naik	Mohammad Ayam	3612

Legend

(a)	QM of 1st Mn Bty HK/SRA
(b)	QM of 2nd Mn Bty HK/SRA
(c)	QM of 3rd Med Bty HK/SRA
(d)	QM of 4th Med Bty HK/SRA
(#)	Artificers
(*)	Artillery Clerk
(##)	Shoeing Smith

Gnr	Sajjan Singh	4837
Gnr	Bachan Singh	3706
Gnr	Kishen Singh	4875
Gnr	Dashand Singh	5428
Gnr	Naranjan Singh	4692
Gnr	Gurbachan Singh	3744
Gnr	Kartar Singh	7611
Gnr	Hakim Singh	4837
Gnr	Bag Singh	7880
Gnr	Nasib Singh	7545
Gnr	Anan Singh	7598
Gnr	Indar Singh	7612
Gnr	Babu Singh	7865
Gnr	Sohan Singh	7720
Gnr	Jarnail Singh	7506
Gnr	Jagar Singh	4670
Gnr	Harbans Singh	7734
Gnr	Banta Singh	7912
Gnr	Banta Singh	4812
Gnr	Warean Singh	7548
Gnr	Sapuran Singh	7544
Gnr	Jan Singh	4656
Gnr	Tara Singh	7730
Gnr	Tahal Singh	3776
Gnr	Dalip Singh	7700
Gnr	Ajit Singh	7509
Gnr	Haud Singh	7863
Gnr	Naranjan Singh	3823
Gnr	Ranjit Singh	7542
Gnr	Mehan Singh	4678
Gnr	Indar Singh	3784
Gnr	Karnail Singh	7913
Gnr	Ishar Singh	4019
Gnr	Bahkshish Singh	7735
Gnr	Narajan Singh	7515

Naik	Sulaklan Singh	2960
Naik	Mohammad Illahi	3336
Naik	Ilam Din	4025
Naik	Enayat Ullah	3370
Naik	Sher Jang	3170
Naik	Karim Din	3367
Naik	Laklin Din	3315
Naik	Mohammad Shariff	4982
Naik	Mohammad Khan	3605
L/Naik	Sowaran Singh	3994
L/Naik	Dial Singh	3696
L/Naik	Sohan Singh	3707
L/Naik	Balwant Singh	3725
L/Naik	Kalyan Singh	7519
L/Naik	Harbans Singh	3724
L/Naik	Sardara Singh	2837
L/Naik	Sandgara Singh	3675
L/Naik	Bur Singh	3942
Langri	Teja Singh	156
Langri	Teja Singh	121
Tptr	Balwant Singh	7533
Gnr	Uggar Singh	4788
Gnr	Baghwan Singh	7567
Gnr	Mohan Sing	4636
Gnr	Puran Singh	4794
Gnr	Sarain Singh	3991
Gnr	Jagir Singh	7621
Gnr	Kaka Singh	7881
Gnr	Sawaran Singh	4833
Gnr	Parilan Singh	7838
Gnr	Teja Singh	3716
Gnr	Ragbir Singh	3033
Gnr	Hari Singh	4776
Gnr	Jagan Singh	7514
Gnr	Hakin Singh	4658
Gnr	Darshan Singh	7738
Gnr	Harbant Singh	7518
Gnr	Babu Singh	7879
Gnr	Shan Singh	2562
Gnr	Pyara Singh	7573
Gnr	Dimak Singh	4795
Gnr	Kartar Singh	7642
Gnr	Mohan Singh	7557
Gnr	Dalip Singh	5420
Gnr	Kartar Singh	5410

Gnr	Jora Singh	7873	Gnr	Bakhtaur Singh	7863
Gnr	Sawaran Singh	4633	Gnr	Sadhu Singh	4704
Gnr	Jamail Singh	7716	Gnr	Bur Singh	7739
Gnr	Dalip Singh	7546	Gnr	Jara Singh	7911
Gnr	Balwant Singh	7691	Gnr	Labh Singh	7541
Gnr	Aubar Singh	4736	Gnr	Rayjindar Singh	4674
Gnr	Kartar Singh	3732	Gnr	Kehar Singh	7536
Gnr	Mohan Singh	7692	Gnr	Darshan Singh	4720
Gnr	Bant Singh	5465	Gnr	Ajmir Singh	5464
Gnr	Mokand Singh	7855	Gnr	Indar Singh	7685
Gnr	Kehar Singh	7559	Gnr	Gurbachan Singh	5421
Gnr	Rup Singh	7511	Gnr	Gomand Singh	4885
Gnr	Asa Singh	7569	Gnr	Gulbant Singh	7551

Appendix 5: List of Prisoners in Shamshuipo Camp Whom I Know Well as of 21 March 1942

Rank	Name	Unit	Rank	Name	Unit
Maj Gen	Maltby	GOC of Troops in South China	Maj	Branson	HKVDC
			Maj	Jarvis	HKVDC
Brig	Peffers	HQ CC	Capt	Robertson	HKVDC
Brig	McCleod	HQ CC (CRA)	Capt	Atkinson	1stHKRegHK/SRA
Brig	Clifford	HQ CC	Capt	Waters	1stHKRegHK/SRA
Brig	Wallis	HQ CC	Capt	Knowles	12th Coast Reg RA
Cmdr	Millet	RN	Capt	Jones	2nd Royal Scots
Col	Hopkins	RAOC	Capt	Campbell	2nd Royal Scots
Lt Col	Simpson	HQ CC	Capt	Miller	2nd Royal Scots
Lt Col	Penfold	12th Coast Reg RA	Capt	Warrrack	RAMC
Lt Col	Field	5th AA Regiment RA	Capt	Lynch	RAMC
Lt Col	Lamb	Royal Engineers	Capt	Johnson	RADC
Lt Col	Galpin	FA Staff	Capt	Belton	York and Lancs Reg
Lt Col	Kilpatrick	FA Staff	Capt	Bennett	Presb. Chaplain
Lt Col	Andrews-Levinge	RASC	Capt	James	8th Coast Reg RA
Lt Col	Fredericks	RASC	Capt	Hoyland	8th Coast Reg RA
Lt Col	Wilson	Royal Engineers	Capt	Skipworth	8th Coast Reg RA
Lt Col	White	2nd Royal Scots	Capt	Whittaker	5th AA Reg RA
Lt Col	Shackleton	RAMC	Capt	Barker	5th AA Reg RA
Lt Col	Rudolf	RAMC	Capt	Escott	FA Staff
Lt Col	Stuart	1st Middlesex Rgt	Capt	Hubbard	FA Staff
Lt Col	Cardogan-Rawlinson	2/14 Punjabis	Capt	Thompson	RAPC
Lt Col	Price	RROC	Capt	Wiseman	RASC
Maj	Crowe	1st HK Reg HK/SRA	Capt	Flood	1st Middlesex Reg
Maj	Duncan	1st HK Reg HK/SRA	Capt	Robinson	RAMC

Maj	Mills	12th Coast Reg RA	Capt	Strachan	RAMC
Maj	Anderson	12th Coast Reg RA	Capt	Toole	8th Coast Reg RA
Maj	Forrester	12th Coast Reg RA	Capt	Hilton	Royal Engineers
Maj	Stephenson	12th Coast Reg RA	Capt	Woodward	IAMC
Maj	Bemans	12th Coast Reg RA	Capt	Davis	HKVDC
Maj	Templer	8th Coast Reg RA	Capt	Burch	HKVDC
Maj	Morgan	5th AA Reg RA	Lieut	Hoskins	1st HKRegHK/SRA
Maj	Cross	HQ CC RA	Lieut	Willcocks	1st HKRegHK/SRA
Maj	Perry	2nd Royal Scots	Lieut	Vinter	1st HKRegHK/SRA
Maj	Harland	2nd Royal Scots	Lieut	Andrews	1st HKRegHK/SRA
Maj	Walker	2nd Royal Scots	Lieut	Parkes	1st HKRegHK/SRA
Maj	Marsh	1sr Middlesex Reg	Lieut	Simpson	1st HKRegHK/SRA
Maj	Mayer	1st Middlesex Reg	Lieut	Challoner	1st HKRegHK/SRA
Maj	Hedgecow	1st Middlesex Reg	Lieut	Allanson	8 Coast Reg RA
Maj	Guscott	1st Middlesex Reg	Lieut	Dawson	8 Coast Reg RA
Maj	Berridge	Royal Engineers	Lieut	Taylor	5th AA Reg RA
Maj	Parsons	Royal Engineers	Lieut	Hitchcock	5th AA Reg RA
Maj	Foley	RAOC	Lieut	Pike	12th Coast Reg RA
Maj	Browning	5/7th Rajputs	Lieut	Ellis	12th Coast Reg RA
Maj	Curran	RAMC	Lieut	Austin	RAEC
Maj	Brown	RAMC	Lieut	Barford	RASC
Maj	Mold	RASC	Lieut	Chapman	RASC

Appendix 6: Nominal Roll of Prisoners in Shamshuipo Camp Whom I Know Well as of 21 March 1942

Rank	Name	Unit
Lieut	Woodcock	Royal Engineers
Lieut	Jessop	Royal Engineers
Lieut	Harris	Royal Engineers
Lieut	Crawley	Royal Engineers
Lieut	Llewellyn	RIASC
Lieut	Hancock	RIASC
Lieut	Wardell	RAOC
Lieut	Markey	RAOC
Lieut	Wilson	RAOC
Lieut	Hanlon	RAOC
Lieut	Sutcliffe	RAOC
Lieut	McGhee	2nd Royal Scots
Lieut	Rothwell	1st Middlesex Reg
Lieut	MacKechnie	RROC
Lieut	Campbell	RROC

Other Ranks	Name	Unit	Army No.
RSM	Gould	12th Coast Reg RA	5720230
CSM	Meade	2nd Royal Scots	–
MG	Brooks	12th Coast Reg RA	1410966
MG	Cooper	HQ RACC	5415550
MG	Cousins	8th Coast Reg RA	1421493
MG	Berry	8th Coast Reg RA	1061660
BSM	Scragg	5th AA Reg RA	–
BSM	Mills	8th Coast Reg RA	1062585
BSM	Morley	12th Coast Reg RA	1051733
BSM	McMurtry	12th Coast Reg RA	1058692
BSM	Barlow	12th Coast Reg RA	816130
BSM	Allport	12th Coast Reg RA	1064171
BSM	Radford	12th Coast Reg RA	–
RQMS	Lloyd	12th Coast Reg RA	1045690
BQMS	Sumner (a)	12th Coast Reg RA	818673
BQMS	Alexander	12th Coast Reg RA	821969
BQMS	Pettit (b)	8th Coast Reg RA	1033573
BQMS	Dicks	8th Coast Reg RA	1422100
QMS	Daniels	Royal Engineers	–
QMS	Wellwood	Royal Engineers	–
QMS	O'Connor	Royal Engineers	–
QMS	Locke	Royal Engineers	–
QMS	Upton	Royal Engineers	–
QMS	Jordon	Royal Engineers	–
S/Sgt	Amberson	RAOC	–
S/Sgt	Hunter	RAOC	–
S/Sgt	Smith (#)	8th Coast Reg RA	–
Sgt	Eves	8th Coast Reg RA	1414266
Sgt	Gunston	12th Coy RASC	–
Sgt	Martin	12th Coy RASC	–
L/Cpl	Dart	12th Coy RASC	–

Legends
- (a) QM of 20th Hvy Bty RA
- (b) QM of 36th Hvy Bty RA
- (#) Artificer

Appendix 7: Nominal Roll of Indian Prisoners of 1st HK/SRA Regiment at North Point Camp as of 21 March 1942

Rank	Name	Army No.	Rank	Name	Army No.
Jem	Ahmed Khan	2689	Gnr	Wali Mohammad	4756
Jem	Munshi Khan	3169	Gnr	Bagge Khan	4895
Jem	Hazara Singh	2628	Gnr	Ghulam Haidar	4907
Jem	Haranjan Singh	3160	Gnr	Ali Asghar	4945

QMH	Ghulam Rasul	2824	Gnr	Man Jur Hussain	5064
Hav	Gurdip Singh	2869	Gnr	Sher Johan Khan	5091
Hav	Amir Mohammad	3306	Gnr	Magor Mohammad	5111
Hav	Nawab Khan	2825	Gnr	Waris Ali	5131
Hav	Rahmal Khan	2687	Gnr	Sher Bay	5172
Hav	Abdul Rahman	3156	Gnr	Babu Khan	5261
Hav	Mohammad Akbar	3181	Gnr	Malak Sher Khan	7843
Hav	Karam Busc	3085	Gnr	Ghulam Sarawar	7850
Hav	Mohammad Ali	3985	Gnr	Abdul Ghani	7917
Hav	Fatteh Khan	3180	Gnr	Barkat Ali	7923
Naik	Ahmed Din	3328	Gnr	Shaffi Mohammad	7933
Naik	Mohammad Iqbal	5177	Gnr	Fagus Ali	7927
Naik	Maula Busc	3344	Gnr	Bag Ali	7966
Naik	Allah Gar Khan	3036	Gnr	Dil Mohammad	7980
Naik	Mohammad Aslam	3272	Gnr	Mohammad Sadij	8004
Naik	Arjan Singh	2961	Gnr	Mohammad Hussain	8020
Naik	Desa Singh	3166	Gnr	Allah Ditta	8045
Naik	Buhd Singh	2988	Gnr	Nur Ahmed	8061
L/Naik	Daray Khan	3058	Gnr	Mehar Mohammad	2547
L/Naik	Mohammad Araf	3179	Gnr	Mohammad Illapi	2751
L/Naik	Sardar Ali	3192	Gnr	Mohammad Hayat	3191
L/Naik	Shahra Khan	3055	Gnr	Rahmat Khan	3325
L/Naik	Ahmed Hassan	3664	Gnr	Saraj Din	3962
L/Naik	Sher Mohammad	2898	Gnr	Hiamat Khan	4645
L/Naik	Afyar Khan	3657	Gnr	Ali Mohammad	4710
L/Naik	Mohammad Fazal	3157	Gnr	Hayat Mohammad	4767
L/Naik	Karamat Hussain	3334	Gnr	Shabir Hussain	4804
L/Naik	Mohammad Alam	3328	Gnr	Hur Khan	4936
L/Naik	Khalas Khan	3643	Gnr	Rahmat Ullah	4958
L/Naik	Darbara Singh	3638	Gnr	Hur Khan	4936
L/Naik	Mehma Singh	7763	Gnr	Rahmat Ullah	4958
L/Naik	Malak Singh	4870	Gnr	Hur Mohammad	5076
L/Naik	Kishen Singh	3834	Gnr	Hur Mohammad	5092
L/Naik	Ishar Singh	4789	Gnr	Mohammad Hussain	5121
L/Naik	Kartar Singh	3010	Gnr	Karam Dad	5735
L/Naik	Manna Singh	5023	Gnr	Mohammad Yusaf	5178
Gnr	Asghar Khan	5065	Gnr	Mohammad Apal	7844
Gnr	Shaffi Mohammad	2718	Gnr	Abdullah Khan	7832
Gnr	Wali Dad	3178	Gnr	Tagi Mohammad	7910
Gnr	Mohammad Ismal	3305	Gnr	Roshan Din	7928
Gnr	Alam Sher	3391	Gnr	Taj Din	7934
Gnr	Magar Hussain	4612	Gnr	Mohammad Khan	7955
Gnr	Karin Din	4625	Gnr	Shaffi Mohammad	8024
Gnr	Mohammad Khan	8050	Gnr	Hakim Singh	7707

Gnr	Mohammad Hussain	7936	Gnr	Gurder Singh	7710
Gnr	Buta Khan	2600	Gnr	Jarnail Singh	7714
Gnr	Farzand Ali	3130	Gnr	Jat Singh	7831
Gnr	Mian Mohammad	3194	Gnr	Karnail Singh	3839
Gnr	Fazal Dad	4608	Gnr	Kundan Singh	7572
Gnr	Magar Khan	4651	Gnr	Tara Singh	2820
Gnr	Ghulam Nabi	4745	Gnr	Kartar Singh	3756
Gnr	Ghasamfar Khan	4853	Gnr	Charan Singh	4866
Gnr	Habib Khan	4897	Gnr	Dalip Singh	4891
Gnr	Khan Bahadur	4939	Gnr	Dalip Singh	5495
Gnr	Qasim Ali	5002	Gnr	Baknshish Singh	4664
Gnr	Sher Bay	5081	Gnr	Dalip Singh	7615
Gnr	Sher Mohammad	5103	Gnr	Haranjan Singh	4631
Gnr	Ghulam Hussain	5128	Gnr	Baktaur Singh	4667
Gnr	Hur Mohammad	5167	Gnr	Darshan Singh	7565
Gnr	Abdullah Khan	5190	Gnr	Ajaib Singh	7595
Gnr	Mehar Din	7821	Gnr	Karnail Singh	7689
Gnr	Mohammad Khan	7849	Gnr	Jarnail Singh	7731
Gnr	Fazal Din	7916	Gnr	Dalip Singh	4033
Gnr	Barkat Ali	7918	Gnr	Ram Singh	7602
Gnr	Mohammad Sharif	7935	Gnr	Dhanna Singh	3642
Gnr	Umar Hayat Khan	7937	Gnr	Piara Singh	5497
Gnr	Khushi Mohammad	7965	Gnr	Jogindar Singh	4884
Gnr	Mayat Khan	7961	Gnr	Ranjit Singh	7536
Gnr	Ghulam Rasue	7978	Gnr	Bachan Singh	7614
Gnr	Ibrahim Khan	8016	Gnr	Basant Singh	7704
Gnr	Rahmat Ullah	8027	Gnr	Jogindar Singh	7709
Gnr	Allah Ditta	8051	Gnr	Ujager Singh	7713
Gnr	Allah Ditta	7938	Gnr	Banta Singh	7695
Gnr	Buta Khan	7939	Gnr	Mehar Singh	7825
Gnr	Ahmed Khan	2897	Gnr	Dalip Singh	3754
Gnr	Hur Illahi	3091	Gnr	Arjan Singh	4733
Gnr	Shamsher Singh	4790	Gnr	Karnail Singh	3691
Gnr	Pritan Singh	7628	Gnr	Jagat Singh	4735
Gnr	Haranjan Singh	3986	Gnr	Jajar Singh	4815
Gnr	Shangra Singh	7663	Gnr	Jaswant Singh	5478
Gnr	Gurdit Singh	7566	Tptr	Ahmed Ali	7791
Gnr	Ajmer Singh	7703	Langri	Naurata Singh	133
Gnr	Mehar Singh	3902	Langri	Bakhshish Singh	155
Gnr	Bikkar Singh	7641	Langri	Kartar Singh	151
Gnr	Mohindar Singh	7635	Langri	Tahal Singh	152
Gnr	Asa Singh	4700	Langri	Naranjan Singh	100
Gnr	Teja Singh	5492	Langri	Ahmed Khan	153

Gnr	Ranga Singh	7571	Langri	Pruan Ditta	125
Gnr	Lakha Singh	7561	Langri	Nadar Khan	120
Gnr	ChainChil Singh	7690	Langri	Gulmaway Khan	133
			Langri	Mohammad Sadij	116
			Maulvi	Kuresh Mohammad	

Appendix 8: The Indians buried by Argyle Street

Army

No.	Rank	Name	Unit	Died on	Disease
3643	L/Naik	Khalas Khan	HK/SRA	2.3.42	Dysentery
2095	Gnr	Ahmed Khan	HK/SRA	10.4.42	Pneumonia
7642	Gnr	Kartar Singh	HK/SRA	7.5.42	Dysentery
4582	Gnr	Inayat Ullah	12th Coast RA	2.7.42	T.B.
5280	Gnr	Ghulam Mohammad	12th Coast RA	10.7.42	Gastro Enteritis
2570	Gnr	Khushi Mohammad	HK/SRA	24.7.42	Anaemia Peritonitis
5085	Gnr	Mut Khan	12th Coast RA	5.8.42	T.B.
782	Gnr	Ghulam Mohammad	HK/SRA	8.8.42	Fracture of Scull
5117	Gnr	Din Mohammad	12th Coast RA	9.8.42	Beriberi
5092	Gnr	Shah Jang	HK/SRA	23.8.42	Entro Colitis
5149	Gnr	Amit Hussan	HK/SRA	26.8.42	Beriberi
5137	Gnr	Abdul Raham	HK/SRA	14.9.42	Jaundice
7959	Gnr	Jemedar Khan	HK/SRA	17.9.42	Dysentery
3361	Gnr	Allah Yar Khan	HK/SRA	16.10.42	Dysentery
5294	Gnr	Mohammad Din	8th Coast RA	19.10.42	Dysentery
8143	Gnr	Fazal Hag	HK/SRA	26.10.42	Ulcerative Colitis
4994	Gnr	Nanam Din	HK/SRA	29.10.42	Entro Colitis
8162	Gnr	Shah Jahan	HK/SRA	1.11.42	Pulmonary T.B.
7523	Gnr	Farman Ali	HK/SRA	3.11.42	Entro Colitis
7649	Gnr	Nrazin Singh	HK/SRA	14.11.42	Entro Colitis
2898	L/Naik	Sher Mohammad	HK/SRA	23.11.42	Malaria T.B.
8040	Gnr	Rahmat Khan	HK/SRA	24.11.42	Beriberi
5447	Gnr	Muzzafar Khan	HK/SRA	3.12.42	Beriberi
2897	Gnr	Ahmed Khan	HK/SRA	16.12.42	Beriberi, Malaria
4898	Gnr	Ali Mohammad	HK/SRA	16.12.42	Beriberi, Malaria
7860	Gnr	Suleman Khan	HK/SRA	19.12.42	T.B.
8034	Gnr	Shah Newar	HK/SRA	25.1.43	Beriberi
5059	Gnr	Nut Muh	HK/SRA	15.2.43	Malaria T.B
5071	Gnr	Lal Khan	HK/SRA	8.3.43	T.B.
8480	Gnr	Blag Ali	HK/SRA	9.3.43	T.B.

Appendix 9

Item	Weight in grammes	Remarks
Rice	440	As at present
Flour	120	As at present
Atta	50	Additional
Fish	100	Double present ration
Meat (fresh)	120	Additional once per week
Sugar	5	As at present
Salt	10	Double present ration
Tea	3	As at present
Vegetables	300	Increase of 30 grammes, but that 30% to be green vegetables of good quality, e.g. spinach, cabbage and onions
Beans	50	Increase of 47 grammes
Ghee	20	Additional
Peanut oil	20	As at present

Appendix 10: List of Argyle Street POWs

Hut No. 1

Name	Nationality	Name	Nationality
Capt Cole, N.S.	British	2/Lieut Forsyth, I.N.M.	British
Lieut Offer, J.C.	British	Lieut Poltock, W. D.	British
Capt Thomson, B.C.A.	British	Capt Van Langenberg, C.	British
Capt Flynn, J.L.	British	Capt Evans, B.I.	British
Capt Head, B.A.	British	2/Lieut Millar, A.W.	British
Capt Blair, I.J.	British	2/Lieut Ross, J.E.	British
Capt Norris, J.A.	Canadian	Capt Johnstone, G.	British
Capt Philip, R.W.	Canadian	Capt Egerton, R.W.J.	British
Capt Philip, D.G.	Canadian	Lieut Llewellyn, N.	British
Maj Prasad, K.	British Indian	Lieut Ferguson, G.P. *	British
Maj Simpson, K.S.	British	Maj Stansfield, H.C.	British
Capt Woodward, J.J. *	Australian	Lt Hancock, F.C.S.	British
Capt Flood, G.W.	British	2/Lieut Poole, P.J.	British
Maj Guscott, R.T.	British	Lieut Paterson, T.	British
Capt Price, C.	Canadian	Maj Hayes, L.	British
Capt Billings, G.M.	Canadian	Maj Mayer, R.W.	British
Capt Hill, S.O.	British	2/Lieut Cole, K.	British
2/Lieut Geer,R.G.	British	Maj Marsh, H.	British
2/Lieut Lebedeff, A.	Russian	Capt Hudson, J.H.F.	British

Lieut Spearey, A. .	British	Maj Heane, C.W.	British
Capt Mathers, D.A.F.	British		
*Hospital Staff			
		Total: 41	

Hut No. 3

Maj Berridge, R.L.	Irish	Lieut Crowley, B.E.	Irish
Maj Grose, D.C.E.	British	2/Lieut Robson, R.C.	British
2/Lieut Simpson,T.S.	British	Lieut MacAlister, D.	British
Lieut Pope, C.	British	Capt Cartwright-Taylor, H.C	British
Capt Dewar, J.G.B.	British	2/Lieut Lawson, G.	British
Lieut Evans, A.F.	British	Lieut Rowell, R.W.	British
Lieut Jessop, H.	British	Lieut Harris, J.R.	British
Capt Dand, A.A.	British	2/Lieut Wakefield, J.T.	British
Capt Rees, G.F.	British	2/Lieut Franklin, F.P.	British
Maj Watson, J.	British	Maj Parsons, W.W.	British
Lieut Stoker, W.	British	Lieut Perry, A.E.	British
2/Lieut Carter, B.S.	British	Capt Penn, A.H.	British
Lieut Andrews, W.R.N.	British	Maj Flippance, F	British
Capt Waddell, C.J.	British	Lieut Wilson, J.M.	British
Lieut Tebbutt, H.	British	Lieut Cooper, G.H.	British
Lieut Mackichan, A.S.	British	Lieut Adam, J.	British
Capt Wood, G.O.	British	Lieut Sweeney, J.N.	British
Maj Smith, J.	British	Maj Cook, E.	British
Capt Waters, J.T.	British	Maj Redmond, F.A.	British
Lieut Lapsley, R.	British	Capt Smith, S.G.	British
		Total: 40	

Hut No. 4

Capt James, T.A.	British	Capt Lomax, J.A.	British
2/Lieut Hunt, K.A.	British	Lieut Beattie, L.D.M.	British
Capt Thomson, A.C.M.	Canadian	Sub Lieut Parkinson, R.B.	British
Rev.Capt Deloughery, F.J.	British	Capt Skipwith, P.J.T.	British
Lieut Potts, J.H.	British	Lieut Toull, E.	British
Maj Templer, C.R.	British	Lieut Dawson, H.P.	British
2/Lieut Trapman, J.A.	British	Maj Hook, H.W.	Canadian
2/Lieut Simpson, R.K.M.	British	Maj Hodkinson, E.	Canadian
2/Lieut Challinor, R.H.	British	Maj Bailey, J.A.	Canadian
Lieut Parks, P.B.	British	Maj Beaman, W.H.	British
Maj Baird, K.G	Canadian	Lieut Willcocks, W.J.	British
Capt Atkinson, A.G.	British	Lieut Vinter, J.S.M.	British
Maj Duncan, H.L.	British	2/Lieut Hoskins, P.J.	British
Lieut Ellis, S.E.	British	Capt Simon, G.N.	British
Lieut Pipe, J.	British	Capt Camp, H.G.	British

Capt Hammett, B.W.	British	Capt Roberts, W.J.	British
Maj Anderson, E.W.S.	British	Maj Forrester, B.T.C.	British
2/Lieut Burgess,O.B.	British	Maj Robinson, J.E.C.	British
Maj Mills, A.O.G.	British	Capt Strachan, A.W.B. *	British
Capt Hoyland, W.H.	British		

Total: 39

Hut No. 5

Mne Chamberlain, F.W.	British	Pte, Loncraine, D.C.	British
AB Glover, W.M.	British	B.Q.M.S. Barman, C.E.	British
AB James, W.H.	British	L/Bdr Holland, R.	British
Cpl Moulton, J.	British	Gnr Dinner, E.	British
AB Bartlett, J.	British	Pte Kaluzhny, K.A.	Polish
Mne Kilroy, J.	British	Gnr Eastwood, F.L.	British
Mne Pearce, J.	British	AB Felsted, G.J.	British
Mne Hulme, S.	British	Pte Cheeseborough, J.R.	British
Tel Walker, R.W.	Canadian	Spr Price, L.	British
Cpl Holden, H.	British	Bug Rogers, H.A.	British
Pte Jones, J.	British	Pte Franklin, A.E.	British
Spr Black, T.F.	Irish	Pte Prince, G.	British
Mne Hamer, W.	British	Pte Robertson, W.G. *	British
Gnr Skinner, O. *	British	Gnr York.N.J.	British
L/Sea Coleman, J.	British	Gnr Brain, J.	British
AB Laurence, W.R.	British	Pte White, G.A.	British
Pte Woods, W.A.	British	Pte Gardner, W.J.F.	British
Sig Latter, F.C.	British	Pte Novikov, V.	Russian
Sig Howell, D.	British	Pte Schiller, M.	Russian
Gnr Cumming, R.	British	Spr McMaster, W.D.	British
Spr Bhumgara, G.	Iranian	L/Cpl Hobbs, K.W.	British
Pte Sprague, W.	British	Sig Smith, N.L.	British
Gnr Petersen, K.W.	Danish	Pte Burch, L.R.	British
Pte Pinna, C.L.	Portuguese	Sgt Tupper, H.O.	British
L/Cpl Lee, R.E.	British	#Cpl Mattison, T.D.	British
L/Sea Harverson, C.J.	British	#In Medical Isolation Room, Hut 2	
Sgt Bullimore, F.	British		

Total: 52

Hut No. 6

Sub Lieut Odell, H.O.	British	Lieut Cockle, H.M.	British
Sub Lieut (E) Fraser.	British	Lieut (E) Ford, A.C.	British
Surg Lieut Dawson-Grove, A.W. *	British	Lieut (E) Buckle, F.	British
Lieut McDouall, J.C.	British	Lieut (E) Blakeney, B.F.	British
Sub Lieut Nash, W.	British	Sub Lieut Young, P.E.	British
Lieut Stephenson, W.R.E.	New Zealand	Sub Lieut (E)Benn, L.A.	British
Lieut Watson, K.A.	British	Lieut Kilbee, L.D.	British

Lieut Hindmarsh, D.E.	British	Sub Lieut Ambrose, F.W.	Australian
Lieut Dudley, G.C.	Australian	Sub Lieut Westwood, E.W.	Australian
2/Lieut McLeod,W.J.	British	Capt Dinnie, R.C.	British
Pay Sub Lieut Macleod, F.	British	Capt Padwick, E.H.	British
Sub Lieut Smith, J.B.	Canadian	2/Lieut Snoswell, F.T.	British
Capt White, A.S.	British	2/Lieut Stevens, E.P.	British
Capt Carter, L.T.	British	2/Lieut Matthews, C.	British
Sub Lieut Young, J.W.R.	British	Sub Lieut Winter, D.A.	British
2/Lieut Mann,T.	British	2/Lieut Valentine, F.	British
2/Lieut Davies, M.M.	British	2/Lieut Couper, L.R.	British
2/Lieut Lempard, W.C.T.	British	Capt Rossini, F.W.	British
2/Lieut Baxter, B.N.	British	Maj Campbell, D.	British
Capt Lane, S.F.	British	Maj Manning, C.J.	British
Lieut Cmdr Stevenson, L.J.	British		
*Hospital Staff	(E) Engineer		

Total: 41

Hut No. 7

Maj Paterson, J.J.	British	Lieut Col Trist, G.	Canadian
Maj Moody, R.E.	British	Maj Stevenson, W.M.	British
Lieut Col Shackleton, C.O.	British	Lieut Col Fredericks, E.C.	British
Lieut Col McCurdy, J	British	Lieut Col Smith, W.J.L.	British
Maj Ryan, G.L.	Irish	Maj Kerr, S.R.	British
Lieut Col Home, W.J.	Canadian	Wing Cdr Sullivan, H.G.	British
Lieut Col Penfold, R.J.L.	British	Maj Browning, J.M.	British
Lieut Col Wilson, J.B.	British	Lieut Col White, S.	Irish
Lieut Col Galpin, A.W.	British	Maj Crowe, J.P.	British
Maj Merthyr, Lord	British	Maj Morgan, W.A.C.H.	British
Lieut Col Mitchell, E.J.R.	British	Maj Wood, W.de B.	British
Lieut Col Gray, G.E.	British	Maj MacAulay, T.G.	Canadian
Maj Hedgecoe, S.F.	British	Lieut Col Rudolf, H.P.	British
Lieut Col Price, J.H.	Canadian	Lieut Col Lamb, R.G.	British
Lieut Col Levett, E.	British	Lieut Col Shaw, S.	British

Total: 30

Hut No. 8

Capt Wiseman, E.P.	British	Capt Barker, A.R.V.	British
Maj Curran, E.J.	British	2/Lieut Joyce, D.W.	British
Lieut Richards, R.S.	British	Capt Thompson, T.A.	British
Lieut Barford, W.S.	British	Lieut Taylor, H.J.	British
Lt.Andrews, G.M.	British	2/Lieut Hobbin,W.R.	British
Lieut Pontin, A.	British	Capt Hitchcott, E.A.J.	British
Capt White, G.W.	British	Lieut Plummer, R.I.	British
Maj Mould, K.S.	British	2/Lieut Guinness, A.H.	British

Name	Nationality	Name	Nationality
Lieut Purvis, L.S.	British	2/Lieut Turner, M.H.	British
2/Lieut Barrow,J.	British	2/Lieut Carr, J.R.	British
Capt Scotcher, W.J.	British	Lieut Edwards, H.G.	British
Capt Hooks, T.	British	2/Lieut Elliott, F.A.M.	British
Capt Gidley, A.S.	British	Lieut Hanlon, M.C.V.	British
Capt Chapman, A.V.	British	Lieut Sutcliffe, J.	British
Lieut Shrigley, R.J.	British	Lieut Wardle, J.	British
P/O Thomson, F.A.	British	Lieut Markey, W.	British
F/O Hennessy, F.P.	Australian	Lieut Wilson, G.	British
F/Lieut Hill,D.S.	British	Maj Foley, M.	British
Maj Colquhoun, A.R.	British	Capt Howard, R.W.	British
Maj Rochfort-Boyd, C.	British	Tailors shop in this hut	
Capt Whittaker, J.G.	British		

Total: 40

Hut No. 9

Name	Nationality	Name	Nationality
Sub Lieut Baker, W.E.	British	Lieut Bailey, H.P.	British
Sub Lieut Fogwill, W.	British	Lieut Goodwin, R.B.	N.Z.
Lieut Rickett, C.A.L.	British	Lieut Carey, F.R.L.	British
Sub Lieut Miller, R.	British	Sub Lieut Smith, C.K.S.	British
Lieut Wood, R.B.	British	Sub Lieut Munro, D.M.	British
Lieut Moodie, J.	British	Sub Lieut Huidekoper, A.W.	Netherlands
Sub Lieut Youngman, J.L.	British	Sub Lieut Ross, W.S.	British
Pay Sub Lieut Robb D.S.	British	Sub Lieut Ross D.P.	British
Lieut Brown A.R.	British	Sub Lieut Burling.W.J.	British
Sub Lieut (E) Lendsbert A.L.	British (E) Engineer	Sub Lieut Lamble R.D.	British
Lieut Trenchard –Davis C.	British	Lieut Manning F.C.	British
Lieut Cmdr Swetland S.J.	British	Sub Lieut Hood T.H.	British
Sub Lieut Gray N.W.H.	British	Sub Lieut Glover H.C.	British
Lieut Eardley H.C.	Australian	Sub Lieut Mayne G.S.O.	British
Sub Lieut Knox C.F.	British	Sub Lieut Thornhill J.T.McC.	British
Sub Lieut Grant F.C.	British	Sub Lieut Baker R.C.	British
Sub Lieut Ross J.S.	British	Lieut Smith R.R.T.	British
Lieut Rutherford.R.	British	Sub Lieut Robinson C.R.	British
Lieut Brown J.T.	British	Sub Lieut Baukham V.	British
Cmdr Vernall	British	Lieut Cmdr Grenham J.C.M.	British

Total: 40

Hut No. 10

Name	Nationality	Name	Nationality
Maj Bishop W.A.	Canadian	Capt Belton, P.	British
Capt Warrack A. *	British	Lieut Prior, J.T.	British
Capt Willoughby R.	British	Capt Bird, G.V.	British
Capt Turner G.C.	British	Lieut Browne, H.W.	British
Capt Hubbard A.	British	Lieut Morahan, B.J.B.	British

Lieut Navey G.	British	Sub Lieut Nissin, A.	British
Maj Parker	Canadian	Capt Pinel, C.E.	British
Maj Young C.A.	British	Capt Squires, W.	British
Maj Atkinson F.T.	British	Capt Bramble, H.C.	British
Capt Valentine R.K.	British	Maj Cross, G.W.	British
Lieut Goldman L.	British	Maj Darland, N.	British
Capt Strellett D.	British	Maj Bottomley, J.H.	British
Capt Blaker C.	British	Maj Sherry, J.P.	British
2/Lieut Schiller G.	Russian	Capt Thursby, E.N.	British
Lieut Field B.C.	British	Capt Martin, A.H.	British
Capt Jones C.R.	British	Capt Escott, F.	British
Capt Glasgow K.V.	British	Lieut Austin, F.S.	British
Capt Millar H.A.W.	British	Maj Pirie, J.R.	British
Lieut Hunter T.D.	British	Capt Pinkerton, D.	British
Pay Lieut Sommerfelt A.	British	Lieut Macgregor, J.K.R.	British
##Maj Boxer C.R.	British		

Total: 41

Hut No. 11

Lieut Wilby G.S.	British	2/Lieut Cooke, S.J.	British
Lieut Crozier D.J.S.	British	Lieut Nigel, F.G.	British
Capt Hamilton K.C.	British	2.Lieut Sleep, R.	British
Capt Barnett K.M.A.	British	Lieut Burt, S.J.C.	British
Maj Stewart E.C.	British	Lieut Davis, D.E.	British
Capt Clark W.C.	British	Maj Jarvis, S.	British
Capt Cole C.W.L.	British	Capt Way, J.R.	Australian
2/Lieut Wright A.M.J.	British	Lieut Calvert, C.H.	British
Lieut McLellan D.	British	Maj Branson, V.C.	British
Lieut Redmen J. *	British	Capt Burch, R.T.	British
Capt Robertson K.S.	British	Lieut Russell, J.	British
Capt Braude A.N.	Australian	Lieut Scott, H.H.	British
2/Lieut Coppin A.D.	British	Capt Davies, R.R.	British
Capt Parsons T.B.	British	Lieut Palmer, G.T.	British
Lieut Tamworth I.P.	British	Capt Egal, R.	British
Capt D'Almada C.P.	Portuguese	2/Lieut Skvorzov, A.V.	Russian
Lieut Ribeiro F.V.V.	Portuguese	Capt Botelho, H.A.de D	Portuguese
Lieut Alves J.M.M.	British	2/Lieut Brett, F.	British
Capt Rodrigues J.S.	Portuguese	2/Lieut de Silva, P.M.N.	Portuguese
2/Lieut Clark D.H.	British	Maj Williams, H.G.	British
2/Lieut Carruthers M.C.	British		

*Hospital Staff

Imprisoned along with Cmdr D.H.S. Craven, Lieut Cmdr R. S.Young and Lieut H.C. Dixon.

Total: 41

Overall total: 405

Note: The original number of men that were transferred from Shamshuipo to Argyle Street as of 28 April 1942 totalled close to 650 men. Of these there were 113 ORs, comprising 20 NCOs including myself and 93 batmen. The remainder were officers. The total number of officers as of 22 January 1944 is 405 excluding 135 men that have been transported to Japan and Formosa in late 1943. Of the 135, nearly half were batmen and NCOs. The remainder are officers including the general staff. These men previously occupied Huts 2, 12, 14 and 16. Hut 13 is the cookhouse and ration store, whilst Hut 15 is the ablution block (see layout of the Argyle Street Camp on p. 170).

Apprendix 11: Batmen groups and general duties

The batmen have been sorted out into groups as follows:

No. 1 Group

B.Q.M.S. Barman	Group Commander
Pte McDougall	Gnr Dinner
Pte McMillan	Pte Hall
L/Cpl Fowler	Pte Richmond
Gnr Snell	Spr Price
Gnr York	

No. 2 Group

Sgt Sutherland	Group Commander
L/Bdr Roche	Gnr Cumming
Gnr Eastwood	Gnr Webber
Gnr Brain	Pte Prince
L/Bdr Holland	L/Bdr Birkinshaw
Gnr Hannington	

No. 3 Group

Cpl Mattison	Group Commander
Pte Francomb	Pte Smith
Pte Smith F.	Cpl Holden
Pte Smart	Pte White
L/Cpl Bushell	Cpl Moulton
L/Cpl Hobbs	

No. 4 Group

L/Cpl Pickles	Group Commander
Gnr Blazey	Pte Evans
Pte Pederson	Sig Howell
Pte Sprague	Sig Latter
Gnr Skinner	Gnr Elsworth
L/Cpl Earnshaw	

No. 5 Group

Sgt Tupper	Group Commander
Pte Hastings	Spr Moore
L/Cpl Taylor	Spr Black
L/Bdr Robinson	Spr James
L/Cpl Sawyer	Pte Jones
Pte Bradley	Pte Woods
Pte Normandale	Pte Loncraine
Spr Black	

Note: This group shows 14 men owing to the strength of the hut being 13 plus.

The present duties of the batmen and the batting to their various officers are as follows:

Rank	Name	Employment, etc.	Rank	Name	Employment, etc.
BQMS	Barman	Hut Commander	Pte	White	Batting and I/C Hut Canteen
Sgt	Tupper	Batting and I/C drains			
Sgt	Sutherland	Batting and I/C Bread Issue	Sig	Latter	Batting and Hut Bin daily
Cpl	Mattison	Ration Storeman	Pte	Howell	Batting only
Cpl	Moulton	Cook permanent	Pte	Sprague	Batting and sanitary
Cpl	Holden	Batting and no heavy duties	Pte	McDougall	Batting and sanitary
L/Cpl	Hobbs	Batting only	Pte	McMillan	Batting and sanitary
L/Cpl	Bushell	Batting only	Gnr	Hannington	Batting and sanitary
L/Cpl	Sawyer	Batting only	Gnr	Brain	Batting and sanitary
L/Cpl	Taylor	Batting only	Gnr	Dinner	Batting and sanitary
L/Cpl	Fowler	Batting only	Spr	Richmond	Batting and Hut Messing
L/Cpl	Pickles	Batting only	Pte	Smart	Permanently sick
L/Bdr	Holland	Batting and sanitary	Pte	Cheeseborough	Hospital Orderly
L/Bdr	Birkinshaw	Batting only	Gnr	York	Batting, no heavy duties
L/Bdr	Roche	Batting only	Gnr	Cumming	Cook permanent
Pte	Wood	Batting only	Spr	Price	Cook permanent
Pte	Bradley	Batting only	Pte	Prince	Cook permanent
Spr	Moore	Batting only	Pte	Hastings	Cook permanent
Pte	Loncraine	Medical Room orderly Permanent			

Apprendix 12: Batmen who left Argyle Street on 8 December 1943

L/Bdr Burkinshaw 12th Coastal Regt RA
L/Bdr Roche 8th Coastal Regt RA
Gnr Snell 12th Coastal Regiment RA
Gnr Blayney 5th AA Regt RA
Gnr Webber 5th AA Regt RA
Gnr Elsworth 5th AA Regt RA
Pte Hale 1st Middlesex Regt.
Pte Francomb 1st Middlesex Regt.
Pte Normandie 1st Middlesex Regt.
Spr Richmond Royal Engineers
Spr Moore Royal Engineers
Spr James Royal Engineers
Pte Smith Royal Army Service Corps
Mne Sanderson Royal Marines
Mne Hancock Royal Marines
Mne Rogerson Royal Marines

L/Cpl Taylor Royal Engineers
L/Cpl Fowler 2nd Royal Scots
Pte McMillan 2nd Royal Scots
Pte McDougall 2nd Royal Scots
Pte McKay 2nd Royal Scots
Pte Haughey 2nd Royal Scots
L/Cpl Pickles Royal Army Ord.Corps.
L/Cpl Bushell Military Police
Pte Evans Royal Army Pay Corps
L/Cpl Sawyer Royal Army Vetinary Corps
Pte Howe Royal Army Med.Corps
Pte Albistone Royal Army Med.Corps
AB Coite Royal Navy
AB Hooker Royal Navy
AB Williams Royal Navy
Tel Bell Royal Navy

Mne Sutherland Royal Marines
Mne Glover Royal Marines
Mne Handsley Royal Marines
Pte Whiting HKVDC
Pte O'Grady HKVDC
Pte Clibborn HKVDC
Pte Altrice HKVDC

Tel Goodwin Royal Navy
Tel Franklin Royal Navy (NZ)
Stoker Hodgson Royal Navy
Sgt Simpson DDC
Pte Tull DDC
Sgt Kernaghan Dockyard Police Royal Navy

Notes

1 Unusually for pre-war buildings in Hong Kong, these still exist.
2 The mansion was called 'Ho Tung Gardens' and was situated at 75 Peak Road. It still exists today. Ho Tung himself lived in Macau during the war years.
3 The site is now the Kowloon Park, though four of the original barracks buildings have been preserved.
4 In fact, Joe Henson would become one of the oldest POW's at Shamshuipo, while his wife would be a civilian internee. She would pass away in Stanley Camp on 16 April 1944.
5 John Vinter survived the war, and passed away in 1997.
6 Now King George V School.
7 Nichols survived the war, ending it as a prisoner in Japan.
8 All three officers survived the war.
9 Gollege and May would survive the infamous *Lisbon Maru*, though Gollege himself would die when the plane flying him home from Japan crashed. Wilson would die as a POW in Japan of acute gastritis.
10 Squires would survive the war.
11 Thompson survived the war and was later awarded an MBE.
12 This building still exists, being used to house several different kindergartens.
13 Maltby survived the war, being imprisoned in Taiwan and Shenyang, China.
14 In September 1942, Sergeant Waterhouse would be shipped with the 'hard men' in the first draft of POWs to Japan, and Blofield would be on the third draft.
15 Ghulam Mohi-Ud-Din would be lost on 19 December and has no known grave. Dalip Singh, who died in 1943, also has no known grave.
16 Adjutant of the HKVDC, and therefore a regular officer. Thursby survived the war.
17 Gray survived the war.
18 Willcocks had been captured as the Japanese took the southernmost part of the Redoubt. Two of his Indian signalmen had been killed.
19 Captain Thomas Pardoe of Fortress HQ was killed in this manner.
20 Nurses Brenda Morgan was killed and Kay Christie wounded.
21 Frank Daniels survived the war.
22 Lance Sergeant Frank Ewens was lost on 24 December and has no known grave. Herbert Ealey was on the fifth draft to Japan. James Stopforth would be executed in 1942 after a failed escape attempt.

23 Henry Searle would be lost in the sinking of the *Lisbon Maru* in October 1942.

24 The Canadians reported a number of men injured at Lei Yu Mun by an air attack at that time; they were taken to St Albert's Convent. Presumably the 'twenty men' lost were also injured, as there are no reports of HK/SRA deaths on that day.

25 Torquil McLeod was one of the senior officers shipped to Taiwan and then Shenyang, China, as POWs.

26 Robert McPherson would be killed on 22 December, along with Horace (Vic) Morris, Ronald Bliss, John Singleton and Cyril Walker (though there is some doubt about Walker as CWGC claims he died in January but has no known grave). Frank Haynes died at BRH in 1943 of dysentery. Of this whole group, only Wilfred Markey and Arnold Collinson survived the war.

27 Alex Sutherland was on the fifth draft to Japan.

28 Robert O'Connell was on the third draft to Japan.

29 George Ryan survived the war.

30 Walter Peters was on the third draft to Japan.

31 Henry Marsh survived the war.

32 William Hoyland, RA, survived the war.

33 Potts survived the war.

34 Hermione and Wendy Wilson spent the war interned in Stanley.

35 The Aberdeen Industrial School. Herbert Millet survived the war.

36 Ian Blair, of C Company Punjabis, survived the war.

37 George Tinson, MC.

38 Jack Smith survived the war.

39 Killed on 20 December.

40 CWGC records for this day report the deaths of one Havildar and seven gunners from the HK/SRA (mainly 1 Mountain Battery).

41 Henry Duncan commanded 3 Medium Battery. He survived the war.

42 Herbert Dawson, 8th Coastal Regiment, RA, survived the war.

43 Clarence Cooper had died of wounds from Belcher's on 15 December.

44 Christopher Holberry was on the first draft to Japan. Albert Yearling survived the war.

45 Caesar Otway was one of the two officers on the first draft to Japan. Fred Field, commanding the 5th AA Regiment, survived the war.

46 Fred Thompson and Ian Tavendale would be on the *Lisbon Maru*. Thompson died in the sinking. Tavendale survived, but died of dysentery in Japan shortly after.

47 There were two Sgt Walkers whom this may have been. Both were on the fifth draft to Japan.

48 Dr E. W. Kirk was at the War Memorial Hospital. He survived the war.

49 CWGC records show nine HK/SRA gunners killed that day, mainly from 1 Mountain Battery, who were probably these.

50 After the war the surviving men testified against Colonel Tanaka, who was tried at the war crimes trial and subsequently sentenced to death.

51 Hugh McKechnie survived the war.

52 Stanley had not yet been established at this time. On 11 February, Barman notes that the civilians were transferred to Stanley on 20 January.

53 Postwar author of *Darlings, I've Had a Ball!*

54 James McGhee would be lost on the *Lisbon Maru*.

55 Harry Rudolf would be on the sixth draft to Japan.

56 Herbert Dobson died of these wounds on 23 January.

57 For a list of patients at that time, see Appendix 1.

58 Cedric Shackleton, William Bartlett, Phillip Knightly, and Gerald Harrison survived the war. Ken Brown was on the sixth draft to Japan.

59 Osborn won the only VC of Hong Kong, defending his men during the retreat from Jardine's Lookout.

60 Hankow Barracks was in fact the name for one side of the camp, and Nanking Barracks was the other.

61 Richard Penfold survived the war. John Eves and Alfred Lloyd were on the *Lisbon Maru*, but only Lloyd survived.

62 Edwin Soden was on the *Lisbon Maru*.

63 Lindsay Ride and Francis Lee went on to found the British Army Aid Group.

64 Most likely David Henderson, Royal Scots, who would be lost on the *Lisbon Maru*.

65 For nominal roles of POWs known to the author, see Appendices 4 to 7.

66 Gordon Bennett survived the war.

67 Douglas Clague, Lynton White, John Pearce, and David Bosanquet escaped successfully. Clague became a very important member of BAAG, and both he and Pearce were successful businessmen in postwar Hong Kong (where Pearce still lives at time of writing). Alec Pearce, John's brother, also survived the war. L/Bdr Robinson is presumably Richard Robinson, who was on the fifth draft to Japan.

68 Alfred Lloyd would be on the *Lisbon Maru*.

69 Alex Warrack was on the sixth draft to Japan.

70 Fred Bullimore and Albert Pontin survived the war.

71 Sidney Hedgecow survived the war.

72 Charles Earnshaw would be sent to Taiwan with the senior officers.

73 Stanley Kerr survived the war.

74 For a list of batmen at Argyle Street, see Appendix 2.

75 Peter Belton and Henry Selby survived the war.

76 Barman noted that he was reunited with his family in 1946 and was fully compensated for his secret activities in assisting the conditions of the prisoners of war in the camps at Shamshuipo and Argyle Street. The British government recognized this and fully supported him financially in the business he had in Cardiff before the war, which included the education of his family. Major General Maltby and the remaining staff officers of Argyle Street camp reported to the British government of his undercover work in our interests to help wherever possible.

77   Robert Simpson survived the war.
78   Jack Grenham, George Prince, and James Sutcliffe survived the war. Arthur
      Francomb was on the fifth draft to Japan.
79   William Sprague survived the war.
80   Alf Bennett, a Japanese speaker, survived the war.
81   Thomas Mattison survived the war.
82   They died of avitaminosis and enteritis respectively.
83   Barman noted that the diphtheria outbreak claimed 500 victims, which was
      almost one man in ten and of these, more than fifty died.
84   Possibly Henry Cole, who was on the fifth draft to Japan.
85   David Lam, following his release, crossed the border into China and became
      a BAAG stalwart.
86   Arthur Dewar survived the war.
87   Sapper Moore was shipped to Japan on the fifth draft and survived the war.
88   Cedric Blaker survived the war.
89   Woodcock in fact survived. Knowles did not.
90   Fred Thomson had been wounded in the neck during the fighting. He
      survived the war.
91   Eric Elsworth was on the fifth draft to Japan. George Flood also survived
      the war.
92   Arthur Strachan survived the war.
93   Simon White survived the war, ending as the Senior British Officer of the
      POWs in Hong Kong.
94   Richard Penfold survived the war.
95   Ronald Snell was on the fifth draft to Japan. Ronald Holland also survived
      the war.
96   Donald Howell and Anthony Atkinson survived the war.
97   See Appendix 9.
98   Henry Handsley was on the fifth draft to Japan.
99   See Appendix 8.
100   Jack Fraser survived the war.
101   Thomas Roche was on the fifth draft to Japan.
102   James Robinson was on the sixth draft to Japan.
103   John Hastings was sent to Taiwan with the senior officers. Ken Hobbs also
      survived the war.
104   Hugh Haughey would be on the fifth draft to Japan. Major Parsons also
      survived the war.
105   For batmen groups and general duties, see Appendix 11.
106   Desmond Loncraine survived the war.
107   Alex Fowler would be on the fifth draft to Japan. John Browning, Kenneth
      Glasgow, and Arthur Perry also survived the war.
108   Joseph Haddock survived the interrogation. Manuel Prata did not.
109   Barman noted that Lieutenant Haddock was the unfortunate one. He
      received a Japanese trap message from a Chinese lorry driver, whom he had
      in the past been receiving news of the world situation. As soon as Lieutenant

Haddock saw the blank piece of paper on top of the cistern in the officer's toilet, he must have realised that it was a trap set by the Japanese.

110 Doctor Selwyn-Clarke survived his interrogation, but never fully recovered physically. Many of his team were executed.

111 John Hale would be on the fifth draft to Japan.

112 John Cadogan-Rawlinson survived the war.

113 At the time of writing, the Argyle Street Camp Commandant's house still exists.

114 Presumably Kenneth Allanson.

115 Joseph Randle was on the fifth draft to Japan. Alfred Chainey also survived the war.

116 John Cheeseborough, Gordon Ferguson, William Robertson, and Leslie Smart survived the war.

117 Stoker Hodgson, Harold Bushell, and Ronald Sanderson were on the fifth draft to Japan. Frank Chamberlain also survived the war.

118 Peter Hoskins survived the war.

119 For a full list of batmen who left on 8 December 1943, see Appendix 12.

120 Austin Spearey survived the war.

121 Ben Hammett survived the war.

122 George Simon survived the war.

123 Latimer Cleave was on the sixth draft to Japan.

124 Joseph Fraser survived the war.

125 Norman Llewellyn survived the war.

126 Ralph Shrigley did not survive interrogation. He died on 28 June 1944.

127 Thomas Hunter survived the war.

128 Sergeant Tupper survived the war.

129 Ernan Dinner survived the war.

130 Barman noted later that apparently each of these two bombs' explosive power was equal to 20,000 tons of TNT, which is something beyond our comprehension. Hiroshima was apparently the target for the first bomb.

131 After the war, like a lot of evacuated families whose father did not come home, the Gollege family remained in Australia.

Index

Wada, Hideo, Lieut, 108, 140, 172, 236
Waichow, 110, 125
Wake Island, 193
Wales, 124
Walker, C., 39
Walker, C., Sgt, 69
Walker, L/Sgt, 209
Wallis, C., Brig (HQCC), 1, 181, 182, 184
Walrus, 12
Wanchai Gap, 2, 14, 29, 31, 40, 41, 44, 51
Wanchai, 52
war diary, 94
War Memorial Hospital, 40, 44, 48, 54, 57, 72, 76, 82, 89, 94, 125, 212
War Office, London, 94
Wardle, J., Lieut (RAOC), 206
Warner, Cmdr (RN), 120
Warrack, A., Capt (RAMC), 117, 120, 138, 169, 190, 205
Water Police Station, 202
Waterhouse, Sgt (HK/SRA), 24, 55
Webber, Gnr (8th Coast Regt RA), 157, 173
Wedemeyer, A., Lieutenant General (US), 258, 259
Wellwood, P., QMS (RE), 221, 222
West Administrative Pool, 2, 3, 5, 6, 11, 16, 18, 20, 25–27, 29–31, 38, 40, 47, 48, 51–53, 56–58, 60, 61, 67, 69, 78
West Fort, 7–10, 13, 24
West Group headquarters, 2, 23, 25, 28, 36, 40
Whampoa Docks, 249
White, Maj (RA), 110
White, S., Lieut Col (Royal Scots), 155, 161, 167, 169, 173, 182, 194, 197, 227, 230, 231, 234, 235, 248, 251, 256, 257, 259–262
Whitfield Barracks, 6–8, 143, 202, 217
Whitney, P., Capt (RAMC), 80
Whitstable, 188
Willcocks, W., Lieut (HK/SRA), 31, 229

Williams, QMS (RASC), 222
Wilson, H., 48, 218
Wilson, S/Sgt (HK/SRA), 13, 25, 48, 55, 218
Wilson, W., 48, 218
Winkworth, Pte (Middlesex), 181, 184
Wiseman, E., Capt (RASC), 36, 65, 73
Wong Nei Chong Gap, 13, 16, 19, 27, 41, 45, 51, 56, 62, 64, 78
Wong Nei Chong Valley, 66, 67, 78, 80, 94
Wong Nei Chong, 2, 30, 55, 59, 61
Woodcock, K., Lieut (RE), 142
Woods (twin sisters), 82
Woods, Lieut (RASC), 137, 138
Woods, Pte (Middlesex), 180
Woods, Sgt Maj, 222
Woodward, J., Capt (RAMC), 194

Yale, Lieut Col (HK/SRA), 78, 81
Yearling, BQMS (HK/SRA), 61
York, N., Gnr (12th Coast Regt RA), 173
Young, R., Lieut Cmdr (RN), 192
Yunnan, 194, 195
Young, Sir Mark, Governor, 4, 38, 76
Yaumati Ferry, 9, 11, 24

Zhitomir, 211
Zindel (Red Cross), 235, 236